The Outdoor Life
BEAR BOOK

Edited by Chet Fish

 Outdoor Life Books

Stackpole Books

Published by

Outdoor Life Books
Grolier Book Clubs, Inc.
380 Madison Avenue
New York, NY 10017

Distributed to the trade by

Stackpole Books
Cameron & Kelker Streets
Harrisburg, PA 17105

Library of Congress Cataloging in Publication Data
Main entry under title:

The Outdoor life bear book.

   Includes index.
   1. Bear hunting — Addresses, essays, lectures.
2. Bears — Addresses, essays, lectures.   I. Fish, Chet.
II. Outdoor life.   III. Title: Bear book.
SK295.095 1983   799.2'774446   83-17249
ISBN 0-943822-22-X

Fifth Printing, 1987

Manufactured in the United States of America

Contents

Preface

Bears stir our imagination and arouse our curiosity more than any other big-game animal. So it's not surprising that readers of *Outdoor Life* magazine, year after year, are treated to the most exciting and informative coverage of the grizzly, brown, black, and polar bears of North America.

If there's one label that fits all four, it's *unpredictable*. Bear unpredictability is nowhere more evident than in the chapters of this book. These are personal accounts by people who have met bears in almost every situation imaginable.

Long before I became editor-in-chief of *Outdoor Life*, I learned from Bill Rae—my predecessor—the great drawing power of bear stories. An issue of *Outdoor Life* without a bear story was rare indeed during Bill's tenure.

The stories in this book were selected from the best that have appeared in the magazine during the past thirty years. Another editor might have made different choices. That's not to apologize for my own. I like these stories for a variety of reasons, and I believe you will, too.

Here are the most terrifying bear attacks, the most challenging and rewarding bear hunts, and the most intriguing investigations of bear natural history. Good reading to you.

CHET FISH
Editorial Director, Stackpole Books
Former Editor-in-Chief, *Outdoor Life*

PART

I

WHEN A BEAR ATTACKS

Sow Bear Attack

Jim Heiney

January, 1979

It was one of those crisp, clear autumn days when it feels good just being alive. The sun had climbed above a high ridge to the east and a morning breeze had set the golden aspen leaves in motion. September is a lovely time to hunt the mountains. There had been a frost at dawn, but now the day was warming and I unzipped my jacket as I picked my way across a brushy saddle.

I'm a guide and outfitter and I hunt Area 42 in the high country of central Colorado. I'm 40 and I make my home in Paonia. On this particular morning I was making a quiet drive, hoping to push a small band of elk within range of three bowhunters I had stationed along game trails on down the canyon.

The men had come out from Pennsylvania and seemed to be good guys and experienced hunters. Only one of them posed a problem. He had a bad cough that erupted every few minutes. I knew it would be tough putting an elk within range of his bow if he warned them with his hacking.

Three other archers were scheduled to arrive as soon as these fellows tagged their bulls. I don't enjoy taking large groups of hunters. I prefer to concentrate on furnishing a quality hunt. The previous fall my 10 bowhunters had taken nine elk, which I consider outstanding results nowadays.

I glanced at my watch . . . 9:15 a.m. Time for me to begin the drive. I don't usually carry a bow myself when I am guiding hunters, but on this particular morning I had my old recurve and a few arrows in a hip quiver. My hunting license entitled me to take a cow elk, and since my hunters all wanted bulls, they voiced no objections to my claiming a young cow if I had the chance. I have seven kids and elk meat is an important item in our family budget. As it turned out, it was lucky for me that I toted that old bow and a few arrows.

I cut through a narrow stand of aspens, keeping my eyes peeled for fresh tracks, then I looped into a pocket of spruce timber where I thought the elk might have bedded down for the day. They weren't there so I figured they were still ahead of me on down the canyon.

Just as I cleared the timber and entered a small park I spotted a black bear 100 yards or so ahead. It was a huge sow with two cubs. She wasn't feeding, but was on the move at a steady clip. I suspected she had winded one of my hunters down below.

She was a lovely reddish brown and with each step her pelt shook and glimmered in the sun. I could see no rubbed spots. I smiled as I watched her and her cubs move across the little park before me. I was thinking that when I told my hunters they had spooked a bear to me, they probably wouldn't believe the tale.

I began guiding in 1964 and since that time I have seen many bears in the Colorado Rockies. Most of them are wary and have a great fear of man. Every bear I'd ever seen had always high-tailed once it knew I was nearby.

I watched and waited for the bear's reaction as she moved across the wind and approached my scent stream. I figured she would bolt and run for cover at any moment. I remember thinking, "Surely that old gal has my scent by now." Then I realized that she was no longer moving away from me but seemed to be bending around slightly and increasing her gait.

It must have been instinct that made me look around for a nearby tree. I'm 6 feet 2 inches tall and weigh about 200 pounds. If I had to climb, any little tree wouldn't do. I saw a likely spruce some 50 feet away, and just as I turned around I saw the sow break into a lope and head my way.

I thought she had at last caught my scent and was trying to escape but had misjudged my position. I began to walk toward the spruce. When she saw my movement, she came in a rush, her jaws snapping together like a huge trap. I still did not believe that she was coming for me, but was only trying to lead her cubs to safety somewhere away from the stench of man.

I broke into a dead run for the tree and though I had only a short distance to travel, I barely managed to make it up into the limbs before she reached the trunk.

As I wormed my way up the tree, a tangle of limbs caught my hip quiver and spilled the arrows. I heard them clattering through the limbs below me. I still had my bow in my left hand. The one arrow I had knocked earlier was still under my index finger.

"Get out of here," I yelled at her as she came up after me.

I remember my surprise at the great ease with which she moved up the tree and through the limbs . . . pure strength and power.

And still I did not believe I was going to be attacked by a bear. She was just running me up a tree, I told myself.

"Get going!" I shouted at her, my voice sounding very hollow.

And then she curled her lips and snapped viciously at my left foot. I had on a new pair of western work boots, and I tried to plant that big heel squarely on the end of her nose. My foot grazed the side of her mouth. She grabbed at my jeans with her right paw as I went higher and circled the trunk. Her movement was faster than mine and she closed her jaws on my left foot. I gasped for breath and expected to feel the bones in my foot splinter, but she didn't bite down. She only mouthed my boot. I jerked free and kicked her face again.

I climbed higher and circled away from her, trying to keep the tree trunk between us. Limbs popped as I pulled my way upward with my shoulders and back. And still she came.

In my climb I lost my bow but I still had that one fiberglass arrow clutched in my left hand . . . and now I realized that it might be the difference between living and dying.

As I pushed off a limb, she closed her jaws on my foot for the second time. My heart came up into my throat as I expected her to crush it, but again she didn't grind down with power and I was able to jerk free. The bite was much harder than the first, but still not hard enough to do real damage. In thinking back I wonder if she was testing the fierceness of her adversary with those first two bites.

I was backed up against several large limbs and couldn't climb unless I turned my back on the bear. I wasn't about to do that. She snapped at my foot again and I closed my fist on the feathers of my arrow and jabbed hard at her face. The razorhead glanced off her forehead. Before I could strike again, she had my foot in her mouth. This time I felt her teeth break through the leather and sink into my arch and instep.

I screamed, but strangely the bite didn't hurt too much. I jabbed again at her face with my arrow.

Up until now her movements had been very deliberate, almost in slow motion, but suddenly she seemed to go into a rage and lunged and snapped at my feet and legs with abandon. I jabbed frantically with my arrow to fend her off.

I had my left arm hooked across the top of a limb near my head, and it is a good thing I did, for the limb I stood on suddenly snapped under my weight and my legs fell down about her head and shoulders. Instantly she seized my right leg with her paw and bit through the top on my boot and into the calf of my leg. I felt her teeth scrape across my shin bone and realized I was looking death in the face.

I screamed aloud, but again I felt no great pain. She jerked and tugged at my leg and tried to back down the tree. I held on with all my strength, for now I knew I had to stay in that tree to stay alive. If she got me to the ground I'd be a dead man in seconds.

I poked at her head with my arrow several times, and when the broadhead sunk into the base of her black, shiny nose, she let out a bellow and released her hold on my leg. I scrambled for another limb.

Almost instantly she was back at me again and her first snap caught the bottom of my trousers. She jerked and shook her head like a puppy playing with a sock as she tried to dislodge me from my perch. I came down again and again with my arrow, but it had no effect. Finally my trousers ripped and just in time, for in another second or two she would have had me out of the tree. I could hold on with only one arm and it was about exhausted.

Blood gushed from the wound in her nose, and she snapped and ground the piece of denim she held in her mouth. It was then that I noticed the point of my broadhead had been slightly bent by the force of my blows on her skull.

When she came again, the first bite put her teeth into my leg just below the calf. Then, just as her big head began to twist and turn in an effort to shake me out, I brought the arrow down again.

This time fortune was with me and the broadhead sank deep into her left eye. When I jerked upward to strike again, blood spurted from the wound. Still, she showed no sign that she was hurt.

When she attacked again, I kicked her hard with my left foot, but she managed to hook her paw around my leg and pull it into her waiting jaws again. She bit down hard and I remember thinking that if she shook me again I would not be able to stay in the tree.

Then suddenly she turned me loose and began backing down the trunk of the tree. My breath was coming in great heaves and my tattered pants were soaked with blood. I couldn't believe she was going down. I didn't move a muscle as I watched her go to the ground. When she turned to walk away, I could see blood streaming from her nose and eye.

For the first time since the attack begain I felt light-headed. Suddenly I realized how exhausted I was, and my arms and legs began to tremble.

As I stood up there amid those broken and bloody limbs, she turned and began to amble away as though nothing had happened. She moved with indifference and it seemed as if she was trying to remember where she had been going before it all started. She may have been thinking of her cubs.

I have no explanation for what I did next. I would like to believe I was trying to warn the others, but I can't say that with any conviction.

All at once I could hear myself cursing at her at the top of my lungs. My voice seemed to come from some faraway place.

At the sound of my voice she stopped and stood motionless for a moment. And then slowly her gory head turned and I could see that one black eye glaring at me. One side of her face was bathed in blood. Then she snapped her jaws several times and came for me again.

It was terrifying. I gasped in horror as she burst up through the limbs and grabbed for me with her bloody head. Her breath reeked of raw flesh and blood.

I knew if the arrow's shaft broke I'd be defenseless. I tried to protect myself with the battered broadhead, but I had little chance of hitting the other eye. I remember thinking that if she only knew that, all she had to do was bite down and then jump out of the tree. Her great weight would pull me from the branches to the ground where she could rip me to shreds.

Once again she bit me near the knee, but turned loose when I kicked her with my other leg.

I could tell from her body motion that she was trying to find a way to get higher in the tree. She was reaching with her hind legs for support. If she found it she would soon be striking at my mid-section. Panic was welling up in my gut.

Then abruptly she turned her head and peered down through the limbs. And just as she had done before, she began to back down the trunk.

When she reached the ground she ran a few steps and then raised up on her hind legs, her nose bobbing in the wind. A moment later she dropped to all fours and I watched as she loped back the way she had come, probably to retrieve her cubs.

It was over.

Seconds later I understood why she had broken off her attack when I heard the hacking cough of my hunter a short distance away. It was music to my ears. The bear must have heard him coming before I did. I called out and he came to help me. The other hunters were rounded up. They gave me first aid and got me off the mountain and to a hospital.

I was battered and bleeding, but had no broken bones. And I was alive. It took 27 stitches to close my wounds. I was treated for shock and laid up for a few days, but I came out of it in pretty good shape considering how close to death I'd come.

At the time of the attack I had a .357 Magnum handgun at home. I didn't carry it often because of the bowhunters. Some archers are real purists and I was afraid they might object. Since that morning two years ago I have traded my .357 for a .44 Magnum handgun. If you ever hunt with me, you can bet a month's pay that it will be strapped to my hip.

You know, it's funny, but I don't feel any hatred for that old sow, or any other bears. I saw two bears last hunting season and could have killed both. I kept my eyes on them and gave them a wide berth.

The Colorado game authorities investigated the attack, and told me that they could hunt the sow down with a pack of hounds and destroy her. But I told them I did not want the bear killed and felt no hostility toward her. Again, I can't tell you why, but it may have something to do with my feeling that she was only trying to protect her cubs. Sometimes I wonder if that old girl and I will ever come face to face and if she would know me. I am sure I would know her. And if she came at me again, I know what I would do.

Man-Eating Black Bear

Ted Gorsline

August, 1978

It's unlikely that 16-year-old George Halfkenny saw or heard the bear approach. The boy was fishing from a logjam on the north bank of Lone Creek, a stream that flows from east to west in the northeastern corner of Ontario's Algonquin Park.

Fishing was good; the boy already had four brook trout stuffed in the pockets of his jacket. His success may have intensified his concentration on the small pool in front of him. His mind was on trout.

He faced south. The bear came from the north. It came quietly; the forest floor was carpeted with wet leaves and pine needles. The creek was swollen with spring runoff, and any sound the bear may have made was masked by the roar of the water.

Young Halfkenny was among friends, enjoying the company of his brother, 12-year-old Mark, and 15-year-old William (Billy) Rhindress. The three boys were separated. George was alone, and Mark and Billy were fishing another, nearby section of the stream.

They were within 400 feet of power lines and a road. Billy Rhindress's older brother, Richard, 18, would soon come in his car to pick them up. From the fishing area, it was only an hour's drive back to the boys' home at Canadian Forces Base Petawawa.

George had fished this section of the creek many times before with his father, Warrant Officer George Halfkenny of the Eighth Canadian Hussars. The boy's father was no stranger in the bush. The year before he had led a Canadian Forces Survival training expedition into remote Yukon Territory.

Young George had learned a great deal about bush survival from his father. He and his companions carried a knapsack and extra food and clothing with them on this short, day-long fishing trip. As a member of the Canadian Airborne Regiment Cadet Corps, young Halfkenny had taken at least two wilderness-survival courses.

The bear probably made its attacks at between 5 and 6 p.m. on Saturday, May 13. His first victim, George, had no chance. The struggle, if there was one, was brief. The bear surprised the boy from behind and either killed him where he sat or forced him into the stream and killed him in the shallow water.

Later R.G. Tasker, a pathologist from the Pembroke District Hospital reported, "George Halfkenny suffered a broken neck and left collarbone, six broken ribs on the right side, and a punctured right lung."

The bear did not run away after it killed Halfkenny, as bears often do. Instead it picked up the body in its jaws and dragged it for 10 yards along the north bank of the creek, then crossed the creek, and dragged the boy's remains 50 yards into the bush on the south side of the creek.

Predator biologist George Kolenosky of the Ontario Ministry of Natural Resources speculates that the attack may have been a case of mistaken identity. Perhaps the bear thought Halfkenny was a rival bear.

"The boy may have been hunched down by the stream," Kolenosky said. "That way his outline would not resemble that of a man. Bears have very poor eyesight. The bear might initially have been attracted to Halfkenny by the smell of fish in his pocket. The bear killed the boy very quickly. It may then have smelled blood and associated the boy's remains with food."

Kolenosky examined the immediate area carefully. There was little doubt that the bear had been feeding in that area for a week or two. In a small nearby marsh, the grass was heavily grazed, and Kolenosky found a number of bear scats.

"The bear had eaten nothing but grass," Kolenosky said. "He was obviously hungry, but so are all black bears in Ontario in mid-May."

Kolenosky and two other expert trackers from the Ministry of Natural Resources, Stuart Strathearn and Dennis Voigt, visited the scene of the tragedy and tried to reconstruct the terrible sequence of events.

The men think Mark Halfkenny and Billy Rhindress met their fates together, suddenly and unexpectedly, while looking for George. The boys either met the bear as it dragged George's body into the bush, or came upon the animal at close quarters as it guarded the corpse.

Staff Sergeant Tom Parker of the Pembroke detachment of the Ontario Provincial Police said there was nothing to suggest the two young boys had come to the rescue of George. They probably didn't know he had been killed.

But again, the bear's attack was savage and swift. It killed the two boys within a few feet of each other. One paw struck Mark on the head, causing brain damage and hemorrhage. Billy's neck was broken and his throat lacerated.

The bear dragged both boys 15 yards, up to within 10 feet of George's body. The bear then fed on all three bodies and buried the remains under debris from the forest floor.

The bear ate much of one corpse and at least part of the others. From the signs the bear left, the mostly flattened grass, it was evident to searchers that the animal had lain beside its victims.

Late that evening Richard Rhindress drove to the rendezvous site, the place where the power transmission lines and the old road crossed Lone Creek, and waited for the return of the three fishermen.

Eventually, Rhindress became impatient and went looking for them. Fortunately he chose to travel along the north side of Lone Creek. Still, at times, he must have been within a few hundred feet of the killer bear. Had he walked along the south side of the creek in his search, he could well have become another victim.

Richard went back to his car and honked the horn. No reply. By 12 p.m., he was convinced something was seriously wrong, so he returned to Canadian Forces Base Petawawa.

Rhindress approached Mrs. Charlotte Halfkenny, mother of the missing brothers.

Mrs. Halfkenny immediately contacted Lt. Col. Bob Billings of the Eighth Canadian Hussars. Billings sent 200 men to the search area that night and more men the following morning. In all, about 250 men from the Canadian Forces, Ontario Provincial Police, and Ministry of Natural Resources took part in the search.

None of the searchers realized they were looking for bodies and a killer bear. Everyone assumed the boys were lost. It is illegal to carry firearms in Algonquin Provincial Park, so no one had a gun.

By 9 a.m. Sunday morning, the searchers had not seen any trace of the boys. Corporal Curtiss, who headed up the Ontario Provincial Police investigation, contacted Constable Ray Carson at the O.P.P.'s North Bay detachment.

At 8 a.m., Carson had just finished working the night shift, but by 9:15 he was on the way to the site. Carson is a veteran O.P.P. dog handler with more than 10 years experience in locating lost persons.

Over the years, he had gone through two successive tracking dogs, Cloud One, and Cloud Two. The dog with him now was Cloud Three.

Richard Rhindress told Carson where he had last seen the missing boys and the area he had searched.

By now, four Canadian Forces helicopters had joined the operation. Two worked over Lone Creek in the area where the boys were last seen.

Lumberman Gordon Stewart, with more than 40 years experience in the bush, warned the searchers that a bear might have killed the boys. "We've got so many bears around here," he said, "I thought we might have trouble last year."

Stewart, who himself has had many confrontations with angry black bears in that area, said seven bears had been seen in the vicinity earlier in the week. "The day before, five bears were seen within two miles of the site," he said.

There hadn't been a killer black bear in the vicinity of Algonquin Park for more than 80 years. However, chopper pilots who flew over the Lone Creek section of the park during the search said that they had seen an unusually large number of bears.

Constable Carson and his German shepherd Cloud Three scouted through the area Richard Rhindress had already searched—the area north of Lone Creek. Like the other searchers, Carson saw no reason to carry a gun.

Carson reasoned that he was looking for lost, living people. Everywhere he went within the search area he saw choppers and hear soldiers with loudspeakers. Carson did not believe the boys could fail to hear the loudspeakers or wave down a chopper if they were in that area.

"They must have wandered far back in the bush," he thought to himself. And so Carson headed deep into the forest, hoping to cut a fresh track that his dog could follow. By now the Lone Creek area was so crisscrossed with human trails that Carson felt Cloud Three would have a hard time distinguishing the lost boys' tracks from others.

While on their way out of the search area, just north of Lone Creek, Cloud Three began to act up.

"It looked to me like she was following an animal or perhaps an old track left by Richard Rhindress," Carson said. "Cloud is trained to follow human beings, not animals, and so I didn't encourage her to keep on the trail."

Carson and Cloud Three spent a fruitless day wandering far beyond the periphery of the search area. They found no sign of humans.

"I kept putting two and two together and coming up with three," Carson said. "Something didn't make sense."

By Monday morning, Warrant Officer Halfkenny had learned his sons were missing and had returned from Texas to join the search. Like everyone else, he expected to find the boys alive. He had taught them how to survive in the bush, and he accurately predicted they would be found within 300 yards of Lone Creek.

During the search, Carson came to like Warrant Officer Halfkenny, who was obviously very proud of his sons. Halfkenny said young George, ". . . doted on his brother Mark and was sure to look out for the younger boy."

By Monday morning, there was still no sign of the boys. It just didn't make any sense. Something was very wrong. Constable Carson decided to retrace with Richard Rhindress the exact steps the boys had taken when Rhindress had seen them walk into the bush.

Carson and Rhindress hadn't walked more than 100 yards up the south shore of Lone Creek when Carson and Cloud Three found George's jacket and fishing rod in the creek. The jacket was snagged on a knot on a log that protruded from the stream. The arms of the jacket were pulled inside out and faced upstream. In the back of the jacket right between the shoulder blades, there was a small hole.

Carson immediately thought the hole, which later proved to be a cigarette burn, was a bullet hole.

"For the first time I began to suspect foul play," he said. "Now I believed we were looking for bodies and not lost boys." Carson's belief was reinforced by a drag mark that led from the pool, crossed a moss-covered log, and went down the bank of the stream.

Constable Carson and Lt. Col. Bob Billings called all the men out of the bush and regrouped them in a long line along the power-line road.

The road crossed Lone Creek at right angles. One hundred men would walk into the bush and search the bush directly north of Lone Creek. Another line of 100 men would search south of Lone Creek. Carson went to his car and strapped on his .38 Special revolver. The searchers moved shoulder-to-shoulder through the thick brush.

At 6:15 p.m. Monday night, the men at the extreme south end of the line on the south side of Lone Creek sent up a yell: "We have found the boys, and there is a bear with them."

About 20 of the searchers gathered to witness the scene, including the father of two of the missing boys. Faced by so many men, the bear reluctantly retreated into the bush.

Ray Carson shouted to the men and told them not to follow. He realized that if they hoped to kill the bear they must not drive it from its food. The searchers dispatched a message to the Ministry of Natural Resources in Pembroke and asked for a man with a gun to come and kill the bear.

Conservation Officer Lorne O'Brien had just sat down to supper. As a 26-year veteran of the Ministry of Natural Resources, he had killed many nuisance bears. He could not believe he was being asked to shoot a man-eating black bear.

Lt. Col. Billings dispatched a Canadian Forces helicopter to Pembroke. O'Brien grabbed his Model 94 Winchester and a box of 150-grain Silvertip cartridges and then rushed out to meet the chopper.

In the interim, the searchers managed to find another .30/30 rifle. The 250 men were now armed with two .30/30's and a .38 Special.

Corporal Curtiss from the Ontario Provincial Police, Carson from the O.P.P., O'Brien from the Ministry of Natural Resources, and an officer from the Canadian Forces stalked the man-eater. Unfortunately, the light was beginning to fail. The sky was overcast and darkness would soon fall. The men were in a race against time.

None of the four men who went into the bush to stalk the bear had been present when the bear and corpses were found. After several minutes of searching, they failed to find the bodies.

Corporal Curtiss and the Canadian Forces Officer returned to the power-line road to find a man who knew exactly where the bodies were. They took one .30/30 rifle with them for protection.

While they were gone, O'Brien and Carson found the bodies. They saw the bear move off the bodies, and retreat into thick cover. O'Brien could have shot the bear in the rump, but he didn't want to risk wounding the animal and losing it.

Carson reasoned that if they remained still, the bear might come back. He believed that if the other men returned, they might drive the bear back into the bush and lessen O'Brien's chance for a shot.

Carson called Corporal Curtiss on his two-way radio, explained that O'Brien and he had found the bear, and asked the men to stay where they were.

The two men took up kneeling positions. O'Brien faced the bodies, which were about 40 feet away. Carson kneeled too but faced in exactly the opposite direction. That way the men had all directions covered.

Twenty-five feet in front of Carson was a pile of logs and thick bush. If the bear charged from there, Carson did not think he could stop it with his revolver.

Carson was scared, and he is not a man who scares easily. Carson and his second tracking dog Cloud Two had once hunted down a dangerous, accused murderer named Donald Kelly. Kelly vowed the police would never take him alive. When Carson caught up to him, Kelly went for his gun. In the ensuing gun battle, Carson and his partner shot and captured Kelly but Cloud Two was killed.

Now Carson was reliving that same kind of tense situation. Suddenly, he sensed movement to his right. In Carson's opinion the bear was deliberately stalking them.

"He was stalking us all right," he said. "The bear would come a bit, hesitate, and then come some more. I'm sure he was stalking us."

Carson tapped O'Brien on the shoulder and pointed to the bear. The range was only about 60 yards, but by this time the light was very poor and the bear was partly obscured. It was coming along the edge of a small swamp. Thick grass and tamarack trees obscured part of its body.

O'Brien swung smoothly and fired almost the instant his rifle bore on the bear. In the dim light, red flame flashed from the muzzle of the short-barreled Winchester. The bear dropped so fast that Carson later asked O'Brien if he had shot it in the head.

No sooner had the bear dropped than it was back on its feet. O'Brien flattened it again. The bear tried to escape into the thick forest, but it now was obvious the bear was hurt. Its front shoulders functioned, but it dragged its rear quarters.

Every time the bear rose or moved, O'Brien fired. At the same time, Carson fired with his .38 Special revolver.

The bear pulled itself about 10 yards, let out a bawl, and died. O'Brien and Carson walked up to it and put two final shots into it.

Those who were close to the tragedy were visibly shaken. O'Brien said, "I feel like a gunfighter in the Old West, who has acquired a reputation he doesn't want." Constable Carson said, "Any man who tried to pretend he was a hero for being part of the team that killed the bear would have to be sick. It was so awful, so tragic. If there is ever another search for young kids who have been killed by a bear, I don't want to be part of it. I wish to God it had never happened."

A coroner was brought in to examine the bodies. Gordon Stewart, the lumberman, and his sons were recruited to help bring out the bear. They remarked on the animal's fine condition.

Steward said, "The fat was rolling like jelly on that bear." His son Tim added: "It was in the best shape of any bear I've seen in the park this year."

The head of the bear was sent to the Animal Research Center of Canada's Department of Agriculture for rabies tests. The tests proved the bear was not rabid. The animal was examined by the Ministry of Natural Resources in Pembroke. It appeared to be in perfect health.

But since man-eating black bears are so rare, various parts of its carcass have been sent to different university and forensic science labs for further analyses. Various remains from all three bodies were found in the bear's alimentary tract.

Biologist George Kolenosky called the incident "bizarre and abnormal." He said nothing like it may happen for 85 years, but cautioned, "Some biologists predict bear attacks will become more frequent in years to come.

"As the number of bear-people contacts increases in areas like national parks, where the bears are protected, the bears will lose their fear of man at an increasingly fast rate.

"Some biologists in western Canada already argue that grizzlies in some of our parks are beginning to regard nonviolent man as a potential source of food."

Perhaps the same grisly situation will arise with black bears.

The Killer Bears

John O. Cartier

January, 1983

Lee Randal Morris, a 44-year-old geologist, was the black bear's first kill. Morris had gone for a walk near a wilderness oil-drilling rig in Alberta, Canada. He was mauled to death and partially eaten on August 14, 1980.

The bear was covering the remains of his grisly meal with dirt and grass when he turned his attention to 21-year-old Marty Ellis and 24-year-old Carol Ann Marshall. The couple had left Cantex No. 10 rig an hour later than Morris and were walking the same route Morris had taken.

"We were about 300 yards from the oil rig's campsite, walking between spruce trees near a small creek when the bear charged out of some underbrush and came straight for us," Ellis, a heavy-equipment operator, said later. "Carol was terrified, so much so that I had to half carry her a few feet to the nearest tree that was big enough to climb. There were two large spruces growing very close together, and my idea was to help her climb one while I climbed the other.

"But that bear was so fast we had no chance at all. We had barely started climbing when he swarmed onto us. He went for Carol first, and he got her when we were about four feet up the trees. I was holding her with all my strength, but the bear swatted her from my grasp and out of the tree with a single swipe of a front paw. He seized her neck in his jaws and shook her. He must have killed her instantly. Then he dragged her into the bush."

At this point Ellis was unaware that the bear had already killed Morris and that he was carrying the woman to the same spot where he had partially buried the remains of his first victim. This short lapse of time gave Ellis the chance to climb about 20 feet up the tall spruce, where he thought he would be out of reach of the killer bear. He was woefully wrong.

16

When the brute reappeared there was no question that he intended to kill Ellis, too. He rushed straight to the tree and began climbing. He went up so fast that Ellis frantically climbed higher and began screaming for help. Many times the berserk beast rushed up and down the tree, trying to drag him down.

"I was about 30 feet above ground the first time he lunged at me," Ellis later told Royal Canadian Mounted Police (RCMP) investigators. "He was so close I could smell his foul breath. I kept hanging onto branches with my hands and kicking him in the head with my feet. After I'd kick him enough times he'd retreat down the tree. Then he'd come back up, breaking branches and clawing bark. Each time he got close, he seemed to be larger and his eyes were wild with rage. I was now 40 feet up the spruce trunk, and it was dangerously thin. I was so terrified that I wasn't aware of my blood flowing from cuts made by scrambling through branches."

Ellis recalls that the bear got close enough to kick in the head six times. He figures about an hour passed before a 12-year-old boy appeared and almost became another victim.

The rest of the story is most accurately told by Corporal Maurice Chislett of the RCMP. Chislett was at the scene a few hours after the attacks, and he discussed them with me at length.

"The attacks were classic examples of accidents waiting to happen. All the ingredients were there," Chislett told me. "The scene was set when the Hudson Bay Gas and Oil Company moved the drilling rig into deep wilderness 25 miles northwest of Zama, a tiny community of about 250 persons. We had the age-old problem of man encroaching on a beast's home territory. This particular bear decided to retaliate. The people involved weren't even aware of his presence. None of the victims were armed, and they had no reason to believe they should be armed. Some newspaper accounts of the tragic killings were accurate up to this point, but theatrics got in the way of truth regarding the part played by the 12-year-old boy, Reagan Whiting.

"Whiting, like the others, had left the campsite to go for a walk. He did not respond to Ellis' screams for help because his yelling was drowned out by the loud noises of the nearby drilling rig. The boy simply happened upon the attack scene. Then Ellis spotted him and shouted at him to run for help. Though some newspaper accounts credited Whiting with outrunning the bear, this is certainly not the case. No human outruns an enraged bear. We believe that the bear was so intent on killing Ellis that he purposely let the boy escape."

Chislett went on to tell me that Whiting dashed back to the rig and told his father, Bud, a consulting engineer, that Ellis was fighting off a bear. The elder Whiting grabbed a .300 Winchester Magnum and raced to the scene with his son. When he got there the bear was on the ground and immediately charged. Whiting fired three rapid shots, one of which hit the oncoming bear and rolled him over. The huge brute got up, roared with rage, but then turned and lumbered away into the bush. Ellis hastily came down the tree and the three people retreated to the campsite.

"It was at this point that we received the news of the tragedy by radio, and Constable C. R. Elias and I immediately patroled to the scene," Chislett told me. "When we got there the two bodies had already been found by a gang of rig workers who armed themselves and went looking for the missing victims. Ellis was in shock, as were many other people at the site. Darkness fell with no further sighting of the bear.

"We contacted wildlife personnel and they sent helicopter pilot Don Stubb to the scene early the next morning. He spotted the wounded bear from the air, landed his aircraft nearby and killed the animal with four shots from a .30/06. We later sent the clothes of the two deceased to our RCMP crime lab in Edmonton for comparison with stomach contents of the 310-pound bear. The stomach contents included parts of Morris' shirt and blue jeans."

Chislett seemed very concerned about the bear attack problem. I got the impression that what happened near Cantex No. 10 rig was just one more incident in a growing number of horror stories. I wondered if this could be true, so I decided to find out.

Because bear attacks on humans always rate a great deal of newspaper coverage, and because most of them occur in western Canada, I contacted an important Canadian newspaper and surveyed its files on the subject. My contact was Patricia Garneau, librarian for the *Edmonton Journal*. Garneau dug out clippings on 13 bear attacks that occurred during 1980 and 1981. Consider these examples.

Rancher Vinko Mamic was fixing a fence on his property near Prince George, British Columbia, when a grizzly grabbed him by his arm and threw him to the ground. "I got up, grabbed a piece of wood and began banging the bear in the head," Mamic later told hospital attendants. "He grabbed my right leg and flipped me to the ground again. His jaws were so massive that he got both my knees in his mouth. He could have easily killed me, but for some reason he backed off and stood staring at me. I got up and ran for my truck which was parked two kilometers away. I stumbled and almost passed out several times. My ripped and torn clothing was covered with blood by the time I got there."

Mamic was mauled so badly that his wife, daughter and five sons worked feverishly to keep him from bleeding to death before even trying to get him to the hospital in Prince George. At the hospital he required extensive surgery and a two-week stay.

Ernest Cohoe, a 38-year-old Calgary resident, wasn't so lucky. He was fishing in Banff National Park when a bear crashed out of the underbrush and clamped massive jaws around his head. The bear apparently thought he killed his victim because he left the scene after his sudden attack. Cohoe, though his head was horribly mauled, staggered to a nearby housing development for help. He survived six hours of surgery in a Calgary hospital, but died a week later.

Fifty-year-old George Brisch of Summerland, British Columbia, went for a walk on a Sunday morning in August 1980. His remains were found in the bush four days later. There were signs of a violent struggle about 200 yards from Brisch's car that was parked in an abandoned gravel pit. Human remains and clothing were scattered over such a wide area that wildlife officials suspect that more than one bear made the attack.

Lawrence Gordon, 33, of Dallas, Texas, met a similar fate in Montana's

Glacier National Park sometime in late September 1980. He was the third person killed by one or more grizzly bears in Glacier that year. His remains were found on October 3, and so was his camera. Park officials developed the exposed film and studied pictures of Gordon's ransacked camp. They theorized that the victim returned to his camp and was photographing the destruction when the killer bear attacked.

The details of fatal attacks can only be guessed at, but the stories told by those who survive are always horrifying. Faye Smith, 23, of Circle, Alaska, told reporters about an attack that began when a bear stepped on her head.

"We were camped at a fishing area 25 miles from Dawson City," Smith said. "There were six adults in camp, and that's the main reason why the three of us lived. Early in the evening we watched a big grizzly patrolling the nearby river for fish, but bears aren't unusual in that country and we weren't overly concered when we went to bed. My husband and I were asleep in one sleeping bag under a tarp when I felt a tremendous pressure on my head. I could barely scream, but when I did the bear began slashing and biting both of us."

From this point on, as with most victims, hysteria blurs the victim's memory. RCMP Constable Ralph Jolley, who investigated the maulings, offered this account.

"As soon as the grizzly attacked the Smiths the uproar awakened James Taylor, 28, who was in a nearby tent," Jolley said. "He saw the bear and threw a coffee pot at the animal. The grizzly instantly shifted his attack to Taylor and began biting and mauling him. Richard Smith picked up his wife and tried carrying her away from the scene. But the bruin noted their escape attempt and ripped into them again."

Jolley estimated that the bear probably took less than two minutes to maul the three persons. Then he quickly left the campsite. But the ordeal lasted for several hours. The other three people in camp hastily carried the victims—who were barely conscious, bleeding profusely and in severe pain—to a boat where they were taken to a nearby island in the river. A fisherman who was camped there used his boat to help ferry the party upstream to Dawson City.

"The victims were in really bad shape by the time I saw them," Jolley said. "They were partially covered with dried blood and dirt, and all had deep cuts. Two of them had puncture wounds."

Because such maulings are so horrifying and because they have been increasing, wildlife officials are giving them a great deal of attention. Listen to Jerry Kemp, an Edmonton-based wildlife biologist and consultant on these matters.

"At least 10 persons were attacked, four fatally, in Alberta and British Columbia alone during 1980," Kemp began. "The bear problem could easily increase for logical reasons. Oil and gas drilling rigs are pushing farther into remote areas, agriculture is still expanding and wilderness recreational activity continues to boom.

"The key to solving the problem is educating people rather than trying to change the habits of bears. We need specific garbage management plans because garbage dumps definitely attract bears. Park planners must also study bear distribution patterns when designing and maintaining parks. We have to develop ways to keep people out of bear concentration areas and make the areas that humans use less attractive to bears."

Rangers at Glacier and Yellowstone national parks are now making strenuous efforts to keep people and bears apart.

"We call it a bear management program, but 90 percent of it is people management," says Glacier ranger Bob Morey. "Bears are especially attracted to cooking and garbage odors, so we no longer allow open-fire cooking in some areas. We recommend that campers not sleep in the same clothes they wear while preparing food and we advise hikers to wear bells to alert bears to the presence of humans. This eliminates the surprise element when people and bears meet unexpectedly. In some areas where the trouble potential is high, we stop all camping."

One unique idea for keeping bears and people apart involves an experimental bear "exclosure." Glacier rangers are using the exclosures— high chain-link fences—in places that are most popular with bears. It is like a zoo in reverse. The campers are fenced in at night and the bears are fenced out.

Removing problem bears from more developed areas is getting increased emphasis. When park rangers get the slightest hint that a bear may cause trouble, they tranquilize it with darts and transport it far back into remote wilderness. These animals are fitted with radio transmitting collars to track their movements. If a given bear returns to a problem area, it may be necessary to kill the animal.

Will bear management plans reduce maulings and killings? There's little doubt that they'll prevent some, but ranger Morey offers sobering thoughts.

"More than three million people visited Glacier and Yellowstone parks in 1981," he said. "We look for an attendance increase of 20 percent this year. Inevitably, the more people in bear country the greater the number of bear confrontations . . . no matter what the precautions. When you enter wilderness, nobody can guarantee your safety."

Of more significance, perhaps, is the fact that bears often lose their fear of man if they aren't hunted. In parks where bear hunting is banned, the bruins learn that humans are harmless. Some bears simply regard us as defenseless prey, far easier to catch and kill than rabbits.

We Hunted Down a Man-Killer

Gordon D. Gosling

November, 1970

Harvey Cardinal had not a moment's forewarning that it was his last day on earth.

He must have realized that there was some risk in tracking a grizzly through pockets of very thick spruce. Guides with whom he had worked said afterward that although he'd had no previous encounters with grizzlies, he had a deep respect for them.

But Cardinal was carrying a rifle that he considered adequate, an old .303 military Enfield. And if he thought about danger at all that cold January morning, he probably figured that he knew what to expect and could deal with it if it came.

Cardinal was 38, a Beaver Indian from the Moberly Lake Reserve southwest of Fort St. John, a town at Mile 50 on the Alaska Highway above Dawson Creek, in northeastern British Columbia. He had been a trapper, hunter, and guide all his life, working for other guides and outfitters in the area. Chunky of build, weighing close to 200 pounds, and about five feet 10 inches tall, he was a strong, husky woodsman, slow of speech and movement, not much afraid of anything except grizzly bears. Unmarried, he spent more time living off the Reserve than on it.

The evening before, Cardinal had gone to visit friends at the Doig River Indian Reserve, a Beaver community of about 30 families 50 miles north of Fort St. John. He had heard a strange story there.

The Indians in that area hold rights to large trapline blocks, within each of which several families are allowed by law to trap. By contrast, whites generally hold trapline rights individually.

21

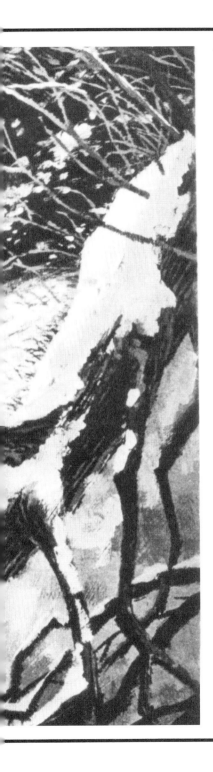

As Cardinal walked by, the grizzly burst from cover in a murderous fury and killed him with a single blow to the side of the head.

One of the Doig River Beavers, running his trapline in 40-below cold that morning, had come across the tracks of a bear.

The date was January 13, 1970. Ten inches of snow was on the ground, and for 10 days the temperature had stayed below zero, falling to minus 30° or lower night after night. At that time of year and under those conditions, the bear should have been in winter quarters. The fact that it was out and prowling was something of a mystery to the Doig River people, and it stirred up more than a little excitement.

The reason will never be known for certain, but I believe that the animal had not hibernated at all during the winter, perhaps because of mild weather. That part of British Columbia had experienced temperatures well above normal all through the fall and early winter, up to the first week in January, when the mercury plummeted and stayed down for more than two weeks. I think this grizzly had not bothered to den up in the warm weather, and when the cold spell came he just kept on traveling, perhaps goaded by hunger.

The trapper who found the tracks was sure of two things: the bear was big, and it was unquestionably a grizzly. The claw marks in the tracks made by the front feet proved that.

Nobody in the isolated community at Doig River wanted anything to do with the maker of those tracks if he could avoid it. With few exceptions, the Indians of British Columbia prefer to steer clear of grizzlies.

Harvey Cardinal usually shared that feeling, but this was a special case. In midwinter the bear would very likely be carrying a good pelt, prime and unrubbed. Such a pelt, uncured, would be worth around $150 in hard cash. That was money a north-country guide without winter employment could use, and Cardinal made up his mind to go after it.

Shortly after daylight the next morning, Cardinal went to the place where the trapper had hit the grizzly tracks. He picked up the trail and followed it into an area of logged-off openings alternating with stands of aspen and thick young spruce. The snow was not deep enough to require snowshoes.

When Cardinal did not return at nightfall his friends at the Reserve began to worry. And when nothing was heard from him the next morning the worry mounted into real fear that the bear had attacked and injured or killed him.

Half a dozen of the Doig River men made up a search party and set out to investigate. They followed the tracks of Cardinal and the bear for two miles, across openings and through timber and finally into a tangled thicket. There they found what they feared they were looking for—Harvey Cardinal's body.

It was a grisly scene. The ground around the body was tracked-up and bloodstained. The man's clothing had been torn to shreds. He lay on his back with both arms raised in a hands-up position—frozen in the bitter cold of the night. A fair share of the upper body had been devoured.

Grizzlies are notorious for their savage possessiveness and short tempers if anything threatens to rob them of food to which they have laid claim. The Indians knew that in all probability the man-eater was in thick cover nearby, perhaps only a few yards away—watching, working up a murderous rage, getting ready to rush the entire party. There was nothing they could do for Harvey Cardinal at that point and no purpose in risking more lives. This was a matter for the police.

The searchers backed off, turned, and hurried for the road. They drove 20 miles south to the store and post office at the little town of Rose Prairie, where the nearest phone was available, and phoned their report to the Royal Canadian Mounted Police at the Fort St. John post.

Because a bear was involved, the Mounties contacted the Fort St. John office of the British Columbia Fish and Wildlife Branch, where I am stationed as a conservation officer, and asked for a man to accompany them to the scene.

I was in the field that morning. Senior Conservation Officer Jack Mackill, a 20-year veteran with the Branch, took the call and agreed to go along.

Mackill and several police officers drove at once to the place where Cardinal had left the road to go into the woods. They were able to get a panel truck to within a half-mile of the scene of the killing, and they followed the tracks from there. Since they were dealing with a grizzly that had reportedly killed a man, Mackill was carrying a 12 gauge shotgun with slug loads.

The death scene was fully as horrifying as the Indians had described it. Cardinal's body lay in a thicket, torn and mutilated, and it was obvious that the bear had fed heavily on its victim.

Mackill and the police pieced together the story of the attack as best they could from the evidence in the snow.

Cardinal had been surprised and killed in a lightninglike attack that came from behind without warning. He had not had time to release the safety of his Enfield, and the leather mittens he'd been wearing were still on his hands. The bear had killed him with a single blow of a forepaw to the side of the head, a blow so savage that it shattered the entire skull.

Although the area was badly tracked up, the men could easily imagine what had happened. Apparently the grizzly had lain quietly in ambush, in thick stuff no more than a few feet away, perhaps hidden behind a log or a windfall as bears often do. He must have let Cardinal walk by. Then, once the man was past him, he had exploded in murderous fury, pouncing on his victim in no more than two or three leaps.

I doubt that Cardinal felt the blow that killed him, and if he saw or was aware of the bear at all it was for only a fleeting instant.

Newspaper accounts, basing their conclusions on the fact that the bear had attacked from the rear, said the animal had deliberately stalked the man through the brush to kill him for food. But those of us who investigated the affair disagree with that version. Fred Harper, a regional wildlife biologist with the Fish and Wildlife Branch who went with me to hunt the grizzly down, summed up our collective opinions.

"The attack probably was unintentionally provoked by the victim," Harper said. "He got too close to the bear without knowing it was there, and it jumped him without warning. Though the animal was old and battle-scarred, I do not believe that any of its physical peculiarities were sufficient to have stimulated the attack."

Fresh tracks around the body, apparently made 24 hours after the attack, indicated that the grizzly had been on the kill again that morning. Jack Mackill and the police made their investigation very cautiously, with guns in hand, knowing that the bear was probably lurking nearby and might decide to attack at any instant.

When they had put together as much of the story as possible, they covered Harvey Cardinal's body with a blanket and carried it out to their truck, keeping a sharp watch all around throughout the half-mile hike.

Fred Harper and I returned to the office of Fort St. John late that afternoon. Jack Mackill told us the story.

Nothing quite like it had ever happened before in our part of British Columbia, and we were all agreed that the bear had to be destroyed. Whatever the grizzly's reasons for attacking Cardinal, now that it had killed and fed on a human the odds were great that it would repeat the performance. We could not leave so dangerous an animal in the woods.

Though this was the first instance of a grizzly turning man-eater that ever came to our attention, it was not the first time one of the big bears had attacked a man in our area. Luckily, the earlier affairs had turned out better.

Two such attacks had occurred before my time at Fort St. John. In both cases the victims were big-game guides. In one incident the guide was on foot and escaped the bear by jumping over a 20-foot cliff. The other attack was more unusual, though the girzzly had good reason for what it did.

The bear had been wounded by a hunter and had got away. The party followed it, and it rushed out of thick bush and attacked the guide while he was on horseback. The man was cut up badly, but he remained conscious and walked out for help. The bear disappeared and was never seen again.

A third attack happened in late October 1968. The victim that time was an experienced hunter, Mike Markusich of Port Alberni on Vancouver Island.

Markusich was hunting moose east of Mile 135 on the Alaska Highway. In four inches of snow he came across grizzly tracks going into dense spruce. He had no bear license but decided to see where the animal was headed.

The bear had a moose kill about 300 yards ahead in the bush and had been feeding there. With its belly full, it had walked 50 feet away and lain down to keep watch, in typical grizzly fashion.

As in the case of Harvey Cardinal, the bear let Markusich walk by before it moved. Then it struck.

Markusich neither saw nor heard the animal. His first warning of the attack came when the bear's jaws clamped down on his head and face from behind. Before it let him go, he suffered two jaw fractures and severe lacerations on the face, neck, and back. He eventually lost the sight in one eye. (I interviewed him in the hospital not long after the incident, and he could not speak. He had to nod or shake his head in answer to my questions.)

The attack lasted only seconds. Then the bear dropped Markusich and ran off. As far as is known it never came back to the moose kill.

Markusich was able to walk and drag himself two miles out to the road, where he collapsed and was later picked up by a passing motorist.

Jack Mackill and I investigated that case thoroughly. As far as we could determine, the bear had not been wounded earlier. It was protecting its kill and had attacked in blind anger when the man came too close.

At daylight the morning after Cardinal was found, Mackill, Harper, and I climbed into a big chopper rented from Okanagan Helicopters, a first-class flying service operating over most of British Columbia.

Our pilot was Maynard Bergh, the service's 51-year-old base manager at Fort St. John, who has been flying copters since 1940, has logged over 7,000 hours at their controls, and is rated one of the best in the business.

In the seven years I have been stationed at my present post, Maynard has flown me on many game counts and predator-control missions. Countless times he has put me down close enough to a particular animal to enable me to classify it as adult or juvenile and even to determine its sex. If anybody could locate this grizzly from the air, hidden as it would be in dense cover, Bergh was the man.

We went armed for what we intended to do. This was no hunt for sport, and we wanted weapons that would kill no matter what the circumstances might be. Harper was carrying a .375 Magnum Browning in Safari grade; Mackill and I had 12 gauge shotguns. Jack's was a Model 12 Winchester with the plug removed, giving him five shots without reloading. Mine was a Browning over-and-under. We carried both buckshot and slug loads.

We flew directly to the scene of the killing, and a few minutes of circling revealed a line of bear tracks headed north. The grizzly had cleared out sometime during the night—we guessed right after dark. He no longer had any reason to hang around in that neighborhood, and the presence of the Indian search party and later the police had almost certainly disturbed him. He was traveling steadily.

Tracking the bear from the air, which was the only way we could hope to overtake him, proved very difficult. The terrain was level, as is most of that part of British Columbia except for creek draws and river breaks. The tree cover is aspen with very dense scattered stands of spruce. There are a few clearings devoted to grain crops and the grazing of horses (it's not cattle country), but the bear had avoided the clearings.

To follow the tracks we had to fly just above the treetops. The snow on the ground was light and fluffy, and at our height the main rotor of the helicopter blew it into the tracks and filled them instantly.

The four of us strained our eyes to the limit. Try as we would, however, we could not follow the track for more than a few hundred yards at a time. Repeatedly it disappeared into thick spruce stands where we could see nothing, leaving us the frustrating chore of circling until we picked it up again.

About five years before, oil-exploration crews had cut seismic lines through the area at one-mile intervals. If it hadn't been for those lines, 35 feet wide and straight as a fire break, I doubt that we could have stayed on the track. We could spot the trail where the bear had crossed one of the lines, fly on to the next in the general direction he was traveling, and pick up the track again.

It took four hours of this aerial tracking to cover eight miles. Probably the bear had made better time than we did. Finally his tracks went into a very thick isolated stand of spruce about a half-mile long and half that wide. We circled the 80-acre tangle twice, but no tracks came out.

We were sure we had the grizzly cornered at last.

We had decided at the outset that we would kill the bear from the air if we could. Mackill, Harper, and I strongly deplore the aerial hunting of any game, but this was no time for ethics or sportsmanship. We had come to destroy a killer, a man-eater, an animal that was a potential menace to any human he encountered. We meant to do it quickly and humanely.

We searched the 80 acres of bush for 20 minutes without seeing a sign of the bear. Then, in a little opening below us, something big and brown moved out of one thicket and into another. We had no chance for a shot, but at least we knew where the bear was and we had him on the move.

It took us 10 or 15 minutes to find him again. Twice during that time Bergh made a quick circle around the perimeter of the spruce to make sure the grizzly had not slipped out. Finally the bear moved into an open place, and we got our first good look at him.

To me, one of the most surprising things about that bear hunt was the way the grizzly reacted to the chopper. All the while we were tracking him I had visualized him running at top speed to get away, or turning on us, upreared on his hind feet, cutting the air in a rage, daring us to come down.

But he did nothing of the kind. He showed neither anger nor concern. He just walked away, and even after we started shooting he did not hurry. I got the idea that he was too old to care.

The bear was on my side of the copter, and I quickly emptied both barrels of the Browning into him. When we autopsied him later we learned that although my buckshot had not hit a vital organ, some of them had penetrated the body cavity to the stomach and would have killed the bear eventually. Yet he didn't react in any way to those two shots.

The grizzly walked out of sight into thick spruce again, but Bergh was directly over him now, just above the trees, and in a minute the bear came into the open once more, on Harper's side 60 feet below us.

Fred's 300-grain soft-point from the .375 Magnum smashed into the grizzly's right shoulder and blew up in the lungs and heart. He fell, pushed himself ahead a few feet to the edge of a thicket, and was dead in seconds.

Maynard set the helicopter down at the border of the thick stuff, and the four of us climbed out for a closer look at the killer animal we had destroyed. What happened next almost piled tragedy upon tragedy.

Jack stepped down from the bubble and walked back along the side of the copter, checking the loads in his Winchester in case the grizzly was not dead. We were taking no chances. We knew that more than one "dead" bear had come suddenly to life.

Jack's mind was intent on his gun and the bear, and he didn't notice the still-spinning tail rotor of the helicopter. He walked into it and was knocked down as if he had been sledged.

Jack escaped instant death narrowly indeed. The spinning rotor struck him on the side of the head, in front of and above the right ear, knocking away a fragment of skull a half-inch wide and half again that long. His doctors said afterward that he came within a hair of being killed outright.

Jack was unconscious, and for a minute we thought he was dead. When we saw that he was still alive we gave up all thought of checking out the bear and loaded Jack back into the chopper for the half-hour flight to Fort St. John. Fortunately, the fragile rotor that had felled Jack wasn't seriously damaged and the chopper could still fly.

Mackill was treated at the Fort St. John Hospital, and at 6 o'clock that evening he was put aboard a Canadian Pacific jet flight for Vancouver as a stretcher patient. Eight hours after the accident, surgeons in Vancouver General Hospital removed bone fragments from his skull.

Prompt help and medical skill saved Jack's life. He has recovered completely and has since been transferred to Williams Lake, leaving me the Senior Conservation Officer at Fort St. John.

On Saturday, three days after the grizzly killed Cardinal, Harper and I went back to bring in the bear's carcass for examination, to see whether we could learn the answers to the riddles in the case. We were assisted by half a dozen members of a Fort St. John snowmobile club headed by Grant Slatter. We drove to within two miles of the place in a light truck and went the rest of the way on three snowmobiles.

The weather was still bitterly cold, and the grizzly was frozen hard. We rolled the carcass onto one of the snow machines, took it out to the truck, loaded it, and brought it back to Fort St. John to thaw overnight in a Forest Service warehouse there.

Grizzlies are notorious for their stench, which is hardly surprising, considering that they feed on carrion much of their lives. By morning this one smelled so bad that we moved it outside for an autopsy. Even there, the job was very unpleasant.

Harper and I did the autopsy in 25-below cold. We learned less than we had hoped, but we did prove that we had destroyed the right bear. Its stomach contained human hair, a piece of denim cloth from Harvey Cardinal's shirt, and not much else.

The grizzly was a very old male, weighing about 500 pounds and was severely battle-scarred. The pelt was poor; its hair was only two or three inches long and was iced up on the back from exposure to snow and cold. The face was scarred, probably as a result of a fight with another bear, but the injuries were old and had healed. Part of the pad on the right-front foot had been torn off.

The teeth were badly worn, the two upper canines broken across and split in half. But apparently the bad teeth had not bothered the bear much, for we found two or three inches of fat under his pelt and he showed no evidence of having gone short of food. Hunger may have contributed to his attack on Cardinal, but it was not hunger of long duration. He had come through the winter in good condition.

Tests were made to determine whether the bear was rabid, but they proved negative.

About the only conclusion Harper and I could reach was that the grizzly had jumped Cardinal simply because the man got too close, and had fed on his kill afterward as he would have fed on a moose.

One question will never be fully answered: why was the bear out of winter quarters in such frigid January weather? But for that odd bit of behavior, the whole strange affair would never have happened.

Unusual as this case was, there is a lesson to be learned from it: grizzly bears are unpredictable, dangerous animals, and humans who deal with them in any way had better keep that fact in mind.

Killer Bears of Alaska

Jim Rearden

March, 1981

Do grizzly bears hold grudges? How dangerous *are* grizzlies? Ask Al Thompson, a 44-year-old Division of Fish and Wildlife Protection officer (game warden) who patrols Alaska's Kenai Peninsula. He won't commit himself on the first question, but he doesn't mince words on the second.

Al and his wife Joyce moved north from Casnovia, Michigan, in 1968, and they went deep into the Alaska Range to claim a mountain-backed, lakefront homestead. Their only neighbors were moose, caribou, wolves, and bears.

"There were eight grizzlies living near," he told me. "We knew and named them all."

One night a grizzly tore out the side of the temporary cabin they slept in. They frightened it off. Another bear packed off an outboard motor and dumped it into the lake. Others chewed on their snow machines.

One night their dog barked an alarm. Al picked up his fully-loaded .44 Magnum revolver, stepped out of the cabin, and found a big grizzly standing on hind legs peering down at him. Al didn't want to kill it, so he aimed carefully at the sky but near to the bear's head and fired. The magnum bucked five times, but the bear stood, weaving and threatening. Then Al heard Joyce and saw her .30/06 poke over his shoulder and point at the bear.

"It swayed a bit more, then dropped to all fours and left," Al said.

The bear hung around for weeks, and it got cranky when the Thompsons neared the alder patch it was in, warning them with growls. Rifle fire didn't frighten it. A visiting hunter finally killed the bear.

In 1971 Al and Dick Dykema, who also is a warden, hiked 15 miles

The bear was trying to tear Joyce out of her sleeping bag. I grabbed fur and punched the grizzly as hard as I could with my fist.

into the Kenai National Moose Range to bowhunt for moose. Al killed a bull with a 60-inch spread, and Dick got one with a 55-inch spread.

In 1972 Al decided to hunt in the same area to try to get an even larger bull. This time Joyce went along. Al took his 65-pound bow and glass arrows and carried his .44 Magnum. Joyce took her .30/06. A friend with horses was to come after the meat; Moose Range is closed to mechanized equipment.

Before the hunt Joyce made meat sacks, ironing them so they would take less space in packs. It was near dark when, after an 8½-hour uphill hike, they reached their campsite in the highlands between Skilak and Tustumena Lake.

Next day they built a lean-to of poles and plastic, cut firewood, and picked up scraps left by other campers. The following dawn the Thompsons were out stalking moose. They saw two bulls, but they couldn't get close enough for a shot with his bow. That evening a full moon flooded the Kenai with light.

The Thompsons follow a routine when camping, as do most Alaskans who live in bear country. Al laid his revolver on a piece of yellow paper towel so he could see it in the dark. The flashlight went in a certain spot, as did the loaded rifle. That night Al left his sleeping bag partly unzipped so he could reach the rifle or pistol quickly, if need be, but Joyce zipped hers shut. The campfire burned out, and the Thompsons slept until about 3:30 a.m.

Al and Joyce told me what happened after that as I sat in the lovely log cabin home they've built overlooking the Kenai River. Al is a rugged 180-pounder, 5 feet 9 inches tall, broad shouldered, powerful. Joyce is slender, tall, and athletic. A smooth scar four or five inches long runs from Al's left eyebrow to the top of his head. His left arm has great puckers in it where huge teeth once penetrated. His voice was strong, but there was a faint feeling of wonder in it as he talked, as if he still had difficulty believing what happened.

"I came awake, sensing something was wrong, a feeling anyone can get who has spent a lot of time in the woods," he told me. "I whispered to Joyce, 'Dont'move, something's out there.'

"My hand slid out for the rifle, then it was as if a mad bull had lunged into our lean-to. A bear came right through the top, and in seconds the place was a shambles.

"I tried to lift up the rifle with my right hand, but it flew off into the dark. The bear was trying to tear Joyce out of her sleeping bag. I reached over and grabbed fur, I think around the ear, and hit as hard as I could with my right fist.

"The bear immediately turned on me. I had no time to grab my .44 or the flashlight. The bear grabbed my left arm and tossed me into the corner of the lean-to. Before I could move it leaped and grabbed my scalp with its teeth, then picked me up and ran into the night, clutching me with its right front paw and shuffling sideways on hind feet. That's when the claws ripped me, leaving a great Z-shaped wound, which is now a scar on the side of my chest.

"After shuffling on its hind feet for a while, the bear dropped down. Still holding me with its right paw and still gripping my scalp with its teeth, it ran on its left forefoot and two hind feet in kind of a rocking lope. Then my scalp tore away, and the bear dropped me onto a mossy hummock. By then it had carried me about 80 feet.

"I knew my only chance was to convince the bear I was dead, but I didn't want my belly up with my vitals exposed. With my right arm—my left arm was useless—I held myself belly down.

"I held my breath until I almost passed out, playing dead, while the bear chewed on my back and batted me on the side of my head with its claws.

"I think it left because I played dead. I didn't move until I couldn't hear it.

"Joyce might have spooked the bear off. She had white long johns on and had crawled out of her sleeping bag. She was standing trying to see where I was. She was unhurt.

"I staggered to my feet, wondering if Joyce was all right. I went back to camp and Joyce. Blood poured down my face.

"It was up to Joyce then. She found the rifle and lit a fire. She bandaged me with the meat cloths she had packed, got me into the two sleeping bags, and put me near the fire. She gave me aspirin and strong tea with a lot of sugar in it. It was three hours until daylight, and we had to decide whether Joyce should leave me and go get a helicopter, or if I could make it out on my own.

"I didn't want her to go along with that bear still around, so at daylight we started walking. My head lay on my left shoulder because I'd been hurt on the right side and it had weakened my neck. I carried my .44 and Joyce had the rifle. We half expected the bear to waylay us.

"I didn't dare stop. About a mile from the highway I sat down, but I knew I'd never get up again if I didn't go on. I finished hiking those 15 miles, beating Joyce to the highway. I stopped the first car and asked the driver to call an ambulance."

Three doctors worked for hours stitching together the great gashes in Al's body. He needed six pints of blood. For two days he hovered between life and death, but on the third day Joyce saw color in his face and a glint in his eyes.

Al later heard that a party of nonresident hunters on horses had been in the same area earlier. They were trying to get pictures and had chased a brown bear sow with two big cubs. One of the hunters wounded the sow.

That isn't the end of the story. On November 10, about six weeks after the September 23, 1972, attack on the Thompsons, and only 10 miles away, hunter Leland C. Collins, of Anchorage, was after a moose when he came across a brown bear sow with two big cubs. The bear heard or saw Collins, who later told Al, "It came bounding, looking for me."

Collins shot, hitting the bear in the head, and momentarily drove it off. Then the bear came back and Collins got another shot into it. He drove it off again, but not before the bear managed to slash his head and chest.

Al was still bandaged from his attack when he visited the just-hospitalized Collins.

"His wounds were the same as mine," Al said. "The bear that chewed on me apparently had only one large tooth—the upper right canine. I had a big groove from it in the bone of my arm where it partly destroyed the main nerves, and in my scalp. From the bite marks it looked as if the other teeth were worn or broken off, and my arm expecially was mashed more than punctured. Where the bear hit into my back there was one big hole, and then other, much smaller, tooth marks. The marks on Collins were similar."

Though his left arm was still almost useless, and he was weak and bandaged, Al joined Dick Dykema and a state trooper in a search for the bear that mauled Collins. They flew in by helicopter.

"I had a grudge against that bear," Al said. "I think it was the same one that got me. I carried a slug-filled 12-gauge autoloader across the crook of my bum left arm.

"We found tracks and a lot of blood where Collins had hit the bear. Once we went around a big pile of brush. The bear came out behind us, so we were right on top of it. Other troopers were in the noisy helicopter, flying nearby to protect us. They weren't woodsmen and didn't understand that in the woods you don't want noise. The bear got away."

The next day Al, Dykema, and troopers again searched for the bear. By this time Commissioner Chapple, Al's boss, learned that the still shaky Thompson was on the revenge trail, and he ordered him out of the woods. Dykema and others continued the hunt on horses. But the bear was never found.

Al doesn't hunt with a bow now because of his bear-damaged left arm, but he still hunts with a rifle. Last year he tracked and killed a crippled grizzly that threatened a fishery research crew. He has no fear of bears or hatred for them, but he has a lot of respect. He now carries super protection when he patrols in bear country—a sawed-off double 10 gauge filled with 935-grain handloads.

Al is scarred for life. He is tired of the attention he's been given because of the attack, but he agreed to tell OUTDOOR LIFE about his experience because he feels it might help others. Al is aware that bear attacks are increasing in Alaska. Action by the Carter Administration, which establishes vast new parks, wildlife refuges, and wilderness areas in Alaska, probably will attract more visitors, and bear attacks will increase.

If a woodswise, experienced, and armed hunter with Al Thompson's savvy can get mauled, what chance has an unarmed and inexperienced person when a bear attacks? Practically none.

My incomplete Alaska bear files include details about six human deaths from bear attacks and 10 severe maulings since 1972 [written in 1981— *Editor's note*]. Most attacks involved brown/grizzly bears (scientists consider Alaska's coastal brown bear and the interior grizzly as a single highly variable species). Prior to about 1970 Alaskans could expect an average of one severe mauling by a grizzly each year. Some victims died, some didn't.

Why the increase in attacks? Bob Hinman, deputy director of the state game division, thinks it is a matter of numbers.

"Alaska's brown/grizzly population is probably at its highest in several decades," he said.

Alaska's human population also is increasing. There are more vistors each year. "With more people in the woods, and more bears, there is more chance for interaction," Hinman added.

The impact of current game-management practices and hunting also may have triggered more attacks. Most of the huge old bears with nine and 10-foot hides have been killed by hunters, leaving a growing population of younger animals. This gives more hunters a chance to take a bear, and a seven or eight-foot hide is a nice trophy. But young bears are more feisty than old ones and more likely to attack. Carl Williams, who lived with Alaska's brown bears for 40 years (see "My 40 Years with Bears", OUT-DOOR LIFE, February 1980) believes young bears are like human teen-agers—they have to prove themselves.

The National Park Service (NPS) is concerned about the safety of vis-itors to Alaska's parks, while also wanting visitors to have maximum op-portunities to see bears. John Cook, NPS area director for Alaska, proposed regulations for Alaska's new parks that would allow visitors to carry fire-arms for protection from bears. This is a break from past NPS policy. Even today visitors to Alaska's new national monuments are advised by rangers to carry firearms.

The park service has reason to worry. There have been 13 known attacks by grizzlies in Mount McKinley National Park in 60 years, and nine of these occurred since 1971. The attack increase is linked with a tremen-dous increase in visitors. In 1971 about 44,500 people visited McKinley; in 1979 there were 251,000.

Two killings by bears have taken place in Alaska's Glacier Bay National Monument. In 1976 a grizzly killed Alan Precup, a 25-year-old Illinois camper. His partly eaten body was found after a four-day search.

In July 1980 a young black bear in the Monument apparently killed and ate Thomas Shulz, a 27-year-old camper from Juneau. Rangers killed the bear, but they could find no abnormalities about the animal.

Ignorance was largely responsible for some recent bear maulings. Most persons who were mauled had no experience with wild bears. Many are city-bred and were raised on Disney's nature pap. Idealistic youngsters from almost any city in the nation can put together a pack, and in a few hours they can fly to McKinley Park or elsewhere in Alaska where wild girzzlies are the dominant species.

Crowd a bear to get a better picture and you're likely to get slapped with a clawed paw. If you hike in thick brush, you may surprise an old griz, and it may react by slapping you down.

Park bears can't be hunted, so they have little fear of or respect for man. They learn that there is food in packs, tents, and cars. Rangers in McKinley Park had to shoot a sow in July 1980 when it repeatedly tore into tents for food.

Dr. Fred Dean, leader of the Alaska Cooperative Park Studies Unit at the University of Alaska since 1972, outlined this common park situation: "You're backpacking in bear country and a bear threatens or charges. Your first reaction is to drop the pack and climb a tree or give the bear something to chew on besides you. The bear digs into the pack and finds food. What is that bear going to do the next time he encounters a backpacker?''

Dr. Dean agrees that there probably will be an increase in bear attacks in Alaska. He thinks that most of the attacks will occur in new parks because park bears have little fear of humans and because most visitors will head for those parks.

In 1955 while researching an article on Alaska's brown bears for OUT-DOOR LIFE ("The Shy Killer" October 1955), I found only one reliable report of a brown bear eating a human body, and that was a man who drowned and washed ashore.

Since 1974 I have added to my files five cases of Alaska bears eating their victims. Two were grizzlies, two were black bears, and one was either a black or a grizzly.

In August 1974 Jay B. Reeves Jr., a 38-year-old postal employee and amateur photographer from Anchorage, Alaska, flew to Cold Bay, headquarters for the nearby Izembek National Wildlife Refuge. There he asked refuge manager Bob Jones and his assistant John Sarvis about a place where he could camp and photograph brown bears.

Reeves pitched his tent on the banks of Frosty Creek, an area often used by brownies. He was not armed.

The next morning a fisherman happened on Reeves's camp. It had been torn up by a bear. The fisherman couldn't find the photographer, and he reported what he had seen to airport security officers at Cold Bay. They searched the area on foot but didn't find Reeves. They returned to the airport to get a helicopter for a wider search.

As they circled, they flushed a brown bear from an alder patch 400 feet from Reeves's camp. There they came across a human head, ribs, and part of a pelvis. Their only firearms were handguns. A rifle was sent for. The bear again was flushed, and John Sarvis shot it. Jim Faro, a state game biologist who investigated the case with Sarvis, Jones, and others, pieced together what likely occurred, and gave me a copy of his report.

The big male brownie, weighing an estimated 550 pounds, with forepaws 8½ inches across, and an 8½-foot square hide, probably entered Reeves's camp looking for food.

As the bear tore into his tent Reeves, barefooted and without his jacket, apparently fled. The bear caught and killed him, and then carried his body into the alders and fed on it.

Bears attack humans for several reasons: They are hungry; they are protecting a kill that a human has blundered upon; they are protecting cubs; they are surprised and act defensively. Some bears hold a grudge for a past wounding, as in the Al Thompson mauling. A bear that loses a fight with another bear may attack a human to bolster injured pride. Bears have great dignity and pride. As with other animals, including man, some bears are probably natural soreheads and attack just for the hell of it.

The spectacular nature of bear attacks and the resulting publicity can give the impression that Alaska is filled with bears just waiting to maul visitors. Not so. The chance of a bear attacking a reasonably prudent backpacker is slight. Bears are naturally shy, and most flee at the sight of man, especially in areas where they are hunted. The Mount McKinley National

Park statistics should be reassuring: 1.4 million tourists (including about 200,000 who hiked off the road system and camped at least overnight) visited between 1971 and 1980, and in that time there were no deaths due to mauling and only nine reported maulings.

You can improve the odds by following Al Thompson's basic rules: no food in camp and a clean camp area; a firearm and flashlight in a handy place when sleeping (though firearms are not allowed in Alaska's "old" national parks or in national parks in other states). Avoid camping in a pass that bears and other game commonly use, or on major trails. Make plenty of noise when traveling in brushy or timbered bear country so you don't surprise a grizzly (many hikers wear a small bell or place rocks in a tin-can rattler). Don't crowd a bear to get close-up photographs.

My records show that most of those who survive bear attacks have played dead, as did Al Thompson. An attacking bear will usually bite and claw so long as its victim struggles. When the victim lies still, most bears leave. Sometimes a bear stands and watches his victim, waiting for movement. It will resume biting at the slightest move, as many victims have learned.

Grizzlies can climb trees, though most won't, and a perch in a stout tree has saved many lives. Unfortunately there are often no climbable trees where you may encounter a grizzly. Also don't run from a bear, unless there is a nearby tree or other shelter. Bears are tempted to chase fleeing prey.

When in bear country pack a rifle with the wallop of a .30/06 or better. Be prepared to use it day and night. You might pack a rifle for a lifetime and use it just once, but that one time could justify all those years of packing.

Unless you're a gilt-edged expert at using it, forget that .44 Magnum. It's good only when the bear is right on top of you, and by then you've waited too long. The .44 may save your life, but the chances of being mauled by a determined grizzly are good if that's your only protection.

If you do everything you should, as Al and Joyce Thompson did, and a bear still mauls you, what then? Here's Al Thompson's advice: "Never give up, no matter how much a bear has chewed on your body or how much you hurt."

A Grizzly Scalped Me

**Eddie Dixon
with Bus Hamilton**

April, 1967

Roy Hamilton came into our moose-hunting camp on Boss Mountain that cold October night with news that stirred everybody up. He thought he and the hunters he was guiding had seen a grizzly that afternoon.

They had caught a glimpse of a bear running off through a thick growth of fir. When they walked up to the place they found what was left of the decayed carcass of a cow moose, most of it eaten, that the bear had been feeding on. We decided later that a hunter had shot her early in the fall, out of season, and had left the carcass out in the woods to rot.

"I didn't see enough to be sure," Roy told us, "but I don't think that bear was a black!"

I'm a Shuswap Indian, living on the Canim Lake Reservation east of 100 Mile House, in British Columbia 200 miles north of the United States border. It also happens I have only one good arm.

I was 44 at the time, and working as a guide for Bus Hamilton, Roy's father, with whom I am telling this story. He operates the Ten-ee-ah (Shuswap for moose) camp for fishermen on Spout Lake north of Lac la Hahe in summer, and in the fall outfits and guides hunters in the mountains east of his place.

This was the fall of 1963. We were camped on Boss Creek, in rough, heavily timbered country a few miles west of Wells Gray Provincial Park, which has some of the finest snow-peak scenery in that part of British Columbia. It also has an abundance of mountain game. The park itself is closed to hunting, but the area around it is top country for moose, caribou, sheep, and goats.

There were six hunters in the party. I was guiding two from Las Vegas, George Riddle, a steel company contractor, and Cleo Cripps, who heads

40

a firm that makes and installs air-conditioning equipment. Riddle was 56. Cripps was approximately 20 years his junior.

We were using a sleeping tent but doing our cooking outside. Although it was only late October, the weather up in that high country was cold, and there were about eight inches of snow on the ground. Conditions were pretty rough for hunting and, likely for that reason, we weren't having much luck with moose, the game we wanted most.

Then Roy Hamilton came in with his story about the bear he had seen, and my two hunters lost all interest in moose hunting.

"What are we wasting our time on moose for, if there's a grizzly?" George Riddle asked. "I'd rather have one bear rug than a dozen moose."

Cripps agreed, and the three of us started to lay our plans for the next day. Roy told me exactly where to find the moose carcass. We'd have a look at it the first thing in the morning, and if we failed to find the bear, we'd wait around for him. Sooner or later, he was almost sure to come back to eat.

About that time, Bus Hamilton, who was in charge of the party, sounded a warning.

"Don't forget what you're after," he said. "Nobody ever knows what a grizzly will do. But if you shoot him and don't kill him, you'll likely have a fight on your hands. Keep your guard up."

I guess we didn't take him as seriously as we should have. I have lived in bear country all my life, and I've had plenty of dealings with blacks, but I had never hunted grizzlies, and neither had the two Las Vegas hunters.

We rode away from camp at daybreak the next morning in a light fall of snow. A miserably cold wind was sweeping through the timber. Riddle was carrying a .30/06 Winchester Model 70, and Cripps had a Winchester .300 Magnum, also a Model 70. My rifle was a 6.5 mm. Norwegian Krag, a converted military rifle.

Between a quarter and a half a mile from the place Roy Hamilton had described, we stopped, tied our horses, and went ahead on foot. We were getting close to the spot when I heard ravens squawking like sixty up ahead.

"The bear is home," I told Cripps and Riddle in a low undertone.

"How do you know?"

"Hear those birds? The bear is keeping them away from their breakfast."

We were 90 feet from him, moving carefully through fairly open jackpines, before we saw him. It was plain to me in the first instant that he knew we were there.

He had heard or smelled us, and was standing broadside to us beside the moose remains with his forefeet up on a log, swinging his head from side to side and sniffing to get a better snootful of our scent.

Hunters who have had wide experience with grizzlies have told me since then that it's almost a sure bet a brizzly intends to come for you if he lets you get as close as 90 feet. There is very little chance that a man can approach that close without the bear knowing it, and by that time the bear has made up his mind what he is going to do. If he had decided to clear out, he wouldn't have been there. If he's still there, you better expect trouble.

My hunters hesitated an instant for fear of hitting me, and the bear lunged down to bite at my head.

I didn't know that at the time, but I guess it wouldn't have made any difference. We didn't lose a second. I touched Cripps on the shoulder and pointed the instant the bear came into view, and Riddle barked, "Let him have it, Cleo."

The .300 Magnum bellowed, and the bear dropped off the log and spun in a series of cartwheels, just like an overgrown cat. I saw a patch of red start to spread on his side, but it was too far back. I had a hunch there was trouble coming.

I slammed a shot at him, but it had no effect.

"Keep shooting," I yelled at the two hunters. "When that bear lands, he's going to come for us."

I was right. The grizzly charged the instant he got his feet under him. Bawling and growling, he smashed through a thick growth of small cedars. We could see only his back. I shot again in the hope of stopping him, but missed, and then he broke into the open 50 feet away, and we were all shooting at once.

In all, we hit that grizzly six times as he was coming at us but didn't knock him down. He was hit twice in the mouth, once in the throat, twice in the chest, and once in a foot. Those six wounds were in addition to Cleo's first hit just behind the ribs.

At one point, a shot belted the grizzly back on his rear. He slowed, skidded to a stop, and went down on his haunches for a second. Then he was up and coming again as if nothing had happened.

I'd had three shells in my Krag to start with. There was only one left when the bear came out of the thick brush. I used it, and there were no more. In that same instant, I heard Cleo yell, "My gun is empty!"

I'm one-armed, as I mentioned earlier. I was working in a sawmill back in 1959 when a small stick fell against the headsaw. I reached for it, and my left hand went down between the saw and the table. I couldn't get hold of anything to yank myself free, and the saw, chewing into my sleeve, pulled me down three times.

It was either my neck or my arm, so I let the arm go. It was severed below the elbow.

Now a steel hook replaces my left hand. I get along with it pretty well, but it's awkward for some jobs. A one-armed rifleman can't reload as fast as one with two hands, for instance, and I knew that I was going to have to go into a bear fight with an empty gun.

"Split up!" I yelled.

Cripps dodged 10 or 12 feet to my left, Riddle about the same distance to the right. For some reason, the bear had his eye on Riddle and swerved toward him. I saw that he was poking fresh shells frantically into his rifle, but I knew the grizzly wouldn't give him enough time.

It all happened in a second or two. I was a few years younger than Riddle, and I thought maybe I could move faster. Besides, I was the guide, and it was my job to keep that bear off my hunter if I could.

As the grizzly came around a small jackpine, I took one quick step and jabbed the stock of my rifle in his face to divert him.

The bear grabbed the stock, put his teeth clear through it, split it as if spikes had been driven in, and tore the butt plate away. In the same instant, he slapped the rifle out of my hands with a forepaw, and I saw it go spinning into the brush 30 feet away. Then he walloped me on the shoulder and knocked me flat.

I shoved my steel hook into his mouth to keep him away from my face, but he took care of that about the way he had the rifle. I didn't lose my hook, but the hard fiberglass cuff will carry his teeth marks as long as I wear it. He bit down once, cuffed it aside, and grabbed my good arm in his jaws. I felt him crunch down, and I thought that arm was a goner too, but although his teeth went all the way through, they luckily missed bone.

I suppose it's only natural for a man to have strange thoughts at a time like that. The thing I remember most clearly about that savage attack was the bear's horrible foul breath in my face. He had been feeding on moose carrion, probably for two or three weeks, and the smell was so bad I seemed to be rolling in the stuff.

The whole thing happened too fast for me to know when Cleo and George got more ammunition into their rifles, but the bear was standing right over me, and they both hesitated for a second or two for fear of hitting me.

The bear let go of my arm and grabbed my head in his jaws. If he could have gotten a little better hold, he would have crushed my skull like an eggshell. As it was, his teeth slipped and peeled away my scalp all the way from my right ear up to the top of my head. He even tore the top part of my ear away from my head.

That was the last bite he got at me, thank God! Cripps and Riddle fired almost together, from less than 10 feet away on either side of the grizzly, and the bear collapsed and rolled on top of me. Their presence of mind and quick shooting were all that saved my life. In the next few seconds, that grizzly certainly would have killed me by crunching my neck or head.

The bear had not stopped bawling and raging for an instant.

George and Cleo couldn't see much of me for bear blood, and for a minute they thought they had shot me as well as him. They admitted later that this was the worst fright they had during the whole affair.

The grizzly was lying on top of me, my good arm was useless, and I couldn't get up. They had to pull me out from beneath the bear and help me to my feet. When I looked around at the grizzly, he was still moving and trying to raise his head. I was half out of my senses.

"Brain him," I begged, "before he gets up again."

George took care of it with a shot in the head, and then they turned their attention to me, wiped the worst of the blood off, and gave me what first aid they could, including bandaging my torn scalp back in place.

We were in a pretty bad fix: five miles from camp in rough country with heavy timber and deep canyons, and I was hurt so badly I wasn't sure I could stay in the saddle without help. My right arm was paralyzed, and a steel hook isn't worth a great deal on a horse.

Cleo went back and brought the horses up, and they boosted me onto mine. I hooked the reins over the horn and let the horse have its head.

When we got close to camp, George rode ahead to get the car started and warmed up. We had 35 miles over a rough gravel road to drive to 100

Mile House in addition to the horseback ride. But just four hours after the bear had knocked me down, I was in the office of Dr. Peter Mudge there, and he was starting to patch me up.

I had spent 55 days in a hospital at Williams Lake at the time I lost my arm, and that was enough hospital to last me a lifetime. Anyway, I didn't feel too bad, and Dr. Mudge agreed that he could repair me about as well in his office.

It took him 2½ hours to finish the job—scraping my skull, sewing my scalp back in place, fixing the torn ear, cleaning and closing the deep bite in my arm, and loading me with antibiotics. I required 44 stitches in all. The part I liked least was the skull scraping. The doctor went right down to the bone, and that really hurt.

I was a little weak and groggy for a few days because of the blood I had lost, but I recovered very fast. In three weeks, I was back guiding for Bus. I had better luck on that trip, too. I took two hunters out for moose, and they both killed good bulls the same afternoon. It was too late in the day to get back to camp, so we siwashed out in the snow that night.

The story of the bear attack was carried in newspapers over most of Canada and in many places in the United States. It even appeared in The New York Times. One paper headlined it, "Bear Scalps Indian."

The grizzly weighed about 400 pounds, but as the story circulated he grew heavier and I grew older. He finally wound up at something over 800 pounds in the newspaper accounts, and I got to be more than 50 years old. I still chuckle at some of the clippings.

The day after we killed the grizzly, Roy Hamilton and another guide went back to take the hide.

Cleo and George said at the time that they were through hunting grizzlies for life. I don't know whether they have kept that resolution or not, but I do know one thing. If I ever have a run-in with another one, I doubt it will be because I go looking for him. The next time I might not have partners along with the coolness and courage of Cleo and George. If they had lost their heads or run off, I'd have been a dead Shuswap.

PART

II

OBSERVING AND CONTROLLING BEARS

We Tag Live Bears

Al Erickson

July, 1957

We were after bears, and equipped for it. The live-trap was an eight-foot section of 36-inch steel culvert, with a steel drop door at one end and boarded up at the other with two-inch planks reinforced with steel rods set six inches apart. The trigger mechanism was arranged so as not to trip until a tug of at least 35 pounds was put on the bait. We figured that would rule out skunks, porcupines, coons, stray dogs, and other lesser fry. We wanted bears, nothing else.

For bait we had a quarter of a young deer that had died a natural death at the Cusino Wildlife Experiment Station operated by the Michigan Department of Conservation in the upper peninsula, near the town of Shingleton.

We loaded the 500-pound trap onto a pickup truck, drove to a place where we'd seen bear sign, and lugged the clumsy contraption a few yards to what looked like a good spot. Dragging the slightly ripe venison back and forth along an old woods road, we laid a scent trail leading to the trap. Then, fastening the bait firmly on the trigger, we headed back to the station.

We could hardly wait for morning. If we caught a bear it would be the first, so far as we knew, ever taken anywhere in the country in a live-trap and for the purposes we had in mind. We drove out shortly after daylight, and even before we climbed out of the truck we saw that the trap's door was down. We'd caught something.

It was a bear, just as we'd hoped, and it was plain he didn't take kindly to the proceedings. He wasn't going crazy, trying to tear the culvert apart, or anything like that. He was wasting no energy at all—just sitting calmly on his haunches, awaiting developments. But when we peered at him he stared back in a decidedly jaundiced fashion.

49

We'd trapped this bear for scientific reasons—as a beginning toward a wildlife-research project aimed at solving a few of the riddles in the life history of black bears. We intended to measure and weigh him, fix a numbered metal tag in each of his ears, then turn him loose unharmed. We realized it was a rough assignment, and the fact that none of us knew anything about handling live bears didn't make it any smoother.

We began by loading the trap—bear and all—on a truck and driving to a platform scale. By weighing the trap with the bear in it, we could figure his weight later by deducting the weight of the trap.

The weighing accomplished, we proceeded to the ear tagging. We'd had a series of three-inch holes cut in the sides of the culvert for ventilation, and also on the theory that it might be possible to slip a tag into the ear of a captive bear through one of these apertures. But a couple of trials convinced us it wouldn't work. The bear wouldn't cooperate. There was only one alternative—to somehow anesthetize him with ether.

That meant making the trap airtight. We started by stuffing rags into the holes, but the bear unstuffed them as fast as we poked them in. We then tried wooden plugs driven firmly into place. They stayed. Next we wedged the door tight, banked dirt around the bottom of the trap, and began administering ether by pouring it through one small unplugged aperture. Before we were through we'd used 3½ pounds of it.

Then we hauled the inert bear out, tagged his ears, measured him, and later watched a very drunk bruin reel off into the woods. When we weighed the empty trap later we found that our first captive wasn't much of a bear—he weighed only 115 pounds. But it took us a whole day to handle him.

That was in August 1952. By the summer of 1955 we repeatedly tagged, measured, weighed, and released a bear in 20 to 25 minutes after arriving at the trap. Our methods have improved, and so have the results, but basically we still rely on the same procedure—catch, anesthetize, handle, and let 'em go.

There's nothing new about marking birds, animals, and fish with metal bands or tags. Audubon fixed silver-wire leg bands on birds in 1803. That was the first time it was tried in this country, but others had done it before elsewhere. For the past 20 to 30 years wildlife biologists have used the same method to study fish ànd animals as well as birds. Metal disks have been attached to gills and fins of trout, salmon, and muskellunge, and numbered tags have been clipped in the ears of deer, sheep, and moose.

But bear banding is relatively new. We believe our Michigan project is the first of its kind ever attempted, and we've been doing fairly well with it. During the summer of 1955 we caught and released 34 blacks. By last fall the total had mounted to 109. Of that number about 90, so far as we know, are still roaming the woods wearing our ear tags. To date 17 have been killed and reported to us by hunters. In addition, we have retrapped and released 13 more, so we're beginning to find out some of the things we hoped to learn about black bear behavior. The project is now in its third year, and before we wind it up we hope to turn between 150 and 200 tagged bears loose in the woods.

Working with that many bears proved a novel and lively job. As game biologist on the project, I had two summers jammed with excitement and surprise.

I can't say we had any close calls. The average trapped bear is far more philosophical than most persons would think. But bear behavior varies widely, and when an ornery one comes along or one that weighs 425 pounds (the heaviest we caught), the tagging crew has its hands full.

I've been asked many times what we hope to accomplish by doing this. Since those who ask usually are sportsmen who foot the bill for just about all wildlife research, I'd like to explain the project's purposes in detail.

To begin with, the black bear is growing in importance as a game animal. In Michigan some excellent bear dogs have been bred and trained in recent years, several organized hunts are held each season, and the bear is coming to be more and more appreciated by sportsmen. That's also true in other sections of the country.

Then, game biologists know little about the black bear. The things we're not sure of, but guess at, would fill a book.

How long does he live, for example, and how far does he travel? Does the female breed every second year? If she loses her cubs the first summer does she breed again without delay? How old must cubs be to survive the loss of their mother? Should blacks be protected? What are their exact food requirements, their reproduction rate? When do they start and stop breeding? Under what conditions do they hibernate? What's the surplus population that can safely be harvested each hunting season without depleting the breeding stock?

We launched our trapping project in the hope of finding answers to some of these questions. We need to work out a bear-management program that will keep pace with the growing importance of the black as a game animal, and insure an adequate harvest of the crop as well as the future of the hunting. We believe the results of our live-trapping will help us to do that.

It was while I was a student at Michigan State University, majoring in wildlife biology and working for the conservation department during the summer, that we caught our first bear. A few days later, while I was away from the Cusino Station, other biologists trapped a second and we believe, a much bigger black. But he refused to accept confinement, ripped the reinforced planking out of the trap's rear end, and went on his way. That ended both trap and project for that year.

The following summer two or three bears were taken, but no one had much time to devote to the job. One of the captives was interesting, however. It was a female, and when the trappers visited the set they found her two young cubs sitting on top of the trap waiting for ma to get out.

I returned to the station in the spring of 1955 and began the bear-trapping program on a full-time basis. We set our first trap June 15, again using a chunk of venison for bait. By that time we were using a trap of a new design, with no apertures and with a welded steel back replacing the reinforced planks. It certainly looked bear-proof, and proved to be so. But there was still a chance for the bear to make trouble when we opened the door and hauled him out.

We found a black in our trap the next morning. I still don't know his weight, but we guessed it at 350 to 400 pounds. He was too big for us at this stage of the game, mostly because we weren't prepared. We had only a one-pound can of ether with us, and that wasn't enough. We'd learned that ether did a quicker and more effective job if it was sprayed into the trap (calked and banked to make it airtight) through one small opening, rather than poured in.

So we loaded our spray gun and let the bear have all the ether we had. We allowed him about 10 minutes to become unconscious, and when there was no longer any commotion in the trap we opened the door and hauled him out. He was limp but not unconscious, and when I snapped the first tag into his ear he jerked his head around and made a grab for me. Then he tried to roll to his feet.

We threw a noose of half-inch rope around his neck and snubbed him to our pickup, hoping to hold him long enough to finish the job. But he came out of the ether as if he hadn't had it, snapped the rope with one lunge, and departed on the run. We haven't seen him since though we operated the trap in his neighborhood for several weeks.

We took two more bears in that same set the next two nights. Ready with an ample supply of ether, we handled and released them without incident. Our project was off to a flying start.

What we needed now were more traps. We had two and we began work on four more. Meantime, someone suggested we test the live-traps used in taking deer for research and stocking purposes. They're built of one-inch lumber, 12 feet long, four feet high, and three feet wide, with a drop door at each end. We added floors to a couple, tucked them into the woods, and baited them.

They were all right for catching bears but no good at holding them. The first morning we found one sprung but minus a drop door. The bear had ripped it to splinters and walked out. Next night the other trap also took a bear, but when we got to it in the morning it looked as if a small bomb had exploded inside. The trap was ripped and chewed to kindling, and blackie had gone out via a hole in the top big enough to pass a small elephant. That ended our efforts to catch bears in deer traps.

By mid-July we had six culvert traps operating, and had worked out a smooth and effective procedure for handling the bears after they were anesthetized.

We quickly learned that the ether's effects didn't last long enough to permit tagging, measuring, and weighing unless we administered more of it as we went along. So, after much experimenting, we devised a metal cone with a pad of sponge rubber around the inside of the large end which would fit snugly over the muzzle of almost any bear, big or little. The small end was closed with a pad of thick cloth. By spraying ether on the pad and alternately holding the cone in place and giving the victim a whiff of air as the need arose, we found we could keep the situation under control.

We anesthetized 34 bears that way the first summer. In addition, we put three to sleep a second time when they wandered back into the traps. Three stopped breathing from the effects of the ether but were revived by artificial respiration. We've had about as good success since.

We lost four bears during that summer. Two died from heat and exhaustion during periods of extremely hot weather. One was shot in the trap by a hunter who evidently was scared off before he got the trap open. The fourth was a cub, and it was the only bear to die from the ether. We didn't have the cone with us that day, and when we tried to anesthetize him by pouring ether on a rag held over his nose, he got an overdose.

We trapped our biggest just about the time we thought we had all our problems licked, but he convinced us otherwise. We'd been getting reports of an unusually large bear in the vicinity of Blaney Park, about 30 miles southeast of the station, so we trucked a culvert trap there and went after him. We spread sand in front of the door, and for three or four days in a row we found tracks showing that he's walked up to the trap, peered in, sniffed the bait, and backed off. We decided later that one reason for his unusual caution might be that the 36-inch culvert was a tight squeeze for a bear his size.

His tracks whetted our determination, so we built a special trap with an open grid in the back in place of the usual steel plate. We figured that maybe if he could see through the trap he might not be so skittish. Also, since air would be moving through the culvert, he'd be able to smell the bait better.

The new trap worked the first night, but we didn't catch the bear. He reached in from the back end, through the grid's bars, hooked the bait, and tripped the trigger. The same happened on two more nights. We didn't get him and he didn't get our bait, but when we covered the grid with heavy wire mesh the temptation proved too much for him.

A local man who was watching the set for us phoned to report that we'd trapped the biggest bear in northern Michigan. The word spread quickly, and when we got there we found a gallery of about 75 excited spectators waiting near the trap.

We closed the trap's open end with a heavy tarp and went to work. The ether took effect unusually fast, perhaps because the bear filled the trap so completely there wasn't much air space around him. When he became unconscious we opened the door, got the ether cone over his nose, and clipped in the ear tags. Then I crawled in the trap to haul him out, but I couldn't budge him. Since there wasn't room for two of us in the trap with him, we tied ropes around him and dragged him out. The measuring was uneventful, save for the fact that the ether cone was proving to be too small for the bear, but I had misgivings when we got ready to weigh him.

We'd worked out a simple and fast weighing method, mounting a steel tripod in the back of our pickup and equipping it with a cable and winch much like those used by tow trucks to hoist wrecked cars. All we had to do was roll our bear unto a square of stout canvas, run a length of chain through steel rings sewed in the corners, wrap him up, hook a heavy-duty spring balance into the chain, hang it on the cable, and winch him off the ground.

The system worked fine, but we hadn't used it on anything as heavy as this bear. It took four or five men to roll him onto the canvas, which barely reached around him. We brought the corners together, hooked on our scales, and started to crank the hoist. Before he was clear of the ground there was a loud ripping—and the tarp tore as if it were paper.

By that time the bear was coming to. We jammed the cone on his nose and poured ether to him. I was determined to weigh him, for I felt sure he'd set something of a record for us. So we hurriedly tied his four feet together, looped our chain through, and hoisted him. The needle went around to 425 pounds. Then we lowered him, untied his feet and stepped back a respectful distance.

He opened his eyes, blinked, raised his head, and looked around as if wondering where he was. Then he rolled to a sitting position, his head lolling down. Again he took a look around, and tried to get to his feet. He took a step or two, and fell sprawling. I've never seen anything quite so funny as a bear reviving from ether, and this big lug put on a wonderful show for our entertainment.

He got up and fell down three or four times, stared back at us, and shook his head many times before he finally managed to stay on his feet and lumber off. That's the last we've seen of him, and there have been no further reports of him hanging around Blaney Park.

As the work went along, we made some interesting tests with baits and soon came to the conclusion that venison was tops. Our supply was limited, for we got it only when someone had the misfortune to kill a deer on the highway, but it proved most effective. A bag of beef bones ran a close second.

Chickens didn't work. Highway-killed rabbits, woodchucks, and porkies did no better and—much to our surprise—fish were a complete dud. We baited traps with bags of fish offal and with net-killed, unmarketable fish we got from commercial netters on Lake Superior, but the bears would have nothing to do with them.

I don't think this means that the black is a deer predator and develops his taste for venison as a result. In the wild he probably gets a crack at deer meat only now and then, mostly by accident, when he kills a fawn or comes across a dead deer. But he certainly relishes it.

We noticed that the bears became more finicky in their choice of bait, and therefore harder to trap, as summer advanced. They come out of hibernation in early spring ravenously hungry, especially females with young cubs, and then they'll eat almost anything. Despite our experience, old bear trappers have assured me that fish are hard to beat as bait at that season. But when the berry crop matures, starting with wild strawberries in June, blackie seems to care less and less for meat and is harder and harder to entice with it.

Anothing thing that surprised us was his aversion to putrid bait. He doesn't object to meat being mildly high—say a haunch of venison three or four days old in hot weather—but if it gets stronger than that he doesn't want it. Consequently, he kept us busy changing baits frequently.

With the culvert traps, we were limited to big baits. The bears wouldn't go in them for tidbits. More than that, we needed baits large enough to stand a good solid tug. When you expect a bear to trip a trigger set at 35 to 40 pounds, you have to give him somthing hefty to pull on. We found a quarter of deer about right.

We tested a variety of other baits supposed to be almost infallible, such as honey and molasses, and found them next to useless. We poured small pools of molasses in front of the trap doors, and time after time a bear would walk up to them, sniff, and turn away. Honey was only a little more attractive. We even tried peanut butter, smearing it on stumps and logs near the traps. The story got around that we'd discovered a new sure-fire bear lure, but the truth is they didn't go near the stuff.

We had only one disappointment in connection with the project. We were eager to capture females with cubs, then run the cubs down on foot or tree them with Big Blue, a rangy bluetick I'm training for bear hunting, catch them, and add facts about them to our records. Though large bears are hardest to handle and provide the most fireworks, the young animals are the most valuable to the research we are doing.

But we haven't had any luck taking females with cubs. Several times family parties came to the traps and looked things over, but not one sow with youngsters in tow ventured inside. Why? We have no theories, though it may indicate abnormal caution on the part of mother bears with cubs.

In the middle of the first summer it occurred to me that we could run a bigger line, and maybe take more bears at less cost, if we used ordinary steel traps in place of the culvert type. I didn't like the idea of using regular bear traps, which usually grip an animal above the foot and are so powerful they often smash ankle bones. But I knew that northern Michigan bounty trappers frequently caught small bears by the pad of the foot in No. 4 coyote traps which held them without much injury. I figured that if we used a No. 4½, somewhat bigger and stronger than the coyote size, we could hold all but a few big blacks and do the job humanely.

The advantages were obvious. One man could carry a dozen steel traps and set them in a forenoon. We had to truck our live-traps, and it took a crew of three half a day to move and set one. Steel traps would speed the proceedings and boost the catch.

The drawbacks were equally obvious. Once we caught a bear we'd have to rope him, tie him up, and anesthetize him—all without benefit of our airtight culvert. But I like to handle animals, and I knew that a determined and careful man can do wonders with a rope. So, doping out a plan that we thought would meet the requirements, we got a few No. 4½ traps and made the sets.

The system worked like a charm. In five days we caught four bears, the biggest a 163-pound female, trussed them, fed them ether, tagged, measured, weighed, and turned them loose. We figured we were getting pretty good at this business—until we got a bear that made us wonder.

We didn't catch him. He came as a bonus. John Arduin, a state predatory-animal control officer, got a request to liquidate a nuisance bear that was hanging around a farm near Newberry.

John set a standard bear trap, and next morning the farmer found a bear in it. He didn't go close enough for a good look before he phoned Arduin. "You caught a cub," he reported. "Come get it."

John called me, and three of us went along with the tagging equipment. When we arrived we found that the "cub" was a male that turned out to weigh 320 pounds. We hadn't tackled a bear that big outside the live-traps, and I felt a little hesitant. But the bear was taking it reasonably easy, so we sailed into him just as we had the smaller ones.

We'd made a neck noose for handling our steel-trapped bears, fastening a T handle at one end of a six-foot length of iron pipe and a loop of strong rope at the other. By dropping the loop over a bear's head and twisting it snug, we could control him much as a stockman leads a bull with a nose ring and staff.

I worked in close to the big fellow, and he obligingly rolled over on his back. It was no sign of surrender, but it gave me the chance I wanted. I got the noose around him and tightened it. He fought like a tiger but couldn't get loose. Next we snared a hind foot with a loop of rope, and after that it wasn't hard to get ropes on two more feet. The trap held the fourth.

We spread-eagled him on his back, tied him down, and were ready for the ether. Getting the cone in place and keeping it there is the most ticklish part of the job, for while the noose holds the bear's neck securely his head is still free and his jaws can snap like a rat trap. The trick is to ease the cone down to within a foot or so of his nose, have a helper attract his attention for a second, clap the cone over his jaws and throw your body and arms down on his head, and stay there until the ether takes effect.

That 320-pounder took some rassling, but in less than a minute we were squirting ether onto the cloth and he soon quieted down. Half a pound of anesthetic put him out cold.

This bear was by no means the toughest and most troublesome one we took. That distinction went to a 173-pound female that stepped into one of our No. 4½ traps in mid-September. The trap was the last we visited at the end of the day and it was close to dusk when we arrived. She hadn't been caught more than half an hour, we judged, and she was fresh and fighting mad—growling, bawling, raging, and lunging at us the length of the chain.

Getting ropes on her was a wild hassle, and putting the cone over her nose was wilder. Then, worst luck, the ether froze on the pad (it was a sharp, frosty evening) and we couldn't put her all the way out. She was half conscious while we tagged, measured, and weighed her, and she resented every part of it. Before we could untie her foot, she came to in a combat state.

We threw a couple of hitches around her neck and snubbed her to trees while we freed one foot at a time. Then we flipped the ropes off and moved back, expecting her to head for the woods. Instead, she took a few steps, stopped and looked us over, ripped out a surly growl, and came straight for us.

It was lucky we had Big Blue with us. He ducked in, his hair standing the wrong way, and the old girl turned on him. While she chased him all over the place, we climbed into the truck. Then I called Blue off. The bear never ran away. The last we saw of her she was standing in the brush, her face wrinkled in hate, watching us rattle away.

We still hope to trap her again some summer when she has a pair of cubs. I'd like to keep a record of the offspring of a she bear with that much cussedness and spunk.

Project Polar Bear

Jack Lentfer and Lee Miller
as told to Ben East

June, 1968

Т he bear, a medium-size boar weighing about 400 pounds, was down but not out, in a patch of very rough ice.

Ten minutes before, while hovering overhead in a helicopter, we had whopped him in the rump with a hypodermic syringe loaded with an immobilizing drug and fired by powder charge from a gun resembling a 28 gauge shotgun. The animal had paid no attention to the needle, which had delivered its dosage on impact, and he was now on the way to becoming a helpless polar bear.

He walked into the rough ice and slumped down on his rear end with his front feet braced wide apart, about to lose control. We set the helicopter down and started for him on foot. To finish our job we'd have to drag him out to smooth ice.

When we got to the bear it was apparent that he was not completely drugged. He didn't try to fight us off, but he dug his claws in and hung on. We finally got him to a smooth place, and then, to our astonishment, he stood up on all fours as if nothing had happened. We ran for the helicopter to get a second syringe, but before we could get back to him he was walking off across the ice.

Our eyes must have bugged out. A bear that can walk can fight, and one lick is all that this 400-pounder would have needed to stop us.

We had to take to the air again and fire a second shot into that bear to get things under control.

That young boar was one of 31 polar bears that the authors knocked out with the drug gun, measured, tagged, weighed, and then watched walk away unhurt on the ocean ice off Point Barrow, Alaska, in April of last year. This, the first major tagging program ever attempted on these animals, was a project undertaken by the Alaska Department of Fish and Game as part of a long-range polar-bear study (similar tagging work had been carried out previously with black, grizzly, and Alaska brown bears). We—Lentfer, 36, and Miller, 35—work for the department as game biologists stationed in the Anchorage office.

Before 1967 ended, Norway and Canada carried out similar polar-bear-tagging programs. That summer, Norwegian biologists measured and marked a total of 51 bears, hunting them off the arctic coast of Europe from a boat. Lentfer was privileged to be a member of that party. And last fall, Canada tagged another 20-odd bears in the Hudson Bay area.

The tagging programs are part of an international effort by five countries—the United States, Canada, Denmark, Norway, and Russia—to learn more about the white bear of the ice fields and to set up management programs, including hunting regulations and kill limits, that will guarantee his continued existence.

Surprisingly little is known about the polar bear's life history and ecology. How long does he live? How widely does he roam? How often does the female breed and have young? Do all the bears that inhabit the arctic ice belong to the same race, or are there individual races, belonging to separate populations, off the coasts of Europe, Asia, and North America?

Are these animals carried around the polar region with the drift of the ice fields, so that a bear may be off Russia or Norway one year and north of Canada or Alaska the next? Or are there stationary populations that live out their lives off a given coast or in the vicinity of certain big polar islands, so that each country can claim a permanent bear "herd" of its own?

These are questions that no one can yet answer. Although the polar bear is of almost universal interest to hunters and many hunters rate him the most beautiful trophy on earth, much of his way of life remains unknown.

Most important questions of all: what is the polar bear's total population and how many of his kind can be harvested safely each year? Once again, nobody knows. The U.S. Bureau of Sport Fisheries and Wildlife recently pointed out that the population has been guessed to be 8,000 to 20,000. But even such figures as those are based on tenuous assumptions and sketchy data and cannot be considered valid.

The mystery surrounding these animals is not surprising. Their home is a bitter, hostile world of ice and sea, snow and gale, and long winter darkness. Most of the polar bear's life is spent on the trackless ice, hunting seals among the pressure ridges and along the open leads, sometimes traveling 30 to 50 miles a day on a pack that may be drifting at about the same rate. There is little chance to study him as land animals are studied.

But this intriguing animal is going to have a tougher time keeping his secrets from now on. Alaska, the only state in this country having a polar-bear population, and the U.S. Bureau of Sport Fisheries and Wildlife are leading a determined program of polar-bear research. The tagging project of the Alaska Department of Fish and Game, which we carried out, was one of the first steps.

We located bears by flying from Barrow in a helicopter and a Cessna 185, both chartered. Merric Inc. of Fairbanks supplied the copter and pilot. Bobby Fischer of Barrow supplied the plane. We used both aircraft to search for fresh bear tracks on the ice. When a track was found we followed it with the copter. Tracking conditions were best on days having fresh snow, bright sun, and little wind.

Once we got close to a bear its weight was estimated and the gun was loaded with a projectile syringe carrying a drug dosage based on the bear's estimated weight. If there happened to be open water in the vicinity, we used the copter to chase the bear away from it. We also tried to keep bears out of rough ice.

Once things were right, we went in close for the shot. The needle in the rump didn't bother the bears; most of them just kept running.

After a bear was hit we circled until it went down, which took from three up to 13 minutes if the dosage was right. Now and then, if we underestimated the size of an animal, we had to resort to a second shot. Once the bear was down we landed and walked in.

The animals were stupefied by the drug, immobilized and completely helpless as we rolled them around for marking and measuring.

Drugging, handling, and even weighing these big short-tempered brutes may sound exciting, but we did not have a single close call in a month of the work. However, there were enough unexpected incidents, such as the one we related at the beginning of the story, to keep the job from getting dull.

Each bear was given a metal tag in one ear and a nylon tag in the other. The tags were numbered and they carried a legend advising that a reward would be paid for their return to the Fish and Game Department.

The bears were also tattooed in the upper lip with numbers that will make possible the identification of any bears killed by hunters, even if the tags are lost. Alaska game regulations require that the hides and skulls of all bears taken be submitted within 30 days to a representative of the game department for examination.

In addition to those permanent markings, a small bright-colored marker, visible from the air, was fastened to an ear of each bear. These markers, meant to be only temporary, were to prevent redrugging any animal already tagged and tattooed. In the white world of the ice fields, those markers really stood out.

As a further aid to identification, color-coded nylon collars were fastened around the necks of fully mature animals. It was hoped that these collars would remain in place for a year or two.

Also, a red dye—a type that deposits a thin red line in the teeth, similar to a growth ring in a tree—was injected into the body cavity in some cases. This dye will be a help in determining the age of any animal from which a tooth may someday become available.

Each bear was measured and finally, by rolling him into a net and hooking the net to a scale hung below the copter, lifted and weighed.

The results of the weighing will interest sportsmen. There has been a lot of guesswork among hunters about polar-bear weight, and some of the guesses have been wild. Rarely has a hunter killed one of these animals under circumstances that permitted actual weighing, but tales have been told of males that weighed a full ton.

The biggest we weighed pulled the scale to only about 800 pounds, but some up to 1,200 pounds have been weighed in earlier research in Alaska, and they may get bigger. Clearly, though polar bears fall well short of a ton, they do rival the Alaska brown in size.

Most of our bears were on their feet again within two to five hours after being "shot," and some recovered in 30 minutes. Once the effects of the drug wore off, the bears appeared none the worse for the experience. Several were sighted later, sporting their colored markers and going about their seal hunting and other affairs.

One of our most amusing experiences came in dealing with an old sow that gave us a hard time without raising a paw.

She was big for a female, around 600 pounds, and was accompanied by a husky yearling cub. We "shot" them both, but before the drug took effect she led the cub to the edge of a nearby open lead. There he collapsed as he was supposed to, but the old lady refused to go out.

Her hindquarters failed, as usually happened first, and she sat down on the ice. But she was hitching around, and there was danger that she'd roll into the water. If that happened, she might drown, and even if she didn't, we wouldn't be able to haul her out. One way or another we had to keep her on the ice until she was sufficiently doped to be handled.

We ran to the helicopter for a rope, fashioned a lasso, and got the noose around her neck. She was too far gone by that time to give any real trouble, but we felt as if we'd roped a stubborn old cow, and she was heavy!

"Reminds me of a song," Lee grunted. "The one that goes 'I don't want her, you can have her, she's too fat for me'."

The sow passed out five minutes after that, and we rolled her away from the lead and went to work.

Because of the possibility that at least part of the world's polar-bear population is carried clockwise around the arctic on the drifting ice, international cooperation is essential if research and management programs are to be carried out and the future of the bears safeguarded.

Such cooperation seems assured as a result of a meeting at Morges, Switzerland, last January under the sponsorship of the International Union for the Conservation of Nature. Eight working polar-bear specialists—two each from this country, Canada, Norway, and Russia—met there to compare notes, exchange information, and lay plans for future research. A single delegate from Denmark was unable to attend, but that country—which has a polar-bear population in Greenland—is also interested in the program and is expected to participate.

The U.S. delegates were Lentfer and James W. Brooks, Bureau of Sport Fisheries and Wildlife, former chief of the game division of the Alaska Department of Fish and Game.

At the meeting, plans were laid for a continuing study of the polar-bear population, and specific phases of the program were assigned to each country. Canada, Norway, and the U.S. will continue tagging and field studies, with the Alaska game department carrying out the tagging in this country. Russia also is expected to launch a tagging program.

In addition, the Bureau of Sport Fisheries and Wildlife will work on techniques for taking bear censuses. Canada and Russia will make a study of skulls, and Norway will study blood samples—all three projects aimed at determining whether all polar bears belong to one race. Alaska will undertake a study, based on tooth formation, of ages and life span, and efforts will be made to learn the polar bear's reproductive rate.

All of the information will be pooled, through the international union that sponsored the meeting in Switzerland.

Concern over the future of the polar bear has been expressed in many quarters in recent years. At the end of 1965 the Boone and Crockett Club eliminated the animal from the list of trophy game that the club accepts in its North American Big Game Competitions. There were two reasons for this action: 1) the element of unfair chase involved in hunting with aircraft, and 2) the unreliability of information about the world polar-bear population and about a safe annual-harvest figure.

"The polar bear is an international carnivore of major importance," the club's statement read. "In recent years the pursuit of these bears has increased tremendously, and their exact world status is ill defined."

Effective July 1, 1966, Alaska put polar-bear hunting on a permit basis, a further reflection of concern about the danger of overhunting. At first, 350 permits were allowed each year, but that restriction has been removed, and a permit now is required only when the bear meat will not be utilized. There is a cutoff date for permit applications of March 1, and each guide is allowed to take out only six hunters.

"The seriousness of man's inroads on the over-all bear population is not precisely known," Jim Brooks states.

Probably 1,300 to 1,400 polar bears are taken each year, including 200 to 400 taken in Alaska, where guides charge as much as $2,000 for a hunt. The annual kill in Norway is around 300, of which only about 40 are taken for trophies (the rest are killed for their pelts by commercial hunters). Russia halted all polar-bear hunting in 1956, and that ban is still in effect.

Most of Canada's kill occurs in the Northwest Territories, where, with rare exceptions, only residents are allowed to hunt. The average annual kill there for the last few years has been about 500 bears. Kill quotas have now been set for 25 arctic settlements. These quotas are intended to limit the annual take to 386, the kill figure for about 10 years ago.

If reliable population estimates can be made and the reproductive capability (minimum and maximum breeding age, and the average number of litters produced by a female in a lifetime) can be determined, then we will know how many polar bears can be taken safely each year, and hunting can be controlled accordingly.

Everyone interested in the white bear of the arctic will hope that the Swiss meeting will lead to fruitful results. The ice bear is a splendid game animal, and we can't afford to take chances with his future.

The Kodiak Bear War

Jim Rearden

August, 1964

Something brand-new and extremely effective in bear-control equipment made its appearance on Kodiak Island, Alaska, last fall. It consisted of a .30-caliber M-1 Garand semiautomatic rifle, mounted on top of a Piper plane so that it shot four inches above the prop, fired electrically with a button on the control stick, and was capable of firing its eight rounds so fast the shots blurred. When the clip was empty it could be reloaded in flight, through a sliding door in the cowling of the aircraft.

Equipped with a Nydar sight and zeroed-in at 150 yards, this ingenious little replica of a fighter plane could throw its lead inside a three-foot circle at that range.

In a brief period in the fall, the gun-mounted Piper killed 13 Alaska brown bears. Before it was available, the same type aircraft was used earlier in 1963 to kill 22 other Alaska brown bears with a gunner shooting out of the rear seat of the aircraft.

The whole operation was carried out by the Alaska Department of Fish and Game, but, while legal, was done with such secrecy that it was nearly impossible for the public to learn facts. Personnel doing the control work did no talking, and it was difficult for even other employees of the department to get information on the program. Rumors flew thick and fast.

A letter to the editor of OUTDOOR LIFE dated November 26 brought the first details to this magazine. An Anchorage man wrote that he had heard bears were being shot from an aircraft with a mounted M-1 rifle. "I was shocked and could hardly believe it," he said.

Then on January 16, 1964, a group of Kodiak guides sent a telegram to the editor saying there had been "a tremendous increase in the bear kill in the area this year with the Alaska Department of Fish and Game taking the initiative." It asked OUTDOOR LIFE to present the facts to the public.

What were the facts? What extraordinary circumstances had led the state conservation agency to use such a lethal engine to kill animals considered by many the finest big-game trophies on the continent?

The 35 brown bears (one report put it at 45) were killed as part of a fight a handful of cattlemen on Kodiak Island have waged against cattle-raiding bears along with the federal and state governments. The Piper with the M-1 belongs to Joe Zentner, a rancher, and it was used to kill Kodiak bears from the air for 10 years before the gun was mounted on it. It was converted into the gun-mounted fighter at the request of the State of Alaska.

The pilot who used the new equipment was Dave Henley, a one-time Kodiak cattleman who had been a full-time pilot for the department since 1960, and who until May, 1963, continued ranching as a sideline. He had sold his ranch shortly before using the mounted M-1, but he was still president of the Kodiak Stock Growers Association (an office he later resigned).

Bear-control work on Kodiak Island is not new. The big browns have been killing livestock on the island ever since the Russians introduced cattle there around 1795. Ranchers fighting them in recent decades have used rifles, traps, snares, lye, and even poison. Tom Nelson, who ranched on Kodiak in the 30's and 40's, hunted with a pack of imported redbone hounds and killed 115 bears.

Before Alaska gained statehood, the U.S. Fish and Wildlife Service gave the ranchers assistance in killing predatory bears. Then in January, 1960, Alaska assumed management of its own wildlife as a state, but neither that year nor the next did the Department of Fish and Game become involved in the bear war, mostly because few cattle were killed and ranchers were handling things themselves.

For 10 years, or since Zentner acquired his airplane, an average of 10 bears annually had been killed from it. Ranchers probably accounted for about as many more on the ground. In other words, about 20 bears a year have been killed for at least a decade.

And how did this sit with the law? A section of Alaska's game regulations provides that game may be taken "in defense of life or property." Hence, court conviction for killing brown bears out of season or in an illegal manner on a Kodiak cattle ranch is improbable.

Came the year 1962 and the bears started taking more cattle. At the request of the cattlemen, the Fish and Game Department helped to destroy individual cattle-killers from small planes and from the ground. There was no publicity. Outsiders heard nothing about it. The program was a continuation of the policy established by federal game officials years earlier.

In the spring of 1963 the picture changed. Killings by bears increased, and letters, telegrams, and phone calls to Alaska's Governor William A. Egan, Senator Ernest Gruening, and Commissioner Walter Kirkness of the Fish and Game Department mounted with each cow lost. The ranchers wanted more help. They even asked Senator Gruening for a supply of 1080, the deadly poison used by the Fish and Wildlife Service against coyotes and their predators in many Western states.

As a result, the control program was intensified. In the fall, the M-1 was mounted on Zentner's airplane. There are conflicting reports on the total kill, but it is clear that the Fish and Game Department killed at least 35 brown bears from the air and ground in the ranching section of Kodiak during 1963. Ranchers killed another four on the ground, and sportsmen, mostly from the nearby naval base, killed six in the ranching area.

But there were two important differences in 1963 when the cattle kills by brown bears rose to a new high. One was that a general "thinning" type of control was used. Bears on cattle range that were even suspected of endangering cattle—not just known killers—were destroyed. Some guides claimed bears were killed 20 miles from the nearest cow. Department employees who did the control work reported the farthest kill was 10 miles. Be that as it may, the thinning type of control created a furor.

And the spark that outraged Kodiak guides and sportsmen was the mounting of the M-1 rifle atop Rancher Zentner's Piper—that and the policy of secrecy. Many knew small planes had been used to hunt down bears in the past, but this was different.

What happened, I learned later, was that, in May of 1963, Ovid McKinley, a protection officer at Kodiak, helped ranchers by hunting down stock-killing bears as he had in 1962. Johnny Morton, an experienced pilot, was hired partly to help with bear-control work, and the two men killed six bears from a plane in short order.

The idea of shooting a brown bear, one of the world's finest trophy animals, from the air, is anathema to sportsmen. But these men were charged by a state agency with protecting property for individuals whose livelihood depended on livestock, and sport certainly was farthest from their minds.

At any rate, McKinley, busy with law-enforcement work in the multimillion dollar salmon fishery, could not spend enough time on control to satisfy the ranchers. They asked that Dave Henley, the department pilot who had also been a cattleman, be given the bear-control job.

The department went along. Henley, a former Mustang pilot with two enemy planes to his credit, shot down on his 23rd combat mission, flew with Gilbert Jarvela, a Kodiak bush pilot for 15 years and also an Army Air Corps pilot. Jarvela is a representative serving his second term in the Alaska legislature. Alternating at the controls and behind the gun, in a brief period while the bears were in high open country, the two racked up a score of 16. That made 22 for the year. The public was not informed of their work.

Then, in the fall, the rifle-mounted Piper was added to the stew. Henley killed 13 bears with it, and it became impossible to keep the work quiet. How do you explain an airplane parked at an airport with an automatic rifle mounted atop it? That's when the storm broke.

Small wonder, too. Guides and conservationists suddenly learned that the president of the Kodiak Stock Grower's Association, former owner of a cattle ranch, was flying a "fighter plane" after brown bears with authority to kill them anywhere within the ranching area, an airplane owned by a rancher, representing the state of Alaska—all under a cloak of secrecy.

Letters, wires, and phone calls went to Juneau and Washington from angry Kodiak guides and sportsmen and from wildlife protectionists in other parts of the state. It was then that the gun-mounted aircraft was grounded, allegedly because of "an insurance snarl."

"Insurance hell!" snorted rancher Zentner to me. "It was political pressure." Other ranchers agreed. "The department hasn't lived up to its agreement," Zentner said disgustedly.

At the height of the row, critics of the bear killing appealed to OUT-DOOR LIFE to bring the matter to the attention of sportsmen and conservationists throughout the United States. In a harshly critical telegram, 10 of the leading guides on Kodiak—Herb Downing, Darrell Farmen, Kris and Leonard Helgason, Alf Madsen, Joe Maxwell, Park Munsey, Bill Pinnell, Bill Poland, and Morris Talifson—asked this magazine to "look into the facts and present them to the public."

"There has been a tremendous increase in the bear kill in this area this year," the guides charged, "with the Alaska Department of Fish and Game taking the initiative. While the total kill has been obscured by rumor and unreported kills, it appears that the state of Alaska, using aircraft, is destroying nearly as many bears as guided trophy hunters are taking. The state intends to carry on next year, killing any bear in the general area. This will lead to the extermination of brown bears on the northeast quarter of Kodiak Island, which in turn will mean drastically reduced hunting seasons over the entire island. Some cattlemen admit that extermination of brown bears from Kodiak is their goal."

In November, a month and a half earlier, James E. Hemming of Anchorage, a federal Department of Health employee and president of the Alaska Ornithological Society in Anchorage, asked OUTDOOR LIFE to send a representative to probe the bear killings.

Rumors had reached him from early summer on of a heavy bear kill by Kodiak ranchers, Hemming said, and while attending hearings of the Wilderness Society at Anchorage in September he heard for the first time that bears were being shot from low-flying aircraft.

"I was shocked and could hardly believe it," he wrote, "but it proved true. Most of the killing is being done by a former rancher who is said to be violently antibear, shooting from an aircraft with an M-1 rifle mounted on the roof and using tracer bullets."

OUTDOOR LIFE immediately sent Hemming's letter, of which the foregoing is only part, to Jim Brooks, director of the Alaska game department's division of game, for comment. We quote two paragraphs from Brooks's reply:

"It is apparent . . . that Mr. Hemming has considerable knowledge concerning the bear-cattle conflict on Kodiak Island. While there are minor errors in his letter to you, he seems to have presented the over-all picture in a surprisingly accurate way.

"This problem on Kodiak Island is pacing the Department of Fish and Game in the difficult position of extending protection to the cattle ranchers while safeguarding the bears. Obviously, these two responsibilities are inimical, and it is difficult to reassure all groups that our handling of the problem reflects a realistic weighing of contrary interests."

OUTDOOR LIFE'S response was to assign me to make a complete and impartial investigation and report facts. This article, based on records of the Alaska Department of Fish and Game, the U.S. Fish and Wildlife Service, the Bureau of Land Management, and interviews with ranchers, guides, game officials, legislators, businessmen, and sportsmen is the result.

The Kodiak bear war is a highly controversial subject, charged with emotion, beset by widespread disagreement, involving people, politics, the economy of a new and sparsely settled state, land-use policies of both federal and state agencies, and complex wildlife-management programs. Two basic facts are clear, however. There are more cattle on Kodiak today than ever before, about 1,600, and there are also more brown bears on the island than at any previous time in its recorded history. Game biologists estimate there may be 2,000, with litters of triplets, twins, quadruplets, and single cubs occurring most frequently in that order. Conflict between bears and cattle is inevitable.

The problem started when the Kodiak National Wildlife Refuge was created by executive order of President Roosevelt in 1941. It took in nearly 75 percent of the island, and most of the bears of the island are found on the refuge. Hunting is allowed. The area outside the refuge was administered by the U.S. Bureau of Land Management, the federal agency that administers most of the public lands in Alaska. A small area was assigned the city of Kodiak, and another chunk was taken when the Kodiak naval reserve was established. (Uncle Sam owns some 95 percent of Alaska and will still own almost three quarters of it even after Alaska selects the 28 percent to which it is entitled under the terms of statehood.)

Beginning in the 1930's, the Bureau of Land Management saw fit to lease various Kodiak areas to cattlemen, and there's the rub. Bill Poland, former Kodiak city manager, and a guide, put his finger on the origin of the problem when he told me, "The ball was dropped when the federal government created the Kodiak refuge for brown bears, while another bureau of the same government was leasing the land immediately adjoining for ranching."

The ranchers do not own their ranches, but lease them for 20 years, with the lease subject to renewal. Leases specify that the lands are open to public entry—for hunting and fishing. A rancher may sell his improvements to another, and transfer the lease.

From all the noise and fury, it would be easy to get the impression that half the population of Kodiak Island is in the ranching business. Actually, there are only nine leases in the problem area. A ranch of around 20,000 acres is about average. One I visited, 50 miles from the town of Kodiak by gravel road, has 22,000 acres, 26 miles of fence, 10 separate pastures, and about 300 cows.

All the ranchers lost cattle to starvation, bogs, from falls off steep mountainsides, and to disease (federal range experts estimate these losses at five percent) as well as to bears. Many persons believe that the browns are often blamed for killing animals that have died from other causes. If you find the months-old remains of a cow-critter, how do you determine what killed it? Is a bear always guilty when a cow simply disappears? Does cattle hair in bear droppings prove anything, other than the fact that the bear swallowed cattle hair? Bears, of course, feed on almost anything dead they find.

Kodiak ranchers vary in their attitudes toward brown bears. One is a licensed, registered guide, and has the reputation of knowing what a bear thinks better than a bear does. Others also recognize that bears are of great value. Some ranchers hate bears with an unreasoning passion and make no bones of the fact that they'd like to see them all destroyed. One in particular continually advocates the use of poison for controlling bears.

One old-time rancher, there since 1932, lost track of the number of cows bears had killed when the figure reached 150. He can't recall how many bears he has shot.

Another told me that in the 11 years he has raised cattle on Kodiak, bears have taken 46 head. A third rancher, the guide whose ranch lies nearest the refuge, believes he lost 61 head of cattle to bears in 1963 alone, and Zentner, who owns the hunting Piper, figures a loss of 30 head to bears in 1963. He found 11 of these, and the others just disappeared. "After there's green grass and the animals are strong, you know they don't just go off and die," he explained.

The Kodiak ranchers leave no doubt about what most of them think of the relative importance of bears and cows to the future of Alaska. The stronger the cattle industry, the better for the individual rancher, they feel, and that means more grazing leases on public land and more ranches.

One cattleman, a former resident of Colorado and new to the business on Kodiak, put it bluntly. "Expansion of ranching here is inevitable," he said, "and the logical area to move into is the refuge." Another, a part-time rancher with an almost missionary zeal about the cattle business, was even more frank. "With our expanding population, people are looking for a place to live, such as Kodiak Island," he told me. "The Indians didn't stop them in the West, the mountains didn't stop them. They pushed on because they were pioneers. The same thing will happen here, and the bears will have to give. It's only a matter of time."

What about the value of Kodiak's brown bears? Obviously, the esthetic value defies a monetary evaluation. But a study made in 1959 showed that resident and nonresident hunters spent $343,500 that year to bag 147 bears on Kodiak.

During the years 1960–63, sportsmen killed 353 brown bears in the Kodiak-Afognak area. Probably less than 10 percent of these were killed on the ranching area.

Kodiak guides have a substantial investment in their businesses. Alf Madsen told me he has more than $100,000 invested in camps and guiding equipment, unquestionably the largest such investment on the island. Guided hunts bring many thousands of dollars to Alaska annually, and the bulk of the business of Kodiak guides depends on Kodiak's brown bears.

I personally talked with six of the guides who sent the wire to OUT-DOOR LIFE, and found that they agreed with selective use of the hunting plane, but every guide insisted that the work be done in a discriminating manner under direct supervision of a competent game biologist.

"If a bear needs killing, kill it," Park Munsey said flatly. Munsey has been a Kodiak guide since 1955 and is a leading spokesman for guides and sportsmen on the island. "But first we have to agree that a bear has to be killed—and a bear miles from livestock doesn't have to be killed," he added.

Munsey's comment is typical. The "thinning" type of control drew violent objections from all persons interested in the bears' welfare.

The guides complained too about the game department's failure to issue a clear, written statement of policy covering the situation, something the public can depend on and the department's own people can follow.

Finally, they want the operations made public. Said Munsey of the 1963 operation, "Nobody would discuss it. We couldn't get information. It was obvious that nobody wanted to get caught holding the bag."

Kodiak Island is rugged real estate. Attempting to hunt and kill on the ground specific bears that have destroyed cattle has proved almost impossible. The dense vegetation in spring, summer, and fall, when the bears kill most cattle, and the almost vertical, alder-clad ridges and deep cuts and draws makes finding a particular bear from the ground unlikely. Even an airplane is virtually useless during the height of summer vegetation. A bear can slip into the jungle growth, and a pilot simply cannot see it. In 1960, a professional California bear hunter with hounds was hired by the state and federal government for the season to hunt bears on the ranches. Ranchers and game experts alike agreed the attempt was a failure.

"It cannot be done from the ground," says Commissioner Kirkness in discussing bear control. "To be selective, only one method is available to us—hunting from an airplane."

It has to be remembered that trying to shoot a marauding bear on a kill can be a hair-raising business. Tom Felton proved that when he rode out one black night after a brown that had downed one of his yearlings.

Tom is a cattleman who came to Kodiak from Montana in 1932. He lives in a low-ceilinged, one-room log cabin that's an echo from the West of 50 years ago, with a stove, sink and hand pump, gasoline lanterns, Frederic Remington prints on the walls, and rifles hanging within easy reach.

On this particular rainy night, he heard a commotion among his cattle, snatched a rifle, threw a saddle on a horse, and hurried out to investigate. Before he reached the scene, he discovered there was only one shell in the rifle.

Thirty feet from the bear, he spotted it standing over its kill. At that point his horse showed it didn't care much for the situation, but Tom stayed in the saddle and turned his light on the bear.

It reared up on its hind legs to face him, surly and growling. Holding his flashlight in one hand and the rifle in the other, Tom slammed his one bullet into its middle, clearly hearing the plunk as it hit. The bear dropped to all fours and ran into the timber, and Felton left right then. But at daylight he went back, found the bear, and finished the job.

The attempt to keep last year's program secret probably stemmed in part from the fact that the control work in 1962, when about 15 bears were killed by the department, was successfully kept under wraps.

Further, Oscar Dyson of Kodiak, hand-loading sportsman, commercial fisherman, and member of Alaska's Board of Fish and Game, admitted, "I agreed with the boys it was probably best not to say anything." The 10-member board in Alaska establishes policies and promulgates all fish-and-game regulations.

While most of the attention in the dispute has been paid to the conflicting interests of the ranchers and guides, actually there is a big third party to this quarrel, the sportsmen of Alaska and the entire United States.

Alaska is the last great, primitive storehouse of wildlife remaining in this country. How that wildlife is managed, how bears are safeguarded throughout the state, how predator problems are handled, and how all trophy game of the state is protected is as much a matter of legitimate concern to a hunter in California, a Boone and Crockett Club member in New York, or any sportsmen between, as to Kodiak residents.

The present strife is important because precedents are being set, and policies for the future may well emerge from it.

What is the solution? Can Kodiak Island, and other brown-bear ranges of Alaska, have both cattle and bears? If so, how is bear control to be handled? Which is more important in the long run to the economy and welfare of Alaska itself, and which will best serve the long-range public interests of the whole country.

Those are troublesome questions, and you can get many answers anywhere in Alaska. Some of the ranchers want to see all the bears destroyed. On the other hand, some Alaskans think the best solution would be to buy out the cattlemen and turn all of Kodiak into a brown-bear refuge. "After all, the bears were here first," I heard often.

One thing is obvious. Ranching and bear hunting are both businesses highly important to the economy of a new state wealthy in a wide variety of natural resources but short on people and money. Kodiak cattle are valued at $250 to $400 a head, depending on who sets the price. The guides say that each brown bear taken is worth $2,000, when taken by a trophy hunter. The livestock inventory and ranch improvements on Kodiak are conservatively valued at $1,000,000. Losses to Kodiak ranches due to the great March 27 earthquake in Alaska totaled more than $50,000.

Many believe Alaska can have ranching and bear hunting if the cards are played wisely. Gilbert Jarvela, Kokiak's representative in the state legislature, is one. "We need all the industry we can get," he told me. "Ranching is an industry, but so is guiding. I think we can keep both."

Even Park Munsey, a leading critic of last year's bear-control work, says, "I think ranching has a future here when a few problems are solved, but it should be limited to the areas now committed." Other prominent guides agree.

The brown-bear population of Kodiak Island will not be endangered as long as the present refuge is not invaded or reduced in size. Fortunately for the future of the brown bears over all of Alaska (Jim Brooks thinks they total about 11,000), a hunge chunk of the state's best brownie country on the Alaska Peninsula has so far been kept exclusively for the use of wildlife. An application for a grazing lease there was denied in 1958, after a committee of federal agencies decided that the approximately 2,710,000 acres between Port Moller and Port Heiden were more valuable for wildlife than ranch stock.

Various ways of cooling off Kodiak's present hot war between bears and cattle have been proposed. One rancher hung bells on his sheep. He later found bear dung with one of his bells in it; the bear had eaten the sheep, bell and all. Cattle ranchers have tried bells without much success.

A 10-month open bear season has been in effect on the ranches (eight months is allowed elsewhere on Kodiak), but no serious hunter will hunt on the ranches because the bears are too scarce there.

Alaska's representative in Congress, Ralph J. Rivers, sought another solution in 1960 when he introduced a bill that would have required the U.S. Department of Interior (Fish and Wildlife Service) to pay damage claims to ranchers for cattle killed by bears, but the bill did not pass.

Commissioner Kirkness issued a written policy statement last January, saying it is the task of the Alaska Department of Fish and Game "to develop a tolerable compromise between cattle ranching and bear conservation," and calling for a four-point program of study under a game biologist, maximum hunting on the ranch area, and a minimum of bear control.

The proposal that has attracted the most attention is one to build a nine-foot bearproof fence across the 16-mile base of the Chiniak Peninsula, isolating the ranches from the rest of Kodiak.

Estimates of cost range from $100,000 to $750,000. Some favor the plan, others are dubious. "It would be a good thing, but financing is the problem," Kirkness says. Oscar Dyson of the Board of Fish and Game told me, "The value of the bears and the cattle killed in this controversy in 1963 alone was close to $100,000, if you use the values the guides set for bears. A fence is not as crazy as it first appears." Alf Madsen, Kodiak's dean of guides, thinks a fence the only answer.

There are others who wonder whether any fence can be built that will keep a full-grown brown bear from going where he wants to go. A big brownie has been known to drag a 1,000-pound steer half a mile up an almost vertical mountainside, through alder thickets a man can hardly penetrate.

OUTDOOR LIFE was told that Senator Barry Goldwater of Arizona is willing to introduce a bill appropriating $750,000 for the fence. "Before that kind of money is spent we want some experimental work done to find out whether a really bearproof fence is possible," says Bud Roddy, executive director of the Alaska Sportsmen's Council. Commissioner Kirkness has called on his game division to make studies on fences and brown bears.

Whatever is done, it's a safe bet that the eyes of sportsmen, trophy hunters and conservationists throughout the South 48, as Alaskans now call the states below the Canadian border, will be on Kodiak Island and its bears and cattle ranches for some time.

What Sportsmen Say

What do the leaders of organized sportsmen, in Alaska and elsewhere, have to say about the Kodiak bear war?

"The National Wildlife Federation and its affiliate, the Alaska Sportsmen's Council, have long been concerned about the incompatibility of the Alaska brown bear and domestic livestock on Kodiak Island," Tom Kimball, the Federation's executive director, told OUTDOOR LIFE. As former director of the Colorado Game and Fish Department, Kimball has had long experience in dealing with problems involving cattle and wildlife. He is also spokesman for the largest sportsmen's organization in the country, with affiliates in all 50 states.

"In my opinion, the decision to introduce cattle grazing to these islands off the coast of Alaska, which contain a large population of one of North America's largest carnivores, was a tragic mistake," he says.

"Kodiak Island possesses only limited areas suitable for grazing, because of the rigors of weather and the Alaskan climate. At best, these are marginal grazing lands and produce a rather insignificant return on the investment.

"Events have proved the complete inability of the brown bear to live with domestic livestock. As a consequence, the livestock permittees took matters into their own hands and initiated a systematic program to eliminate bears from the grazing areas. Many of the techniques employed were against the law.

"To correct this situation, the Alaska Department of Fish and Game has attempted to use its own methods to control stock depredations. I have been assured by Alaska game officials that the number of bears taken is relatively insignificant so far as the over-all population is concerned and that control is limited to the grazing areas.

"Since almost everyone agrees, however, that the brown bear and livestock are completely incompatible in the same range, there is a very serious question as to what the future will hold for the perpetuation of these fine game animals. One has only to refer to the history of the grizzly in the western United States. Being smaller than the brown bear, he was probably less capable of depleting livestock herds. Yet, because of the livestock industry, he has been extirpated from most of his former range, and only a very limited number remains, in extremely remote wilderness areas where little or no grazing is permitted.

"The brown bear found on Kodiak Island is world famous. There is no question is my mind that the economic as well as the esthetic value of this animal is as important as any of the renewable resources on the island, and it should be given the highest possible priority in both the land and wildlife-management programs which are developed for the future well-being of Alaska."

The Alaska Sportsmen's Council, made up of 12 of the state's leading conservation organizations, takes an equally strong position.

"I think we should recognize certain facts," says A. W. (Bud) Roddy of Juneau, executive director of the Council. "First, the areas involved are public lands. The people in the ranching business have leases from the Bureau of Land Management for the use of this land, and these leases are binding on both parties. I am not in a position to state whether the lessors are complying with all the provisions of the leases, but there should be a review to determine whether all parties are fulfilling their obligations.

"In spite of earlier predictions that any livestock venture would be of short duration on Kodiak Island, I think all parties concerned should now recognize that we are going to have a livestock industry in this area, although it may be of a marginal nature.

"I think all parties also should recognize that we are going to have a bear population in the area, and that this bear population is of real value not only to the guides and outfitters but also to sportsmen throughout the United States. Any rules and regulations for the management of livestock and bears should take into consideration the rights of all the people involved.

"We are opposed to the use of planes or to unnecessary control work. We are also opposed to the use of poison in bear control, on Kodiak Island or any other area. We have suggested that the Alaska Department of Fish and Game step up its investigations to determine the actual extent of bear predation. We believe bears are being blamed in many cases where cattle have died from other causes. At the same time, we must recognize that any losses the ranchers sustain are serious to them, and everything possible should be done to alleviate the problem.

"We have recommended that the game department investigate the feasibility of fences, and we have urged further research to determine from what areas the bears are entering the grazing lands. We also believe there is a possibility of live-trapping some bears in the grazing areas to move them.

"We feel, too, that the ranchers have a responsibility to assist the game department and others who are endeavoring to improve the situation. They should recognize that, although the bears become a nuisance at times, they are of value to all the people of Alaska. Our Sportsmen's Council hopes the cattlemen will join with us and the game department in working out a fair solution."

The Grizzly: Is He Villain or Victim

Bill Schneider

January, 1977

Harold and Diana Peterson and their two children, 11-year-old Karen and 7-year-old Seth, of Des Plaines, Illinois, were looking for excitement on their vacation in Montana's Glacier National Park. They found more than they wanted.

On the morning of August 7, 1975, they planned to hike to Grinnell Glacier, which is reached by way of one of the park's most popular trails. They rose early, making it to the trail head before any other hikers. The wind blew in their faces as they quietly walked along. After three miles, the family was strung out, and Karen was about 100 feet out front.

When Karen turned a sharp bend in the trail, she heard a growl just below her. She looked down and saw the gold-colored fur of a grizzly bear. Her involuntary scream startled the bear—and it charged. It grabbed her by the head and threw her into a rock ledge.

Karen's father rushed up the trail and leaped on the bear's back, grabbing it around the neck. The bear quickly broke one of his arms and severely lacerated the other.

Tossing him off, the bear bolted down the trail and ran smack into little Seth. It knocked him down with one swat on the back of his head. Then, apparently confused, the bear raced back toward Karen and her father. When Harold yelled, it veered off the trail and disappeared into an alder thicket.

The ordeal lasted only a few seconds, but it left the family in shambles. Diana had run off for help. So it was up to Harold, as disabled as he was, to get his children to safety. And he did.

When Peterson reached Josephine Lake, he was lucky to find a park naturalist with a group of tourists. After doctors in the group administered first aid, the family was rushed to the nearest hospital. Physically, the Petersons survived. But their mental wounds may never heal.

The questions raised by their experience add another chapter to a continuing controversy. Their ordeal revived the periodic debate over the conflict between grizzly bears and humans who use the same area at the same time.

This debate was intensified in 1976 when a female grizzly with three cubs killed a young woman hiker in British Columbia's Glacier National Park. Last year grizzlies also injured three persons in Yellowstone National Park and another three in Montana's Glacier Park.

So questions are being asked: Are our Western parks and forests, inhabited by grizzlies, too dangerous to permit humans to visit them? Should the bears be annihilated from these areas to "make them safe" for people?

To both questions, park officials answer no. The parks are preserves, they say, where nature works the way it's supposed to—in relative harmony. The grizzly is a vital part of this arrangement.

The grizzly once ranged over most of Western North America. Then the white man began blazing trails of destruction into the Western wilderness. In a scant 175 years, the grizzly's habitat was whittled down to a few islands in its former range. Alaska and Western Canada still have sizable grizzly populations. But south of Canada their numbers have declined from perhaps one million or more to less than 1,000.

The grizzly's last strongholds in the lower 48 are Glacier and Yellowstone national parks and the surrounding national forests. Realizing this, park administrators often put the bear first in management decisions— even if it means excluding people. At the same time, park employees are doing everything they can to prevent confrontations between grizzly and man.

But management plans didn't prevent that day of terror for the Petersons. Could it have been prevented? Perhaps, if the family had stayed together and made a lot of noise coming up the trail, they might not have startled the bear.

On the other hand, this may have been "a statistic waiting to happen," as Clifford J. Martinka, the park's research biologist, puts it. Martinka and most other serious students of the grizzly believe there will be a few such confrontations so long as people frequent grizzly country—regardless of preventive management.

Martinka is right, of course. Witness another incident that occurred later that year. On September 7, Michael Coppes and Martin Evans were hiking to Rockwell Falls in the southern part of the park. Their fun ended abruptly when they spotted two grizzlies—one a silvertip and the other almost white—about 50 to 60 feet up the trail. Coppes's recollection of what happened next is "hazy." But the two men fled for separate trees, as the white bear raced after them.

The bear caught and mauled Coppes. Then it left him and pulled Evans out of his tree, which wasn't tall enough, and gave him a similar beating.

Suddenly, it was over. The bear turned and sauntered off, leaving the battered hikers to struggle two miles to the trail head.

Seven days in the hospital and a few hundred stitches later, their wounds began to heal. But their mental scars remain.

"His caved-in forehead and dark, deep-set eyes will never leave my memory," Coppes recalls. "There is no hate or remorse that fate caught us unprepared on that day. I am only thankful that luck had been with us, and we will both get a chance to take another hike some day."

How common are these confrontations? Are they frequent enough to warrant drastic action?

Unfortunately, the park doesn't have a complete and documented history of the adverse relationship between man and bear. For example, rangers don't know how many tourists driving into the park actually stop their vehicles to take a backcountry hike, thus exposing themselves to the possibility of meeting a grizzly.

Using the available records, though, one can still draw some fairly sound conclusions. Since 1913, 127 persons have died in Glacier Park from vehicle accidents, drownings, falls, hypothermia, and so on. Since the park was created in 1910, grizzlies have killed only three persons. Meanwhile, at least 26 million tourists have visited Glacier. Obviously, the chance of getting killed or mauled by a grizzly is remote.

During an 18-year period (1958–75), grizzlies injured an average of about one person per year. During the same period, yearly visitors numbered from 642,100 in 1964 to 1,571,393 in 1975. Even if only one fourth of the visitors took a backcountry hike, a realistic estimate according to Bob Burns, visitor protection specialist at Glacier, the chance of getting mauled was something like one in 250,000.

All park officials can do is take every precaution. People entering the park are warned about grizzlies and are given suggestions on backcountry behavior, Burns explains. "Then, we put signs at trail heads warning people what they can do to lessen the probability of an incident. There's plenty of warning. We just don't know if people heed it."

Park rangers ask hikers to notify them of bear sightings. If a bear (grizzly or black) acts suspiciously, chases someone, or destroys a camp, the trail is closed immediately.

"We closed 40 trails and campsites last year (1975)," Chuck Sigler, chief park ranger, said. "Sometimes we even close an entire drainage."

If a bear continues to cause trouble, rangers tranquilize it and move it to a more remote section of the park. If it becomes a persistent troublemaker, it may be destroyed. But park policy doesn't call for the routine destruction of any bear that attacks a human. For example, Martinka feels a sow injuring someone while attempting to protect cubs may not be justification for killing her.

Martinka also feels that some trails and campsites have been wrongly set out in high grizzly-use areas. Fishing is also a problem in the backcountry, he maintains, because the smell of fresh fish or discarded entrails attracts bears. So the park occasionally eliminates or moves campsites away from popular fishing sites.

Some tourists think too much about grizzlies and too little about other hazards. Because of extensive news coverage of grizzly attacks, Glacier has become known as a bear park, according to Burns.

"So people come here thinking about bears," he says. "But they don't think about drowning or the dangers of mountain climbing. So they're more careless."

Statistically, the chance of grizzly trouble occurring is slim, but that's of little comfort to those who are the victims of it. Five young women learned all about that last September, and one of them isn't alive to tell about it.

The Many Glacier drainage, the same area in which the Peterson confrontation took place, had more than an average number of grizzly sightings and minor incidents that season. Most of the trails were closed, but the Swiftcurrent Campground, a major drive-in facility, was open.

The five University of Montana students found their intended trail closed, so they reluctantly pitched their tents within 200 yards of the ranger station and turned in.

About 6:45 a.m., a bear ripped into one of their tents, clawed at the closest camper, Mary Pat Mahoney, and retreated. Seconds later it returned, dragged the girl away, and killed her.

Why? No one knows. Dr. Charles Jonkel, reknowned bear scientist at the University of Montana, sat on the board that inquired into the tragedy. He says: "It was probably triggered by increased human use of the backcountry and inadequate supervision by the Park Service caused by budget cuts and shortage of personnel." However, he added, the bear's behavior was definitely abnormal. The campground probably should have been closed along with the trails, he concluded, but the district rangers acted correctly under the present bear-management plan.

The grizzly is a big, fierce-looking, dangerous animal. It makes good copy for the newspapers. "There's something about bears and wolves that automatically makes people's hair stand up straight," Jonkel says. Witness the local paper that carried a banner headline in three-inch type: GRIZZLY KILLS GIRL.

At Glacier, there can be a serious auto accident, and there's hardly a line about it in the local papers. But if someone gets mauled by a bear, it's all across the nation in a hurry. Backpackers who hike Glacier all their lives without getting involved with grizzlies aren't news.

This gives the public a biased view of the grizzly, and it complicates park management. Worse, it sours people on efforts to protect the grizzly. "A responsible press is essential if the grizzly is to be preserved," Jonkel says. But it's hard to work up enthusiasm for saving something that's viewed as a killer of human beings.

This attitude toward the grizzly is not new. In 1804–6, Lewis and Clark explored the West and told of seeing an "awesome white bear." Writers and orators read the early journals and repeated and exaggerated them. The grizzly was Ursus horribilis, the horrible bear.

Biologists and other wildlife professionals concede that the grizzly is a potentially dangerous animal. They maintain that it is a solitary creature that wants to be left alone in its habitat and one that rarely attacks man.

Be that as it may, to many persons the bear is still Ursus horribilis, and they are intrigued by reports of its horrible exploits.

I went to Glacier many years ago, fresh from college and eager to brave the wilderness. And I was afraid of the bear I had heard about. I worked at Glacier for four summers, hiking the backcountry nearly every day. In years since, I've spent many weeks backpacking in the park. I've met about a dozen grizzlies face-to-face. What happened? The bears fled like rabbits.

In 1967, about two weeks after grizzlies killed two young women, I was fighting forest fires in the park. That day, two of us were told to check out the fire line, which at that point dipped into a deep, brush-filled ravine. At the bottom, we heard an ominous rustling in the nearby bushes. After going on about 50 yards, more noise in the ravine prompted us to make quick glances over our shoulders. There stood a large, skinny-looking grizzly—exactly where we had just been. We must have passed within 15 feet of it.

After thinking about my personal experiences and my researching into the history of grizzly incidents at Glacier, I never wonder why there are so many grizzly maulings. I wonder why there are so few. Each summer, several hundreds of thousands of hikers trek into remote corners of this great park. Yet bear confrontations are rare, and they would be even more so if people would abide by the rules of the wilderness.

As for the "statistics waiting to happen"—those few incidents that occur regardless of precautions—we can only learn to accept them as part of life in the wilderness.

GRIZZLY COUNTRY CARE

For women

Stay out of grizzly country during menstrual periods.

Don't use perfume, hair spray, deodorants, or other cosmetics. There is some evidence that bears are attracted and even infuriated by these scents.

If you meet a grizzly

Most important, try to remain calm. If the grizzly stands his ground and doesn't seem aggressive, stand still. Don't run! This may excite the bear into pursuit.

Don't move toward the bear. Start looking for a good tree to climb. If the grizzly moves toward you, get up it fast. Make sure it's tall enough to get you out of reach. (Only very young grizzlies can climb trees.) Before starting for the tree, it may help to drop something like a pack or camera to distract the bear.

If you can't get up a tree, play dead. Lie on your side, curl up and clasp your hands over the back of your neck. Grizzlies have often bypassed people in this position.

The Black Bear as Fisherman

George W. Frame

February, 1973

At 3:10 a.m., the sky was quite bright in spite of the cloud cover that continually hung over the valley. The black bear that I'd nicknamed Potbelly came out of the woods at a brisk walk, crossed 50 yards of tide flat, and then stopped at the edge of the stream. He looked around for a few seconds before he spotted four chum salmon on a redd about three yards away in the foot-deep water.

The bear immediately jumped into the stream and churned forward as fast as he could go. Water and fish splashed in all directions as Potbelly made a final thrust to the redd where he'd last seen the fish. But the predator was too late. Dozens of salmon for a distance of 10 or 12 feet in all directions scattered to safety. Potbelly stood still and looked in apparent confusion at the churning water. He then bounded upstream, splashing as he ran. Three times he lunged at fish, and each time he missed.

After about 40 yards of this futility, the bear paused for a moment, spotted another fish, and then lunged at it, biting the salmon behind its head. Potbelly realized almost at once that his catch was not a plump, unspawned female, so he released his bite. He turned and then splashed his way back downstream. On the next try he caught another salmon, but he released that fish, too, and then ran some more, panting heavily. With the next lunge, Potbelly's head went completely under water, and he came up with a fat, thrashing female salmon. The bear quickly walked ashore and lay down on the streambank to eat the fish's eggs.

Clumsy-looking, but skillful at fishing—as Potbelly's efforts showed—Alaska's black bears have aroused the wrath of generations of commercial fishermen. Each year from early July to early September, the bears feed almost entirely upon spawning salmon. On such a diet, the bears grow fast during the short summer and build up enough reserve fat to survive the many months of winter inactivity.

Potbelly was one of 18 black bears—mostly juveniles and adults—that I was watching as they fished their way through eight weeks of the salmon-spawning season. Before then, no research had been done on salmon predation by black bears. Recent *brown*-bear research, however, has shown that browns often kill about one in every 10 salmon before the fish have a chance to spawn. This is fewer fish than you might expect, but it is a dollars-and-cents loss to Alaskan fishermen.

My research took place on a salmon-spawning stream in Prince William Sound, about 130 miles east of Anchorage, Alaska. The project was supported by the National Marine Fisheries Service Auke Bay Laboratory.

The project headquarters was a former U.S. Bureau of Commercial Fisheries field station that had been built several years earlier on the edge of the tide flat near the stream. The seven small cabins served as living quarters, kitchen, bathhouse, boathouse, and office. Besides myself, two permanent employes and two summer workers lived at the station. One of the temporary employes was from Arkansas, and the other was a fisheries student from Michigan.

Black-bear research was quite a change for me. Only a few months before, I had been in East Africa studying the black rhinoceros. I had gone to Africa with the Peace Corps, and had ended up working with Canadian biologist John Goddard on the rhinos. I've been interested in wildlife since my boyhood on New Jersey's tidal marshes, and my experience with the rhinos had convinced me that wildlife management was my future. I returned to the States and enrolled at the University of Alaska, where I was a student when I was doing the black-bear research.

My primary job was to study the year's run of spawning pink and chum salmon as they returned to spawn and die after several years at sea.

The area around the present spawning stream was once entirely under water at high tide, but the great Alaska earthquake of 1964 had lifted this region about five feet. Now, the tidal flat that surrounds the stream supports only short vegetation—ideal for bear-watching. Four 15-foot towers were placed along the stream's bank as vantagepoints for watching both bears and fish.

Within this exposed part of the stream, 26,000 chum salmon and 27,600 pink salmon returned to spawn during the summer of my study. Densely wooded mountain slopes that border the tidal flat furnish shelter and abundant berries for the bears to eat before the start of the salmon run.

About two weeks after salmon began entering the stream, the first black bear started fishing. A week later, on July 14, several more bears showed an interest in fishing. As the salmon became more numerous and easier to catch, all 18 black bears abandoned the berries and fed almost entirely upon fish every day until mid-September.

I soon learned to identify individual black bears by sex, size, color, and scars. After a few days of watching the animals, I could also spot some minor variations in individual fishing and feeding methods, though the tactics were basically the same. The bears spent more than twice as much time eating salmon as they did catching them.

During daylight hours, at least one of the 18 black bears could always be seen fishing or feeding on salmon near the stream. There were peaks of bear activity on the tidal flat at dawn (3 a.m.–5 a.m.) and dusk (5 p.m.–10 p.m.). Because the tidal flat was surrounded by mountains, and the weather was nearly always cloudy, the change from daylight to dark wasn't very distinct.

Generally, bears did not remain out of the woods and along the stream for more than a half-hour or so at a time. After fishing and feeding, each black usually returned to the woods carrying a fish with him to eat at his leisure.

I occasionally followed the bears into the woods to watch them. I was extra-cautious because the visibility was limited, and the blacks could climb trees faster than I could. Once I followed a trail around the base of a large tree and came face to face with a black walking toward me not more than a yard away. Both the bear and I took off in opposite directions.

Blacks kept a little more than half of the salmon they caught; all the remaining captured salmon were immediately abandoned in the stream or along its banks. Often, when a bear caught a salmon in its mouth, I heard a distinct crunch—but some of the abandoned salmon were able to swim, and disappeared among the schools of spawning fish. All in all, the blacks showed a strong preference for female salmon.

The basic method of fishing used by the black bears was to bite the fish just ahead of the dorsal fin, although several times they captured fish by the belly or tail. One bear had the curious habit of standing upright on its hind legs for three or four seconds every time he made a catch. A black stood in the water to inspect his catch; one paw was usually curled around the fish, supporting it against the bear's chest. The bear then released his bite and turned his head down to look at the fish. Frequently, the bear seemed to sniff the fish's anal area. Sometimes, however, a bear seemed to "sense" whether the salmon was an unspawned female while the fish was still in its mouth. Occasionally, the bear carried the fish ashore and inspected it by pressing it to the ground with one or two paws, sniffing the anal area, or biting a hole in the belly.

Though the black bears ate both live and dead salmon, they were selective about it. Usually they fished for salmon for their eggs, and most of the female salmon that were captured and eaten were unspawned. Relatively few of the male salmon that were eaten were unspawned. At times, the bears seemed content to feed upon dead salmon that had been caught and abandoned by other bears, or else they fed upon fish that had spawned and died a natural death. Generally, the bears stuck to only one method of feeding at a time.

The activities of a bear I called Moon are typical for a black bear with a freshly caught, unspawned female salmon. Moon was the largest bear, and she was generally a loner. I named her for a large, white crescent on her chest.

Early one afternoon, Moon had just caught a large, unspawned female salmon. The bear lay down on bank of the stream and then used her teeth and claws to tear open the fish's body cavity, spilling eggs out onto the ground. With one paw Moon held the body cavity open while she licked out the eggs. She then held the salmon with both paws and ate some of the fish's skin and flesh. Except for the eggs, which were always eaten, Moon and other bears ate other parts of their freshly caught salmon less than half the time.

When Moon finished eating the flesh, she turned her attention to the spilled eggs and licked all of them from the ground, along with much gravel. The bear then got up and walked slowly toward the stream to catch another salmon. It had taken Moon a little more than 15 minutes to eat as much of her fish as she wanted.

I frequently saw bears wandering on the tidal flat as they looked over the carcasses of salmon that had been captured, partially eaten, and then abandoned by other bears. I saw a typical example of this one morning at about 8:30, when a bear I named Scrufty came wandering along the streambank. With nearly every fresh carcass that Scrufty came upon, he bit the head lightly, sniffed the anal area, and then squeezed the salmon's belly with his jaws. Scrufty ate three out of every four of the carcasses that he examined, although he never found any significant amount of eggs. Scrufty most often ate the head cartilage, brains, and eyes—all in one bite.

The other feeding method was upon carcasses of chum and pink salmon that had died naturally after spawning and were lying on the gravelbars and along the water's edge. Even though many of these carcasses were decaying and infested by maggots, bears spent a little time feeding upon them. It was not uncommon to see a bear, such as Brownie—a not-very-pretty, cinnamon-colored black bear—walking along the edge of the water inspecting each carcass or standing with his forepaws on a rotting fish and tearing it apart with his jaws. From these carcasses Brownie and the other black bears, usually ate only its head cartilage, brains, and eyes.

The black bears in my research showed an ability to recognize un-spawned pink and chum salmon, and the bears at least temporarily dis-carded most males or spawned female fish that they caught. Although the bears often ate only the eggs before they abandoned their catch, the animals later returned to discarded carcasses to eat most of the remaining flesh. There was very little waste, and I estimated that black-bear predation re-moved 2,240 unspawned female salmon from the stream during the eight-week spawning season. An equal number of unspawned males were killed, but many were not immediately eaten. This total is about eight percent of the salmon that entered the spawning stream.

My study indicates that the amount of salmon lost to black-bear pre-dation in Alaska is far less than is generally believed. Most salmon caught by bears had already completed spawning, and a significant number of spawned-out fish that had died naturally were also eaten. Removing these thousands of expended fish from the stream probably prevents stream-pollution from that source, and may greatly assist survival of the salmon eggs by leaving a greater supply of oxygen and less chance of fungal infection. Allowing the black bears to harvest eight percent of the annual spawning run is a small price to pay for the survival of an animal so magnificent and so representative of the Alaskan wilderness.

Today I'm back in East Africa. I received my undergraduate degree from the University of Alaska, and I am now doing graduate research through the Utah Cooperative Wildlife Research Unit at Utah State University. In Africa, on the Crater Highlands at the eastern edge of Tanzania's famed Serengeti Plains, I'm putting the finishing touches on my research report about the black bears. I still think about Scrufty, Moon, Potbelly, and the other bears that I watched during that fine summer in Alaska, half a world away.

III
THE LORE OF BEAR HUNTING

A Bear on Your Own

Dwight Schuh

October, 1982

What makes black bears so fascinating? Is it their cryptic nature? You know they're sneaking around somewhere, but you never see them. Or maybe it's their unpredictability. One time a bear may appear as mysteriously as a puff of black smoke; the next time he may crash through the woods with the finesse of a bulldozer, demolishing logs and uprooting boulders. Maybe it's the element of potential danger. Authorities agree that black bears pose little threat to human life, but still, any bear can rearrange your plumbing if he wants to, and that fact always adds spice to a bear encounter.

Whatever the reasons, bears do catch the fancy of many people. Bears are challenging to hunt and make fine trophies. Since they've been elevated from the status of unprotected predator to big-game animal across the United States, tag sales have risen fast, and once-liberal seasons and bag limits are being tightened to protect overhunted populations in some areas. The growing demand is reflected in exploding tag costs. For example, in California for 1982, the nonresident tag jumped from an insignificant $1 to $75.

That's all well and good, but how do you hunt something you never see? Heck, you've been chasing deer in good bear country for 20 years and you've never even seen a bear *track*, let alone one of the animals that make them. Would you see any more if you went out and said you were bear hunting?

Indeed, bears are enigmatic, and for that reason many hunters who want rugs for their den walls hire guides who own hounds or who spend months putting out baits to attract bears. There's nothing wrong with that and if you're short on time and long on money, do it. But what if you're an independent cuss like me who insists on doing things on your own? Do you have a prayer of shooting a bear without a guide?

Yes, you do. That isn't to say that suddenly calling yourself a bear hunter will change your luck. If you've hunted nothing but deer and elk, you'll have to learn some new tricks. You have to hunt a bear on its own terms. But once you accept that fact and learn to do it, you're qualified to be your own bear guide. And you'll score.

If one universal bear hunting method exists—other than hunting with hounds, which is a specialized form of hunting few of us will take up by ourselves—it's baiting. Some persons question the sporting and ethical aspects of baiting because it seems too easy. The fact is, planning an effective bait hunt takes as much knowledge and work as any other kind of hunting. And even though baiting can be deadly, it poses little threat to bear populations. Collecting, storing and distributing huge quantities of bait is a task few hunters will stick with long enough to collect a bear. In many areas where the country is as flat and dense as a jungle, baiting is the only feasible way to hunt bears. Without bait you'd never see one. But check the laws in your area. Baiting is illegal in some states.

To get a rounded view of baiting, I talked to hunters across the country. Ray Grenier, Babe Stojonac and Bob Faufau were just three of the hunters I interviewed. Grenier is an ardent 28-year-old from New Hampshire who's killed eight bears in his first five years of bear hunting. He took four in Maine and four in New Hampshire; Stojonac, who lives in Chicago, has taken 16 bears over bait in Michigan and Ontario; and Bob Faufau has killed six bears, including a 700-pounder, in the past six years in his home state of Wisconsin.

The idea of baiting is to create a food source that will hold bears in one small area and will pull them into your view for a shot. To do that you have to feed them well. Table scraps that keep Fido smiling won't even make a bear lick his lips. Stojonac said he stocks 600 to 700 pounds of bait on each of the eight to 10 bait stations he sets up throughout the season. Every weekend Grenier buys (at 6¢ a pound) 500 pounds of meat scraps from a slaughterhouse to keep at least four of the bait stations fresh.

Meat scraps may be the most common baiting material, but other foods also work. Some hunters collect used cooking grease from restaurants. During Ontario's spring hunt, Stojonac has local trappers save beaver carcasses for him, and he nets spawning suckers from creeks near his hunting area. These baits work in either the spring or fall, but in fall when bears are putting on fat, sweets such as applies and other fruits may be even better baits. Faufau uses pastries. During summer he stores dozens of cases of stale sweet rolls in a walk-in freezer. The use of meat has been banned in Wisconsin, but even when it was legal, Faufau found that pastries worked better.

"I've seen bears throw meat aside to get to sweet rolls," he told me. "In Wisconsin you can hardly make a bear eat fish. I've put carp on a pile and they laid there and rotted because bears ate the bread first."

Baiting doesn't demand extensive scouting to pinpoint a bear's haunts. The strong smell of a bait pulls bears to you. Still, you have to be in the animals' proximity. Grenier begins his scouting at home by looking at topographic maps. In spring he looks for south slopes where the first green grass will attract and hold bears. For fall hunting he prefers draws and canyon bottoms that serve as travel routes for bears. Stojonac, too, puts baits near creek bottoms where thick, dank vegetation makes traveling bears feel comfortable. Faufau baits near tag alder and spruce swamps where bears hide during the day and come out to feed on berries at night.

You want to get away from other hunters, too. This can be tough in parts of the Midwest and East. Bears are sensitive and an encounter with other humans could run them off your bait. In New Hampshire, Grenier often backpacks his baits as far as three-quarters of a mile from the nearest road, particularly to get away from houndmen, who hunt by driving roads. Chances are good they'll locate and run any bear that's hitting a bait near a road.

Grenier chooses bait sites systematically. Before the season opens, he picks eight or 10 "test sites" on his maps. Then at each site he leaves a pile of meat and sprinkles anise oil, a strong licorice-smelling liquid, on logs and bushes to create a good scent. After a week or two, he stops maintaining unproductive sites and heavily baits active sites. By the time the season opens, he wants to have four active bait stations to assure alternatives should hunters disturb one or two, and to allow hunting under various weather conditions. One may be ideal when a north wind is blowing, another might be better when wind is from the south.

Most hunters use tree stands for blinds so they can get off the ground where a bear is unlikely to see them. Even more important, a tree stand gets your scent off the ground so a circling bear won't smell you as he might if you're on the ground.

That doesn't mean ground blinds don't work. Stojonac used them for many years because Michigan law prohibited the use of tree stands (bowhunters now can use them). Stojonac built a square framework of logs, then covered it with dense branches. He cut holes for visibility and shooting. In such a blind you're eyeball-to-eyeball with a bear, which is interesting in itself, but if all goes wrong, it can be downright exciting. In Ontario, Stojonac had set up this way when a small black bear rambled into the bait 20 feet from the blind. Stojonac drew his bow and shot the bear. The animal whirled and crashed straight into the blind, knocking Stojonac flat and breaking his glasses and thermos jug. The bear plowed out the back of the blind and sprinted another 50 yards before falling dead in a lake.

You can decide for yourself whether to use a tree stand or ground blind. Just make sure that your blind is on the downwind side of the bait. Bears have incredible noses.

Setting up a good bait and blind isn't the end of baiting. As Grenier said, "Any fool can haul food into the woods and get a bear to eat it. The trick is to get a good shot at that bear."

First that means attracting an animal to the bait during daylight. Grenier thinks the less suspicious a bear is, the more likely it is to come in during the day, so he takes great precautions. Most baiters, including Grenier, hunt only in the evenings. Bears normally come to a bait in later afternoon and stay nearby until daylight the next morning. If you go to your blind at 2 or 3 p.m. and stay until dark, you'll be waiting and undetected when a bear comes in, but if you walk to your stand early in the morning, you may spook bears that have been there all night.

Grenier also watches the weather. He hates blustery days because he can't predict where his scent will go.

"If you have a hot bait, stay out of there when conditions are bad," he said. "Otherwise you could ruin all the work you've done."

Grenier keeps his bait areas free from human sign. His baits contain only pure food—no paper or other litter. When working with baits he wears rubber gloves, and when going to his blind he always wears rubber boots, which hold in his scent better than those made of leather.

Bears are tough and must be hit perfectly for a quick kill. That's especially true because their thick fat and loose hides can seal a bullet or arrow hole and their long fur soaks up blood, which almost guarantees a skimpy blood trail. Bowhunters in particular must place their blinds close to the bait for a sure shot. The average bow shot is made from a distance of 20 to 50 feet.

One of the best shots is a diagonal angle from back to front through the lungs. Stojonac goes to great lengths to get that shot. He cuts all bait material into small chunks so a bear can't wander off with a big chunk but must stand at the sight to eat. He points out that if you dump bait in the middle of a clearing, a bear can eat facing any direction, but if you pile it against the near side of a tree or big rock, the bear must turn his back toward you. Stojonac carries that idea further by using small logs to build a crib, which looks like the corner of a split-rail fence. He places bait inside the V so that a bear must put his head right into the crib to eat. Built in proper relation to the blind, the crib ensures that an animal presents the right quartering-away angle for a perfect shot.

Another successful form of bear hunting is what I call spotting. You spot animals from a distance and stalk within rifle or bow range. Spotting doesn't work just anywhere. The country has to be steep enough for you to see from one side of a hill into another or open enough for broad visibility. Best spotting conditions are found in the mountainous West.

You have to know bears' feeding habits to consistently spot them. In the spring, bears seek lush green feed. In northwest Montana, Arlie Burk, who's killed about 30 black bears and four grizzlies, said many hunters simply drive back roads and look for bears in borrow pits, where lush grass and clover grow in late April and May. Burk prefers to hike into the foothills to glass grassy meadows and avalanche chutes, where bears come out to feed on skunk cabbage and glacier lilies. He also knows that a group of ravens and golden eagles may indicate a winter-killed deer or elk, and he'll watch that spot closely for bears. Wherever spring seasons are held in the Rocky Mountains and Pacific states, this kind of hunting is possible.

Spotting is most commonly associated with spring hunting, but a person who knows the habits of bears in a given region can successfully use this technique in the fall. Unlike deer and elk, which make predictable yearly migrations, bears are opportunists that migrate randomly, depending on availability of feed. Tim Burton, a wildlife biologist with the California Department of Fish and Game, has worked on bear studies for years.

During spring and summer, Burton said, bears roam small home ranges, but come fall they may head out suddenly and follow some inexplicable sixth sense as far as 12 miles to the richest food sources. In California, those sources could be acorns or manzanita berries. If salmon runs are heavy, bears may migrate to coastal streams. In northeast Washington, bears follow ripening huckleberries from the lowlands in midsummer to high country in fall, where backcountry hunters may spot up to a dozen bears a day in old burns and natural openings. In Arizona, Jay Elmer often finds bears feeding on mast in September and on prickly pears at the edge of the desert in October. Prickly pears are such a favorite food that Elmer has seen as many as eight bears in an evening gorging themselves on juicy "cactus apples."

If there's any secret to spotting bears, it's patience. Even under ideal conditions, bears are scarce compared to other big game, so seeing one takes a lot of looking. Elmer said he started bear hunting by walking and watching as he always had for other big game. It didn't work. Then one year he just sat on a high rim for hours, watching one canyon. That did work. Even though the oak trees there are dense, he found that if he watched patiently, he'd eventually see black hair ghosting among the trees, and he frequently heard bears before he saw them as they rolled rocks and ripped limbs from trees to get acorns. By patiently waiting and watching, he was able to kill six bears in six years.

Patience also worked for Ralph Flowers in jungly western Washington. From 1950 through 1975, working as a professional hunter for the Washington Forest Protection Association, Flowers killed 1,100 black bears. Hunting from May through August, when bears were most active, he'd park himself every morning and evening on a stump on one side of a canyon to watch a brushy clearcut on the other. Eventually he'd see black movement in the brush or would hear a bear smashing open logs as it looked for insects.

In that country, Flowers often could get a shot at 200 yards or less simply by waiting until the bear moved into the open, but in more expansive country, you may have to stalk within range. Bears have poor eyesight, which gives you an edge, but their senses of smell and hearing are excellent. To be successful you must be very careful to move noiselessly and you must always pay attention to wind direction. Bears also show little curiosity, as a deer might. One rainy spring day in Idaho, I spotted a bear across a canyon and circled way around to get the wind in my favor. I crept within 20 yards when my cuff hooked a twig that made a faint snap. The bear leaped like a squirrel onto a big yellow pine and scurried up without ever looking my way. With that kind of hearing, bears are hard to stalk at close range. You can't make mistakes.

If topography or vegetation don't lend themselves to spotting, you can try a method I call ambush hunting. It is similar to spotting except that you use it where visibility is limited, and watch one spot for a particular bear. Doug Menzies, a conservation officer with the New Hampshire Fish and Game Department, has perfected this approach. Menzies watches abandoned apple orchards or hardwood forests with rich mast crops in northern New Hampshire. Studies show that bears in New Hampshire feed heavily on corn and apples in September and on acorns and beechnuts in October. Menzies scouts promising feed areas and looks for dung piles and scratched-up ground and leaves where bears have pawed for mast. When he finds heavy bear sign, he makes a ground blind 50 to 60 yards away on the downwind side in the morning and the last two hours in the evening. He shot his first bear this way in an apple orchard in 1975, and he's killed three since—in 1979, '80 and '81—by watching oak groves.

Perhaps the most overlooked but potentially successful and exciting form of bear hunting is calling. Reed Peterson, a high school football coach who lives near Phoenix, Arizona, has called in 42 bears during the past 20 years. Many of them have been exceptionally large boars. Peterson thinks bear calling is much easier than most people think.

"You don't even have to be a good caller," he said. "Calling in a bear is simply a matter of knowing where the bears are. You can't call a bear in front of Valley National Bank."

In Arizona, Peterson concentrates on the transition country between scrub oak and desert where bears feed on prickly pear cactus in September and October. Then he calls much as he would for coyotes. Using a Circe cottontail call, he squeals and shrieks on the call for a minute, rests 15 seconds, calls for another minute, rests 15 seconds and so on. He gradually shortens the call and blows more quietly. He makes only one change from coyote calling. Rarely does he call from a coyote stand for more than 10 minutes, but he'll stay in one place for 30 to 40 minutes when he's bear hunting. During one hunt, Peterson and a friend were using a call when they saw a bear come over a rise a mile away. Peterson called for 45 minutes until the bear finally rambled within good rifle range. Peterson is emphatic that such calling will work anywhere.

"The sounds you make with a predator call don't necessarily imitate a dying rabbit," he said. "Those sounds are almost a universal distress call and any predator will come to investigate."

There may be other tricks that will take bears, but these are a few of the proven methods. If you adapt one of them to your hunting area, you'll find that you don't have to hire a guide to get one of those mysterious black bears. You can do it on your own.

Grandpa Was a Bear Hunting Man

George Laycock

August, 1979

One of my frequent fantasies has me poking along a forest trail on a pleasant autumn afternoon shortly after the opening of grouse season. Then I round a curve and suddenly come face to face with the biggest black bear I have ever seen. If this dream were to materialize in the hills of southern Ohio, the bear and I would renew a conflict that began between our ancestors a couple of hundred years ago. When the earliest of my predecessors came to the wilderness of Ohio in the 1780's, bears wandered the woods freely. The black bear that invaded the forest clearing where a pioneer's little farm stood made an error that was often fatal. The average settler was a fine shot; he had to be. And the bear was considered an enemy as well as a source of meat and fat.

But the Ohio settlers did not pursue game out of necessity alone. I'm convinced they had a ball hunting bears. Besides, buckskin-clad hunters knew that killing bears would bring them local fame, smiles from the maidens, and praise from the neighbors who believed there wasn't room for both bears and domestic stock in the same country.

This conflict between hunter and bear gave the bruin a special status on the frontier. The black bear was a glamour animal, and the exploits of bear hunters were often recorded in diaries, journals, and family histories.

I've spent many delightful winter evenings poring over old accounts of frontier hunters. This article is drawn largely from those sources.

One of the first Ohio bear hunters to gain fame was Samuel Pope, who was noted for killing three bears in one day. But the hunt Pope himself remembered most vividly began one day when his dogs roused a huge black bear. Hoisting his flintlock rifle to his shoulder, Pope fired a fast shot. The bear, only superficially wounded, let out a bawl and began loping down the trail with the dogs in hot pursuit.

While he jogged along trying to keep the dogs and the bear in sight, Sam struggled to reload his rifle. When he caught up to the bear, he found it had turned on the dogs and was going after his favorite hound. Infuriated, Pope rushed up, put the muzzle of his rifle next to the bear's head, and pulled the trigger. Nothing happened. His loading had been a little too hasty.

The bear charged Pope, who backpedaled, tripped over a log, and fell. The bear caught him by one heel, and the dogs plunged back into the affray. They hung on with such tenacity that the bear released Pope and turned on the dogs again.

Pope staggered to his feet, pulling his tomahawk from his belt. With repeated blows he chopped the bear to death. But Pope was so badly cut and bruised that he barely made it back home.

Pope's three-bear day seemed impressive until I found the story of Barley Monroe, who dispatched five bears in one day. At the time, Isaac Bonser was erecting a grist mill on Bonser Run. A mill was vitally important to a settlement in those days, so all ablebodied men left their homesteads to the care of their wives and went to spend time helping Bonser build the mill, which was a considerable distance from Bonser's home.

Mrs. Bonser, meanwhile, busied herself with the garden and her weaving until Mrs. Lindsey, her nearest neighbor, dropped by to visit. As the two ladies chatted, they happened to look across a little clearing toward the broad waters of the Ohio River and saw a bear come out of the Kentucky woods on the other side. Then four more bears came out, and all five bears waded into the river and began swimming toward the clearing. The women, without weapons because their husbands had carried the rifles along to the mill, were calm at first but decided it was time for action when the quintet of bears had almost reached shore, Mrs. Lindsey's dog, Watch, a bear-fight veteran, was beside her. Mrs. Lindsey shouted "Bear!" and Watch set up a yowling that brought the Bonser hounds running. The pack rushed down on the bears as they emerged from the river. Within minutes, the dogs had every one of the bears up trees.

Barley Monroe, a neighbor, was hunting in nearby woods and heard the dogs. He knew the hounds had something important at bay. The old hunter came puffing into the clearing, took aim, and dropped one of the bears out of its tree. He continued to reload and shoot until all five bears were on the ground. Monroe nodded politely to the ladies and vanished into the forest. The bear meat and grease was divided among the families of the local settlement, and Monroe became a legend along the length of the frontier.

To the early settlers, the fat of the bear was nearly as important as the meat. "The fat," says one old record, "was rendered into oil then put away into deer skins neatly and cleanly dressed for the purpose. The oil served many valuable purposes, supplying the place of butter and hog's lard. He could fry his venison and turkey in it, and if he had neither of these, it was admirable sop for corn dodger." Bear grease mixed with dried venison and parched corn was regarded as one of the greatest delicacies of a hunter's larder. Sometimes, as in the case of Ben Reed, bear grease could be collected right outside the cabin.

Ben and his wife, Patty, came to the Ohio wilderness from Virginia in 1805. He cleared a patch of woods for corn, built a cabin, and shot deer and other wild game for meat. He had one large black hog, which he kept in a pen. One day, Reed purchased a white hog as a mate for the black hog.

By the time he had gotten the new hog home and put it in the pen, it was nightfall. Reed went into his cabin, lowered himself wearily onto a bench, and waited for Patty to finish fixing supper. Suddenly, he heard one of his hogs squealing as if butchering day were at hand.

Reed rushed out of the cabin and saw what he thought was the black hog dragging the white hog around the pen. But when he got closer, he realized that a black bear was attacking his new white hog. The bear saw Reed and started to turn on him. But Reed's dog came to the rescue, harassing the bear from the rear. Reed and the dog soon had forced the bear up a tree. Reed shouted for Patty to bring his gun. "With well-directed aim," Reed recalled, "I brought him down." Not only had he saved the new hog, but he also added fresh bear meat and cooking oil to the family supply.

Bear-up-a-tree stories abound, but occasionally one finds an account of frontier hunters having to deal with a bear *in* a tree. In January, 1821, James Samuel and Smith Stephenson were working in the woods when their hunting hounds opened up with loud baying at the base of a hollow tree.

Samuel, believing the dogs had treed a possum, stuck his head in the cavity for a glimpse and quickly drew back. His eyes were big as teacups. It was a bear. Stephenson ran off to get a gun while Samuel stayed with the dogs and tried to hold the bear at bay. But the agitated bear jumped out of the tree and went for the hounds. Sanuel, not wanting the bear to escape, grabbed his pole axe and landed a blow on the animal's head. The bear, stunned but far from dead, leaped backward, still tangling with the dogs. Then Samuel connected with a second blow, dropping the bear in its tracks.

Stephenson returned with a horse and some extra help. The bear was lifted across the saddle and, according to the story, was so big that it dragged the ground on both sides of the horse. The bear was said to have weighed 400 pounds, and the whole settlement enjoyed bear in the following days.

One of the most dramatic early-Ohio bear confrontations was in 1813. John Farney, a Jackson County settler, was hunting one day when he came across a black bear larger than any he had ever killed. Farney and the bear saw each other at the same instant at fairly close range. The giant bear charged, but Farley was not worried. He confidently drew his gun to his shoulder, sighted on the bear's head, and pulled the trigger. Click. Farney's gun failed to fire. And the giant bear continued to close on him. The hunter dropped his gun, now useless, and whipped his tomahawk from his belt. He threw the tomahawk as hard as he could at the rushing bear. But the weapon just glanced off the bear's broad, black head and fell into the bushes. And the bear kept on coming.

The bear was on him now. Farney drew from his belt his last weapon, a long hunting knife, and began to slash wildly at the bear. The bear swiped at him with its massive paws. Claws raked through his buckskin shirt. Again and again the knife struck home as bear and hunter rolled over and over, battling to the death. Finally, the bear slumped into a heap. It twitched a few times and lay still. Weak and exhausted, Farney dropped to the forest floor and rested until he had regained enough strength to dress the bear out and start for home. Farney not only survived hand-to-claw combat with a bear, but also lived to become commissioner of the county. He lost his taste for close encounters with bears, however. As history records it, "He never saught (sic) another bear fight."

By the early 1800's, black bears were beginning to disappear in Ohio. As opportunities to kill a bear diminished, any sighting was discussed with great excitement, and the successful hunter told and retold his story. When there was a question about whose shot actually brought a bear to earth, the dispute could easily end up before the magistrate. This happened in 1831.

The bear in question was said to have been the last one ever killed in Jackson County. Two brothers named Massie spotted the bear first and had time to get off one shot, which only wounded the animal. The bear raced off into the distance. There was snow on the ground, and the brothers trailed the bear throughout the afternoon. But they pushed the bear right past another hunter, Bill Whitt, who promptly shot it. By the time the Massies came upon the scene, Whitt was hanging the bear in a tree to dress it.

A heated argument followed, with Whitt claiming the bear was his because he delivered the fatal shot. The Massie boys insisted that they had shot the animal first, then trailed it for many hours, and that this made the bear their property. Whitt, outnumbered, finally gave in and surrendered the bear to them. But he was so convinced that he had been wronged that he later sued the brothers. The account does not tell us the decision of the court, but it does say that the Massie family had eaten the meat. Perhaps that settled the question of ownership.

Sometimes the bear came out the winner in old Ohio. One afternoon in the fall of 1832—bears were so scarce by this time that many people had never seen one—people in the village of St. Clairsville heard a commotion on Main Street and ran to their doors. They saw Isaac Ruby, astride his big gray horse, waving his hat above his head and shouting at the top of his lungs, "Bear! Bear!" Behind him came a large, fast-moving black bear. Later estimates said that 120 people chased the bear through St. Clairsville.

The bear might have made it all the way down Main Street if a funeral procession hadn't crossed the street in front of it. Cut off, the bear wheeled and jumped over a fence into the church graveyard, then ran off across John Thompson's farm and made for the woods. It was while the throng was crossing Thompson's farm that Andrew Orr and his dog drew close enough to the escaping bear for the dog to attack. Orr urged his dog forward. But the dog, who was at least as confused as the bear, attacked a calf instead. "The chase," says the account, "was somewhat impeded by the crowd's trying to get the dog away from the calf." This gave the bear the edge. It escaped into the woods and was never seen again. "Mr. Orr's dog," wrote the historian, "was never afterward looked upon as being worth much for bears, even by his owner."

Another bear made good its escape by comandeering a boat. George Cochran, who moved to the Ohio frontier in 1799, found a bear swimming in the Scioto River. Cochran had left his gun back in the cabin and was afraid that if he went back for it, the bear would escape. Cochran ran down to the river's edge, pushed his boat out into the stream, jumped in, and grabbed a paddle. His plan made the taking of the bear seem easy. He would simply cut off the animal's escape and make it swim until it became exhausted and drowned. Then he would drag it out of the river.

But the bear, instead of swimming away from the boat, turned toward it. As the bear began to climb in one side of his boat, Cochran climbed out the other side. There he stood, chest deep in the Scioto and helpless, as his boat and the bear drifted around the next bend in the river and out of sight.

Few Ohio bear hunters ever had a more frightening experience than Samuel Jackson. In the fall of 1809, Sam was hiking along the trace that followed Sunfish Creek, three miles east of Sinking Springs, when a bear appeared. It was a large one and Sam's thoughts turned at once to ways of taking it. The bear, fat from the fall feeding, disappeared into a cave in a rocky cliff.

This complicated Jackson's job. He was going to need help to kill the bear and get it out of the cave, so he ran off to the nearest cabin. There he found John Lowman, who was equally eager to kill the bear. Lowman took a glowing ember from the fireplace and accompanied Jackson back to the cliff. First they piled leaves at the entrance to the cave and set them afire with the ember. Then they stationed themselves 30 yards away, their rifles pointed at the cave entrance. The smoldering leaves soon filled the cave with heavy smoke, and the choking bear emerged into the fresh air. Jackson fired, wounding the bear. But instead of going back into the smoke-filled cave, the bear fled to another but smaller cave and pushed its way inside.

Once more the hunters set a leaf fire. Smoke curled up around the rocks and into the cave. But the bear did not come out. After an hour of waiting, the men were uncertain about the safest course to take. To wait longer seemed futile. To crawl into the cavern and search for a black bear in the dark seemed foolish. They decided to go home and think about it until evening, then come back to reassess the situation.

Back at the cave, Jackson and Lowman searched the area but found no evidence that the bear had come out. There was only one thing to do if they were to get their bear. Jackson volunteered. Taking a torch in hand, he lowered himself to hands and knees and began working his way into the cave, hoping to force the bear out. Once inside, he shoved the torch into the blackness and suddenly froze: there lay the giant black bear, facing him. But Jackson's fear was short-lived, for the bear was dead. His shot had been fatal. Only one problem remained: the bear had to be moved out of the cave.

Lowman joined Jackson in the cave, and they began the task of moving the animal. With Lowman in front pulling and Jackson behind pushing, they inched the heavy carcass toward the entrance. Somehow the bear had squeezed through the small, rocky opening while alive, but getting its dead weight back through the hole would be a problem. Lowman preceded the bear out of the cave while Jackson continued to push. Inch by inch, they forced the bear into the rocky opening. The more they struggled, the tighter the bear became wedged.

Lowman, preoccupied with trying to pull the bear out, did not notice that his scuffling had rekindled the smoldering leaves from the fire they had built earlier in the day. Dense smoke filtered in through cracks in the rocks around the bear and soon filled the cave. Jackson, coughing and crouching low against the cave floor, was trapped.

Lowman thrust his hands between the bear and the rocks and gradually succeeded in opening a space. Then, lying on his back, he braced both feet against solid rock and, taking a grip on the bear's front legs, strained desperately to pull the bear free while Jackson pleaded to be saved. Lowman thought he would pull his arms from their sockets. Finally, he felt the bear moving toward him. He soon had it out of the entrance, and Jackson, gasping for air, pushed past the bear and out of the smoke-filled cave.

Lowman lived to be an old man. After the bears were gone and only the memories remained, he often retold this story of the last bear in Jackson County and how he helped kill it.

On occasion we still hear stories that leave us wondering if there might be a few bears holding out in the more rugged areas of the forest hills of southern Ohio. There are occasional rumors. A neighbor of mine told me of a farmer near Peach Mountain who has been on many Western hunts and knows bear tracks when he sees them. The farmer reports having found bear tracks in the soft earth of his barnyard.

If bears are there, I wish them luck. One thing is certain: any bears remaining had extremely unfortunate ancestors, because back in the days when the earliest settlers came to Ohio, Grandpa was a bear hunting man.

One for
the Bears

Jack O'Connor

January, 1964

At Annette Island, the airport for Ketchikan, Alaska, my wife and I left the big jet on which we had flown from Seattle, Washington, and transferred to an amphibious plane. We were to make a stop at Wrangel and then land at Petersburg, Alaska.

"Do you mind if we take our rifles into the cabin?" I asked the pilot.

"No," he said. "You people bear hunters? Look, I'll show you some bears on the way up."

And he did. The unpredictable Alaska weather was on its best behavior that day. It was brilliantly clear, and when the weather is good the Alaska Panhandle is one of the most beautiful areas to be seen on this globe. We flew low, often below the tops of thickly timbered island mountains still deep in snow, past narrow gray beaches washed by the dark and restless sea. Once the pilot spotted a black sow with two little cubs grazing on a narrow strip of sedge between the heavy timber and the sea, and later, in a quiet cove, we saw a big, lone, brown bear.

Robert Chatfield-Taylor, a friend of 20 years' standing, was to hunt with us. He had gone ahead and the plan was for us to transfer our rifles and duffel to Ralph Young's bear-hunting boat, the Umatilla, get our licenses, eat a quick lunch and take off. I had hunted with Ralph in May 1956, in the days when the annual limit on bears was two of the big Alaska browns and two blacks and I had got the works. Now it is one brown and three blacks.

In not much over an hour Eleanor and I had joined Bob for lunch while Ralph Young and his wife, Jo, did some last-minute chores. Then we bought our licenses and got our stuff down to the sturdy Umatilla. Bob was well armed with a handsome Griffin & Howe rifle for the 7 mm.

Remington Magnum cartridge and a second rifle, which is known as the
.380 Taylor, a .375 on the same short Magnum case used for the .338, the
.264 Winchester, and the 7 mm. Remington Magnums. Eleanor had only
her 7 × 57 Mauser, a battered little musket she has used on safaris in
Tanganyika, Mozambique, and Angola. I took along a custom-stocked Winchester Model 70 in .338 with a 4X Leupold scope and a 22-inch barrel.

"I know a place for blacks not far from here," Ralph told us as we
moved out to sea from the harbor at Petersburg. "We ought to hit it about
5 o'clock, and that will give us plenty of time for a hunt. A guy I had up
here for black bears last season knocked off two dandies over there in one
afternoon."

On schedule, we slid into a long, narrow arm of the sea and anchored.
All around us were steep, wooded mountains coming down to the water
and capped with snow. The place where we were to hunt was a big, grass-
filled valley between a huge glacier and the sea.

The water was dotted with the black, oily-looking heads of seals and
little white chunks of ice that were miniature icebergs broken off the glacier
at the head of the bay.

Ralph tows behind the Umatilla a fiberglass skiff with a powerful
outboard motor. Presently we were in it, scooting over toward the bay.
All of us were dressed in the Alaska bear-hunter's uniform of hip boots
and down jacket.

Standing up and steering, Ralph had a better look into the meadow
than the rest of us. "Well," he shouted presently so he could be heard
over the roar of the motor. "I see a couple of bears."

He cut off the power and rowed in. We all got out in knee-deep water
with Ralph trailing a line so he could tie the skiff to something on the
shore. We could see two black bears, both busily chomping grass, one
right in the middle of the meadow, the other about 50 yards from the heavy
timber that bordered it. Both looked as if they'd make nice trophies.

"It will be nice if Eleanor can get her black tonight," Ralph said. "Then
we'll have a little of the pressure off. Three good browns and three blacks
in two weeks is a pretty big order."

We waded ashore, and Bob and I watched while Eleanor and Ralph
made the stalk. They disappeared in the timber to our left, and as I watched
with my binoculars I'd glimpse them occasionally as they flitted through
the trees. The bears kept on feeding. I expected to hear a shot at any
moment.

Then, to my surprise, I saw Eleanor and Ralph emerge from the woods
and walk straight back toward the skiff across the meadow. The bear
feeding there saw them and galloped off, but the one by the woods paid
no attention.

"Rubbed," Ralph explained when he and Eleanor joined us. "Neither
hide worth a hoot."

We didn't know it at the time, but that was the first tough break of
many we were to have on this trip. Luck is the most important ingredient
of any hunt. Give a man enough of it, and he doesn't need good equipment,
much skill, or much time. Take luck away from him, and he's dead. On

my first Alaska bear hunt with Ralph, the weather had been pretty bad with many days of hard, continuous rain, but we had seen lots of bears. Most of the pelts were good. Our stalks were successful, and our luck was consistently good. On this trip the results were just the opposite. If anything could go wrong, it did go wrong. That's Finnegan's Law.

It was Bob's turn to stalk a black bear the next day, and as it happened Ralph had to stay with the skiff because of the way the tide was running. That turned out to be bad break No. 2. Bob had a long stalk to make, and when he finally ran out of cover, the bear still looked pretty far away. Bob took a solid rest over a log and held the horizontal crosswire in the scope even with the top of the bear's back just above the point of the shoulder. Then he squeezed the trigger. Bob saw hair fly precisely where he had held, and he also saw the most startled bear in Alaska trying to get out of there.

Our next snafu was on Baranof Island. We went whizzing down another long, narrow arm of the sea toward a lovely valley at the end. On either side were steep, wooded mountains that rose from narrow, rocky little beaches.

The valley was about a mile long and half a mile wide. It was surrounded by heavy woods and snow-capped peaks. Ralph suggested that Bob, Eleanor, and I go ashore and wait for him around a little point at the right edge of the valley while he made the skiff fast.

Probably what happened subsequently was my fault. While Ralph was tying up the boat, I was glassing the open meadows and the edge of the timber to my left. I had glanced at the timber and the arctic willows to my right about 200 yards away but had really paid little attention to that area.

When Ralph joined us, he almost jumped out of his pants.

"Look, for heaven's sake, look," he said.

In the waist-high arctic willow right at the edge of the timber to our right were the backs of two fine bears, a boar and a sow. The boar was dark brown, the female as light as a mountain grizzly.

"You people are certainly alert," Ralph said. "Who's going to shoot?"

"Let Bob have it," I said.

And this was yet another piece of bum luck. Ralph didn't know much about Bob's shooting, as the only time he'd seen him perform he had missed a black bear. He resolved to get Bob close. Actually, the bears were within 200 yards, and Bob could have climbed up the hillside 20 or 30 feet. He could then have taken them at his leisure. But the way it worked out, Bob hadn't gone 100 feet when he stepped on a dead branch. It cracked. Both of the bears stood up, took one horrified look at the four people plotting against them, and plunged into the woods. Discouraged, we climbed up on the bank and started glassing.

A couple of hours later, a big bear walked out of the woods a mile away and clear across the meadow. This time Bob insisted that Eleanor and I make the stalk. The wind was puffy but consistent, and it looked as if we could skirt the woods and get a shot at the bear.

That was a long mile through muskeg, muck, willows, bog, and down timber. When we were within 100 yards of the spot where we had planned to shoot, what wind there was died. We sneaked on. Then I felt a puff of wind on the back of my neck. I knew that was it. The bear smelled us and took off.

As we plodded back, Ralph shook his head. "I don't want to sound discouraged," he said, "but I've got a funny feeling about this trip. With luck we could now have three fine bears. It isn't often you see three good, unrubbed bears in one valley in one afternoon. But we don't have a thing."

The next day our bad luck let up on us for a few hours. Ralph decided to try a couple of other spots from the same anchorage. On our first stand we saw, high on the hill above us, a handsome sow with three little teddy-bear cubs feeding in the alders that had grown up on a snowslide. They were about 500 yards away, and we watched them for about half an hour, expecting all the time to see a male show up. When none did, we went back to the skiff and went around a point into another valley.

Before we could get ashore, we saw a big male brown bear feeding at the edge of the woods on the left side of a little semicircular valley. Ralph cut the motor and began to row in, but the big bear waddled slowly into the woods and disappeared.

"Let's go ashore and wait," Ralph said. "That bear wasn't running when he disappeared. I don't think he saw or smelled us, and I don't think he is frightened. Maybe he'll come out."

"If he does, you take him, Bob," I said.

We found the moss-covered trunk of a tree that had floated ashore during some storm many years before and waited behind it. A wind sprang up, but it was in our favor. Clouds skidded across the sun. Back in the timber, a blue grouse hooted.

Then, on the far side of the little valley about 300 yards away, three panicky blacktail deer came boiling out of the woods.

"Watch," whispered Ralph. "Something scared those deer, and it has to be a bear."

For five minutes nothing happened, and then a big brown waddled out of the heavy timber and began feeding on sedge.

"Can you hit him from here?" Ralph asked Bob.

I saw Bob take his 7 mm. Remington Magnum rifle off safe and begin to aim. Just in case the bear would need another shot to keep it from getting into the woods, I got the scope of my .338 on the bear.

When Bob's rifle cracked the bear went down. It lay struggling for a moment. Bob shot again and it lay still. His first shot with a handload had driven the 175-grain Nosler bullet through both shoulders, and when Ralph skinned it we found the bullet rolled up under the hide on the far side. His second shot had gone squarely through the lungs.

A cold, clear stream lay between us and the bear. It came almost to the top of my hip boots and as I edged my way across, I stepped on a slick stone and went down like a wounded hippo.

"You're really bright," Eleanor said as I floundered out, dripping. "If you'd gone 30 feet upstream you'd have found the water less than a foot deep."

Bob's bear was a nice big one that squared out a bit less than nine feet. Its unrubbed pelt was medium brown. By the time Ralph got the bear skinned, the wind was blowing a gale, and I was freezing in my wet clothes. Our little bay was calm enough, but we could see high, white-topped waves out in the wide channel.

"Four of us can't get back in the skiff," Ralph told us. "I'll go back alone and try to bring the Umatilla over into the bay here. The channel outside is a hell of a place when the wind comes up. Once a party I had in here had to sit out all night . . . Anyway, you won't go hungry. You have about 800 pounds of fresh bear meat right here."

So we went back into the woods, built a fire, and waited for Ralph. Piece by piece I dried my wet clothes. Some eagles lit in a tree near us and eyed the carcass of the bear. A juicy little blacktail buck wandered out of the woods across the valley and started to feed.

Eleanor eyed it through her scope speculatively. "If I am going to have to live on meat while the storm blows itself out, I'd a lot rather have venison than bear meat," she said.

But presently we heard the Umatilla's diesel. Ralph anchored the boat in the cove and soon we were aboard getting the chill out of our bones with hot-buttered rum.

Since we were not far from Warm Springs Bay on Baranof Island, we decided to put in there and take a bath in the hot water from the mineral springs. And then we were off to Chichagof. The big bears of the southeastern Alaska islands are the darkest on Admiralty, where they are an even, dark brown. On Baranof, where Bob got his bear, they are a medium brown, and on Chichagof they are blond, as light as the lightest interior grizzlies that are sometimes called sun bears.

On Chichagof, we had another misadventure, if it can be called that. It was a case of too many bears. Never have I seen more bear sign. There were deep trails, droppings, and bear tracks everywhere.

Ralph had seen a big blond male feeding along a little stream in a narrow valley. Then, as he came back to get Eleanor and me, a sow with three beautiful, golden cubs walked out of the timber upwind and not over 100 yards away.

Since mamma bears with cubs can be pretty mean, he asked Bob and me to keep our eyes on the sow and to protect the rear while he and Eleanor stalked the big male. So Bob and I, watching sow and cubs, stayed behind.

Our bad luck followed. By the time Ralph and Eleanor got over to the spot where Ralph had seen the bear, it had fed into chest-high willows. They could hear him but could not see him. They waited, waited, waited.

Finally Ralph told Eleanor to go quietly ahead and to take the bear at close range when she saw him. He walked right behind with his .375 ready.

Suddenly the bear stood up about 20 feet from Eleanor. She was so flabbergasted that she didn't shoot. He faced her for a moment and then dropped to all fours and ran.

She came back shaking her head. "I don't know whether I like this close-range bear hunting or not," she said. "When that bear stood up, I was afraid he'd eat me if I missed him. Then when he ran I wasn't about to shoot him in the bottom. Gee, that was a big bear. When he stood up he looked as big as an elephant!"

Then, back on Admiralty, Eleanor actually took a shot at a brownie. I was watching one valley, Ralph and Eleanor another, when I saw a medium-size brown bear with a good pelt walk out of the woods and start to feed. I watched it for about 15 minutes with binoculars, hoping all the time that Ralph would see it and bring Eleanor over. Presently I saw them come sneaking around the point.

It was a tough stalk. All they could do was bend over and make themselves as inconspicuous as possible, as mostly they had no cover. Part of the way they could keep partly out of sight by taking advantage of the contour of the ground and the banks of the creek, but most of the time they could move only when the bear looked the other way.

Finally, the bear saw something that made him suspicious. He gazed in their direction for a long time, started to feed, looked up again. Then he moved slowly toward the woods, stopping now and then to look back.

I saw Eleanor getting ready to shoot. It was a straight sitting shot with nothing to rest the rifle on.

Then the little 7 mm. cracked. The bear did a nose dive, got up, and headed for the woods.

I galloped clumsily over to them, and together Ralph and I went over to see what we could find out. From the color and location of the blood on the willows, I was certain that it was a muscle wound, probably in the lower neck or brisket forward of the forelegs.

"We'll never see that bear again," I told Ralph. "He's wounded superficially up front."

Ralph agreed. The bear wasn't badly hurt. He had plunged into the woods and had taken a bear trail that climbed up into a saddle between two peaks. His bleeding had almost stopped when he hit the saddle.

Eleanor was a very disappointed gal when we told her she had drawn a blank.

"I think this rifle's shooting off," she said. "The crosswires looked just right when I shot. I had them right on his shoulder."

"Don't feel too bad," Ralph said. "That wasn't an easy shot, and you weren't very far off at that.'

"Anyway, I'm glad I didn't hit him in the guts," Eleanor said. "But I still think this rifle's off. I've killed sitting jackrabbits farther away than that."

I might add that she has also killed running jackrabbits almost as far away. This gal of mine has been shooting a rifle a long time, and generally she's had pretty good luck with one. She shot her first deer, a fine big buck with five points to the side, just 32 years before she wounded that bear. She has hunted in Arizona, Idaho, Mexico, Canada, and she has made three safaris in Africa. Generally, when her little 7 × 57 pops, something falls over.

The next day, I took a crack with the 7 mm. at a rock about 200 yards away on the beach. Bob was manning the glass and he said the shot looked pretty good. We decided Eleanor must have flinched or wobbled.

Our time was growing short now. Neither Eleanor nor I had a bear, and Bob had no black. We went to a favorite spot of Ralph's on Admiralty

Island only to find another bear-hunting boat in there and to learn that the occupants had killed two good browns there.

That lost us a day. We went to get another spot on Admiralty, but rain began to pour down. While Bob and I stayed on the boat, Eleanor went ashore to hunt with Ralph. They saw many blacktail deer, two sows, and several cubs. No big males. They returned chilled and completely soaked.

We had to head back to Petersburg the next day. I took the disappointment in my stride, as I had a fine brown-bear trophy at home. Bob had previously shot black bear, so he wasn't hurting. But Eleanor and Ralph were disconsolate.

"When I tell people about all the lousy luck we've had on this trip, they won't believe it," Ralph told us gloomily.

I didn't particularly care when I came here whether I got a bear or not," Eleanor said. "But now that I have worked so hard for one I've got my dander up."

We were about a mile offshore, rolling along at 12 knots, when Ralph suddenly grabbed his binoculars and did a double-take.

"See that big black over there on the beach?" he asked. "He's a good one with a good hide." He cut the engine until it was barely idling. "Here, Jo," he said to his wife. "You steer the boat. Eleanor and I are going bear hunting."

I have never seen anyone get into a bear-hunting uniform faster than Eleanor did. In about three shakes she had on her hip boots, her rain jacket, and had grabbed her 7 mm. and a handful of cartridges. She jumped into the boat, and she and Ralph roared away toward the not-too-distant shore.

Bob and I watched from the deck. We saw Ralph cut the motor and row ashore about half a mile from the busily feeding black. Then, with Ralph in front, they started the stalk.

The Umatilla was rolling and presently I put down my binoculars to rest my eyes.

"What do you know," Bob said. "That damned bear has lain down on the grass."

I looked, and this was indeed true. I thought nothing of it, since on a previous Alaskan trip I had seen black bears lie down on the grass for a bit of shut-eye. With the glass, I saw Ralph and Eleanor walking toward the bear, less than 200 yards away. They seemed singularly relaxed for people stalking a bear, even a sleeping bear. They got nearer and nearer to the bear.

"I wish Eleanor would be careful," Bob said. "She's going to step on that bear. She's within 20 feet of it, and she can't see it because it's on the other side of the log." Then: "For the love of Pete, she kicked the bear and it didn't move. She must have shot it."

"Either that or it died of heart failure," I said, still watching. "It has been my experience that if you kick a bear, and he doesn't move, he's either dead or drunk."

Eleanor and Ralph came roaring back to the Umatilla in triumph.

"Well," said Eleanor. "I didn't get skunked after all. I killed him with one shot, but I still think this rifle's cockeyed. I held for his shoulder and hit him in the head. I had a good rest over a log, and I really squeezed the trigger. My shot on the brown was left. Now this one is left. I'd sure like to see what this thing does on a target."

We all went back to skin the bear and to take pictures. It was a fine, big, black male, about as big as any I have ever seen. It would weigh, I imagine, around 275, maybe 300 pounds.

After we got home, I took three rifles, one of them Eleanor's 7 mm., over to the Speer 100-yard indoor range to check them. I put up a 100-yard small-bore target, fired a shot from the 7 mm., but couldn't find it through the spotting scope where it hit. I fired another. No luck. Then, clear off the target and on the paper background, I noticed two bullet holes about half an inch apart.

I fired another shot. Now there were three holes, about 14 inches from where they should have been. By using the windage adjustment available with the opposing screws in the Buehler mount and some within the tube itself, I got Little Betsy again shooting where she looked.

When I got back to the house I told Eleanor what I had found out.

"Write and tell Ralph that," she said. "I was never so embarrassed in my life as when I wounded that brownie. The next time I take an airplane to go on a hunt, I'm going to carry my rifle in my lap and treat it like a baby."

Bear That Broke a Jinx

Fred Bear

December, 1966

It says on the label that this stuff should be served at room temperature," Bob Munger said with a chuckle, holding up a bottle of Burgundy and squinting at it against the light. "How in blazes are we gonna get it out of the bottle?"

It was a good question. "Room" temperature in our tent was so low that the wine had congealed into slushy ice. We finally heated it in a pan of water, and it went well with fried seal liver.

We were after polar bears the hard way, camped on the ice 200 miles east of Point Barrow and 40 miles offshore, and hunting with snow sleds. Our tents were pitched on shore ice which, unlike the polar pack that drifts endlessly the year around, is anchored on the beach and doesn't break up until the spring thaw, usually around the end of May. We'd made camp in mid-April, setting up the tents 10 or 15 miles from the outer edge of the anchored ice. We'd be safe and reasonably comfortable for the six weeks we were allowing ourselves for the hunt. The ice on which we had pitched our tents was from five to seven feet thick, and just behind the camp a pressure ridge was piled 30 feet high. It formed a good windbreak and provided us with salt-free ice that we could melt for our water supply. Also, since seals make their spring dens under drifted snow along those jumbled ridges and polar bears hunt them there, we hoped this hogback might be the means to lure a bear right into camp.

We got our wish on that score. Unfortunately, though, the bear arrived before we did, tore up our tents, and left. The guides had put up two of the tents the day before we flew out to the camp, and sometime in the intervening 24 hours, a big bear had come along. We found one tent down and both ripped and torn. We sewed them up, cussing our luck that we hadn't been on hand. We didn't see the intruder again, either, in spite of doing everything we could think of to entice him back.

Our plans for the hunt hit a snag right at the outset. I didn't want to use a plane for spotting bears if I could help it, so we'd decided to try baiting them in. The problem was to find seals for bait.

When there are no leads, or areas of open water, in the shore ice, seals hide their winter breathing holes under snow that piles up in deep drifts along the pressure ridges. When it's time for the young to be born, the female scratches out a den under a drift beside her breathing hole. There the little seal is hidden—unless a bear smells it out first—until it's old enough to follow its mother under the ice. We couldn't find seals in those retreats, and until the weather turned warmer and open water started to appear, we wouldn't have much luck hunting them.

We used a bag of fish soaked in seal oil as a substitute and towed in behind a snow sled to make a drag trail. In the next few days, seven bears passed within half a mile of camp, and we saw the tracks of others a few miles away. But none followed the bait trail.

The wind kept the ice scoured free of snow, too, making it impossible to track them. We'd find a track where snow had drifted at the foot of a ridge, but as soon as the bear turned out across open ice, we'd lose him.

This was my third try at taking a polar bear, and for me it had to be done with a bow or it wouldn't count. My company at Grayling, Michigan, makes archery equipment, and it's been more than 30 years since I've hunted with anything but a bow. After my first two polar-bear hunts, which wound up as fairly close shaves, the polar bear was the only major North American trophy game that wasn't on my list of arrow kills.

I'd taken deer, elk, moose, sheep, mountain goat, caribou, black bear, grizzlies, Alaska brown bears, an Indian tiger, an African elephant, cape buffalo, and lion, all with bow. But up to now, the white bear of the arctic had proved too much for me.

I'd had good shots at very close ranges on both of my earlier polar-bear hunts, but the instant my arrows sliced in, the bears charged and had to be killed by rifle.

It happened the first time in April of 1960. On the ice off Point Barrow, George Thiele and I stalked to within 17 yards of a bear. The bear's rump was toward us, and the guide urged me to plunk in an arrow and then kill him when he turned to fight it. I figured George knew what he was talking about, so I followed his advice. It was a good hit, but the bear came for us like white lightning, and George downed him at nine paces with two shots from a Winchester .300 Magnum.

The second time was in the spring of 1962, again off Point Barrow, with Thiele as my pilot and guide. We got within 25 yards of this bear, and the same thing happened. George killed the bear with a 180-grain load in the head at 10 steps.

I'd filled my license both times but couldn't claim either trophy as a bowkill since the pelts had bullet holes as well as arrow holes in them.

I said in that story, "One of these days I'll collect a polar bear that I can count. When I do, I'll consider that I've killed the most dangerous animal a hunter can tangle with on this continent." Now, in the spring of

1966, I was out on the ice again with a 65-pound-pull Kodiak hunting bow, still of that same opinion and hoping to prove the truth of the old saw, "Three times and out."

To me, the white bear is one of the greatest trophies on earth. He's found far out on almost-inaccessible ice, not much afraid of man, likely to fight at the drop of a hat, and big and tough enough to give a good account of himself. And I'd concluded that hunting him with motorized snow sleds, without the help of aircraft, would be the last word.

A lot of sportsmen share my feelings about the ice bear. He has gained such great popularity as a trophy in recent years that the Alaska Department of Fish and Game recently established new regulations and a permit system, starting in 1967. The season will run from January 1 to April 30, and only 350 permits will be issued. If more than that number of applications are received, a drawing will be held.

Conservationists believe that this system will peg the annual kill at about 300 bears, the average for 1965 and 1966. The Boone and Crockett Club recently removed the white bear from the list of animals eligible for its big-game record competitions, because of the growing use of aircraft in the hunting and uncertainty about the world polar-bear population.

My partners on this hunt were Cliff Robertson and Bob Munger. Cliff is known to just about every movie and TV fan in the country. He is the Hollywood actor picked by the late John F. Kennedy to play the role of Kennedy in a film on the PT boats of World War II. The picture was withheld from distribution after the President was assassinated. Right after our hunt, Cliff won an Emmy award for a TV show he'd done with Bob Hope. An enthusiastic hunter, he wanted a wall-to-wall, white-bear rug.

Munger is a sporting-goods and hardware dealer from Charlotte, Michigan, who had hunted with me many times before. He told the story of one of those trips, the one on which he killed a record-book brown bear on Afognak Island, in "Hunt Against Odds," in Outdoor Life for January, 1963. Bob had taken a very good polar bear in 1960 and didn't want another. He'd cover this hunt with a camera.

In addition to getting a bear, we hoped to make an exciting motion picture for use on the ABC television show, "The American Sportsman," and I also wanted a movie for my own film library. We had a sizable crew of New York cameramen along.

Bob and I flew from Chicago to Fairbanks on April 13 and met the others there. The next day, all of us went on to Point Barrow by charter plane.

Barrow had changed since I saw it last in 1962. Motor sleds had ousted dog teams, and motor bikes were replacing bicycles. Natural gas had come in, and dial phones were common. But some things were the same. A skinny hamburger still cost 90¢ and a can of soda 40¢. A whale had been reported offshore, and we found the Eskimos readying the same whaling gear they'd always used.

The Top of the World Hotel was crowded with guides and bear hunters. Ninety-three bears had been taken up to that time, all with the help of planes, and a number of wolves with planes and snow sleds. I can't help feeling that those sleds can spell the doom of the wolf, the wolverine, and maybe even the caribou. They can travel faster than any animal can run. Used in land hunting, they're deadly.

We were delayed two days at Barrow by a 30-knot wind and swirling snow that cut visibility to zero. The weather cleared on Saturday, April 16, and we flew by bush plane to Bud Helmerick's headquarters in the Colville River delta, 160 miles to the east. Bud and his 21-year-old son Jim would be our pilots and guides. Bud has been in that business for years, and Jim is following in his father's footsteps.

Our first sight of their home from the air reminded us of a lonely lighthouse set in a vast and empty expanse of white. The sea ice ran as far north as we could see, and to the south the arctic prairie sloped up for 50 miles to the Brooks Range. But for all its isolation, the place has every modern convenience. A diesel generating plant churns day and night, and a radio set sputters, maintaining a link with the outside world.

We flew out onto the ice Sunday morning, repaired the bear's mischief, and got the rest of the tents up. We had four big igloo-shaped models and four of the Quonset-hut type, 8 × 12 feet with plenty of headroom. For greater warmth, all were doubled by setting one inside another of the same type. Pitched on hard snow that we leveled off, the resulting four double tents were floored with pieces of plywood and banked with snow.

We heated the cook tent with a stove fed from a tank of bottled gas. Two sleeping tents had catalytic heaters that used white gasoline, and a third sleeping tent was heated by an oil burner. The heaters weren't up to such extreme temperatures, however, and seven men wound up sleeping in the tent that had the oil burner.

The weather stayed rough for days on end, with snow, gale winds, and temperatures down to 20 below. We built windbreaks of snow blocks around the camp and huddled in the tents trying to keep warm. But when we complained about the cold, Bud Helmericks laughed at us. In early March, they'd had three straight days of 65 below at his place on the Colville. "This is a heat wave," he kidded us.

Toward the end of April, Cliff Robertson had to leave for home. He'd hunted hard but failed to kill a bear. Shortly before he left, however, he did take a big bearded seal of the kind the Eskimos call ugrug, a somewhat rare trophy. A week later, the camera crew took off for New York.

Bob Munger, Jim Helmericks, Simon Ned (an Indian guide from the interior village of Allakaket), and I were left on the ice by ourselves. We'd hunt until I killed a bear or the spring breakup forced us ashore. Bud Helmericks would fly back and forth from his headquarters and bring us supplies.

Our first chore was to move camp to a new site. We'd cut a hole through seven feet of ice for fishing, which was fruitless, and so much water came up through the hole that we were flooded out at the old location.

The weather turned warmer with the arrival of May, and seal hunting picked up. The seals were beginning to sun themselves on the ice beside their breathing holes. Though most of the animals were in the open and hard to stalk, we had little trouble killing all we needed for bait. This wasn't work for the bow, however, since it was almost impossible to approach within bow range of them. Also, unless they were killed instantly—it took a shot in the head, even with a rifle—they'd flop into their holes and sink like stones.

We killed the first one by creeping up behind a block of ice and drilling him through the head with Bob's .244 Remington. But we soon found that not many of them could be approached that easily.

We hit on another method, however, that worked very well and also provided some interesting and suspenseful hunting. Bud brought out a small handsled, to the front of which we attached a screen made from a piece of plywood covered with white cloth. A peephole allowed us to watch the seal through the screen.

We'd lie flat on our bellies on the sled and propel it along with out hands. A seal sunning itself snoozes for a minute or so, then lifts its head for a quick look over the ice in all directions. Generations of polar bears have taught them to take that precaution.

By pushing our sled ahead while a seal was napping, and waiting motionless when it raised its head, we were able to get within about 150 yards. With the scope-sighted, flat-shooting .244, that was close enough. It called for a lot of patience. One of my stalks took more than an hour. But it was fun, and it produced.

We made every effort now to bring in a bear with bait. We made scent-trails by dragging skinned seal carcasses behind the sleds in 10 and 12-mile circles all around our camp, dropping chunks of blubber at intervals to keep a bear interested. We also set up a catalytic heater on an oil drum outside our tents and cooked seal blubber on it 24 hours a day, sure that this would get results. Bob and I found that we could pick up the smell of seal oil half a mile downwind from the bubbling pot. Comparing Nanook's nose with ours, we concluded that any bear passing within 10 or even 15 miles could tune in.

We put out seal carcasses for bait 80 yards from our tents. lashing them to ice toggles, and built a blind of snow blocks nearby from which I could shoot. Next, we rigged a device I've used in hunting black bears, running a wire from the bait to a stake inside our tent and hanging a bundle of tin cans on it. Any bear that tugged at one of the frozen seals would be sure to touch off that alarm. And no matter when he came in, day or night, I'd have plenty of light for shooting. The time of continuous daylight was only a few days away now. The sun sliced down in the northwest about 11 o'clock and came up in the northeast a couple of hours later. A bright glow lighted the northern sky all night.

Before we were through, we had 12 seal carcasses in the bait area, anchored so that they couldn't be dragged off. Weighing from 80 to 150 pounds apiece, they made quite an imposing cache of meat.

"You'll get an easy shot," Bob predicted. "Any bear that comes in here will wind up too stuffed to walk away." But no bear came in.

We also hunted hard with the snow sleds, fanning out from camp to prowl the ice for tracks. But with the onset of the arctic spring, we were plagued with wretched weather. There was fog, freezing rain, blinding snowstorms, and—worst of all—whiteouts.

It's hard to imagine what a whiteout is like until you've gone through one. The horizon is lost, and it's impossible to distinguish a snow drift three feet high from a depression three feet deep, even close up. Level ice or hummocks, everything looks alike—or, rather, it all looks like nothing. Your next step may fetch up against a block of ice or pitch you on your face in a drift. Men on foot stumble through a white-out like alcoholics, and flyers dread them above all. Between white-outs and fogs and snow-storms, we went 10 days without a day of hunting weather, and in the end, all our baiting failed to turn the trick.

We knew from tracks and other sign that eight bears had passed within half a mile of camp about the time we were setting it up. But after that, despite the lure of fresh seal meat, scent trails, and our blubber pot, not a bear came within five miles. The only game we attracted were white foxes that found a bag of fish near camp.

We'd probably have done better if we'd camped farther out, nearer open water. But I'd advise any hunter wanting to try that to hire an Eskimo guide who's familiar with those limitless ice fields. Along the edge of the pack, there's always a chance of being set adrift on a floe.

As for hunting with snow sleds, I think it should be done in early April, ahead of the spring fogs, even though seals for bait are hard to come by then. By buying two or three seals at Barrow and taking them out to the camp, that problem could be solved. And camping on the ice and relying on sleds instead of aircraft is certainly a great way to go after polar bears.

We went north of camp one morning to make a seal drag and found the tracks of a good bear that had hit one of our earlier trails. But he'd followed it the wrong way and left it where we'd turned the snow sled around. When that happened twice, we gave up trying to bait a bear.

On the morning of May 11, almost four weeks after arriving on the ice, we took to the air in two light planes in the hope of finding what we'd come for. Bob flew with Jim Helmericks, I with Bud.

It was a clear, beautiful spring day. We flew north toward the open leads that were showing up now at the edge of the pack ice. Just 15 minutes after leaving camp, we spotted a bear walking along the side of a pressure ridge. He was the first one we'd seen in 25 days, and he gave me a great thrill.

The bear was quite a distance away and hadn't noticed the planes. The last thing I wanted was to disturb or anger him from the air. I feel that part of the reason my first two polar bears had turned on us so swiftly and furiously was that we had flown too close in looking them over, putting them in a bad temper. I didn't want that to happen this time.

"He's hunting seals," I told Helmericks, "and he'll follow that ridge for miles until he finds one. Let's give him a wide berth, land a long way ahead, and try to waylay him."

We were about seven miles from the bear when we set the two aircraft down on smooth ice, and he had taken no notice of us at all. We hiked back about a mile in his direction and found an ideal place for an ambush. I crouched behind the pressure ridge, where I'd be out of sight but high enough for shooting no matter on which side of the ridge he appeared.

Jim, Bud, and Bob took cover 20 yards in back of me with the cameras and two rifles. A back-up rifle is a necessary precaution when you're hunting with either bow or gun for an animal as quick tempered as the ice bear.

This one was nowhere in sight now, but if he stayed on his course, we were bound to come together. We waited for 1½ hours, cramped, uncomfortable, and cold, before spotting him coming half a mile away. He looked dark against the sunlit snow as he shuffled along, taking his time, investigating every crack and ice pile he came to, intent on a seal dinner. Everything was going exactly as I wanted it to.

Then, when 400 yards away, he swerved and angled off through rough ice, and I could see he was going to pass me beyond bow range. I hated to leave the spot I'd picked, but my trophy was about to slip through my fingers. There was only one chance to get a crack at him.

I waited until he went out of sight behind upturned ice and then ran for a new hiding place. I made it without his catching sight of me, and when I looked around, my three companions were well hidden in new positions behind me. The bear reappeared very quickly, coming straight at us.

He padded ahead, his long, snaky head swinging from side to side to let his nose take in everyting within range. He paused now and then to look around, the undisputed king of those silent, white wastes. He'd prowled them all his life—in the sun of the arctic summer and the dark of the long night—served well by his keen nose and eyes, his tireless legs, and the thick pelt that shielded him from the bitter cold of both water and wind. Save for the possibility of infrequent encounters with packs of killer whales, he had only man to fear. As far as he knew, there was no man within miles.

I watched him cut the distance to 300 yards, 200, then 100. I could feel my blood pressure going up. Waiting for any major game to walk into your lap is one of the most pulse-quickening things a hunter can do. In the past, two bears of this same kind had turned on me like infuriated cats. I couldn't put them out of my mind as I watched this one come on.

Sixty yards . . . 50 . . . then finally he was within good bow range and still coming. My razorhead arrow was on the string, the bow up, and I was ready to draw when the wind shifted just a little and betrayed me.

The bear jerked to a halt, his body at an angle and his eyes looking straight my way. His nose went into the air, and I could see his black muzzle wrinkle as he sniffed, not quite sure what he'd smelled. From my earlier encounters, I was sure that one of two things would happen in the next couple of seconds: 1) he'd wheel and run, or 2) he'd come at me full tilt. A charge would almost certainly mean another bear killed with a rifle, and that was the last thing I wanted. I didn't wait any longer.

Raising up behind my ice block, I drove an arrow at him. It looked good all the way, and I heard it hit with a resounding smack. Instantly, a red blotch started to spread near his shoulder.

My first two ice bears had charged like thunderbolts. This one ran like a rabbit. I doubt whether he ever knew I was there. He bolted for the pressure ridge, crossed it, and fell dead 100 yards beyond.

He was a handsome trophy—a big, thick-furred boar with 10 gallons of seal oil in his belly. I had broken my jinx at last and killed the bear I'd coveted for so long. It hadn't been done quite the way I'd hoped, but he had been taken in fair chase after a long and patient stalk, with the nearest aircraft a mile away and the bear unaware that it existed.

And there were no bullet holes in that wonderful white pelt. The gap in my trophy list that had existed for so many years was finally filled.

I Hunt a Special World

Grancel Fitz

September, 1956

Away back in 1927, on my first hunt for anything bigger than Pennsylvania whitetail deer, I was lucky enough to bag a very decent moose in northern Quebec. The head was no world-beater, but it was a lot better specimen than is usually found in eastern Canada, and in checking up on its quality I found myself transformed from a carefree venison hunter into a record-conscious trophy enthusiast.

My next big milestone was passed in 1930, on a Wyoming elk hunt. In those days scoring systems were unknown, but the usual index of quality was antler spread. I shot the 51st bull elk I encountered, and he set a new world record for antler spread. From that time on I aspired to shoot a good, representative specimen of every kind of legal big-game animal on the North American continent.

Up to the present there's no official record that any hunter has ever completed such a collection. In pioneer days it was virtually impossible. Stone sheep, for instance, weren't even discovered until 1902. Not a year passes, though, without having such a claim appear in print, and it's been made a few times in my presence.

"Do you have polar bear?" I asked. "Or North American jaguar? Or desert sheep, Barren Ground musk ox, Coues deer, or Atlantic walrus?"

Usually those fellows looked at me as if I'd kicked them in the groin. But even when we exclude the Greenland and Barren Ground musk oxen and the Atlantic and Pacific walruses on the grounds that they can no longer be legally hunted, there are 24 other kinds of animals recognized and listed in Records of North American Big Game. If anybody has ever bagged them all, he should certainly submit the particulars to the Records

Committee of the Boone and Crockett Club, 5 Tudor Place, New York 17, N.Y.

Meanwhile, another objective in my program was reached in 1955 on Kodiak Island, when I became the first man known to have *hunted* every legal species on our lists. But two animals—jaguar and polar bear—I had hunted hard without success.

A few years ago an arctic trip wasn't easy to arrange, and if a polar bear hadn't been needed for a complete collection, I wouldn't have dreamed of going after one. The usual hunt involved a summer cruise among ice floes, when the bearskins are in poor condition. Could be the hunter would sit in a deck chair, rest his rifle on the ship's rail, and assassinate his bear—with as little danger as if he'd shot a zoo bear through the bars of a cage.

Then in 1948 I learned about a pilot named Gene Joiner, of Kotzebue, Alaska. Gene, a tall, intrepid character from Texas, was pioneering a new type of arctic winter hunt, flying out over the frozen ocean in a light, ski-equipped airplane. He'd gone out with a sportsman from Illinois who bagged his polar bear within 70 minutes after taking off from Shishmaref, a tiny Eskimo village northeast of Bering Strait.

I had doubts about the sporting quality of an airplane hunt; it sounded too easy. But at least a plane could put me down on the same ice with a bear, so I booked a hunt with Gene for the following March.

The net result was a frustrating month for Gene, me, and another hunter. None of us even saw a polar bear, and our ideas concerning easy hunting by plane disintegrated. Ice and weather have to be right—and they can be wrong for a month at a time.

Discouraged about the profits to be had from hunters, Gene turned to prospecting—and came up with a fabulous mountain of jade, which in time should yield him a fortune. For my part, I found out far more about Eskimo life and polar-bear hunting that I could ever have learned from a short, successful trip.

Two incidents in that first hunt come to mind. For a week we flew out from Cape Krusenstern, taking a different direction daily in an effort to locate the kind of ice the bears would use. We didn't find it. The beginning of March found open water off Shishmaref, for the first time on record. Although March is often the year's coldest month on the ocean pack, the sea ice—no more than eight feet thick in any winter—can break up with fantastic ease when storms cause turbulent water. So each day we found ourselves flying over open-water "leads" and patches of mushy ice.

One evening, in the restaurant in Kotzebue, a visiting pilot took me aside. "I hear you're finding open leads and mush ice out there," he said. "You shouldn't fly over that stuff on skis. If your motor ever conks out, your number is up."

"The motor sounds wonderful," I remarked.

"A couple of years ago," he said, "I was flying along one day with my motor sounding wonderful. My radio sounded wonderful too. But the next minute, all I could hear was my radio. That day I got out of a treetop. Out where you fellows go, there aren't any trees."

He was a well-meaning lad, though not exactly cheerful. I was sorry to hear, a year or two later, that he'd crashed out.

Soon after that conversation, a blizzard raged for eight days. When it ended we headed for the high arctic, dropping in on Eskimo villages along the way. At Point Hope the natives sometimes kill almost 100 polar bears in a year. That winter only four had been taken, and even farther north we found the ice to be just as impossible as it had been off Kotzebue.

But up there, north of Point Lay and Icy Cape, it was bad for a different reason. The storm had broken up the heavy ice of the main pack, and while the floes had solidly frozen together again, at 30 below, the upended cakes made it impossible to land a plane.

At Point Lay I had another well-remembered chat, this time with an Air Force colonel from Point Barrow.

"As I understand it," I told him, "this ocean is like any other. When you're beyond the 12-mile limit you're on the high seas. What I'm driving at is that while the ice conditions around here are hopeless, I've seen what looks like decent ice away over toward Siberia. It's too far away for the cruising range of our plane, but we might ferry a supply of gas to a sort of advanced base out on the pack and operate from out there. By camping out for a night, we might get our bear with no trouble."

"It's nice to have known you," the colonel said.

"What do you mean?" I asked. "If we don't get any closer than 30 or 40 miles to Siberia, I figure we'll be minding our own business."

"Well," he said slowly, "the Russians are very touchy about spying, and when strange aircraft come near their coast they know it. So don't be an idiot. Stay on our side of the international date line. If the bears aren't on our side this winter, come back some other winter."

It struck me that possibly he had a point.

Things have changed a bit since then, and on my 1956 trip I found that several guides were operating out of Kotzebue and Nome with remarkable success. Under decent weather conditions, such as have prevailed for the last three years, a polar-bear hunt takes no more time than a good deer hunt back home. This unique adventure is bound to become more popular, so I learned all I could about the best way to go about it.

From the sportsman's standpoint, the most significant fact about the polar bear is his general ignorance of man. This is especially true of the males, which do not hibernate. Born on land, they are taken as cubs to the sea ice that's their real home, and many males seem to spend the remainder of their lives out there. The females come ashore to hibernate every other year, when their cubs are born. They spend the rest of their time at sea, where they are completely carnivorous. Living principally on seals, which are very wary, a polar bear has to be a master stalker who uses the cover of rough ice as skillfully as a tiger uses a thicket of brush.

Like other animals, a lot of polars distrust anything they don't understand, and are inclined to withdraw when you encounter them. But you can never tell. Away out on the sea ice, they are often so unsophisticated that they regard men, planes, or even ships with curiosity or indifference. They're so big and strong, remember, that nothing in their native haunts can challenge them, and arctic explorers, including such undramatic scientists as Stefansson and Nansen, have recorded an astonishing number of unprovoked attacks by bears met far offshore.

When a grizzly or a big brownie charges a man without provocation, he does so because he's enraged. In contrast, an aggressive polar bear is merely hungry. He doesn't know man well enough to get mad at him, but he suspects that this strange, two-legged creature would provide a good dinner.

Now about the kind of flying that's involved. Where bears are most plentiful, the ice is often rough. So the flying's done in tiny planes of the Cub type, which can alight and take off where larger planes could not. There's no question that landings on ocean ice are often hazardous. One true instance was reported in "The Cruel Cold" (OUTDOOR LIFE, December, 1955), telling of an accident which resulted in the loss of a hunting plane and nearly cost the lives of three people.

Knowing something of these dangers, I flew along with Gene—whose 11 years of experience have made him a superb judge of what he can and cannot do—but I wouldn't feel safe with any other pilot without having another plane along. Gene himself says it's only sensible for two planes to work together. Then, if one runs into grief, the other can lend a hand or go for help. Two lone planes were lost in 1955. Two others were damaged and the hunters had to be rescued, though the planes were later retrieved.

It's the danger of these flights and landings that puts polar-bear hunting in a special class. Most pilots guarantee the hunter a fair chance at a bear—within reason—but since the pilot runs some risk of damaging or even losing his plane with each offshore landing, each hunter is ordinarily through as soon as he gets one bear. With this sort of hunting, there's no danger for a long time to come that too many bears will be shot. The total take by sportsmen, since airplane hunting from Kotzebue first began, has been less than half the number killed by Point Hope natives in a single year.

However, there is a gimmick in this scheme that can lead to poor conservation and a raw deal for the sportsman as well. One outfitter took out two planes and two hunters. Each hunter had been guaranteed a fair chance, with sex and age of the bear unspecified. So when a female with two cubs was sighted, one plane landed.

"There's your polar bear," the outfitter said, pointing to the sow. "Bust her."

The hunter was in a spot. Here was his guaranteed shot at a bear, all right, and if he refused the female he might not be given a chance at another. He shot the sow.

Then the second plane landed close by. "Shoot those two cubs," the outfitter told the other hunter. "They can't make out without their mother." And the second hunter shot the two cubs.

"Nice work, boys," the outfitter congratulated them. "You've got your polar bears, and the hunt's over."

There's probably no way of controlling this through game laws. When the hunting is done beyond the 12-mile limit, it's questionable whether either Alaska or the United States has any jurisdiction. But a sportsman arranging a hunt can certainly specify that females with cubs don't count.

The best time to hunt is probably in late March or early April, although chances are good, weather permitting, from late February on.

I heard from Gene Joiner occasionally after my first trip to Kotzebue, but I didn't see him again until the spring of 1955, when he came through New York on the last lap of a jade-selling trip around the world.

"How about showing me a big polar bear next season?" I asked.

"I've been out of the polar-bear business since you-know-when," he told me with a grin. "But I still do plenty of bush flying, and I might be tempted to take out a hunter once in a while. In your case, the answer is yes. I'll let you know when conditions are right."

That was the way things stood until late last March, when he wired that there were lots of bears around and that I had better get one while conditions were good. Fortunately it didn't take me long to make arrangements to do the story for OUTDOOR LIFE and get away. On trips for other Alaska game, I had learned what modern air transport can do to get a hunter there in a hurry. So I left New York on a Northwest Airlines plane at 10 a.m. March 26. The same evening, after a leisurely dinner in Seattle, I went on to Anchorage, Alaska, in time to check in at the hotel by 2 a.m. And then, five hours later, the Alaska Airlines took over. By 10:30, on the morning after leaving home, I was looking out over the frozen wastes of Bering Sea as we came down for the landing in Nome.

I was scheduled to stay in Nome overnight and take the airline plane to Kotzebue the following morning, but Gene had flown his hunting plane down to meet me.

"Let's have an early lunch and hunt on up to Kotzebue this afternoon," he suggested. "There's a good chance we might get your bear on the way."

"Are you serious?" I asked. "My parka and mukluks are in my duffel, and it's coming by air freight. I have my rifle and cameras, but nothing to wear."

He looked me over carefully. Anticipating that Nome would be cold, I'd put on a fur cap with good ear tabs, wool hunting socks, heavy tweed trousers, and a couple of wool shirts under an alpaca-lined flight jacket.

"You'll make out," he said. "It isn't much below zero. I have extra caribou-skin socks and fleece-lined flight pants you can use, and this weather is too good to waste. Two outfitters have taken six hunters out from Kotzebue in the last 10 days. Everybody got bears."

It was clear that Gene, the old master, had no intention of being outdone by newcomers to his home range. So an hour later we headed toward Bering Strait, flying over the first good ice for polar-bear hunting that I had ever seen. While it was smashed up enough to give the bears cover for their seal-stalking, there were many places where a good arctic pilot could land. There was no open water. Where the pack ice had recently cracked open, the leads were covered with dark new ice.

We saw bear tracks along these leads, which were dotted here and there with the holes seals keep open for their breathing. We saw some seals, too, lying with their whiskers hanging over the little holes and ready to dive at any instant. But no bear track was very fresh or especially large.

On we flew, past King Island, and it didn't seem long before we were rounding Cape Prince of Wales, the most westerly point of all North America. As the weather was unusually clear, we had an excellent view of Russia's Big Diomede Island and the bold mountain promontory of Mys Dezhneva, or East Cape.

"It's Tuesday, here," Gene said, "but it's Wednesday on Big Diomede and beyond. The international date line runs between Big Diomede and Little Diomede, which is on our side. So when you look west you're looking at tomorrow. Seems funny, doesn't it?"

"Yes," I said. "And it also seems funny that yesterday I had breakfast in New York. Now I'm looking at Siberia."

Turning toward the northeast, we saw a few more old bear tracks, but no bear, and we landed in Kotzebue in time for a good dinner in the most northerly restaurant on this continent. I'll bet that Señor Esteban Salinas, the proprietor, is the most northerly Mexican as well.

Next morning we went hunting. My duffel hadn't arrived, so I wore the same assortment of clothes I'd worn on the flight from Nome. We carried an emergency camping outfit, in case we were forced down on the ice, and enough extra gasoline to fly nine hours.

"From the way the ice looked yesterday, I think most of the bears will be pretty far offshore," Gene said. "Their real home is out there, anyhow."

So we headed far out, over the part of the Arctic Ocean called the Chukchi Sea, and we must have been very close to the international date line when Gene turned north. It was a strange setting for a big-game hunt. On the course we were taking, I knew there wasn't so much as an island between us and the North Pole.

It seemed hard to imagine that there could be any life in those vast, silent reaches of infinitely varied ice. But along toward noon Gene spotted a promising bear track. In was surprisingly hard to follow for more than 100 yards at a stretch. We often lost it for many minutes among the jagged ice blocks. Periodically it crossed patches of wind-sculptured snow so solidly frozen that the heavy animal made no impression on the surface.

Early in the afternoon we picked up the footprints for the third or fourth time.

"Maybe that track isn't as fresh as we thought. Too much snow has blown into—" Gene paused abruptly, then added "There's the bear!"

"Where?" I demanded.

"At the end of the track."

I saw him, then, only 100 yards away. Almost pure white, he was much less conspicuous than his own shadow. He glanced up at us unconcernedly and ambled into rougher ice without changing course as we circled overhead.

"Look him over carefully and tell me if you want him," Gene said.

Gene isn't a naturalist or a hunter so this was in my department. I knew from long study of zoo specimens that the blocky silhouette, the proportionately wide head, and the unhurried, shoulder-rolling gait are signs of age. I noted the extra massiveness around the neck which meant he was a male. I even checked the line of his throat, for old bears often have a sort of double chin. This one had it.

"It's hard to know just how big he is," I said at last, "because there's nothing down there to scale him against. Those chunks of ice can be any size. I'm sure he's old, though, and I'll never be able to tell more about any of them. Let's try to get him."

We flew far ahead of the bear on the line he was taking.

"Throw out those spare cans of gas," Gene said, "and tighten your safety belt. This is going to be rough."

Pushing open the door, I tossed out the four five-gallon cans of gasoline stacked beside and behind me. They burst when they hit the snow-covered ice, making splash patterns that looked strangely like roses. Then Gene set the plane down in a place I'd have considered impossible.

From the top of a pressure ridge we located the bear. He was walking along the edge of a narrow lead, hardly more than 50 yards away. His right side was toward me when I shot him in the shoulder. Down he went, flat on his chest. Then, in an instant, he drove forward with his hind legs and disappeared behind some upended cakes of ice.

Never in the world did I expect that bear to get up. The sudden red spot on his hide had shown me where he was hit, and the 220-grain bullet from my .30/06 would have anchored him if we had been on the same level. But I hadn't allowed for the downward angle.

In the brief time we needed to get over to where he'd fallen, the bear vanished into a field of huge ice blocks. There, as we quickly discovered, he could go a lot faster on three legs than we could follow. So we took off on the blood trail with the plane, and as soon as we saw the bear again, we knew we had a tough job. Although his right front leg was useless, he was making good time through a mile-wide belt of jumbled ice. He had already crossed the treacherous ice of one frozen lead. Several others lay ahead.

"Even if we could catch up with him in there, I doubt that we'd ever get his hide out," Gene said. "We'll see if we can chase him across to the other side."

Banking sharply, Gene made a low swoop that startled the bear in the direction we wanted him to go. But fear changed to defiance when he'd been buzzed a couple of times, and after that he just turned and dared us to fly closer.

I began to admire the great bruin enormously, and every minute I felt worse about messing up the first shot. For we had to go high again and circle around for the next hour, hoping that the route he chose would offer a place where we could land. At the end of that hour, though, we saw him pick out a place to lie down, and there was only one thing to be done.

On the far side of the roughest ice, Gene made half a dozen passes over a proposed landing strip, studying every inch of it before we skidded into a bumpy stop. Then he roped us together before we started on the half-mile walk that we hoped would take us to the bear. In that kind of going, snow may bridge a few feet of open water in a broken floe, and these traps are hard to detect. We found none of them, but we did have to circle around two leads where the thin new ice was dangerous. For the rest, we scrambled over shattered cakes that were higher than our heads, and floundered through drifted snow that was sometimes waist-deep.

There was one innocent-looking stretch where Gene kicked through powdery snow to uncover a square edge of a great flat cake of ice, more than a foot thick.

"Those things are a pilot's nightmare," he told me. "Sometimes they're on what looks like a good landing place, with snow smoothed over them. If you ski runs into one, a lot of things can happen. And none of them are good."

"Something else could happen out here, too," I said glancing at the rough ice field ahead of us. "That bear is mad, and I wouldn't put it past him to ambush us among those ice blocks."

But my bear was either past caring or else didn't know we were around. We found him where we'd last seen him from the air. He was standing quietly, about 150 yards away, when I fired the shots that tumbled him out of sight. We approached cautiously, and he was very dead when we reached him. So his final moment was not as memorable as some that were to follow.

"He's much bigger than I first thought," Gene said, "but he's not as big as others I've seen. You'll never find a richer or a whiter pelt, though, and that's not just guide's talk."

I knew that Gene was right on all counts. With my steel tape we measured this polar bear very carefully before skinning, and he was eight feet seven inches from nose tip to the end of his tail bone. That's a big bear. My Kodiak Island brown bear was only 2½ inches longer, and his skull measurements rate him as the largest bear of any kind ever taken by a sportsman in any part of the world.

We had to forget about additional measurements for the time being. It was getting late. We were a long way from home, and the bear had to be skinned before he froze.

When we did get the hide off–using the bear's body heat to keep our hands from freezing—it was so heavy that the two of us couldn't carry it to the plane. We tied on a couple of ropes and dragged it. Even this was a job, over the broken ice field, and in a few minutes we detoured to leave the skin at a place where Gene thought he could taxi up to it with the plane. While I went back for the rifle and cameras, Gene slowly and precariously worked the plane up to the hide.

Night had fallen when at last we headed for the Alaska coast. There was no moon, but the northern lights were spectacular. We flew eastward toward their unearthly, wavering curtains of yellow-green light until Gene could see the coastal mountains. Not much later we were circling over the tiny Eskimo village of Kivalina, and there, after the natives had come out with pocket flashlights to show us where to land, we were most hospitably given dinner and a bed in the Alaska Native Service school. Our hosts, Mr. Bingham and his wife, were the only white inhabitants.

Even then our adventure wasn't over. We were still beyond radio contact with Kotzebue, where we were expected before dark. Rescue planes would set out to find us in the morning, but we had a deep suspicion that those pilots wouldn't fly without breakfast. So we could head them off by coming in before the restaurant was open. There was only the slight complication that there was no gasoline to be had in this remote little spot called Kivalina. Our prospects seemed none too bright.

Soon after sunrise, Gene looked at our gas gauge. "Nearly as I can tell, we have enough gas for 37 minutes of flying," he said. "Kotzebue is 40 minutes away. We'll have to glide five minutes."

But we must have had a favoring wind, for we had at least an ounce or two of gas when we came in to the Kotzebue landing strip. We didn't stop to measure it, however.

That's all there was to it, aside from the rather important detail that this story, so far, is all wrong. It has been a chronicle of facts and figures, such as the additional fact that my polar bear's skull will score between 26 and 27 when the time comes for official measurement. As there are now only six known specimens that score 27 or better, my trophy will rank well up in the record list. But the essence of my arctic experience is rooted in facts of another kind.

For instance, there was my first sight of the bear—a huge, powerful, and almost invisible animal. He was a wraith drifting through a place that belonged on another planet, and the silent, liquid rhythm of his movement across his special world was something that might be captured in motion pictures, but not by any of my stumbling prose.

None of it was reasonable by familiar standards—and neither was the next development. As I mentioned, the bear must have been very close to the international date line. He traveled east after the first shot, and if he crossed the date line on the way to his last stand, he was killed the day before I saw him alive. Finally, we brought his hide into Kotzebue on the third morning after I had left New York. That doesn't seem possible either.

Polar Hunt—Old Style

Gleason Taylor

July, 1958

Kingik, one of our two Eskimo guides, clambered to the top of a pressure ridge to look around at the vast, empty world of arctic ice. After a minute, he motioned us urgently to come up beside him. When Billy Weber, the second Eskimo, and Payton and I reached him he pointed ahead, across the white, snow-swept waste.

"Nanook," he said, suppressed excitement in his voice.

It took us a couple of seconds to spot the bears—a big slinky-necked sow and a husky two-year-old that looked as if it weighed 300 to 350 pounds. They were the first polar bears I'd seen outside a zoo, and my heart started to knock like a jalopy with a loose rod bearing.

They were 500 yards off, too far to risk a shot, so the four of us lay hidden among the jumbled ice slabs at the sawtooth ridge crest, and watched them put on one of the most entertaining shows I ever saw.

They were across an open lead or channel from us, at the foot of a second ice ridge that was roughly parallel to the one we were on. The sow was sitting on her haunches, the youngster was frolicking in a snowbank, rolling like a dog, kicking up loose snow and having a ball. He raced to his mother, clouted her a healthy swat on the rump, and ducked away. She rolled to her feet and chased him back to his snowbank. They boxed and romped there for a minute or two and then moved off, still sparring and playing. I was so interested in their performance that it was seconds before I realized they were traveling straight away from us, making our chances for a shot slimmer and slimmer.

This was a polar-bear hunt the hard way. Glenn Pew, my hunting partner for the past 15 years, and I had left our homes at Coshocton, Ohio, where my business is a lumberyard and Glenn's is a 250-acre farm, on

122

March 12, 1956. We flew by regular airlines to Seattle, and then on to Fairbanks and Kotzebue, on the arctic coast of Alaska northeast of the Bering Straits. From Kotzebue we flew by ski-equipped mail plane to Point Hope, an Eskimo village and trading post on the coast 150 miles north. There were early robins on the lawn when we left Coshocton. We landed at Point Hope three days later in a howling wind, the thermometer registering 28 below. As Glenn said, spring comes a little late up there.

Up to a few years ago a polar bear was considered an out-of-reach trophy by the average sportsman in this country, about as attainable as an elephant. Cost and time involved in an arctic hunt ruled out the ice bear for all but a handful of sportsmen. But this has changed to a great degree in the last few years. Bear hunting off Point Hope has soared in popularity, with most of it being done with the help of planes. Enough bears have been killed so that local Eskimos are sore about the waste of meat, and federal game officials are worried over the future supply. Plenty of hunters have shown that a sportsman with itchy feet no longer has to think of a white bearskin rug as a pipe dream, even when he has only modest means at his disposal.

When Pew and I planned our hunt we agreed on one point: we didn't want to use a plane. Not that there's anything wrong with it if it's done right—which isn't always the case if you can believe the tales you hear at Kotzebue and Point Hope. It seems it's not exactly rare for a bear to be shot from a plane, or by a newly landed hunter standing in the shadow of its wings.

It's also risky. Some planes have gone through thin ice, several have been lost, and there have been countless close shaves. The idea of just flying out and knocking over a bear didn't appeal to us, so we made arrangements with Don De Hart of Slana, Alaska, who'd guided us on a successful hunt for moose, caribou, and grizzlies in 1954, to hunt polar bears the way Eskimos do it. We'd use dog teams and Eskimo guides, camp on the ice, and hunt on foot. That way we figured we'd earn our pelts and have fun doing it.

De Hart was waiting for us at Point Hope. He had comfortable quarters ready in a building where supplies and whaling equipment were stored, heated (as all heating is done at that remote outpost) with coal shipped in 50-pound bags by parcel post from Kotzebue. It cost 4¢ a pound postage, which figures out to $80 a ton. At those prices you don't waste any.

De Hart also arranged with the Eskimos for guides and dog teams. For a few days, we planned to hunt the offshore ice at Point Hope for both bears and seals. Pew had a stroke of bad luck the first day. We'd gone 20 miles south on the ice, and on the way back he climbed a pressure ridge, stepped through crust into a hole, and wrenched a knee so badly that he was laid up, for almost a week. That put a crimp in our plans to hunt together.

I put in three days with Nicholas Hank, an Eskimo. We saw a few bear tracks but no bears. I shot a hair seal and got a big kick out of the way Hank retrieved it. The Eskimos carry a weighted line with a wooden float at one end that's shaped like a top. Four stout cod hooks are attached to an ivory bar set in the pointed end of the float. If the hunter kills a seal

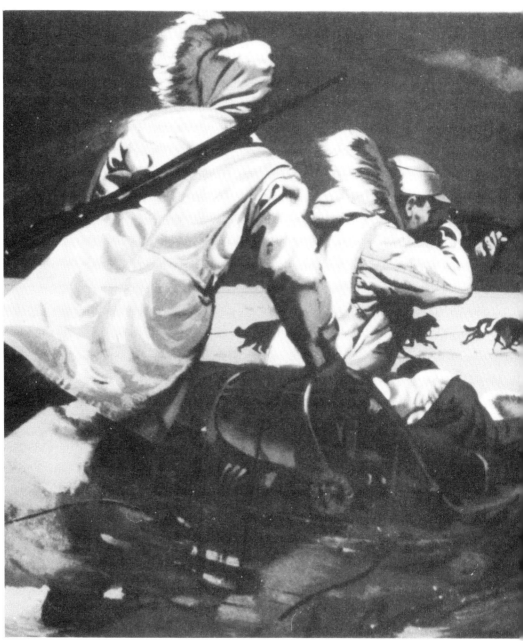

Both teams were running hell for leather, with sleds bouncing and jolting, but I tried a shot as soon as we got within range.

in an open lead beyond his reach, he whirls the weighted line around his head, casts the float beyond the dead seal, snags it, and hauls it in. Eskimos can throw the thing up to 50 yards and pinpoint the cast accurately enough to retrieve an object as small as a duck.

At the end of three days it was plain that Pew would have to postpone his hunt a while, so I went ahead with my plans. William Payton, a young hunter from New Mexico, had arrived at Point Hope two weeks earlier with Dan Moore of Washington and had come down with a hard case of flu that put him in bed for a week. Moore completed his hunt, taking an exceptional bear, a 10-footer with a skull that measured 25⁹⁄₁₆ inches. We'd met him, en route home, when we flew into Kotzebue.

Payton was well enough to hunt now, so he and I tackled the ice together. We planned to leave Point Hope at daybreak on March 19 with Billy Weber and Laurie Kingik and their dog teams. We'd go north along the coast 60 miles to Cape Lisburne, which looks northwest into the open Arctic Ocean, camp on ice, and stay until we killed our bears.

The sun was coming back now from its long winter in the Southern Hemisphere. It still climbed only a little way into the sky to the south, but at least we'd have daylight for our trip. The two sleds were loaded the night before, and at first light Billy and Kingik raced their dog teams out onto the ice and headed north. It was 30 below, with a bitter wind blowing and thick snow sweeping across the ice. But we were dressed for the cold and didn't mind it. I wore long-handled wool-and-cotton underwear next to my skin, then insulated underwear and a quilted eiderdown jacket, and pants over that. My parka hood, worn over an ordinary wool cap, was insulated, and the Eskimo women had sewed a band of wolf fur around the opening next to my face. Without that fur band a man would suffer frostbite in a few minutes.

I wore insulated gloves under Eskimo-made wolfskin mittens hung on a cord around my neck, so I could pull off the mittens to shoot in the gloves without worrying about them.

Our footgear also was Eskimo, and nothing better for the purpose has ever been developed. We wore wool socks next to our feet, then caribou-skin socks with the hair in, and over those sealskin mukluks, also worn hair-in to avoid wetting. Our feet were warm in the bitterest weather.

That was a day I'll always remember. Kingik was driving 11 dogs, Billy 13. There was one dog in Kingik's team that wore a skin apron to protect her udders from the extreme cold. Either team could handle a load of a full ton. Every dog was impatient to get started, and they whined and howled as they were being harnessed. Once under way, they ran like crazy the first two or three miles, and Billy and Kingik had their hands full.

"We follow shore," Billy told me. "Go out on ice, maybe get lost." It was a sensible decision, for even after full daylight the low rocky shore was blotted out by snow.

Once the dogs settled down they traveled at a steady trot, and we alternately rode the sled and ran alongside. Travel is easy on the smooth sea ice. An inch or so of frost covers it (that was to give me a bad minute later on) so it isn't too slippery. It's the many pressure ridges that give trouble. Formed when wind and currents jam two ice fields together, tilting big slabs and blocks in a jumble, they rise as high as 20 feet and extend for miles.

Now and then we had to detour around a ridge or an open lead, but if the leads were narrow the Eskimos jumped the dogs across at a dead run, the long sleds going over of their own momentum. Before the hunt ended I saw eight-foot leads crossed in that fashion, and once, when the ice was too rough for a running start, Billy made his team swim a six-foot lead.

We carried our rifles in skin boots tied to the side of the sleds. There was never a day we didn't tip over at least once or twice, and upsets of that kind are hard on guns and scopes, but the Eskimos think nothing of them.

We halted at noon for lunch and hot tea, and at dusk we pulled up in the ice of low, black rocks on the shore at Cape Lisburne. We'd made the 60-mile run between daylight and dark, hauling loaded sleds.

Kingik and Billy scooped out a hole in a snowbank big enough to take our 7 × 7 tent. By next day snow had drifted in snug and tight all around it, and we were comfortable. We'd brought a small Coleman gas stove for cooking and heating, but didn't need it for heat.

Once out of harness the dogs were staked out, far enough apart so they couldn't reach to start brawls. We'd brought along four seals for them. They got their evening ration, the only one of the day, as soon as camp was set up, and they wolfed down the frozen meat with ravenous hunger. After being fed, each dug himself a shallow hole in the snow and curled up in it for the night. By morning, snow had covered them and they were little more than lumps on the smooth, wind-scoured surface. That's the way the arctic sled dog spends his winter nights. Sometimes snow buries and smothers him too, but for the most part they make out all right.

We crawled out next morning to find a blizzard screaming in off the polar ice fields. The wind was so strong we could barely stand against it. Snow limited our vision to less than 50 feet. The thermometer showed 25 below.

There was no chance of hunting that day, so we settled down in the tent to swap yarns. Billy Weber told us of the polar bear he'd killed with a .22 Hornet two weeks before. Hunting seals, he ran into the bear and shot it in the neck at close range. It took to an open lead, and Billy knew that if he killed it in the water he'd be unable to drag it out onto the ice by himself. So he prodded it with the long spiked pole Eskimo seal hunters carry, and harassed it into climbing out under its own power. But the bear didn't stop then: it kept coming. Billy ran, whirling around and shooting with one hand. He finally got in a killing shot with the light rifle. But, as he summed it up, "Eskimo boy fall down, no more Eskimo boy."

The second morning the wind was still blowing too hard for dogs, but the Eskimos agreed we could hunt on foot. We walked four or five miles to the first pressure ridges, detouring around an occasional lead. We found several places where bears had killed and fed on seals, and within an hour Kingik, who'd hunted bears most of his 48 years and had the sharpest eyes I've ever seen, climbed an ice ridge and spotted that sow and big cub I told you about in the beginning.

He and Billy hadn't seemed worried when the two bears started to move off. They'd had enough experience to know what to do. We stayed where we were until the bears went out of sight around a bend in the pressure ridge they were following, then we descended to the ice, worked around the end of the lead that blocked our way, and took after them. At the place where they'd disappeared we climbed the ridge for another look. The Eskimos had played a smart hunch. The bears had turned around and were coming back our way.

We crouched at the ridge top, camouflaged by the white parkas we wore, and waited.

We'd agreed Payton was to have the shot at the sow. Due to his hard luck with flu and all, I figured he was entitled to it.

When the bears were 100 yards off and we knew we had them dead to rights, they stopped to play and cuff each other. There was no chance they could get away now, so we waited. They kept it up for half an hour, working closer and closer, and for me their performance was the thrill of a lifetime.

They were 56 paces away when the sow stiffened and looked straight at us, swinging her long snaky neck from side to side, her nose and eyes little black spots in the white mask of her face.

"Better take her," I whispered to Payton.

He was carrying a Model 70 .300 Magnum loaded with 180-grain Silvertips and scoped with a 4X sight. He put his shot into the bear's chest just below the chin, and she died in her tracks. The shot didn't belt her over; she slumped down, pushed herself ahead half her own length with her hind feet, and died without a struggle. It was a good clean shot, and Payton had every right to be as jubilant as he was.

I'd like to report that the cub got away, but Billy and Kingik couldn't afford that. To them he represented some 300 pounds of meat for dogs and men, plus a six-foot pelt worth $1 an inch at the Point Hope trading post. Kingik anchored him with one shot, and the Eskimos wrote him off as a good day's work.

It's hard to believe, but it took them only about 20 minutes to skin both bears and cut up and bone out the carcasses. They heaped the meat in a pile on the ice. We'd have to risk other bears finding the cache until we could come back with the sleds, but we couldn't afford to take that chance with the pelts, so the Eskimos rolled them into bundles, tied them securely, and looped them to their belts to be dragged along behind on the hike to camp. We got back at 4 p.m.

At daylight next morning the wind had fallen and the sky was clear. "Take dogs today," Kingik said. "Bring meat home."

They harnessed both teams. Payton went with Kingik, I with Billy, and it was a short, fast ride out to the place where we'd killed the bears. We found the meat cache undistrubed, so we went on, planning to pick it up on the way back.

I hardly know, even now, whether to call that the luckiest or unluckiest day of my life. I guess it was a little of both. We'd traveled another hour and were making good time on ice about 12 miles offshore, with Billy and me in the lead, when we heard a frantic shout from Kingik. He was yelling for us to stop in both English and Eskimo. We covered close to 200 yards before the team came to a halt, and then I saw the cause of the excitement. A big bear was lying at the foot of a ridge about 200 yards ahead.

By the time we'd stopped, the bear had seen us. He rolled to his feet, peering, swinging his head, trying to get our scent. It could well be we were the first men he'd ever seen, but he quickly decided he didn't want anything to do with us. Playing it safe, he started up over the ice ridge.

I jumped off the sled with my rifle and threw myself on the ice for a prone shot, but my foot slipped as I went down, and I pitched headlong, ramming the muzzle of the Model 70 into the ice and plugging the end of the barrel with hard frost. Payton came running up and shoved his gun at me, but by that time the bear had disappeared. I was a pretty dejected hunter, but there was nothing to be done about it. We wrote him off and went to work clearing my rifle barrel.

That done, we started out again, and as we rounded that first turn in the pressure ridge there was our bear, ambling along some 600 yards away.

This time the dogs saw him as soon as we did, and they went stark crazy, yipping and howling across the ice in wild pursuit. Kingik and Billy let them run, hoping they'd overtake the bear.

It was a hot chase while it lasted. Billy and I were riding one sled, Payton and Kingik the other, both teams running hell for leather. I tried a shot from the sled as soon as we came within range, but I wasn't surprised to see the bullet chip ice off the ridge above and beyond the bear.

The dogs overhauled the bear fast, and when we were 50 yards behind him he turned to climb a ridge. Eskimo sleds are rigged with a peculiar brake—three heavy iron claws between the runners at the back. To stop the team the driver steps on that brake, throwing all his weight on the claws. They bite into the rock-hard ice two or three inches, yet I've seen excited dogs drag a sled for 50 feet with the brake on.

Bill jammed the brake on and as the sled slowed I jumped off, ready to shoot. But again things didn't go as I expected.

The Eskimos had named me Old Man because of my gray hair, and Kingik told Pew later, "Old Man get excited." I guess he was right. Anyway, as I jumped off the sled I tangled one foot in a rope and went down flat on my back.

I bounced up, tried to kick my foot free, and took a step away from the sled. But my foot was still snared, and as the dogs yanked the sled ahead I went down again.

I scrambled up, and that time I had sense enough to stand still. But it was too late. The bear was 150 yards away, disappearing among the tumbled slabs of the rige. I got off a snapshot, and saw it strike low. He made a couple of quick jumps, and disappeared for good.

I was mad enough to bite spikes. I'd muffed the chance I'd come for. The bear had been a good one. I'd done enough hunting to know I could hardly hope for another opportunity like it.

Things were in a mess all around. The dogs had tangled their traces thoroughly. They were still yipping and yelping, trying to make a fresh start, and the Eskimos were shouting things that sounded suspiciously like English cuss words. It took us 15 minutes to straighten everything out and get ready to move on. Kingik stepped back of his sled to start his team, then looked off across the ice and said calmly, ''More bear come.''

Half a mile away, following an open lead toward us, a good bear was ambling over the ice at a rolling walk. I'd like to say it was the one that got away, but it wasn't. This fellow was coming from another direction entirely.

We'd had enough of the dogs by now. The Eskimos carried sled anchors, round iron bars attached to the sleds by a stout line tied in a ring at one end, with the other end sharpened and bent at right angles like a half a pick-ax blade. By driving this firmly into the ice, they could prevent the dogs from taking off.

We anchored both sleds. Kingik stayed behind with the teams to prevent trouble, while Payton, Billy and I started off, taking cover behind the pressure ridge.

The bear was following along the foot of a second ridge, across the lead from us. He sauntered on, walking out to the lead now and then as if looking for seals. A few times he lay down and rolled like an overgrown dog.

It was an easy stalk. There were gaps in the ridge we were following, but we crossed them without difficulty when his head was turned, camouflaged by our white parkas. Finally he lay down directly across the lead from us, 300 yards away, and curled a forepaw around in front of his face. This is a standard trick of polar bears to hide their black noses from any seals that might pop up.

I realized we were as close as we were able to get. Smooth ice and the open lead separated us, and there was no way to stalk nearer, so I clambered to the top of the ridge and stretched out prone for a shot. Just then the bear sat up on his haunches.

''Can you nail him from here?'' Payton asked.

''I've got to,'' I replied grimly.

My .375 Magnum carried 300-grain handloaded soft-nose bullets and was fitted with a Bausch & Lomb 4X scope. The gun was up to the job if I was.

I centered the crosshairs on his shoulder, and in the second or two before I squeezed off I was finding it hard to believe that I had a polar bear in my sights at last. Then I slammed a shot at him. It walloped him over on his back, and he lay pawing the air. He rolled, belly-down, facing me, and I put a finisher into his chest. That spun him around in a half circle, and he was dead in seconds.

I had killed a good bear. Laid out on the ice, not stretched, his pelt measured eight feet six inches from nose to base of tail.

We went back for the dogs and made a two-mile detour around the lead to pick up the bear. The Eskimos skinned him and boned the meat in short order. We loaded pelt and meat on one of the sleds and headed for our open-ice cache to pick up the meat of the two bears we'd shot the day before. We were back in camp at sundown, and early next morning we started the 60-mile run back to Point Hope.

There was still Pew's hunt to reckon with, so we left tent and other gear for him. We found him with a healed knee, ready to go. We got to the post on Saturday evening. Kingik gave himself and his dogs one day of rest, mostly so he could go to church on Sunday, and at daybreak Monday morning he and Glenn were on their way to Cape Lisburne.

They had an even shorter and luckier hunt than ours. They made the run in 8½ hours, and went out that same evening to the place where Payton had killed his bear. Other bears had worked over the entrails, and they found one big fresh track.

On the way back to camp they noticed the dogs sniffing and looking off to the right. Kingik anchored the sled and went to investigate, and found a young 300-pound bear that had been killed in a bloody fight with a bigger one. The youngster's chest cavity was torn open and his face was very badly clawed.

The Eskimo covered the carcass with blocks of ice to keep other bears and the arctic foxes off. The pelt was an exceptionally fine one. "Get tomorrow," he told Pew. "Skin make Kingik parka."

They drove the dogs out on the ice next morning in clear, fine weather, traveled three or four hours, and spotted two bears coming out of an area of rough ice onto an old lead that had frozen over. The bears were working in their direction, so all they had to do was lie at the top of a pressure ridge and wait. Unaware of the men's presence, the bears kept coming.

Pew took his shot when one bear was 80 paces off, the other 30 yards beyond that. He picked the farther one for its color. It proved to be a good sow, about as big as mine. Glenn was carrying a Model 70 .30/06 and shooting 220-grain soft-points. One shot buckled her front legs, and she fell on her nose. Kingik collected the other one, a bear about the same size, and was skinning, butchering, and boning out both carcasses within 10 minutes after Pew had first put his crosshairs on a patch of white fur. They got back to Point Hope 60 hours after they'd left.

Polar bears the hard way? I guess you could call it that. But so far as Pew and I are concerned, it's the only way to hunt the white king of the arctic ice.

PART

IV
OF MANY
GRIZZLIES

A Grizzly Hunted Me

Andy Russell

September, 1960

There was a time when I thought the only good grizzly was a dead one. Because some of them are cattle killers, grizzlies have lived under a cloud of condemnation in the ranching country of southwest Alberta, Canada, where I have always lived. When I was a small boy, I fed on a rich diet of bear stories—all hair-raising. Only the dramatic bear stories get told, and they usually lose nothing by the telling.

So my first bear hunting was done with the notion that I was ridding the country of a dangerous menace. Later, when I became a big-game guide and outfitter for other hunters, I began to realize that grizzlies have a certain economic value. Although I could never condone the killing of a mother with cubs, even when it was legal, my hunting has been responsible for the death of many grizzlies—far more than most men would see killed in several lifetimes.

I always knew the grizzly as an exciting challenge. He's big, powerful, intelligent. Aside from the polar bear, the grizzly is the only truly dangerous game in the Canadian wilderness. It took me longer to learn that a grizzly could trail a man as a curious observer, then—wounded—become the hunter instead of the hunted.

The grizzly that hunted me ranged the remote high country of the British Columbia Rockies, not far west of my home in Alberta.

I was trying to clear a horse trail over a high pass through some 10,000-foot peaks drained by the North Fork of the Flathead River. It was a wild September day, with fierce snow squalls blowing through the canyons. I had tied my horse and gone ahead afoot to chop out the blow-downs that blocked the dim trail where it curved through high-country thickets. As the light of late afternoon began to fade, a new snow squall roared down

135

He didn't smell or hear me this time. My silent approach along the log had given me a chance to beat his ambush.

from the peaks, swirling clouds of sticky snow through the timber. The renewed storm reminded me that camp was on the other side of the high pass, my horse tied in a timberline thicket far behind and above me. It was time to shoulder my ax and head for base camp. I was hungry and tired.

As I walked along through the storm and gloom of dusk in the timber there came to me a haunting feeling I wasn't alone. I looked back, my eyes searching among the spruces moaning and creaking in the wind. I saw nothing.

I tried to shed my spooky mood by telling myself I was the victim of an imagination aggravated by fatigue and loneliness. But there was still some phantom something close to me in this howling storm. The feeling persisted, and I went on like a small boy walking through a graveyard at midnight, with only my ax for company.

Finally I reached the timberline grove where I'd tied my horse. He'd be welcome company.

The horse was gone. Somehow the gelding had worked the knot in the hackamore shank loose and had headed for camp. There was nothing for me to do but hike on over the windswept shoulder of the mountain.

I was soon above timberline, in the open, but the feeling of being followed wouldn't leave me. I stopped several times to look back through the thickening darkness. In the shelter of the timber, the wind had moaned and hissed; here it pounded around the rock cornices, sometimes threatening to blow me off the narrow trail.

In the daylight, the mountains are not unfriendly to those who know them; but they do not play lightly with those who take liberties on their naked flanks at night. A wilderness mountain range on a stormy night can be the most lonely place on earth. I felt mighty small and insignificant as I fought through the smothering williwaws of drifting snow to the summit.

At the top, the wind beat wild as the wings of a giant eagle with its feet trapped among the peaks. Several times I had to drop flat and cling to the rocks to keep from being blown into space like a rag. Somehow I managed to fight my way over onto the sheltered side, where I could see the cheery light of our camp winking far below.

Then, as quickly as it had come, the storm subsided. Soon stars were gleaming in patches between scudding clouds. I was vastly cheered, but still had that ghostly feeling of being followed. It stayed with me till I met the horse wrangler coming up the trail with my missing mount.

We were soon back at the tents, and never did a piece of canvas, a bright gas lantern, and a glowing tin stove look more like a palace. A hot supper and a relaxing pipe restored me. The battle with the wind and the weird "presence" on the trail were all but forgotten by bedtime.

At the time I was outfitting for a single hunter on his first-Canadian pack trip. Bill was no greenhorn, however, for he'd been ranch-raised in Colorado and had killed deer and elk in his native state. He was particularly eager to collect a grizzly, and I was no less keen to find one. Helping with the guiding was Levi, a Puckish little Welshman who'd been hunting and trapping these mountains "since they wuz holes in the ground." A cook and a horse wrangler completed our crew.

Next morning the wind had died and the weather was milder, although mist hung low on the slopes above our camp. As I stepped out to the horse corral to help the wrangler catch our mounts for the day, I passed beneath a big tree on which I'd hung my slicker the night before. To my great astonishment, there on top of my tracks in the snow were the prints of a big grizzly.

The grizzly had come into camp along the trail from the pass, and the broad print of his rump showed where he sat down to inspect the place. Then he'd circled the tents. His trail led back up the mountains then, and I supposed those tracks up the slope would be the last sign we'd see of the grizzly.

We rode up the trail to the pass through a thick blanket of fog. Here and there, where the tracks were not completely drifted in with loose snow, I could see the grizzly's marks on top of mine, and I recalled my feeling of being followed the night before. Just below the summit, we suddenly rode out into brilliant sunshine, and when we reached the crest we could see out over a magnificent panorama. As far as the eye could reach, snow-draped fangs of peaks stuck up through rolling mist.

The trail crossed the pass high on the side of a deep notch. In the bottom of this gap were long, undulating ribbons of mist flowing through on the gentle breeze. Farther down in front of us, the fog curtain lifted to reveal a snowy timberline meadow like a wilderness stage. Coming toward us on the trail through the meadow was a big silvertip grizzly. We saw him for a second. Then the mist dropped to hide him again.

We came off our horses, Bill and Levi pulling their rifles from scabbards. I uncased Bill's movie camera, hoping to record a kill in magnificent surroundings. Twice the mist lifted briefly, revealing the grizzly still coming. He was ambling along with silvery fur gleaming as it rolled over powerful muscles, his big head swinging low. I heard Bill catch his breath, and the tension was so thick you could cut it with a knife.

As the grizzly drew closer, the mist began to tease us. It would start to lift, then roll back as thick as pea soup until it looked as if the bear would be right in our laps before Bill could see to shoot. When the grizzly appeared again, he was 200 yards below us, for he'd left the trail to head up through the notch. He was as close as he'd get. I saw Levi nod to Bill.

A moment later the rifle shattered the quiet and the grizzly went down roaring and biting at himself. As the bear regained his feet, the rifle slammed again, but this time the bear didn't drop. He went plunging into a dense stringer of stunted firs and was swallowed from our sight over a rise of ground a moment later.

We waited half an hour, not knowing if the bear was wounded and gone or lying dead inside the thick scrub. Bill softly berated himself for not anchoring the grizzly in its tracks. Levi smoked stoically, considering the prospect of a wounded grizzly in the timber. By the time we rode down to examine the tracks, the sun had burned the fog away and the whole country glistened brilliantly.

Our hopes that the bear was down inside the cover quickly evaporated. The tracks showed plenty of blood, but they didn't pause. By the signs, I was sure he was hit twice—once through the right front foot and again through the body too far back. There was arterial blood in his tracks and now and then a bright splash showed off to one side of his trail. We had a badly wounded grizzly on our hands, and the prospect wasn't one we underestimated.

Tying the horses, we began to trail. In a quarter of a mile the galloping tracks flowed to a walk. The fact that the grizzly was headed downhill made me surer than ever he was hard hit, for rarely does a badly wounded animal go up or even along a steep slope. We proceeded carefully, ready for instant action. There was no telling when he might turn on us. The tension built till we wore it like a load. Levi and Bill went abreast flanking the trail with cocked rifles, while I followed a few steps behind with the camera set to record the final close-range fight. Every step was calculated and at no time was more than one rifle allowed out of position by obstacles encountered.

All morning long we trailed slowly through the timber till we came to the top of the ledge where I'd been cutting trail the day before. Here the grizzly went straight down a steep, water-cut chimney into the lower valley, where giant timber towered above the shoulder-high underbrush and huge dead logs lay crisscrossed everywhere. Every tree and bush held a load of snow that was melting fast in the warm sun, and the steady downpour wet us to our hides.

The bear kept steadily down toward the valley floor and a fair-size creek. Here we could see 100 places in almost as many yards where he could wait in ambush. We left the bear's tracks and circled wide to the creek, hoping to pick him up as we eased up the creek. Usually a badly wounded animal will head for water, take a big drink, and bed down.

But we were disappointed—no bear, no tracks. Finally we left the creek to swing back toward the mountain, almost completing a circle three quarters of a mile across. We were baffled by finding no tracks. Either the grizzly had cut out of our circle behind us or he was still somewhere inside it. I called a halt for a council of war, while we sat on a wet log in soaked clothes and ate a belated lunch.

"I don't know how you fellow feel," Bill murmured apologetically, "but I'm bushed. I've got just enough steam left to get back to the horses."

"You've got company," Levi stated dryly. "I ain't use to takin' baths this late in the year. It's about got me down." Then he added, "I don't think that grizzly's as bad hurt as we thought."

While I attacked a sandwich, I considered this. I was feeling a long way from fresh myself. Water had been running out the top of my boots for two hours. But I have a built-in streak of stubbornness and I hate to leave any wounded animal in the bush to die slow. With a wounded grizzly, there's also the chance some other party will stumble over him with disastrous results.

Levi's council was wise, just the same, for I knew Bill was close to the end of his rope—from nervous strain as well as from the wet and work. So I suggested they head back up to the horses while I had one last try alone. Stalking by myself, I'd have a better chance to slip up close and finish the wounded bear.

Levi gave me a long look and silently shook his head. But he didn't argue, just slipped on his rucksack and headed out, with Bill trailing at his heels. Carefully checking my rifle, I swung back to the spot where we'd left the bear's trail and began to track him once more. In less than 100 yards, there was a swish of snow being dislodged from the brush dead ahead. Easng up to investigate, I found the grizzly's nest—all red with blood—under the wreckage of a wind-blasted spruce. For a few yards the tracks went at a plunging run. They slowed to a walk then, and I was surer than ever he was badly hit.

It's slow, lonesome, nervous work, grizzly trailing. The few times in my life I've done it, I've always sworn I'd never do it again. There are men who say they're not afraid in such a spot, but they're either liars or solid bone between the ears. If a grizzly jumps a man in heavy cover, there's time for just one fast shot, and it has to be accurate. A heart shot won't surely stop a close-range charge, for an aroused grizzly can take a rifle bullet through the heart and come on with enough life left to kill or maul several men. So the bullet must be placed with almost pinpoint accuracy to strike such a nerve center as brain, neck column, or spine. Knowing this, and the fact that your quarry may burst from cover any moment, leaves one with the cold feeling of holding his life in his two hands.

Lining up the tracks as far ahead as I could see them, I'd progress a few quiet steps. Then I'd stop and search every bit of surrounding cover. So it went, step by step, until there seemed no end to it. My only comfort was in the wind, which was in my face.

But then, about halfway to the creek amid a mess of down logs and second growth, the tracks began to bend downwind. Maybe he was going to circle and head down the valley, or maybe he was getting set to make his fight.

There's an old quotation that goes something like this: "The pine needle fell in the forest. The eagle saw it fall, the deer heard it fall, and the bear smelled it fall." It's well said, for keenness of nose is synonymous with the grizzly. An old-time mountain man once told me that a grizzly could take one sniff of a man half a mile downwind and tell the color of his grandmother's wedding dress. He wasn't exaggerating very much.

I expected this grizzly to select a hide where he could keep track of me with his nose, for grizzlies don't rely on their rather poor vision. So I carefully backtracked 100 yards, then swung out to cut his circle into the wind.

In spite of the greatest caution, the small creaking of snow under my boots must have given me away, for I hadn't gone 20 yards before I heard him go. In a patch of down logs I found his hide. Now he was on the move again.

This was the beginning of the grimmest game I ever played in my life, when I was the hunted as much as the hunter and the stakes were life itself. Time and again, the bear circled to lay waiting for me to come up along his tracks. Each time I managed to outguess him. But he always seemed to hear me coming in against the wind and moved to try again. Why there wasn't a sudden showdown, I'll never know, but the even pattern of his plan gave me a whisker of advantage.

There was a numbing chill in the air by this time. I'd been tired earlier, but now mere weariness was something to look back on with pleasure. My nerves were strung up like fiddle strings, and it worried me. Good shooting and tenseness don't go well together. I was afraid to give up, for now the grizzly was stalking me, and retreat could be far more dangerous than facing the issue.

Once more the tracks began to circle, this time into the mouth of a timbered draw. As I studied the lay of the land, the wind switched, blowing down the draw in my face. The sun had dipped behind the mountain across the valley, putting this place in the shade. Instead of circling, I began to work straight in along his tracks.

It must have taken me half an hour to go 50 yards, for the cover was thick and the ground strewn with logs. Finally I reached a spot where I could see his tracks cutting the snow on top of the logs for 40 feet ahead, but beyond that not a snowflake was disturbed. With minute care, every inch of cover was combed. I even used my binoculars, but still that last track on top of the log was the end of the trail.

With a feeling not much short of desperation, I put the glasses on that final track, screwing them down as fine as the edge of a knife. At first I saw nothing different about it, but then a little silvery moon of hair showed through the notch in the snow. As I watched, it lifted and fell with the bear's breathing.

Was he so close to being dead he couldn't charge, or was he waiting? It seemed incredible that he'd let me get this close without making a rush.

If I could reach a spot where I could see a target, I could finish him where he lay. I lifted a foot and carelly pushed the snow off a log in front of me, then stepped up on it. The log formed a straight, elevated path leading diagonally past the bear. By carefully pushing the snow off it with my feet, I could ease along in complete quiet.

The bear was well hidden. Scarcely 20 feet separated us when I got to where I could see his hindquarters. He was lying on his belly like a big dog, with his nose thrust under the log. His legs were drawn up ready to pounce. One slow step brought his hump into view. Another step and the base of his neck was in sight. I gently raised my rifle, the gold bead of the front sight settling into the hollow at the base of his neck.

At the shot the grizzly recoiled like a spring and instantly towered to full height with a great roar. Before I could more than open the rifle bolt, he wilted and fell in a heap.

For long moments I covered him, watching for the slightest quiver of motion. He was dead. I sat down on the log, completely spent. My hands shook, spilling tobacco, as I filled my pipe. I was beat, washed out, but soon a feeling of relief and elation began to take hold—seeping into my bones like a stimulant. Going over to the bear, I rolled him over on his back and began to skin.

It wasn't until I had the hide half off that I fully realized just how close it had been. Aside from my final bullet, there wasn't another mark on him except for two badly smashed toes on his right front foot. The blood marks on the side of his trail had been drops thrown off this front foot. I had misread the signs. If he'd wanted to, this bear could have left the country, and the paw wound wasn't enough to slow him in a fight.

It all added up to a sober reflection or two as I finished the skinning and folded the big hide into my pack. Weary but feeling good, I began the long climb back up the mountain. It was early evening by the time I reached the break in the lava rim, where I'd turned back when clearing trail the night before. My tracks were still visible, and when I sat down on a stump to rest I noticed another trail in the snow at the top of an open lane in the timber. Going up to investigate, I found the tracks of a grizzly half full of snow. As I followed them curiously, they unfolded a story.

Apparently the bear had heard my ax the previous evening and come down from the ridge for a look. He had trailed me for miles. Twice his tracks showed where he'd circled ahead of me to wait in the thick, snow-shrouded trees as I passed within 10 steps of his nose. In one place, under the low branches of a big spruce, his track still showed clearly, and I spotted a gap in the print of his left front foot where a claw had broken off. I'd been seeing that broken-clawed track all day. I pulled the hide out of my rucksack and looked at the claws, just to be sure. It was the same bear.

The whole picture of the past 24 hours unfolded. This old bear had come down off the mountain the night before, trailing me clear to camp to find out what I was doing here in his private empire. When we ambushed him next morning, he only tried to get away, not showing fight till he was crowded beyond endurance.

No man can truthfully say that he knows grizzlies, because individual bears vary as much as different people, but here are a few things I've learned about big bears. Largely, the grizzly is not a trouble hunter. Some cattlemen claim the grizzly is destructively carnivorous. Actually, the grizzly is as omnivorous as man, and, when hungry, will eat most anything he can swallow.

A mother grizzly trains her cubs with unswerving devotion and a strong belief in a sound spanking when it's necessary. There are no delinquent cubs. Few sights are more rewarding or entertaining than a she grizzly with cubs at heel, although the view can be best appreciated if you're watching at a distance with binoculars. Sometimes the mothers will attack if they think their cubs are threatened. The grizzly loves to play. He respects man, but not to the point of cowardice, and he can be an avalanche of destruction in a fight. Relatively long-lived, a grizzly may reach the ripe old age of 50 years. He's an aristocrat of the wilds and should be treated as the most valuable of all our big-game animals.

Experience has erased my boyhood notion that the grizzly should be shot as a dangerous predator wherever he's found. When I hunt him now, it's with a feeling of vast respect and recognition of his rights. I hope that some day a great-grandson of mine will be able to match wits with a grand animal that can fight back. He'll experience the chill and thrill of holding his life in his own hands, and he'll learn something important about living.

Footrace
With a
Grizzly

Howard Copenhaver

May, 1955

Two of my brothers, Gene and Wendell, and I had guided six elk hunters from Cleveland into the mountains 30 miles from our home ranch on the north fork of the Blackfoot, in western Montana. We were camped on Danaher Creek, at the head of the south fork of the Flathead. That's prime game country. It was September, but snow had come early and the ground was still patched with it—enough for tracking. Prospects looked rosy.

Late the second afternoon one of the hunters killed a nice bull on Hay Creek, about 2½ miles above camp. It was dark when he got in, but at daylight next morning I rode out with two packhorses—a grown elk is too much for one—to bring the kill down. We do so as soon as we can in this country, on account of bears. An elk or deer is likely to be half eaten overnight.

Bears are more plentiful and hungrier some years than others, and that fall of 1948 was a bad one. The berry crop failed completely and the bears were on the prowl day and night, hunting for anything that would fill an empty belly. So I wasn't surprised to see bear sign several times as I rode up along the creek.

Half an hour from camp I hit a jackpine thicket that stopped the horses, so I tied all three of them and went on afoot to find the elk and pick a trail up to it. I hadn't walked far when I crossed another fresh bear track. The farther I went the more sign I saw—enough to convince me I'd be lucky to find the elk in one piece. I started to hurry, impatient to run the bear off and salvage what was left of the meat. But I was too late. When I got to the place where the bull had been dressed out I found only a few leavings and a broad trail where a bear had dragged the carcass off.

How would you feel if you'd outfitted a party of paying guests, herded

143

them a hard day's ride into the mountains with all their supplies and gear on pack animals, set up camp, and spotted the hunters in first-class game country, only to have a thieving bear lug off the first kill? Well, I felt the same way. I started out to find that elk and take it away from the bear.

I had hunted all my life and outfitted and guided for close to 20 years. With that much experience, I should have taken a second look at the bear tracks before I did anything else. But I was mad as a bee in a raided hive, and I overlooked that little detail. The sign I'd seen farther down the creek had been made by a black bear and I took for granted that this was one of the same breed. I knew he was big, though, for the elk he'd dragged off would have dressed close to 400 pounds. But that's all I noticed, and I've asked myself plenty of times since how fool-careless a man can get. The answer came too late to do me any good.

The trail was easy to follow. He had taken the elk up and around the side of the mountain, and he'd made easy work of it. After 300 yards or so the track dropped into a series of deep washes and then angled up a steep slope toward an isolated stand of thick spruce, just the spot for him to stop and cash in on his night's work. I'd find him in there somewhere, with what was left of his loot. That likely wouldn't be enough to pack out, I decided, getting madder by the minute.

I halted at the edge of the timber and went down on one knee for a look. Twenty-five feet uphill from me a patch of dark fur moved behind a log, and then I made out the outline of an ear and saw an eye staring in my direction. He had seen me first.

The rifle I was carrying was mighty light for the job. Many years ago, as a kid, I shot a box of 8 mm. shells at a coyote about 1,000 yards off. I didn't kill the coyote, but the big rifle battered my shoulder so that I still flinch with any gun that slams back at me. Consequently I tote a little .25/35. I know it sounds screwy for a man in my business, but I do better with it than with the big bruisers.

It wasn't rifle enough for a big bear, even a black, but I figured if I hit him at the butt of an ear I wouldn't have any trouble. He had the ear conveniently exposed over the log and I was so close I couldn't miss. I brought the rifle up, slow and easy—and in the same instant the bear came up, fast and hard. He reared on his hind legs at my first movement and let go a roar that was enough to knock my hat off.

That roar changed the whole situation. I knew at last, a little late, that I wasn't dealing with a black. I had walked into a grizzly as short-tempered as a stick of dynamite, and all of a sudden the little .25/35 seemed useless as a popgun.

We looked each other over for 10 seconds that seemed like a quarter of an hour. I don't know what the grizzly thought of me but I had time to realize that he was a handsome old sorehead. His dark silvertip coat shone like frost, even in the dim light under the spruces. I held the gun on his neck and waited for him to make the next move, hoping it wouldn't be in my direction.

When he did nothing, I took a cautious step back, and then another. He stayed put and I kept backing up until I had a reasonable distance between us. Then I dropped down into one of the washes and got out of there fast. But I still didn't intend to lead the packhorses back to camp empty, and I knew I'd have to kill the bear if I wanted to claim the elk.

I decided to come at him from above and try a shot in the open, at something more than 25 feet. I made a big circle and worked warily down the hillside to the upper edge of the spruce thicket. I thought I knew exactly where I'd find him. He'd be on the elk, waiting for me. But I guessed wrong.

I was down on one knee again, trying to see under the branches, when he cut loose with another roar so close behind me that I thought he must be looking over my shoulder. I spun around and stared him in the face—just six yards off.

He wasn't a pleasant sight. He was up on his hind feet like a man, eyes blazing, lips curled in a rumbling growl, the hair on his neck and shoulders all standing the wrong way. He looked 20 feet fall and he scared hell out of me!

How he got that close without giving himself away I'll never know. We went back the next day, when the affair was buttoned up, to look over the sign and piece the story together. He had come out of the thicket on the downhill side, picked up my track and trailed me as a hound trails a rabbit, following me while I circled to get above him, stalking me with the stealth of a cat.

The snow was frozen and as crunchy as breakfast cereal, yet he'd crept to within 18 feet of me—we later measured the distance between our tracks with a steel tape—without a whisper of sound. Then he stood up and bawled his blood-chilling challenge, ready for the final rush. They say an unwounded bear won't stalk a man, but this one certainly did.

I'd never stop him before he got to me with the .25/35 and I knew it. He'd be on top of me before that little bullet took effect. There was only one way out. If I could find a tree and reach it in time, I'd climb. A grizzly can't follow you into a tree.

It was a thin chance, for there was just one tree of the right size anywhere near, and it was between me and the bear. When we paced it the next forenoon we found I was 10 feet from the tree and he was eight. But I didn't have time to think. I must have acted from instinct, or maybe it was something they had drilled into me in the Navy, that a surprise offense is often the best defense. I yelled in his face, a screech that would have done credit to a Black-foot buck, and jumped for the tree.

How I made it, slamming into him that way, I still can't figure. My yell must have startled him for a second or two, and my headlong rush kept him off balance just long enough. I was in the tree when he started for me and out of reach when he arrived. I've been asked quite a few times since whether I had any trouble reaching the first limb. For the record, I never touched it. My first jump put me in reach of the third or fourth limb up. I didn't climb. I sailed into that tree like a flying squirrel.

When I started my dash, I had it in mind to take my rifle with me, but when I reached a safe perch 15 or 20 feet off the ground I didn't have the gun. I looked down and saw it lying two or three yards from the base of the tree, with the bear smelling and cuffing at it.

The grizzly really blew his cork over my get-away. He danced around under me, bawling and raging and clawing bark, tearing up the ground like a baited bull. I could see the elk carcass in the spruce thicket, about 20 yards away, and I kept hoping the fresh meat would lure him off. Finally it did. He turned and lumbered downhill, stopping every few steps to throw back a warning growl. When he reached the elk he lay down on it, but kept his head turned my way.

The first thing I wanted was my rifle. It still lay a few steps from the trunk of the tree. I gave the bear 15 minutes to settle down and get interested in the elk. Then I started inching toward the ground, lowering myself from one branch to another.

I was careful not to make any commotion, and he paid no attention until I was almost down. Then he seemed to realized all of a sudden what was going on. He lurched to his feet with a bawl of pure hate and came streaking uphill. A bear can cover ground fast for a short distance when he wants to, and I had to hustle to climb out of reach again. He trampled around under me for a while, grumbling and snarling, and then went back to the elk.

I gave him time to lose interest in me and tried another catfooted descent. It brought the same result. He let me get down to the lowest branches, then bounced up and came raging for me.

It's hard to believe, but we kept up that game at intervals for more than seven hours, from 8:30 in the morning, when he treed me, until almost 4 p.m. I have no idea how many times I went up and down the tree, but I was worn to a frazzle and realized I couldn't keep at it much longer. Unless I got the rifle on the next try or two I'd have to give it up. And that meant sitting in the tree and waiting for help to come from camp, something I didn't relish in the least. Gene and Wendell wouldn't start to look for me until dark, and this bear was nothing to blunder into at night. I wanted to save them from that if I could.

But now the grizzly's attitude changed unexpectedly. I suppose he finally decided that he couldn't catch me in the tree and that I wasn't going to risk coming all the way down. When I started down this time he lay on the elk and watched me balefully, growling and blustering. As I reached the lowest branches he stood up and bawled his resentment, but he refused to be tricked into making any more runs uphill unless there was a fair chance of getting at me.

That gave me the opportunity I'd been waiting for all day. I braced myself at my own height from the ground, with my legs tense and ready for a fast ascent. Cautiously I broke off a forked branch, reached out with it and snagged the rifle. Then I pulled it up to me. I felt almost secure as I started back up the tree with the gun.

But back on my perch I began to question my idea of using this pea-shooter on the grizzly, even shooting from the tree. There was only the slimmest possibility that I could kill him with one shot, and once he was hit and went into the thick spruce I wouldn't have a second chance. I had Wendell and Gene to think about. They'd come up along the creek hunting for me. If I wounded this bear he'd likely jump them in the dark and kill one or both of them. He might anyway. Somehow I had to get out of this fix and head them off while it was still daylight.

I suppose I had looked over the hillside a hundred times, but now I took another look and thought I saw a way of escape. As near as I could figure, it was about 60 feet downhill to the elk carcass where the bear lay. Thirty feet the other way, uphill, was a tree I could climb. Beyond that were two more, a little farther apart. With a series of dashes and climbs, I might put enough distance between me and the grizzly for him to forget about me.

The run to the first tree would be risky but it seemed the only way out. I'd have 30 feet to cover while the bear was coming 90. If I could get a running start, I figured I could make it.

As I let myself down to the lowest branches the grizzly growled ominously, and it took all the nerve I had to let go and drop to the ground. I lit running. I heard a gruff bawl as the bear lumbered to his feet and then I could hear him pounding uphill behind me. But my 20-yard headstart was too much for him. I was up the second tree when he got there and I still had my rifle.

He snorted and tore around at the foot of the tree for a few minutes, then gave up and went back to the elk.

The next tree was about 50 feet farther uphill. As soon as he quieted down I dropped and went for it. It was easier this time. He came charging after me, but he had too far to run now to cause me much concern. Nevertheless, it took four trees and a total gain of 75 yards to make him call quits. He chased me up those four, one after another. Then he must have concluded that he'd driven me off at last, for when I came down the fourth time he paid no attention.

I backed away a few yards, one step at a time, to make sure. When he stayed put I took off uphill, watching him over my shoulder. I made a wide circle to get back to the horses, and you can bet your bottom dollar I kept my eyes open all the way to camp.

It was dark when I rode in. I had expected my long absence to cause some anxiety, but my story was greeted with more amusement than sympathy, to my annoyance, and it took my brothers and the rest of the party a couple of hours to realize that I wasn't just spinning a tall yarn. It was hard for them to believe that a bear would keep a man in a tree a whole day. I finally convinced them, however, and before we turned in we had everything arranged to settle the grizzly's hash first thing in the morning.

"If he's still there," somebody put in.

"He'll be there," I predicted grimly "He won't go 10 yards as long as there's a mouthful of that elk left. He won't move unless we move him."

We left camp at sunrise, following Hay Creek for a couple of miles, then riding straight up the mountain to get around the bear. I remembered an open ridge about 250 yards above him that would give us a clear view of the creek bottom, the hillside, and the spruce thicket where he was holed up. We'd post the hunters along that ridge and Gene, Wendell, and I would move down to flush him out. That way there'd be no chance that he'd catch us with our guard down, as he'd caught me the morning before.

It was a good plan and it might have worked, except for one thing we hadn't figured on. Nobody needed to go into the brush and stir that bear up. He was ready to come out without any prodding.

We tied the horses a safe distance back in the timber and moved down to the ridge afoot. Most of our horses will bolt at grizzly sign in a trail, and we knew we'd be asking for trouble if we took them anywhere near the bear. We bunched on the ridge 300 yards from his thicket, directing the hunters to their places. The bear was nowhere in sight but it was a safe bet that he was down there watching us, because all of a sudden we heard a commotion on the hill below and Gene yelled "Here he comes!"

I guess that was the first time my brothers had really believed me, too, for Wendell added, "By gorry, it IS a bear!"

The grizzly boiled out of the thicket and came plowing uphill at a dead run, ready to tackle all nine of us. We let him come to see if he really intended to go through with it. After his first 40-yard dash he reared up on a fallen log, stretching high on his hind legs for a better look. I don't believe it was caution that stopped him. We all agreed later that he just wanted to size us up before he took us on. We'll never be sure, for we didn't wait any longer.

Gene got in the first shot. He belted the bear in the shoulder with a 180-grain Core-Lokt bullet from his .30/06 and the grizzly dropped off the log with a bellow that shook the ground. But he didn't go down. He whipped around, bit at his shoulder, pulled himself together, and came pelting uphill straight at us.

The mountain fell in on him then. I don't remember all the details, for there was yelling and shooting all around me. Not all the shots connected, for I saw twigs clipped off and snow and dirt kicked up behind him and on both sides. But I also saw three or four solid hits.

He kept his footing through the whole barrage but he knew he was licked. He wheeled and started the other way, still roaring, and Wendell spiked him with a soft-nose in the back of the head. He was less than 100 yards from us when he went down.

When we skinned him we found he'd been hit nine times, and any one of them would have killed him, eventually. Yet he had stayed on his feet until that last shot blew his brain apart. I was glad I hadn't tried for him with the .25/35 the day before.

His pelt squared nine feet, as beautiful a silvertip skin as I've ever seen. It makes a fine trophy on our ranchhouse wall. My brothers and I estimated his weight at not less than 800 pounds. Some of the guests who had hunted Alaska browns thought he'd weight more than that. Anyway, this is for sure: No meaner grizzly than that one ever roamed the mountains of Montana!

As for the elk, we salvaged part of it after all. Luckily, a bear begins at the neck and eats back toward the hams, covering his kill with brush and leaves and lying on it between meals. Unless he's driven off, he won't leave until the last bite is gone. This fellow had worked back as far as the loins. I figure he was saving the steaks for a last supper, but we didn't give him time to enjoy it. The hindquarters were still in fine shape and we packed them out.

Grizzly Showdown

By Robert L. Pagel

January 1975

The valley was a three-hour ride from camp. Its lower end was a wet bog, thick with willows that opened out on the Hess River bottoms. It was broken by a series of narrow ridges that ran back like low foothills. We had chosen the place from a study of our topographic maps the evening before. We could ride our horses up the valley to its head, cross a big ridge, and come back to the river along a parallel valley a few miles away. It would be a long hard day, but our two Cree guides, Willie Dick and Jimmie Peters, thought we'd see enough game to make it worthwhile.

My 15-year-old son Bob Jr., the two Crees, and I had no more than ridden onto the brushy flat when a cow moose broke out of a thicket ahead of us, took one wild-eyed look in our direction, and fled in stark terror. She was followed by a long-legged calf.

"That's odd," I said to Bob. "I wonder what got into her."

In five days of hunting in that same general area, at the western edge of the MacKenzie Mountains in Yukon Territory, we had jumped a number of cow moose, but this was the first one that had shown any fear of us. Many of the others had simply stood still and watched while we rode up to take pictures. And when they finally moved out, they left at an unhurried, swinging trot with so little sign of alarm that they seemed never to have seen a man on horseback before. That may well have been so. The area had not been open to nonresident hunters until 1970.

We were still talking about this spooky cow when the same thing happened again half an hour later with an old cow and twin calves. We surprised them at the edge of an open bog, and they fled up the side of the nearest ridge at breakneck speed. At the top, the cow stopped to look back. What happened next was bizarre. With the two calves safely out of

149

sight in thick brush, she made three or four halfhearted false starts in our direction. She would run a few yards down the ridge with the hair on her shoulders standing the wrong way, retreat, and then do it all over again.

We sat our horses and watched. Apparently she finally decided that we were not to be bluffed, so she went over the ridge and disappeared, trailed by the calves. Minutes later we saw them running up the side of the next ridge. We watched them cross four ridges. It was plain that something about us had scared the cow out of her wits.

Twice more in the next hour we came across cow moose that behaved in the same puzzling manner. Each time a calf was with the cow.

I had hunted big game for years but had never seen anything quite like it, and the guides could no more explain it than I. We had blundered into a perplexing wildlife riddle, and I doubted we'd ever solve it.

For me, this hunt was very special. I was introducing my son to the trophy game of the north country—caribou, moose, sheep, and, with luck, grizzlies. I grew up in good pheasant and rabbit country around Kenosha, Wisconsin. We also had excellent winter fox hunting, and I have had a hunt of some kind at least in the planning stage for about as far back as I can remember. That means some 25 years, for I'm 38 now. I have hunted deer in Wisconsin for 24 consecutive seasons.

I was taken by the splendor and awesome beauty of the mountain country of the western United States the first time I saw it many years ago, and I have made many hunts there. My trips have included two for cougar on the North Fork of the Salmon in Idaho, two for elk in the same state, five elk hunts in Wyoming and one in Colorado, and many for mule deer and antelope in some of the best game areas of the West. I had also made two trips to the Yukon prior to the one in 1973 that I'm talking about here.

I'm a vice-president and broker at Loewi and Company, a Milwaukee-based brokerage firm. My spare time and vacations are all spent hunting and fishing. I'm an active A.T.A. trap shooter, belong to the National Rifle Association and a number of gun clubs, have two good Labrador retrievers, and raise and train German shorthairs.

Young Bob has a sister two years older than himself, and two younger brothers, 12 and five. I'm bringing my three boys up to be hunters and sportsmen and to appreciate the beauty and splendor of mountains and woods.

Bob is an honor student in high school in the Milwaukee suburb of Grafton, where we live. He is a two-time Wisconsin subjunior trap-shooting champ.

My son had taken three good Wisconsin bucks and hunted in Wyoming with me in 1971 where he shot a mule-deer buck and a five-point elk. I figured he was ready for bigger challenge. He did too, and he mowed lawns and worked at local trapshooting clubs all summer to earn the money for his share of the cost of the trip.

We booked our 1973 hunt with Lee Trimble of Rogue River Outfitters at Whitehorse, with whom I had hunted before. I knew Lee would supply skilled and efficient guides, first-class horses and equipment, and excellent food. I also knew that he would take the best possible care of our meat and trophies. Lee has exclusive licensed hunting rights in an 8,000-square-mile roadless area some 200 miles east of Dawson. We'd hunt in the Hess River drainage, which had been opened to outside hunters for the first time only three years before. I hoped to take a Dall ram, something I tried to do twice before. I had seen and passed up a number of small rams on my previous trips.

Bob Jr. and I left home in early August and flew to the Yukon by way of Minneapolis, Winnipeg, and Edmonton. We landed at Watson Lake on the Alaska Highway just as rain and fog began to settle in, and we had to wait there three days for the weather to clear before we could fly via float plane to Trimble's base camp at Arrowhead Lake.

We got to camp about noon. Our two guides and the horses were waiting, and we left almost at once for our hunting grounds on the Hess, a two-day ride. That part of the trip was uneventful. We saw quite a few moose, enough to convince us that we were heading into very good game country, but none big enough to be of interest. What followed was anything but uneventful, however. In the next 11 days we were to see 44 bull moose and too many cows and calves to keep count of, 73 bull caribou, 23 sheep (all ewes and small rams, unfortunately), four grizzlies, and one wolf.

We made a spike camp at the end of our first day's ride. There was a promising mountain range to the west, so we decided to stay there and hunt for a day. That decision paid off for young Bob.

During the forenoon we ran across two bull moose, but neither rack would have gone more than 50 inches, so we took pictures and went our way. While we were eating lunch we saw a big sow grizzly with a cub on the next ridge. She was hunting and traveling slowly, and the cub was romping and playing. They put on a great show for us for almost an hour before the old lady winded us and lit out.

Late that afternoon we spotted a band of caribou in a small alpine meadow just below rimrock. Glassing them with the 60-power Bausch & Lomb zoom spotting scope, we picked out one exceptional bull, and Bob and Jimmie started to climb for him.

It took them 90 minutes to get close enough for a stalk. They got within 75 yards before the whole band spooked, leaving Bob no choice but to take a running shot. His rifle was a pre-1964 Model 70 Winchester in .270 caliber and he was using handloads—150-grain Nosler bullets and 58 grains of No. 4831 powder. He bellied down and flattened the caribou for keeps with one shot.

The bull was a beautiful trophy animal, not quite eligible for the Boone and Crockett Club's record list. My son was a very proud 15-year-old that night.

We reached our campsite on the Hess late the next day after seeing dozens of migrating caribou on the ride.

The following morning the weather had closed in so thick that sheep hunting was out of the question, so we decided to go after moose instead. We put in a hard day, glassed a number of bulls without finding anything of trophy size, and got back to camp just before dark, tired but far from discouraged. Plainly, it was wonderful game country.

We put in a day after that trying for sheep with no luck, and then rode into the valley where we found the spooky cow moose that I have already described.

Before we halted for sandwiches and tea about 2 that afternoon, we had glassed four bull moose with racks just under 60 inches and another that would have measured better than 70. But he had very narrow palms, and it would have taken a full day to stalk him and bring him out. We decided to pass him up.

While we were eating lunch I leaned back and started to glass the region ahead with my binoculars. The mist that had clouded the high country all day was lifting now, and atop a ridge at the very end of the valley I made out what looked like a huge bull caribou. He was lying down, apparently asleep.

We broke out the spotting scope, and everybody had a look.

"Big bull," Willie Dick said flatly. "Biggest I see in long time."

I had taken a caribou on my hunt with Lee Trimble the year before and wasn't eager to kill another, but this one looked too beautiful to pass up. Lying there on that high mountain ridge, he was a sight to behold. His rack was huge and heavy, and it was festooned with ragged streamers of velvet blowing in the breeze.

I was watching him when he lifted his head and looked straight in our direction, and that settled it. I wanted this trophy if I could take it.

We rode to the base of his ridge and led our horses partway up to him, switchbacking across low fingers of shale. When the climb became too steep, we stopped. Bob Jr. would stay there with the horses; my guide and I would go the rest of the way on foot.

We topped out on a ridge across a steep shale slide from the bull. He was on his feet, and there was no way for us to get closer. We held the glasses on him for minutes, and that was one of the very few times on the hunt when I saw Willie show any excitement. The range was long. I estimated it at 425 to 450 yards, but I had shot and printed many targets at the 450-yard mark on our club range at home, and I didn't think I'd have any trouble.

I lay prone, folded my down jacket for a rest, and turned my variable 3-to-7X Leupold scope up all the way. The rifle was a pre-1964 Model 70 Winchester .30/06. I used 150-grain Nosler bullets ahead of No. 4895 powder. I was sure the rifle and loads were up to the job.

I took a long rest and settled into the sling. I held the crosshairs just over his back and allowed for the crosswind. Then I took a deep breath, held it, and squeezed off.

The caribou simply sagged to his knees, stayed that way for a few seconds, and died without taking a step. That was great luck for us. If he had gone 10 feet either way, he would have fallen to the bottom of a shale slide where getting him out would have meant two hours of very hard work.

My guide started across to dress him out and cape him while I went back to Bob Jr. and the horses. He and I crossed into the valley that led back to camp. There we met Willie, who was hiking out with the antlers and cape.

Rain started to fall as darkness came on. We arrived in camp a half-hour before midnight, dog-tired and soaked, but young Bob and I were as proud and happy as a father and son have ever been.

It turned out that my bull scored 415 2/8, high enough to win him a respectable place on the Boone and Crockett record-book list of barren ground caribou.

Bob Jr., one of the guides, and I left the Hess River camp right after breakfast the next morning and headed toward the MacKenzie Mountains. The second guide stayed behind with the packhorses to bring out my caribou.

We rode down the Hess for about three hours and reached the willow grove where we had encountered the spooked moose the day before. Our horses were plodding along on a gravel bar when a yearling cow crashed out of the brush 100 yards ahead of us and went barreling into the shallows with water flying. She was obviously fleeing from something in panic. She was running so hard that she stumbled and fell three times as she plowed through the shallows.

I thought wolves were after her and piled off my horse. I yanked my rifle out of the saddle boot and ran twenty feet to one side. There I went prone in two or three inches of cold river water, ready for the shot. In that same instant the guide yelled: "Bear! Bear!"

I had chambered a cartridge, and my finger had already snugged around the trigger of the .30/06. The bear tore out of the brush on the heels of the fleeing moose. He was a beautiful boar grizzly, and his silver-tipped, almost-black pelt rippled like frost as he ran.

If he saw us and our horses, he paid no attention. He was running hard with his head down, intent only on the chase. A grizzly can cover ground very fast for a short distance, and this one was giving it everything he had.

I held the crosshairs just in front of his shoulder and fired. The kill was quick and clean. He piled up instantaneously, and it was all over.

Now we knew the reason for the strange behavior of the moose in that valley—or at least we believed we did. It seemed a safe guess that the grizzly had developed an appetite for moose calves. If he had hunted them with the same deadly determination he had shown in chasing the yearling, it was no wonder that the cows with young were scared of anything that moved—bears, men, or horses.

Two hours after we finished skinning the bear and left the willow bog, we turned up into the mountains to glass for sheep. We were riding single file with the guide ahead, followed by a packhorse. Young Bob came next, and I was bringing up the rear. I pulled my horse up to glass a bull moose in a creek bottom below us. Then there was a sudden wild uproar.

The packhorse blew up, jerked free, and turned to barge back at me. I heard Willie yell, "Grizzly come! Grizzly come!" and then my son was off his horse and had his rifle in his hands. He dropped to a sitting position, and then I saw the bear running hellbent for us.

The guide and Bob had ridden over a rise and blundered onto a grizzly feeding on a moose carcass. Many hunters have learned that you are not likely to drive a grizzly away from a meal of that kind without a fight.

Quite a few have died when they tried it or when they happened to blunder into such a situation, as we had. Many more had been dreadfully mauled.

This bear was no exception. He had probably heard or winded us before we came in sight and was waiting for us, getting more resentful by the second.

As Bob and the guide topped the ridge, the bear let out a blood-thinning bawl and came at them in an angry, headlong charge. A bear may look clumsy when he's going about his everyday affairs, but once rage explodes in him, there is nothing clumsy about the way he moves. The only thing I have ever feared on my hunts is the chance of a grizzly wandering into camp at night and losing his temper while everyone slept. They can be as deadly as dynamite.

Bob fired his first shot when the bear was 75 yards away. It broke a shoulder, we found out later, and the bear went down, thrashing, growling, and roaring. But he got back on his feet as quickly as an overgrown cat and came on again as though nothing had happened.

By that time I was off my horse, ready to back Bob with my rifle if necessary. But he needed no help. His second shot caught the bear in the center of the chest and knocked him down again. He tried to get up but couldn't make it. Bob broke the other shoulder with his third shot, and the grizzly was anchored. Then my son ran around to one side and finished him with a bullet in the neck. The whole fracas had lasted hardly more than a minute.

The bear was a beautiful silver-tipped blond male, every bit as handsome as mine. It was hard to believe that we had both collected topnotch grizzly pelts on the same day. We could have left for home right then, completely satisfied.

We arrived in camp two hours after dark, as exultant as we were wet.

Our time was running out, but we decided to make one more try for moose and rode out right after breakfast. A few hours later, glassing from a ridgetop, we spotted an exceptional bull.

Getting to him proved a lot harder than we expected. We encountered a jungle of bog and brush, and the mosquitoes and black gnats were as bad as I have ever seen them. We tied our horses at last, loosened the saddles, and climbed a ridge on foot.

When we peeked over the crest, we were looking at nine bull moose. They were loafing in an open bog of not more than an acre. Every one of them was in the trophy class. We picked the two best and worked down to within 75 yards of them. Bob shot first and dropped his in its tracks. The one I wanted just stood there looking our way after Bob's shot. My bullet hit in the left shoulder, and the bull folded his legs and died. Bob's bull had a spread of just over 60 inches; the antlers of my bull were two inches short of that mark. Both were handsome heavy heads.

In 11 days of hunting we had taken two fine moose, two exceptional caribou, and a pair of magnificent bears.

There was a pleasant postscript to come. A few months later I had word from the Yukon Government that my caribou was the best taken in the Territory in 1973. They sent me a beautiful plaque and trophy emblem.

And then came a letter from the National Rifle Association telling me that I had won the Silver Bullet Award for my barren-ground caribou, one of the two best taken by an N.R.A. member in 1973.

From the beginning, I had high hopes for our hunt on the Hess. It turned out even better than I'd dreamed.

Of Terrible Courage

Bud Helmericks

February, 1956

Wheat blows like that in the wind," I thought in the split second I watched the grizzly through the .270 Weatherby's 4X scope. The grizzly's powerful form filled the entire field. Behind the low-slung head those massive shoulders were flashing on each side like pistons, the straw-colored mane streamed in the wind, and the last few yards between me and the bear melted away.

This was the fifth time I'd had a wounded grizzly on my hands. There was no question about this bear's intentions. This was it! The issue would be settled here on the open plains where only a few dry blades of grass protruded through the drifted snow. The arctic prairie around me stretched away to the horizon with not even a bush to hide behind, or a hole to crawl into.

A barren-ground grizzly can cover 100 yards in well under 10 seconds, yet you have time to notice a lot of things. You notice that your knees are shaking, and that his ivory-tipped claws flash. His upper lip sticks out in a silent snarl, but you know somehow that the bear is as scared as you are. There's time to feel pity and admiration for the brute, as well as to hope that your rifle doesn't misfire and that the safety isn't on.

He came at me with his head low, and the crosshairs of the scope rested on his neck above and behind his skull as I pressed the trigger. His feet jerked up as if he'd stepped on a sheet of red-hot iron. He then turned a flip and fell facing away from me, all four feet in the air and still feebly moving. So ended as bizarre a grizzly hunt as I have ever been involved in.

It started an hour before with four blasts from a shotgun. The day was May 10, 1954, and Doc and I were camped on the arctic plains looking for the rare barren-ground girzzly. It was early spring up here north of the Brooks Range, and I wasn't sure there were any bears out yet. Caribou were grazing here and there on the white plains and a few parka squirrels raced about on the snow or stood bolt upright near their burrows. We spent hours studying the white landscape through binoculars and telescope, but we found no bears that way.

A diet of corn-meal mush and tea tastes better with a little meat, so when we heard ptarmigan in the willows along the riverbank, we decided to go get some. I had my Browning over-and-under 12 gauge shotgun and a few shells loaded with No. 00 buckshot. There were nine pea-size pellets in each of these shells, hardly a suitable load for ptarmigan, but it was better than using our rifles, especially if Doc could get a flock shot. I trailed along carrying my 8 × 30 binoculars, still looking for a grizzly bear and expecting to spot one at least a mile away.

Ptarmigan have dark heads in the spring, and we soon spotted several dark spots bobbing about in the willow thicket as the white-bodied grouse pecked off willow buds. By this time we were down in the old river bed in shoulder-high willows, and Doc was lining up several birds for a pot shot, figuring at least two of the big pellets would connect.

I was behind a couple of steps when I heard something in back of me. Turning, I saw a large grizzly not more than 30 feet away, climbing up a steep cutbank of the river.

There are few guns with the stopping power of a shotgun at point-blank range, and even at 40 feet I figured the large buckshot on a broadside shot would quickly prove fatal. So when Doc asked what to do I didn't hesitate. "Shoot," I answered.

The grizzly was broadside at about 50 feet when the first charge caught him. Seven-inch fur flew but that was all. The second barrel only tore off more fur. The bear looked a little perturbed but kept right on his original course. Doc reloaded quickly and fired twice more. The large bear flinched at each report and his rear end seemed anxious to get ahead. The steep cutbank and deep snow had slowed his speed, but before Doc could reload again the bear was on top and out of our sight.

We floundered up the slope in the bear's trail and saw him 100 yards out on the plains. He was sitting down like a dog and watching us. "He'll soon be dead," I told Doc, for he had centered the grizzly every shot. "But we'd better get our rifles anyway," I added as the bear sat there looking at us.

The way to kill a grizzly is to hunt ptarmigan, we decided, and congratulated ourselves upon being the luckiest bear hunters alive. But the grizzly didn't seem to know we'd killed him; he was quietly walking away. "There wasn't much blood back there in the snow," I mused as we watched him go, and doubts began to creep in.

As we had only one pair of snowshoes, I was elected to go after the bear. Doc would follow up or down the river with my .30/30 carbine, and I'd try to drive the bear in a circle. I carried the .270 Weatherby just in case I had to shoot from far away.

I only needed the snowshoes when I crossed a small creek or ravine where the snow was drifted deep. It was easy going without them on the plains. I could see the bear a mile away, and I started to head him off and circle him back toward Doc.

The grizzly didn't seem to be hurt, neither did he act afraid of me. I suppose I was the first man he'd ever seen. After a three-mile hike I had him moving toward the river, where I supposed Doc lay waiting.

Already I was within 300 yards and easy shooting range, but I wanted Doc to kill his own bear if possible. The bear kept walking, while I followed along behind like a farm lad bringing home the family milk cow. I had the rifle slung across my shoulder. I wasn't worried, the bear wasn't worried, and Doc was waiting.

Distance is mighty deceptive on the open plains, but somehow the grizzly seemed much larger now. There wasn't any blood in his trail and it was good walking for both of us on the flat, snow-covered prairie. I wondered why he didn't just run off and leave me.

Then I decided to take a few pictures for Doc. After checking the rifle again to make sure it was loaded and ready, I stuck my head through the sling and began to adjust my camera. The grizzly began to slow down. The distance between us was less than 100 yards, then about 70. The bear didn't seem to want to go any farther. He looked all done in. We were on solid footing where quite a little grass showed through the snow. The grizzly looked from side to side as if aware for the first time that I was there. I just had time to think, "I'd better get the rifle. . . ."

The grizzly didn't turn in the about-face sense. He was plodding ahead one moment—and flashing toward me the next. I somehow managed to crawl out of the rifle sling and thumb off the safety catch. What followed was the scene in my scope that reminded me of a field of wheat, the scope waving full of his beautiful fur. The next instant he lay on his back 15 feet ahead of me.

There's something dreadful about the power of a modern rifle when used against the courage of a grizzly bear.

As I walked around him his glazing eyes followed me, while a growl rumbled in his throat. His massive jaws opened trying still to grasp me, but his powerful body wouldn't respond to his fierce will because the spinal cord was severed. If I had missed the spine—

The biggest surprise came when we skinned him, for there, just under the hide, were the big No. 00 buckshot. Each was wrapped in a wad of fur as large as a quarter and several hadn't penetrated the hide at all. Only a few had even drawn blood; they were merely stuck in a layer of fat. Nearly every one of the 36 pellets fired were found on or in the bear, showing how steady Doc's aim had been.

These buckshot loads consistently plowed through 100-pound wolves; yet the grizzly hadn't been hurt at all. Both Doc's and my opinion of buckshot as a grizzly load tumbled, though I'm still sure it would do the job at a very close range.

The home of the barren-ground grizzly (Ursus richardsoni) is the arctic prairies—that enormous stretch of grasslands extending from the end of the trees north to the Arctic Ocean, and from one side of our continent to the other. I understand he is also found on the arctic plains of Siberia and in the Russian arctic. He is a rare animal, but no more so than he has always been.

In much of my arctic hunting I have had the advantage of the early explorer in meeting animals that have never seen a man before. In this regard my accounts of hunting will differ from those who have hunted the grizzly where he is constantly pursued.

The barren-ground grizzly generally lives on roots, plants, parka squirrels, and wolf-killed caribou. He may do a little fishing, for he ranges every stream and river of the arctic prairie clear to the Arctic Ocean, but the rolling plains in the foothills and the grassy mountains themselves are his favorite haunts. Here parka squirrels are abundant, and he digs them up with ease.

At the approach of a hunter, the grizzly will stand on his hind legs with his massive forepaws tucked up like a squirrel, his claws pointing in and down. Here he stands with his head rolling from side to side, trying to see better and get your scent. Then he's gone in a long, easy gallop across the open plain. This grizzly is quick to depart from any kind of trouble, but a fighter to the last when cornered or wounded.

One warm afternoon I watched an old sow and two yearling cubs digging up parka squirrels. I had my 30X spotting scope with me and trained it on the family. It's amazing and a little unnerving to see the ease with which a grizzly lifts and moves enormous rocks or tears up sod.

The parka squirrels didn't wait to be cornered, but popped out of side exits to make a dash for a new burrow. The bulky sow would spot and catch them in a short sprint, as agile as any fox. The cubs were busy catching squirrels too, mainly by stationing themselves at the emergency exits. After an hour's work the family ambled over to a dry, sandy bank and curled up for a nap.

I was busily writing here at my cabin in the Alatna River valley, 50 miles north of the Arctic Circle, on warm June day. Outside my window, the ice on Takahula Lake was about ready to break up. I was watching it when I saw an old sow grizzly with three yearling cubs walk out to loaf on the ice near the cabin. The cubs were about the size of chow dogs. It was about 2 p.m. when I first saw them. The mosquitoes were getting bad back in the brush. That and the heat had driven the long-furred bears out on the ice for rest. The old sow lay sprawled as if she were dead, while the cubs tumbled and played about. The ice must have been cold under the cubs' feet, for they soon climbed on the sleeping mother. I quickly had my spotting scope trained on them and could see the cubs licking their feet.

All was quiet for a few minutes, while the sleeping mother's sides rose and fell. Then two of the cubs began wrestling and pushing each other off the mother bear. The third cub started sniffing in her ear. I had changed to the 60X eyepiece and the bears seemed right in my lap. Next the cub pawed the sow's eye open to see if she were still in there. At this the patient mother stood up and cuffed all three cubs so that they skidded clear out of my field of view.

For a minute she stood there watching her cubs walk back, an exasperated and yet fond look on her old brown face. Finally she yawned and stretched full length upon the ice again. Her sides heaved in a big sigh and she was asleep again. The cubs played and romped about like puppies for half an hour. They boxed, wrestled, and ganged up on one another. Then they'd climb on the mother, and in a short time they'd get swatted again.

In this way they passed the entire afternoon, and I spent one of my most memorable days with a family of grizzly bears. Then as the shadows of the arctic midnight stole across the lake the mother bear led her family back into the brush.

The barren-ground grizzly eats more roots and plants than anything else. His favorite is the wild vetch, often called the Alaska potato. It has knobs on its roots the size of peanuts and he'll literally turn over acres of land with his three-inch claws searching for these roots.

On a balmy day in late September, 1952, Angus and I were hunting Alatna Valley above the junction of the Kutuk River. I saw a big grizzly feeding in an open slide across the valley. The spotting scope showed he had a beautiful pelt, and as Angus had never killed a grizzly, we went after him.

We were on the timbered side of the Brooks Range, and it took more than two hours to climb to where we had last seen the bear. I had my 16 mm. movie camera and was armed with a .357 S. & W. Magnum revolver. Angus carried a .300 Weatherby with 250-grain Barnes soft-point bullet loads. I was in the lead in waist-high willows. The going was hard on the steep slope and Angus had fallen down several times. In fact, we had made so much noise neither of us expected to see the bear.

A perfectly formed spruce, a few yards ahead of me, seemed to tower against the skyline. Like many trees at timberline, it had the shape and look of a large specimen but was really only five feet tall.

A few twigs snapped suddenly. Then the head and shoulders of a grizzly bear appeared over the top of the tree. I dropped, eyes wide at the sight of a bear that apparently dwarfed a tree!

I was about to get the camera in action when the grizzly vanished. I looked questioningly at Angus.

"By gosh, that's the first time I ever saw you fall down," he laughed.

"Didn't you see that bear?" I asked. "It blotted out the skyline!"

"What bear? Where?"

In answer to his question a *crash . . . crash . . . crash* came echoing from the brushy draw. We saw a couple of flashes of the bear as it sailed downhill, and for five minutes, it seemed, we could hear him running in the valley below.

Angus was never able to kill a barren-ground grizzly; you can count on your fingers the sportsmen who have bagged one. A year later I reminded Angus of that big grizzly, and he said, "You know, I'm glad I didn't kill him. Now I know he's wandering the open plains somewhere and I can dream of another hunt. I'm going to try again, you know."

Fortunately for sportsmen, the barren-ground grizzly will always roam the vast arctic plains if we afford him suitable protection. The land here will never be taken up for farms as was the range of plains grizzlies that once lived on the prairies of the United States.

In my experience, there's only one shot that will stop an enraged grizzly cold, regardless of the power of your rifle. That one is a shot into the brain or the portion of the spinal cord between the head and shoulders. Other hits may partly disable him and slow his charge, but they won't stop a determined bear. Even a heart shot won't kill an aroused grizzly in time to save your scalp. I had this point driven home properly one clear September day on the arctic plains.

Robert Hamilton, a mammalogist from the University of Michigan, and I were hunting for specimens at the head of the Itkillik River. We spotted two grizzlies feeding along a little creek. One was large, apparently an old boar; the smaller one was a sow, we guessed. We stalked to within 200 yards, and when the larger bear presented a broadside shot, Hamilton shot him through the lungs with a .300 H. & H. Magnum. The big bear reared up and fell dead. The smaller bear reared up and then came for us.

I had a .30/06 and was shooting 180-grain soft-point bullets. Since we didn't want to kill the smaller bear, I stepped forward to try to bluff it out. When we were about 10 yards apart I shot into the ground in front of the bear. It kept coming. As it neared, I decided, "Well, I won't ruin its skull." Hamilton wanted all skulls in perfect condition.

At 20 yards, I held on its heart and fired. The results were nil, and I heard the whine of a ricocheting bullet. My second shot was exactly the same, including the ricochet. The bear was right up to me as I slammed in the third shot. It centered its head and stopped it.

"You ruined the skull," Hamilton said.

Skinning the bear, we saw that the first two shots had centered the chest, torn through the heart, and passed on through the bear to whine away across the prairie. The last shot, as the scientist complained, had ruined the skull. Contrary to our first guess, we apparently had a sow and a two-year-old cub.

The big sow, which had been unalarmed, died quickly and quietly from a lung shot. The small bear was angry and scared, and all but impervious to the shock of a bullet until its nerve center was put out of action.

The barren-ground grizzly isn't a large bear. The average weight will run around 400 pounds, with 700 pounds an approximate maximum. April and May are the best times to hunt.

They have a beautiful soft pelt that may be seven inches long and their color varies from chocolate brown on the legs and belly to a straw color on their backs. The season has a lot to do with their color. Dark skins are the rule in the fall and early spring. Summer pelts, bleached by the arctic sun, run lighter.

Barren-ground grizzlies become dormant in late September or October and generally come out in May, although you may find one out even in January. They den in cutbanks along a creek, holes in the rocks, or under piles of brush in the mountains.

The grizzly is a gentleman and an animal I have the highest regard for. Once you've witnessed his terrible courage you can't help feeling humble in his presence, even though he lies dead at your feet. I have seen about 100 grizzly bears, and many more have seen me. They have even searched my home for food when I have been away, leaving claw marks on the sink board.

My wife Connie had one of the queerest experiences with a bear I know of. There's a game trail around the lake that goes right past our cabin door. One sunny day Connie curled up in a dry spot along the trail and fell asleep. Later she awoke to some sound—and looked straight up into a grizzly's face. The bear was examining her closely. She didn't move and in a moment the bear walked on around the lake.

Perhaps I wouldn't be here today if it weren't for a big boar grizzly. The first winter we spent on the Alatna River, 1944 and '45, we were 100 miles from anyone by trail. Freeze-up came early and all the game we got was lean. The sun set for the arctic winter and already we were short of fat.

You can live on meat alone with ease, but it must be fat meat. In this climate, you'll die of starvation no matter how much lean meat you eat. Day after day I hunted hard and found nothing. It was November, which meant that we had only a few hours of shooting light each day.

Returning home one evening I saw a grizzly directly across the river from the cabin. Before I could get in a shot he was a long way off, but at the crack of my .30/30 carbine he turned a flip-flop and vanished into the willows.

The snow was a foot deep, and in the fading light I saw blood on both sides of the trail, frothy blood that indicated a lung shot. The bear kept right on going, and darkness forced me to give up the track.

Next day I again took up the trail. I soon came to a spot where the bear had lain down. It was my first grizzly and I was plenty cautious. The trail led through heavy brush into some hills where rocks the size of boxcars lay in tumbled piles. Here the spruce trees grew thick. The bear had lain down several times, always downwind of his trail.

When the trail led through a tunnel under some big rocks, I peered through and saw his tracks going on up the hill beyond. I started to crawl through, and then something warned me to back out and go around.

It was a climb getting over the rocks, but from the top I could see the bear's trail went only a short way uphill and then circled back. I edged forward, pausing a moment between steps. As I peered over the roots of an upturned tree, I saw the grizzly. He lay with his back to me, staring like a mouse-stalking cat at the hole in the rocks where I would have crawled out.

I was so close I could see his breath sending up little puffs of steam, so I held back the trigger as I cocked the rifle. Otherwise he'd have heard the snap of the cocking sear. I drew a bead on the base of his ear and fired. The bear jumped forward and fell dead on the trail.

The bullet I fired the day before had entered high in front of the left hip, ranged forward through the right lung, and passed on out in front of the right shoulder with little or no expansion. The killing shot passed through the skull and lodged under the skin on the far side, mushrooming perfectly.

The bear carried more than 100 pounds of fat, and even with this added amount we just made it through the winter.

When we drifted downriver to the trading post in June I expressed the pelt to a taxidermist to have it made into a rug. But the grizzly had done all it could for me, because the pelt went to the bottom of the North Pacific with the S. S. Yukon, the ship that brought me to Alaska years ago.

Much of my hunting has been done with Eskimos. I once asked an old Eskimo bear hunter what rifle he generally used. It was an ancient .22, a single-shot Remington of falling-block design. He produced several skulls with a .22 hole drilled neatly through them. Several years ago a mammalogist had paid him $5 for one and he'd been saving skulls ever since. As near as I could tell, he'd killed 13 bears with this tiny rifle.

On the arctic prairie there are little mounds made by generations of parka squirrels. The old-time Eskimo would find a bear that was hunting squirrels and then slip around into its path. Prone behind a parka squirrel's mound, the Eskimo would thrust up his forearm with fist doubled to imitate a squirrel, at the same time chirping like an alarmed squirrel. The grizzly would come over to investigate, and get shot in the head. The Eskimo I spoke to indicated about a 10-foot distance. He showed me the correct spot to hit the bear—about midway between the ear and the eye and a little either side of center. I examined the skulls closely and found them surprisingly thin, at that point—little thicker than shoe-box cardboard.

The old fellow finished talking and stared at the teeth of an enormous skull. Then, as if realizing that a little knowledge is dangerous, he cautioned me: "That brown bear, Oklak, is bad one. You don't hit him right, he come for you!" With this he again indicated the spot where you must hit him.

He also told me how old-time Eskimos snared the grizzly in the willows or shot him with a bow and arrow. He explained that they didn't try to kill the bear with an arrow, but that the arrow induced him to charge. They then speared him at close range.

I have no doubt that an arrow or a spear will kill a grizzly, but both kill slowly, mostly by bleeding the animal to death. During this interval the hunter must keep out of the bear's reach, and that undoubtedly would take some doing.

Sometimes a grizzly will come out in midwinter and his coat will be full of ice. He may ice his fur by crossing overflows in rivers, or he may roll in the water on purpose. At any rate, Eskimos claim bullets are useless against such a bear. I know of two Eskimos who were killed by ice-coated grizzlies.

I know of several bears being killed with .22 Hornets, .25/20's, or even .22 rimfire rifles, but a sportsman will do well to stick to the heaviest caliber he can handle. On the open plains a high-velocity bullet of good sectional density is best. Such rifles as the .300 Weatherby, .300 H. & H. Magnum, .270 Weatherby, and .30/06 are ideal. Use medium-weight, soft-point bullets. In the timbered and brushy parts of the arctic I like something with a bit more power—say a .300 with 220 or 250-grain bullets, or even a .375 Magnum.

All future generations should have a chance to hunt the barren-ground grizzly, which is our only surviving plains grizzly, if he's given reasonable protection in the coming years. He's not plentiful now, but his range is remote and he's equipped to survive with regulated hunting.

But remember, when you stalk him on these treeless plains, "You don't hit him right, he come for you!"

Grizzlies in My Path

Jack Turner

June, 1974

About the only conclusion I've come to after quite a bit of contact with grizzly bears in British Columbia is that you can't generalize about them or predict their behavior.

After almost 30 years in grizzly country and several hundred sightings and meetings with them, I've met with only three unprovoked attacks. One I turned aside with warning shots. Another ended with me killing the bear at a range of six feet with one shot between the eyes. That grizzly, which I told about in "World's Biggest Grizzly?" in March 1967 issue of OUTDOOR LIFE, scored $26^{10}/_{16}$ and tied with the then-world-record grizzly in the Boone and Crockett Club's "Records of North American Big Game." My bear now stands No. 3 in the record book.

There were several other charges, but these came because of a misunderstanding or because I provoked the bear, either accidentally or deliberately—for a specific purpose.

But many times I've done something that a grizzly has a right to take offense to, only to have the bear ignore me. I figure bears are like people in that respect. It's just the occasional one that won't be peaceable if given the chance.

Here's the story of one of the angrier bears I've run into:

Several years ago I was traveling near Knot Lake in the upper Atnarko Valley. At dusk I made my bed on the only nearby level, dry spot, which happened to be the middle of a well-established game trail. After unrolling the groundsheet and sleeping bag and then eating, I let my small fire burn out and turned in.

I'd been asleep for some time when I was abruptly awakened by a loud and very close grizzly grumble, accompanied by a lot of crashing in the brush. I had a rifle, but it was very dark under the heavy timber.

Though the bear couldn't have been much over 20 feet away, I couldn't see anything. I felt pretty helpless.

A few tiny embers glowed in the fire. My immediate need was to kindle a flame to provide some shooting light should the animal move in on me.

I grabbed the birch bark I'd put under the sleeping bag to start my breakfast fire. I put it and a handful of twigs on the coals and started to blow a little life into the embers. I got a flame in a few moments, but I managed to fill both eyes with smoke. For a while I could see less than ever. All this time the bear had been circling at about 30 feet, I estimated from the noise, growling and crashing through the dead sticks and undergrowth.

I got some bigger sticks burning and could see 20 feet around. I was able to slow down enough to look at my watch and find out that it was midnight.

That bear, presumably annoyed by being forced to make what I looked on as a minor detour around my camp, raged around the fire until after 4 a.m. By then I'd completely stripped the ground of everything that could be burned for 15 feet around. I hadn't been able to get up sufficient nerve to go beyond the edge of the light for better fuel.

The bear finally departed, but since I couldn't be sure it wouldn't be back, I stayed up and kept the fire going until daylight.

There's an example of a bear that didn't have much to be mad about but was anyway. Here's the other side of the coin, a situation where I *expected* trouble.

I was using a log jam to cross a river crowded with spawning salmon in the Skeena River area. I didn't have a rifle along. About halfway across, I became unhappily aware that on a lower part of the jam to my left were two grizzly cubs eating fish. On my right was the sow, poking a foreleg between two logs.

I was squarely between them, supposedly a cardinal sin. But I kept to my course and hoped for the best while expecting the worst. The cubs stared with interest, and the sow—after a brief, indifferent look—resumed her search between the logs.

In spite of this happy ending, it's not a good idea to get between a sow and cubs. I just happened to be lucky.

I believe that sometimes when a bear bothers someone without being provoked, its bad temper is caused by something unrelated to the person involved. It's just the human's bad luck to encounter the bear when it happens to be angry about something else.

To illustrate, a few years ago I was traveling up the west bank of the Atnarko River at a point where it's about 60 feet wide. I saw a lone grizzly on the east bank in some heavy pine windfall. It was rooting under a boulder.

As I watched, the bear tried to dig out the yellow-jacket nest it had found under the rock. But the boulder was too big to move, and other rocks under the surface made digging too hard. The bear finally gave up after paying a high price in work and many stings on its face.

As the animal left the nest, it came to a large fallen pine densely covered

Since the grizzly had just got on the log, I figured it could get off easier than I. But the critter kept coming.

with branches of up to 1½ inches thick. The trunk was about four feet off the ground, leaving ample room for the bear to walk beneath it. But the bear was mad, so it stood up on its hind legs and lashed out with both powerful front legs in roundhouse swings that snapped the dry branches with the noise of rifle shots. It lopped off branches for about 10 feet along the trunk.

I'm sure that the bear was just venting its irritation. It quite possibly would have swung just as aggressively if it had chanced to meet a person instead of a log.

Sometimes, though, grizzlies will show more tolerance than a person might deserve.

Once I was traveling in the McGregor River country northeast of Prince George. As the area is flat and heavily timbered, I was using a compass to travel cross-country from my base camp to a creek eight miles away. Because of my big pack and because a rifle makes local attraction for a compass needle, I had left my gun in camp.

After several hours, when I was crossing an open glade in the heavy spruce growth, my attention was drawn to a movement about 80 feet to my left. Closer inspection revealed a female grizzly sitting on her rump with three small cubs playing around her. I was young and foolish at the time—I am now older but still foolish—and had a camera in my pocket. I had never before had a chance to photograph a family of three cubs, so I started walking slowly toward them. I figured that as long as the sow didn't stand up, I'd assume she was unconcerned. When she did stand up, I'd stop.

Walking slowly, I got to within 20 feet of the cubs. All four bears quietly watched me. I took several pictures, turned, and walked away. I'd gone about 20 feet when I heard a heavy thudding behind me. I turned around to see the sow galloping straight at me and looking very annoyed.

I impulsively shouted at her, and she stopped perhaps 10 feet away. I wanted her to know I was leaving, but I didn't want to turn my back on her again. So I started to walk backward cautiously, hoping that I wouldn't trip and end up flat on my back. This routine went fine except that for every step I took away she took one ahead.

After we'd gone about 20 feet this way I found myself backed against a fairly thick pile of windfall spruce trunks. She stopped about eight feet from me and growled unpleasantly, probably because she didn't like my stopping my retreat.

I started working my arms out of the packstraps, hoping that if I dumped the pack she would stop and spend enough time tearing into it to allow me a chance to get over the windfall and up a tree. Before I could loosen the pack, she started forward again. Again I shouted. She stopped, stared at me for a long moment, and then turned and walked back to her cubs.

In retrospect I think she was more tolerant than I deserved.

Earlier on that same trip I had found my way blocked by a very thick slide of alder and devil's club several hundred feet long and about 80 feet wide. Searching for a way past this almost impenetrable prickly barrier, I found a fallen spruce going across the slide from side to side about five feet off the ground.

Climbing up onto the trunk with some difficulty with my pack, I started across, watching down in front of me to avoid tripping over branches and loose bark. About a third of the way across I sensed a movement ahead of me. I looked up to see an adult grizzly starting across from the other end.

As the bear had just got on, I figured that it would be easier for it to get off than for me. So I started ahead with the hope that it would turn around and get off when it saw me. The grizzly had other ideas and probably didn't want to get off any more than I did. It kept coming.

When we were about 30 feet apart I stopped, and so did the bear. While I was still pondering the situation, the grizzly started toward me.

As it got closer I rapidly lost my nerve and forgot about pressing my right-of-way. Better a live coward than a dead hero, I thought. I lay belly-down on the log, lowered myself as far toward the ground as possible, and let go to fall the remaining couple of feet. I fought a slow, painful 60 feet to the creek that ran parallel with the log.

With torn pants and many scratches, I jumped into the cold waist-deep water and waded upstream until I reached the far side of the slide. I climbed out and looked back. The bear was still where I'd left it. The animal had turned to watch my progress—with bearish amusement, I'm sure.

Sometimes grizzlies can be bluffed out and sometimes not. Here are two examples:

My family and I homestead in a good grizzly area on a major salmon spawning river, 25 miles by trail from the nearest road. Each fall we pack in our year's supplies by horse from the road. The trail we use generally follows the river.

Several years ago my wife Trudy was leading loaded horses and carrying our two-year-old daughter Susan on a backpack. I walked ahead carrying two narrow sheets of 14-foot-long plywood that we were taking in for boat building. I was practically encased in plywood, with two sheets sticking out seven feet behind and seven feet ahead. There was just a one-foot gap for me to see through straight ahead. I could not see much on either side.

We didn't have a gun along. Both of us were too encumbered to carry one.

As we passed a good fishing spot on a side channel of the river about 40 feet from the trail, I heard a lot of splashing. At the same time Trudy shouted that a grizzly was coming at us from the river.

I swung toward the river to see through my foot-wide gap. By the time I'd turned a sow with two cubs behind her was just about 15 feet away.

She skidded to a stop. I took a step toward her, moving my shoulders from side to side, jerking the plywood back and forth in front of her.

She'd probably never seen anything like that before. After one startled look, she upended and raced back across the channel, collecting her cubs as she went.

Another time I tried a bluff that didn't go so well.

I was traveling alone in the west Kootenay section of British Columbia and made camp for the night on a small stream. After pitching my small bell tent and putting my pack inside, I gathered my fishing gear and went a few hundred feet down to the stream. Having seen little bear sign that day, I left my rifle in the tent.

After half an hour I had enough trout for a couple of meals and returned to the tent. As I entered the small meadow where I'd made camp I came to a sudden stop at the sight of a bear's rump protruding through the tent door. As all my food and equipment was in the tent, I had to do something fast to get the bear out. The only thing I could think of was to startle it and hope that it would run away. I picked up a good-size rock and threw it at the rump, uttering what I thought was a fearful yell.

This did produce results—though not quite what I'd hoped for. The rock hit just behind the bear and rolled under its belly, scaring it. As it quickly turned to get out, the grizzly hit the tent pole, collapsing the tent on top of the animal. By the time it had torn its way through the tent, the bear was scared and mad. Unfortunately its retreat happened to be in my direction. The bear had no idea that I was in the country. But I was in its way, and as soon as I moved it spotted me and came toward me.

By sheer luck a large boulder about eight feet high was close by. I somehow flew to its top before the bear reached me. I'm sure that if it had really wanted to, the animal could have got up on the rock. But it contented itself with circling around the base several times, looking up and grumbling. It finally returned to the tent, rooted about in the mess for several minutes, and then wandered downstream.

I stayed on the rock for 20 minutes or so. Then I established a new record in running over for the rifle. Thankfully I didn't have to use it.

I've only once had a chance to hear families of bears communicating with each other. That was at Nepah Lagoon, a tidal basin on the British Columbia coast that was full of humpback salmon getting ready to ascend nearby creeks to spawn. The lagoon shore was covered with tracks and other sign of the numerous bears that had gathered for their annual feast on spawning fish.

As I quietly paddled a small boat around the shoreline, I scared up a female and two cubs. They ran along a fallen log that sloped uphill. Just as they disappeared in the thick growth at the top, she gave a loud coughing grunt. This was almost immediately answered from a point several hundred feet up the shoreline. Then from two other locations up the hill came similar grunts.

This four-way conversation kept up for several minutes. I could only conclude that the female I'd scared was warning the other bears of an intruder.

Some of my encounters with grizzlies had a humorous side, at least when I think of them in retrospect. Here's one of the best:

I arrived at a cabin in an isolated area near Kootenay where a friend had a base camp he used while prospecting the area. He wasn't there, so I went in, lit a fire, and started a meal. He arrived at dark. As we ate he mentioned that he'd dropped his rifle that day, knocking the front sight off line. He would have to sight it in the next morning.

The next day as I got breakfast, he took several shots outside. He entered the cabin to announce that the rifle was now shooting so well that he could "shoot the head off a flying duck at thirty yards."

After eating we climbed nearby Silvertop Mountain. After several hours, we reached well above the timberline. We had been poking around for an hour or so when we heard rocks rolling on the far side of a small hill. Going around it, we saw a large grizzly hunting marmots in an area of large loose rocks. The bear was only about 100 feet away, and he saw us moving before we could stop. In this seldom-traveled area there was a good chance we were the first people the bear had ever seen.

The animal stood up on his hind legs to see us better. After a while it dropped down and slowly walked closer. When it was about 60 feet away the grizzly again reared up for another long look and again dropped and shuffled closer.

The third time the bear reared up it was only about 30 feet away. The animal looked pretty tall and quite unafraid so Scotty unslung his rifle and worked the action to chamber a cartridge.

Once more the animal returned to all fours. It walked slowly toward us until it was no more than 20 feet away. Again it reared up to stare down at us, turning its great head side to side. Scotty didn't want to shoot, but there was a point where he didn't want the grizzly any closer. So my friend was poised to shoot if necessary.

However, after one more long look the bear dropped down, turned, and walked away.

Scotty left his gun loaded in case we encountered the animal again that afternoon. But we saw no further sign of it. We reached the cabin just before dark. I went in to make a fire while Scotty stayed outside to unload his gun and bring some firewood into the cabin.

After we'd finished eating I said that seeing as I'd been unarmed, I had felt much better knowing that he had been ready to shoot, with that bear looking down at us from 20 feet. Scotty was silent for a moment. Then he said with a sheepish grin: "I'm glad it made you feel better, and I'm glad he didn't come any closer."

Yes, I agreed, it would have been a shame to kill him.

"I didn't mean that, lad. When I went to unload the musket tonight I found out that I forgot to reload after I sighted-in this morning. It's been empty all day."

Bedtime Story

Jack Tooker

June, 1954

Some of the best hunting in North America is to be found south of the Mexican border along the Sierra Madre Mountains, from western Chihuahua and extending down to Tepic. It's full of big game, including some king-size grizzlies. They average larger than our Rocky Mountain bears. In fact, they resemble our old California grizzly which was reported to have weighed as much as 1,100 pounds.

Earl Boyles and I had a clash with these Mexican grizzlies in 1913 that I still remember as clearly as if it happened last season. We hired a guide named Soto and arranged for a hunt in the wild and rugged country west of Tepehuanes. A branch railway runs to this little mining town from Durango. We were told that this part of the country was infested with bandits, which local officials admitted, and as the government refused to give us any protection, our guide Soto reluctantly refused to go.

We were cussing our hard luck in the lobby of the hotel in Durango when a stately looking Spaniard came in and registered. I saw Soto perk up. He recognized the man and went over and talked to him. Soon the two went into the dining room, and when they reappeared half an hour later Soto's face had lost its gloom.

He introduced the man as Mr. Garcia, who said immediately, "My friend Mr. Soto tells me you gentlemen want to hunt. Bears are killing many of my cattle and I will furnish you horses from my remuda and supplies from my commissary to hunt on my ranch for as long as you can stay."

He admitted there were bandits, but said they worked mostly along the San Blas trail and on north. We'd hunt south of the trail, and besides,

The wounded grizzly pounced on Earl like a dog on a gopher as I stood up. I thrust the rifle at the bear and shot him again.

Garcia said he kept on good terms with the outlaws by giving them beef and tobacco—a sort of combined tribute and charity.

"Are there many bears?" we asked.

"Too many!" he said. He went on to explain that Soto had been his foreman for seven years and knew where the bears ranged. Garcia said he was taking out a 12-mule packtrain next morning.

"You mean there are no roads?" I asked.

Garcia shook his head sadly. "Only trails."

The hotel manager helped us get off next morning, and made it a point to warn us about the bandits: We should never trust any of them. If they got the drop on us, they would kill us for our guns and whatever other valuables and money we had.

It took us three days' packing over rough, scenic country to reach the Garcia rancho. There was a large adobe hacienda surrounded by a high rock-and-adobe wall. Walls four feet thick protected the servants' quarters and huge supply buildings. The ponderous doors were locked with huge keys which reminded me of an ancient castle. The place was a fortress.

Bright and early next morning Garcia showed us a cow that had been killed by a grizzly. As we approached the kill a black bear raised up from behind the carcass. Garcia cried out, "Get him! He is kill cow!"

Soto was about to shoot when I stopped him. "That little bear didn't kill that cow," I said, " and if you kill him he may disturb all the sign around the carcass. We're after a much bigger bear than that."

The old rancher was disappointed, thinking we'd pardoned a grizzly, but we went on up and found the tracks of a much larger bear, the girzzly that evidently had killed the cow. We showed Garcia the difference between grizzly and black bear tracks and assured him he had made no mistake when he reported a grizzly had done the killing.

He showed us three old-style bear traps built of logs. One had been torn apart and the logs scattered. Garcia said a foreman had found a grizzly in the trap and had made the mistake of shooting him inexpertly with a .30/30 rifle. The wounded bear tore through the logs as if they had been matchsticks. Later they found the foreman dead; the grizzly was gone, leaving a blood trail. That had happened seven months before and there had been no traps set since. Nor any grizzlies killed, for that matter.

In two days' riding we saw lots of tracks and several kills but no bears. Garcia admitted that only a few kills had been made near the ranch house, and Soto agreed that most of the bears were on the southern end of the place—which was 30 or 40 miles away.

It's always been my policy, when after any kind of big game, to go where they are the thickest and if necessary live there for a while. So I had Soto bring in four pack burros and outfit them for a trip south.

We got started about 10 a.m. and began to see game almost imme-diately. We'd gone perhaps 10 miles through some of the finest country to be found anywhere when 30 or 40 wild turkeys trotted across the trail and stopped in a clearing not more than 60 yards ahead of us. Earl took his rifle from its scabbard and dismounted. The turkeys were so innocent of men they didn't even run when Earl walked toward them. A white gobbler stepped out of the bushes and stretched his long neck, and Earl shot him. Between Monterrey and Tampico I have seen whole flocks of wild white turkeys, but in the Sierra Madres we seldom see more than one or two whites in a hundred.

Soto tied the turkey on one of the packsaddles and we went on. Topping a little ridge, we came to a forest of giant oaks with gray and golden squirrels everywhere and large acorns plentiful. It was typical bear country. A little further on we flushed a herd of white-tail deer with their stern flags flying the up-go and down-stop signals. Then several more flocks of wild turkeys. We also saw grizzly sign and all sorts of cat tracks.

This oak forest extended for miles and ended in a beautiful green meadow with a brook running through it. Earl remarked he'd seen a lot of hunting country but this was the nearest to paradise he could remember.

Soto called a halt here, saying we could easily reach the site he'd planned for our permanent camp at Cavernas de Agua (Water Caves), which was at the extreme southern end of the range of mountains we were following. He made a fire and put the pot on while Earl and I unpacked the burros and unsaddled our horses, hobbling all the animals and putting bells on them. The bells weren't so much to enable us to find our stock in the morning as to keep the cougars, grizzlies, jaguars, and wolves from killing it.

By the time we got camp in shape and unrolled our sleeping bags, Soto had the turkey in the large Dutch oven and biscuits in the smaller one. Cooked to a turn with just the right amount of chili to give it zest, that turkey was really something to satisfy the inner man.

As night came on we lay among the oak leaves or on our bed rolls smoking and dozing in the flickering light of the fire. It was hardly dark before the wildlife began calling deep in the west fork of the Santiago River not far away. Two jaguars began their peculiar coughlike talk, ending with coarse, vicious growls. Wolves howled their lonely plaint, and a little later some owls flitted in through the firelight as if to see what manner of creatures had invaded their domain.

We rolled into our beds and I was soon asleep, though none of us had forgotten the outlaws. Earl seemed especially nervous. We all slept with out side arms on.

The last thing I remembered was the faint tinkle of the bells on our saddle and pack animals. Next thing I knew a roar was echoing in my ears and the ground was vibrating around me as if from a small earthquake. When I finally got free of my bedding, I found the horses and burros milling around the camp, apparently having been badly frightened by some beast. It was remarkable that none of us had been stepped on. Whatever caused the panic wasn't to be seen. It probably lost its nerve before all that human scent as it approached the campfire. But within a few minutes the animals calmed down and started working their way back into the timber. We went to sleep again.

It was daylight when I awoke. Earl and Soto were still asleep, and Soto had his head covered and his bare feet sticking out. I tickled his feet, or tried to, but the naked soles of those feet were about half an inch thick and nothing short of a branding iron would have had any effect. But when I uncovered his head he came to life pronto. He'd gone to bed fully dressed, six-shooter and all.

He went to the creek to wash his hands and face while I placed some dry leaves and twigs on the oak-wood coals that were still alive. We soon finished breakfast and were on our way.

Arriving at the caves about 2 p.m., we found ourselves on the edge of a small version of the Grand Canyon. Five tributaries of the Santiago River converged in the distance. There was water in the cave nearest us, and a spring flowed only a few feet from its mouth. Soto said it was the only water for some miles, and that's why he proposed we camp there.

I took a good look at the animal tracks around the spring at the cave's mouth and chose a campsite about 50 yards back from the water. There were wolf, jaguar, lion, lynx, deer, and turkey tracks around the water, and some of the largest grizzly tracks I've ever seen anywhere. For the next day or two we never went near that spring at night, and when we went for water during the day we could expect to see almost anything from wild turkey to grizzly.

Camp was under a big, spreading live-oak tree. While we were setting up, a spike white-tail deer came in for a drink, and we had camp meat. Soto dressed out the deer and hung the carcass about eight feet off the ground on a limb of the oak beside our beds. I should have known better than to permit that. Soto himself was rarely so careless, but he had decided there was so much game in this area the big meat-eaters wouldn't bother raiding our camp meat.

We spread our sleeping bags across a 14-foot, 18-ounce tarp, folding seven feet of the tarp back over the bags. That made a bed that would stay dry in rain or snow.

We were many miles from the normal range of bandits, yet we didn't relax our guard. It may have been fear of bandits that got us in trouble that night.

There was pretty moonlight, and I lay awake a long time listening to the wild animals. I could hear fighting going on and once the bells of the stock tinkled. Then some of our animals wandered through camp between the spring and our beds. I never suspected they were in trouble.

Finally I dropped off to sleep, and awoke some time later to hear the thudding sound a boxer makes punching a heavy bag. I screwed my head around cautiously. A huge bear was clawing and slugging the deer swinging from the tree beside us. The venison would be easy to replace, so I had no intention of disturbing the bear at such dangerously close quarters. Deciding we wouldn't be bothered if we acted cautiously, I nudged Earl.

I nudged him twice before he moved, but it didn't occur to me to speak a warning. I should have, because Earl awoke with bandits in mind. Before I knew what he was about, he raised up on his elbow, drew his .45 revolver and shot at the erect silhouette of the bear. I had a feeling right then our goose was cooked.

The grizzly jumped and made a sound like a man's "Oh!" at the impact of the bullet. He probably thought a bee had stung him, but Earl, only half awake, fired again quickly. At the second shot the bear looked our way.

I'd already crawled from under the covers with my rifle, and from a kneeling position I fired at the huge bulk as it came hurtling toward us. The shock of the 8 mm. rifle bullet stopped him momentarily. I saw that Earl was hopelessly tangled in his bedding and I yelled, "Roll up in the canvas!" He did, and that's what saved him.

The bear pounced on him like a dog on a gopher and was soon shaking and mauling both Earl and the canvas. I placed the muzzle of the rifle against the bear's shoulder and fired. The bullet penetrated both shoulders, rendering the great forearms useless. The first shot had torn away the upper part of the heart.

The grizzly fell on his side on top of Earl (who no longer struggled) roaring and growling with rage and trying to turn over to fasten his teeth in whatever was under the canvas. When the grizzly's struggles finally stopped I became aware of Soto standing a little away from me with his six-shooter in hand trembling like a leaf.

Together we rolled the bear off Earl, whom we found alive and miraculously without any broken bones. For that matter, he had no open wounds. His hurts didn't show till morning, but the bedding was so badly soaked with bear blood sleeping in it was impossible. We made a fire between the campsite and the spring and sat up for the rest of the night. By daylight Earl could hardly move. There was scarcely a place on his body that wasn't bruised black and blue.

We couldn't find the deer carcass that morning. Some animal had evidently come in boldly after we retreated to our new site and carried away the carcass of the deer while we sat by the fire. The only tracks we found other than grizzly prints were of a very large cat.

Then we tackled the grizzly carcass. Soto and I had managed to get it off Earl during the night, but we couldn't budge it off our bed. It was cold and stiff now and the legs stuck out like bedposts. We had to saddle two horses and drag the carcass out of camp with lariat ropes.

At noon only three burros came in for water and I thought immediately of the tinkling bells I'd heard during the night. Backtracking the stock, we found what had taken place. As a rule burros don't help each other, as many animals do, but they are terrible fighters when cornered. Ours had fought a pack of wolves. There'd been a lot of blood spilled and the wolves had killed, eaten, or dragged away most of our pack animals. We found one dead wolf and a crippled one that we killed.

While Earl convalesced, we killed another deer and hung it in a tree well out of camp. The next morning it, too, was gone. We trailed and killed the raider this time—a large jaguar.

It was several days before Earl could walk or ride, and in the meantime Soto showed me the country. There were no kills around the spring but within half a mile there we many old kills and some fresh bones. Then he took me southeast nearly a mile from camp to where a steep, narrow trail came up out of the great canyon basin. In some places this trail was so narrow a critter would have had difficulty turning around. If a large animal slipped here it would roll for at least 50 yards. There were bleached bones all over the steep sidehill, as well as some fresh ones. I knew the explanation. We'd had a similar set-up on the west slopes of San Francisco

Peaks, just a few miles north of Flagstaff, Ariz. A grizzly there would ambush cattle on the narrow trail and knock them over a deadly dropoff.

"Do these bears do this in daylight?" I asked Soto. He thought they did, but mostly in the evening or early morning.

The trail was crooked and a little brushy point jutted out less than 50 yards from where most of the killing had been done. There was still another place farther down that was completely hidden from our view. It was getting late now and the trail was in shadow. The upper side was just gloomy enough to hide a bear and the wind was right for us also. I saw trees and brush enough to conceal half a dozen grizzlies. Far down the trail we could see a small herd of cattle slowly working their way up to water. They were so far away, I had my doubts they would reach us while it was still light enough to shoot, but we decided to wait anyway.

Earl, back at camp, had said he was going out with his .30/30 rifle and a .22 to try for a deer and young turkey at the spring. Even now Soto and I heard turkeys somewhere above the trail. I got out my wing-bone call and began making turkey talk. They answered and came down on the trail. When they failed to locate the calling turkey, they went on up the trail where we knew Earl would be waiting. We figured that if the turkeys had been unable to locate us, no bear ever could.

The turkeys had only been gone for a few minutes when Earl's .30/30 rifle sounded in the distance. But that wouldn't alarm either the turkeys or a bear for long. Shooting in a country seldom hunted, where thunder showers are frequent, disturbs game little.

Soto and I had just made cigarettes when we heard a slight sound in the bushes above the trail and saw the scrub oak bushes move. No sooner had we ground out our cigarettes than around the curve came a long-horned, spotted steer and three cows. This wasn't the same bunch we'd seen below. These apparently had been on one of the many invisible curves in the trail, and much nearer us.

Just then the lead steer snorted and sprang forward as a grizzly jumped out of the brush and with one smashing blow broke the second animal down in the hindquarters. The last cow reared on her hind legs, spun around like a top, and ran. The second cow was slower in turning and the bear raised up on his hind legs to land a steak maker.

We both shot at that instant. One bullet took effect in the bear's left shoulder, and his cow-killing blow never landed. The cow completed her turn and ran.

The old grizzly roared and wheeled about, looking for his enemy, but finally lost his balance and rolled down the rocky slope to join the crippled cow below. He was dead when he got to him. We shot the maimed cow.

In the ensuing days we killed seven more bears in the vicinity. Earl still carried bruises from his mauling when we got back to Durango. It was the first and last time he ever picked a fight with a grizzly with only a .45 revolver to defend himself. It's dangerous to dream of bandits when there are grizzlies about.

PART

V

WHO KNOWS THE BROWN BEAR?

The Bear Nobody Knows

Ralph W. Young

August, 1957

Because so few people have studied Alaska brown-bear behavior, the field is full of tall tales and legends. One of the most persistent stories about these animals is that they catch salmon by swatting the fish out of the creeks with their paws. I'd like to see a picture of a bear doing this; in fact I'd be willing to make a wager that no one can show me an unfaked, unretouched photograph of a brown bear tossing a salmon out of a creek with its paws. Of course I may be sticking my neck out making such a wager, for I could never preclude the possibility of a brownie doing something no other bear has done before.

I've been studying Alaska brown bears for more than 25 years. They are highly intelligent beasts. Each is an individual, alike and yet unlike others of its breed. It's impossible and even dangerous to generalize on the behavior of any one of them. A brownie may panic at the sight or scent of a man 100 times, but on the next occasion may boil back in a deadly charge. As a professional hunter who's been in on the kill of hundreds of bears, I'm alive today because I take nothing for granted concerning bear behavior.

At times bears do strange things. One summer I guided a California surgeon on an expedition to Alaska's Admiralty Island to photograph brownies. During the trip, we concealed ourselves in a crude blind facing a stream where salmon were spawning, hoping to get some films of bears fishing. We'd just finished eating lunch when an average-size brownie appeared upstream ambling in our direction, obviously looking for a fish dinner. The bear acted no differently than a thousand other bears I've seen in similar circumstances, until it came abreast of our blind.

Then it did one of the strangest things I've ever seen or heard of an

181

Breaking all the accepted rules for bear behavior, the brownie stood there waiting for me to make the next move. Finally I slipped the safety off my .375, drew a bead on his neck, and started to crowd my way past.

animal doing. Acting as though it knew it was performing before an appreciative audience, it deliberately clutched a very dead and putrid salmon in its paw, stood erect on its hind legs, and meticulously wiped its face and neck with the fish, using it as a man would use a wash rag.

I don't consider the Alaska brown bear a dangerous animal in the sense that a rogue elephant or man-eating tiger is dangerous. Either of these animals will hunt and kill a man without provocation—a thing I've never known a brown bear to do. Of course provocation is a big word, and can mean many different things.

Basically, the brownie is a gentleman. Its chief concern in life is survival or, more simply, getting enough to eat. It has no inclination to roam ferociously through the wilderness, or to seek trouble in the accepted storybook manner. But even the best-behaved bears sometimes kick over the traces, and give the whole ursine family a bad name. The two types of bears most likely to step out of character are immature boars, and sows with cubs.

A young brownie of either sex is usually unstable, but the boar particularly is likely to consider himself a tough guy. He loves to strut and swagger, and has the instincts of a hoodlum. He's also a great bluffer, but you can never be sure when he's bluffing and when he isn't. Whenever I meet one at close range, I treat him with deference and respect, always keeping my rifle at the ready. A touchy situation can develop when a man meets an immature boar on a stretch of salmon creek that the bear considers his exclusive fishing preserve. Frequently the bear will try to drive away the two-legged intruder by running toward him in a manner that suggests a charge. These pseudo attacks often look very realistic, and it takes an experienced bear hunter to tell a real attack from a bluff. He'd better be able to, if he wants to live long.

Two years ago I was guiding a hunter on Baranof Island and we met a young boar brownie that may have been bluffing, but I don't think he was. We were wading up a small creek when we saw a bear standing in midstream eating a salmon. We didn't want him for a trophy, so we continued walking toward him, making plenty of unnecessary racket to scare him away. The bear was obviously displeased at being disturbed, but he left his meal and reluctantly walked up onto the riverbank, where he sat down and watched us intently.

We continued upstream, but when we were within about 100 feet of his original position, the bear jumped down from the bank and took a stand between us and the partially devoured fish. Then he went into an act, gesturing repeatedly with his front paw in a sort of "come-on" motion, reminiscent of Dempsey inviting Tunney to come in and mix it up in their famous Chicago battle. It was a clear and unmistakable challenge to fight.

I told my hunter that unless he wanted to kill this bear and count the small trophy on his license, we'd better forget about calling the bruin's bluff. I was certain that this bear meant business, and my hunter agreed.

The brown bear is born with an instinctive aversion to human scent. It's a deep-rooted, basic fear, and it is the reason, I think, why no member of the species has ever been tamed. Lions, tigers, and leopards tame fairly easily, and are trained to perform complicated stunts in public; but not the

Alaska brown bear. Yet, despite this basic fear, a brownie (especially a young male) will sometimes become indifferent to and even contemptuous of humans. It's a behavior quirk I don't understand.

One summer evening several years ago I was traveling down a bear highway toward the beach where I'd left my skiff, when I saw a small brownie ahead of me, lying in the middle of the trail. This in itself was unusual, for bears aren't supposed to sleep in a trail along which other bears travel. But this one was, and it didn't show any inclination to yield right of way. When I'd advanced to within 50 feet of the boar, I decided to give it a whole snootful of man scent.

I picked up a stick, rubbed it in my sweaty hands and over my clothing, and tossed it at the animal. The brownie got up and sniffed the stick, but instead of bolting for cover he stood in the trail looking at me with complete disinterest. He had me on the spot, for unless I retraced my steps and took a long round-about route back to my skiff, I would have to pass the bear on the narrow trail. Of course I could have killed him, but that's a thing I never do except as a last resort.

Slipping the safety off my .375 and holding the gold bead on the beast's neck, I walked down the trail and crowded past the bear. At the moment I was abreast of him, I could have touched his side with my rifle barrel. He didn't even bristle. When I was safely past and 100 feet down the trail, the bear started following me. He stayed with me all the way to the beach, acting very much like a gigantic dog, half curious, half friendly. That little bear certainly broke all the rules of accepted bear behavior.

A female brown bear with cubs is just as unpredictable as a young boar, and in the face of real or imagined danger, much more explosive. Probably no animal on earth is so devoted to its offspring. A sow will never allow her cubs to be harmed, nor will she desert them, as long as she is alive. I always know that whenever someone captures brownie cubs, the mother had to be killed first.

When a sow sees danger to her young, she will sometimes appear to go completely insane, and anyone present in such a situation had best remain as still and inconspicuous as possible. In such a state, the bear may attack anything that moves, and she may vent her fury on inanimate objects such as trees or logs. In time, even the most violent sow will get herself under control, and lead her cubs to more congenial surroundings. But however the fracas ends, a female brownie defending her cubs must be one of the most dramatic spectacles the wilderness can offer. Snapping her jaws, snorting, occasionally giving full-throated, ominous roars, she's the picture of raw, unbridled savagery.

No one must suppose, however, that this violent behavior is typical of a sow under duress. As often as not, she'll try to avoid a hassle. The point is that nobody knows how a bear will react to danger. I once met a sow with cubs that remained as calm as a Jersey cow in a situation that fairly screamed danger to herself and her offspring.

It happened several years ago after one of my hunters had wounded a trophy-size boar that got away. It's a regular part of my job to follow up such bears, and either kill them or make certain they aren't likely to die a lingering death. Trailing a wounded brown bear, especially when the trail is hot, is always hazardous, and this particular follow-up was really tough. The cover into which the big bear had gone was an almost impenetrable jungle of blueberries, salmonberry vines, and devil's-club, plentifully interspersed with windfalls.

After I'd trailed for perhaps a quarter of a mile, I saw movement in the brush directly ahead of me. Assuming that I'd caught up with the crippled boar, I jumped onto a spruce log to be in a favorable position to shoot in case of a charge. From my elevated position, I saw not one bear but four—a sow and three cubs. The female spotted me instantly, but instead of going into an act she sat down on her broad rump and gazed at me placidly. The cubs ignored me.

With the serious business of a wounded bear to finish off, I had no desire to play guessing games with a family of brownies. The range was no more than 50 feet, so slipping the safety off my Magnum, I aimed at a point just above the sow's head and squeezed the trigger. The bullet struck a spruce tree directly behind the bear, and bits of bark splattered on her fur. The brownie didn't move a muscle. She continued to sit there, completely indifferent to both my presence and the roar of the rifle. I fired again, inches from the bear's head, without disturbing her composure in the least.

I was wondering what to do next when the sow, obviously bored, yawned (she actually yawned), spoke to her cubs, and the four of them departed with unruffled dignity. Even more improbable, the pelage of one of the cubs was blue, like that of a glacier bear.

Another known "fact" about brown bears is that they can't climb trees. Any biologist will tell you that a brown bear's long curved claws, designed for ripping and digging, make climbing impossible. Once the giant of the North approaches the size of an average black bear, it becomes strictly a ground dweller for the remainder of its life. Certainly this aspect of brown-bear behavior is law. Or is it?

One evening in August 1954, Jay Broome of Lubbock, Texas, and I came upon a medium-size brownie eating a dead salmon on the bank of a small Admiralty Island stream. Jay had just set up his movie camera to take some pictures when the bear suddenly panicked. Whether it was our scent, or the near presence of another bear that frightened it, we'll never know. But with an explosive snort, it dropped the fish and crashed into the woods. A moment later we saw it rapidly climbing a tall spruce tree. The bear climbed easily and didn't stop until it reached a stout limb 40 feet above the ground. It stayed there as long as we watched. We have the whole sequence recorded on 16 mm. film. (The movement of the bear climbing the tree is clear on the film, but unfortunately it becomes lost in the heavy foliage in any one still picture. Ed. Note.)

On this same reel, the next day, we took a sequence of pictures. The action of this particular bear was fairly typical of one surprised at close range. The bear was nonchalantly crossing a stream when he suddenly spied us. He looked up in amazement, huffed and snorted a bit, came a few steps closer (in this case he was only about 20 feet away), and then wheeled and raced back across the stream. Less often, if a brownie spies a man, he will circle until he picks up the scent, and then panic or go into a rage. Occasionally a bear will make a false charge to drive the intruder out of the area. I think if a man ran at such a time, the bear would take him.

In all the years I've photographed brown bears, I've never had to kill one, through a few have come so close they splashed water on the camera.

Whenever I look at my many pictures of brown bears, I'm reminded of a bit of wisdom I read somewhere: the only thing predictable about brownies is that they are unpredictable. I agree wholeheartedly.

Do Brown Bears Attack?

Earl J. Fleming

November, 1958

He stood quite still, giving me a long hard look. Strength showed in every square inch of him, and in every move he made. His eight-foot height gave him a decisive advantage over me, and I didn't like the sound of his grinding teeth.

Without a doubt he controlled my immediate destiny. "I'm safe for this second," I remember thinking, "because he can't hurt me without getting closer."

Suddenly the great jaws snapped shut, and without another sound the bear dropped to all fours. He sniffed the air without moving. Still testing the air, he took a few steps straight toward me, then stopped, uncertain, and started edging to his left, walking in a crablike fashion that allowed him to face me at a quartering angle while still moving. After going about 20 feet, he stood up again. I could plainly see his nose wriggling as it searched the air for my scent.

He dropped to all fours again, and moved a few feet farther. Suddenly he stiffened, and his head came up. He gave a tremendous *Whoof!*, and then crashed away noisily into the dense surrounding undergrowth.

Interview No. 1 was over.

I sat down sharply on a grass hummock and started breathing again. My mind was blank. Then questions began to come.

I had just encountered my first Alaska brown bear. Our meeting place was at the head of Port Frederick on Chichagof Island in southeastern Alaska.

To study the big brownies was one of the main reasons I'd come to Alaska—to learn about the big fellows' habits, characteristics, and temperaments.

Had this first one been about to charge me? Was he big for a brown bear? Was it the man smell that had frightened him off?

I got up and pushed into the brush on the bear's trail. I wanted to measure his tracks. He'd gone across a snowbank and through soft mud, and here I found good prints, unmarred by slipping. Measurement of the prints completed all research on bear No. 1 in a project that started more than 12 years ago and is still going on.

My interest in guns, cameras, and wild animals goes back as far as my memory. With animals, this interest seemed to increase in direct ratio to the animal's size and reputation for ferocity. I felt a special interest in the big bears.

In the beginning, my observation of bears was informal and had little more purpose than to satisfy my curiosity and give me the pleasure of seeing, stalking, and photographing them, and occasionally hunting one with rifle for meat or trophy. As time went on, however, and I heard more about the bears and saw more of them in the wilds, I began to notice that much information given and accepted was based on what I considered hearsay.

I started asking many more questions about the bears when talking to old-time Alaskans. I remember particularly a conversation with one.

"Are there many big bears around here." I asked, "and are they as fierce as many people think?"

"There's quite a few," he answered, "and they're pleanty mean."

"If I run onto one in the woods, is he likely to take after me?"

"I'll tell you, son," he answered positively. "One out of every two will come after you."

"You've probably seen lots of 'em," I said.

"No, I don't get out in the woods much. But one of my wife's cousins knew an old guide up in the interior years ago, and he told me a lot about them."

In another discussion I was told, "Any time a bear stands up, look out! He's going to come for you."

"That's been your experience?" I asked.

"I've seen a few of 'em all right," was the answer.

These were typical. I asked the same question of 15 people and got 15 different answers ranging from, "One out of two will charge," to "Leave them alone and they'll leave you alone." I had read that one out of 10 bears seen in the wilds will charge on sight.

At about this time something happened that was as revealing as it was incredible. A party of men had gone to the head of a bay one Sunday to fish for trout at the mouth of a river. When they returned that evening, they were an excited group.

"Boy, did we almost get it!" one of them exclaimed.

"What happened?" asked the nearest man.

"Bear charge ya?" asked another.

"Seventeen shots with a .30/30 it took to kill that brute," said the man who'd done the shooting.

"A big one?"

"About 1,500 or 1,600 pounds, I'd say."

Here, I thought, was an excellent chance to get firsthand information. It's not often that you get all these witnesses to an actual charge.

Later, I saw the rifleman alone and asked him, "Was the bear running toward you when you started shooting?"

"He was standing up, measuring the distance from him to us," he answered. "There was no time to waste."

"Where were you?"

"We were fishing off the high bank on this side. The bear was standing by the big log and grass hump just on the other side."

"Did you hit him 17 times?" I asked.

"Well, you can't miss anything as big as one of them boys."

"Did he have a good hide?"

"I didn't go near him. Can't tell when they might be playing possum."

A few days later I had some time off. In an outboard-powered boat, I went to the head of the bay. I measured the distance from the place where the men had been to where the bear had stood. It was 57 yards.

The bear lay dead—nearly 200 yards from his original position. He apparently had run toward the nearest timber, rather than toward the man with the .30/30. His line of flight was roughly at right angles to the line of shooting.

The carcass was bloated, and the skin drawn tight, making bullet holes easy to see. I examined the body carefully, rolling it over with a short pole. Only two bullets had touched the bear. One had gone through the tip of his nose; the other had broken his neck.

Looking the bear over and comparing him with the many black bears, deer, and other game I had weighed, it was hard to believe he was heavier than 650 pounds.

After that, however, all you had to do was mention bears around the cannery, in neighboring villages, or on fishing boats to hear how a man had to shoot a charging 1,600-pound brownie 17 times with a .30/30 to kill it, and even then had escaped death by a narrow margin.

So far I hadn't learned much about bears, but I'd learned something about men, and I hadn't come to Alaska to study men. If I wanted facts, apparently I had to get them first-hand. That's when I decided to make a scientific project of my study.

The next few days were spent making plans. I wanted the study to be as accurate as possible. So I decided first of all that every measurement must be made with a steel tape. Then I resolved that all facts would be written down, not trusted to memory.

Measurements of tracks, strides, and distance between the bear and me could be made with the tape. Things such as the bear's temper, frame of mind, intentions, and rate of speed couldn't be checked as accurately. But I could try to remain calm enough to make decent estimates.

The main object of the study from now on would be to find out what percentage of bears would *knowingly* charge a human, and under what circumstances.

Throughout the study, the word "charge" would be interpreted in the usual sense: a bear coming toward me to attack me with teeth and claws.

In carrying out this study, I would get as close as possible to each bear, using cover when available. By watching how an animal reacted as I stood up and moved about, I could tell if it saw me. And I'd talk to it so I would be sure it heard me. If I could, I'd circle it so it would get my scent, regardless of wind direction.

Three of a bear's five senses—seeing, hearing, and smelling—should be enough to identify me as a human being. I didn't intend to let it use its senses of feeling and tasting.

Animals that I was certain had seen, heard, and smelled me—all three— would be counted as "interviewed." No bear would be tallied twice if known to be the same animal. Cubs still with their mothers would not be counted either, as they follow the lead of old bears. I wanted to get the reactions of as many different bears as possible. All bears met would be entered in a "general" count.

With these rules in my mind, steel tape and notebook in my pocket, and a high-powered rifle in hand, I started out from my home in Hoonah.

The interview count grew slowly. In only about one out of five cases was I able to carry out all three parts of the experiment.

The next four completed interviews were with medium-size bears. They didn't even growl during their interviews. I discovered one thing of special interest: many bears, upon seeing me, would circle to get my scent. This saved me much time and maneuvering.

Case No. 6 in the general count was interesting and unusual. It involved a situation widely accepted as deadly.

It happened while I was groping through head-high grass in August, a time when hay spiders have their webs strung profusely in the meadows. The place was the mouth of Hawk Inlet on Admiralty Island, a well-known habitat of big brownies.

As I blundered along with an arm across my face for protection from the webs, I unknowingly walked over the brink of a steep cutbank, and plunged eight or nine feet. Tumbling into the tall grass at the bottom, I was startled by a series of hoglike snorts, flashes of flying fur, full-throated whoofs, and sounds of animals galloping away.

Collecting my wits, I climbed as fast as I could back to the top of the bank and looked toward the sounds. Nearly 100 yards away, a large brown bear was running. Now and then I glimpsed two small cubs at her heels. They stopped abruptly, and all three of them stood on their hind legs, looking back at me and apparently wondering what had disturbed them.

After peering for a few seconds, the old bear dropped to all fours. Then, followed by the cubs, she came straight toward me at a full run. Naturally I wondered if this was a charge.

The fur on her neck and back didn't appear to be standing on end, nor were her ears laid back. Her mouth was open, but I felt this was for convenience in breathing rather than from anger. I couldn't imagine a bear charging without anger and I couldn't believe that this animal was angry. But if this wasn't a charge, what was it? "Perhaps the bear is curious," I thought.

Knowing I couldn't outrun her in the tall grass, I quickly planned some tactics in case this developed into an emergency. I drew an imaginary line about 20 yards away, with the idea of trying a shot into the air if the big bear came that close. I didn't want to shoot her, for the cubs would starve without their mother. I could fire a shot at any time, of course, but I wanted to let the animal follow her natural inclinations as far as possible. Suddenly, with no sign of fear or anger, the bear turned to her left, seemed to go through the bank, and ran straight to the heavy timber.

I found a well-worn trail, leading from a nearby river, through the bank, and into the timber. Evidently the bear had come back to the trail because it was the quickest way to the woods. The fact that she had run toward me for some distance was merely coincidental.

The next bear worthy of mention was one I met while working for a salmon cannery. My work was in the Dry Bay area, 50 miles south of Yakutat (see "Alaska Comes to Me," September OUTDOOR LIFE), where most of the canning fish were caught. I had the job of counting salmon that commercial fishermen hauled from nearby streams and dumped into a common bin. From there they were taken directly to the cannery in Yakutat.

I lived in a tent near this fish bin. Besides counting fish, I also kept a canvas over the fish to protect them from the sun and from ravens and seagulls. Sometimes a bear would take a few salmon and chew up others. This was bear country.

Before going to bed each night, I made a final check to be sure the canvas hadn't blown back, exposing the fish. One night I found a two-year-old bear on the fish. He'd pulled the canvas back and was standing on the pile, calmly gorging himself on choice sockeyes.

The bear looked up as I came near, then went on with his supper. I stopped about 60 feet from him, and asked him if he realized he was stealing. He answered with a short growl and a sidewise glance. He seemed to be saying, "Look out, bud, or you'll be next."

I was amused by his show of toughness. He wasn't a big brownie, though he was the size of an average adult black bear. I'd seen him around before. He'd impressed me as a pretty good little bear, seldom molesting things, and willing to step aside to avoid trouble. But things were different now—he'd found food. In the animal kingdom, the biggest finder is the keeper, and I was just a smaller beast trying to chase him away from his food. I couldn't help admiring him when he growled at me.

However, I couldn't allow sentiment to interfere with science. I hurled a few oaths at him and yelled, "Get off those fish and stay off!"

The bear's response was so sudden that for an instant I had the uncanny feeling he understood English. Down from the pile he came, grim determination showing on his face as well as in his actions. He came straight for me, walking with the gait so peculiar to angry bears. From the front, their natural tendency to be pigeon-toed seems exaggerated. Their legs, while slightly bowed, look stiff. Their eyes hold steadily on their adversary. In this pose and frame of mind, they usually look a little bigger than they do at other times.

As he came nearer I spoke sharply to him, much as you might to a misbehaving child. He instantly reared up on his hind legs and stood there eyeing me steadily. I thought I saw a change in his expression as I talked to him in a softer tone. In a few seconds he dropped down and began wriggling his nose and sniffing the air. There was no sign of anger now in his expression.

He took a few steps to one side, sniffed vigorously, took a few more steps, and sniffed again. He continued this until he'd completed about one fourth of a circle. His whoof of surprise when he caught my scent was loud and sudden, but no more so than his actions. He made for the brush at top speed.

Just why will a bear see and hear a person—even at close range—and apparently not recognize him as a human? And why will he suddenly become panic-stricken upon catching the person's scent? I have theories, but they're hard to prove or disprove.

It seems as if the nerves from their ears and eyes don't usually connect to whatever part of the brain it is that gives warnings or causes caution and fear. Only the nerve from the nose seems invariably to have this direct hookup.

The most outstanding example of this peculiarity that I've run into concerned an adult bear I found taking fish from a gill net one night in the East River near Dry Bay.

I saw this bear come out of the brush at dusk and wade along the net toward the splashing fish. Putting on my headlamp and grabbing a shotgun loaded with fine shot, I jumped into a boat and started rowing to the net. I didn't want to kill the bear—just drive him away.

While still about 55 yards from the bear, I stopped rowing and waited for him to turn away so that I wouldn't shoot him in the face. A fish hit the net near shore and the bear turned to go after him. As he did, I shot him in the rear end. At that distance the fine shot doesn't injure a bear, but stings. The bear ran splashing ashore and stopped.

I fired another shot over him. The flash of the gun muzzle was large and bright in the gathering darkness.

The bear milled about uncertainly, walking this way and that. I went ashore just downstream from him, intending to drive him into the brush. When he spotted me, he started walking my way.

I turned on the headlamp and put the beam on him. He reared up on his hind legs and stood looking at me. He was a creature from Mars, standing 7½ feet tall, with coal-red eyes glowing.

Yelling and talking to him seemed to have no effect whatever. Even another shot in the air didn't bother him.

Lowering himself again to the ground, he started calmly wading out along the net. He was going back to his fishing! I stood dumbfounded. What was I to do with an animal like this?

By wetting the back of a hand and holding it up, I found there was a light but steady breeze blowing downstream—from the bear to me.

Walking alongshore behind the bear, I went upstream until I was about 40 feet above him and then started wading out into the river to get directly upwind of him. Watching him closely, I went slowly out. I was beginning to wonder if he had a nose or I had any odor.

Suddenly he threw his head up. Instantly there came the loud whoof so common to a surprised bear. Water splashed in all directions as he raced for shore. And he didn't hesitate there. I could plainly hear brush cracking 150 yards away as he raced from the area.

It didn't figure. How could a bear see and hear me, be shot, see a spotlight, hear the report of a gun and not know that I was a human?

Brown bears wait for their noses.

Of all the bears I've run across in the woods, only one was sick. I feel certain he hadn't been shot, though he may have been injured internally in a fight.

Wading down a salmon river on Kodiak Island, I rounded a bend and was greeted by a constant groaning and growling. It was a bear somewhere in the dense undergrowth on my left.

With the aid of my 7 × 35 Bausch & Lomb binoculars, I finally spotted him. He was standing up, chewing a well-rotted spot on a dead cottonwood trunk leaning at a sharp angle above him. He was unaware of me. As I stood watching him, it occurred to me that here was an excellent chance to measure a bear's natural height when standing on his hind legs.

Taking a firm grasp on my rifle, I started toward the bear. Should the moaning and groaning change to a pitch of anger, I could race back down the hill and into the river. I could even shoot the animal in an emergency, but this I didn't want to do.

As I drew near, the bear backed out of sight in heavy growth. But the groaning kept up steadily, telling me the bear's approximate position and frame of mind. Judging from the sounds, he'd stopped about 35 yards away.

I was thankful for his noise for by it I could keep an "eye" on him while I did my measuring. I worked hastily. The distance from the ground to the chewed spot on the snag was seven feet. From his tracks, I judged him to be about a three-year-old.

In the immediate area of the cottonwood snag were numerous beds where the bear had lain. At the head of each bed was a pile of slimy frothy substance that the bear had vomited.

I had the opportunity of watching this bear, off and on for several days. After a few days during which he moved sluggishly and groaned intermittently, he appeared to be normal again.

In my years of guiding and hunting, I've seen the reactions of a number of injured bears of various sizes. Wounded bears usually try to their last breath to escape. I've walked up to several whose backs had been broken, paralyzing their hind legs, and finished them with a shot through the head from a .44 Special revolver. To the last, they tried to drag themselves away by their forelegs.

Sometimes wounded bears, if unable to run or if followed too closely, will try to defend themselves by attacking their pursuers. Such an incident can create excitement of the highest order, especially if the bear's attack is successful. There have been cases of this, and no doubt the number would be higher were it not for the caution of most hunters and guides.

I know it's considered poor strategy to follow an injured bear into heavy cover, without first giving him time to die or stiffen up from his wounds. But—for experimental reasons—I've often followed as closely as I could. In a few cases I've caught up with the bears before they died. A few, when pressed, have tried to drag themselves toward me or catch me with their forepaws. One bear still sticks sharply in my memory.

Walking along a beach on Admiralty Island once, I was surprised to hear gunfire around a point just ahead. As I rounded the point I saw a fishing boat cruising along a few hundred yards offshore. About 200 yards farther along, I saw fresh bear tracks. At nearly the same instant I noticed a large patch of bear hair, blood, and bits of fatty tissue on the beach. The fishermen had been shooting at a bear on the shore and had hit him.

I followed the tracks and blood trail up over a low bank and into a fairly open patch of alders. I went very slowly, spending more time looking around for the bear than walking. After going about 300 yards in 45 minutes, I spotted the bear lying—apparently dead—a few steps ahead.

I threw sticks at the bear and yelled at him. No response. In these cases, however, caution is always in order. I put the end of my rifle barrel just behind the animal's ribs and shoved.

Suddenly, with a low growl, he swung his head and shoulders around so suddenly that I was caught completely off guard. As I involuntarily jumped back, a dry, sharp snag pierced the foot of my left hip boot, holding it fast. The rest of me continued on over backward. In the fall, my right elbow struck an alder sapling hard; my rifle flew out of the hand and landed crosswise almost under the bear's nose. When I tried to move my right hand I found it was paralyzed.

I lay back as far as I could; my left foot held by the snag about two feet from the bear's mouth. Though the suddenness of all this had startled me, I still noticed that the bear's hindquarters hadn't moved, and his growls sounded weak.

That big brown bear and I lay just looking at one another for what I think must have been seconds, although it seemed longer. I tried cautiously to free my foot, afraid to try too hard for fear of arousing the animal to a final effort. I had no desire to have a foot bitten, even by a half-dead bear. Then the growling stopped and I noticed that the bear's eyes looked dazed and unfocused. Feeling safer now, I gave an energetic tug and the boot came free.

The bear seemed not to notice, and in a few seconds his head dropped to the ground and rolled sideways.

He was an old male, measuring nearly eight feet from the tip of his nose to the tip of his tail. His teeth were worn smooth, and several had been broken badly sometime in the past.

I felt good as I returned to camp that day, even if my right hand and forearm ached and my left boot was useless.

Judging from what I've seen so far, I'd say that if any group of bears belong in a separate category, it's the large, old, males. Their advancing age and the scars of life's battle seem to affect a bear's nature much as they do the natures of humans.

As I continued to study brown bears, friends and others gradually learned of my experiments. I seldom told anyone voluntarily for fear of what they might think. The big brown has such a reputation that anyone intentionally seeking him out just for experimental reasons might be suspected of suicidal tendencies.

As people heard what I was up to, they asked questions. Their remarks were usually caustic, or direly prophetic, such as, "Boy, you're really asking for it!'', ''You tired of living?'' Or ''You've been in the bush too long.'' Advice has been free and plentiful. Some has been helpful.

Several people have told me where they've heard of unusually large, or mean bears. I've been glad to get this information, for these are the bears I like to check on.

Almost invariably, when hearing of my project people will ask if I am not scared of the big bruins. The truth is that in most of my encounters with bears I haven't been afraid, though a few times I've felt some concern.

I've seen a good many skinned carcasses of large brown bears. The firmness and size of their great muscles is mighty impressive. I've often wondered how many horsepower a large brownie could develop. So, as a big bear stands, perhaps 15 feet away, growling ominously and working his powerful jaws, knowing what's under that big fur coat is enough to cause some anxiety in any person interested in his own physical well-being.

My sense of danger is always tempered somewhat by the feel of the highpowered rifle in my hands, by my confidence in the weapon, and in my ability to use it. The rifle, however, may seem to shrink a little if the bear is very close, large and angry.

I don't feel that I'm unusually brave. One of the things I've learned from my 35 years of hunting is that almost everyone is afraid of something.

I was born in the cornstalks of Iowa and grew up with all types of guns. I feel confidence in my ability to use them. Regardless of whether this confidence is fully justified, so long as it's there it gives me courage.

The rifle I use now is powerful enough to lend courage to anyone. The caliber is an improved version of the .375 H. & H. Magnum. The rifle, of my own design, is short, light, and handy, weighing 7¼ pounds and having a 21-inch barrel. It's built on an Enfield action, with my own stock, and has an extralong magazine made by welding parts of two Springfield magazines together to accommodate handloads using long bullets.

Loaded with 85 grains of du Pont No. 4350 powder, or a corresponding charge of No. 4064, behind a 350-grain Barnes bullet, or a 300-grain Hornady, it may not be as powerful as lightning, but it seems to kill big game almost as quickly.

During the 12 years I've been studying bears, I've tried to be free to do nothing but observe them during the part of the year when they're out of hibernation. My bank account hasn't always allowed me this pleasure, but when not completely free, I have still been in the woods in bear country. Sometimes I was working for the U.S. Fish and Wildlife Service as a stream-guard, predator-control or enforcement agent, or making surveys of bears and other animals. Other times I was guiding bear hunters, prospecting, photographing, or fishing commercially in salmon streams—always in areas where the big bears lived. In addition, I've spent the remaining parts of many of these years in the woods, prospecting, trapping, guiding, and taking pictures.

The number of bears in the general count now stands at 402. This is the total I've met. Of these, I've been able to interview 81 at distances ranging from 12 to 100 feet. The 81 heard, saw, and smelled me.

So far I've never had to shoot a bear in self-defense, nor have I been injured by one. Occasionally, though, my heartbeat has increased a bit when the hum of my 16 mm. movie camera or the click of a still camera's shutter has alarmed a bear at close quarters, causing the animal to rear up, huffing and growling.

My count represents bears in nearly every place in Alaska where big browns are found, as well as grizzlies in the Alaska Range. It includes all classes of bears under many circumstances. Large, small, male, and female bears; in daylight, in the dark; while feeding; mothers with cubs; bears sleeping, traveling, fishing. And it includes wounded and dying bears. I also studied a number of glacier bears in the St. Elias Mountains.

This study of brown bears has taught me something about two creatures—bear and man.

First the bears: 1. Bears are basically timid. 2. Most bears are curious. 3. They are individuals in their personality traits. 4. Mother bears feel strongly protective toward their young. This is more pronounced during their first year. 5. Cubs stay with their mothers for two years and get most of their education during their second year with her. 6. Cubs will eventually starve or be killed if their mother is killed during their first year of life. 7. Brown bears live mostly on vegetation, supplemented by salmon in season and carrion when available. 8. Bears do not get fish by slapping them out of the water. They catch their fish in the water with forepaws and mouth. 9. Bears seem to be very nearsighted. 10. Any bear possibly will charge if sufficiently provoked or disturbed.

I believe that most bears accused of charging were not actually charging at all. They may well have been coming toward the accuser (this is especially likely to happen if the intruder is downwind from the bear) either from curiosity or in an effort to escape. A shifting breeze can make it impossible for a bear to tell the exact direction from which a frightening scent comes.

Now some facts about men confronted by bears.

Seldom do they underestimate: 1. Size of bears met. 2. Number of bears seen. 3. Size of tracks. 4. Any danger to themselves.

And now here's what's happened to me since I started carrying my st el tape: 1. Bears stay farther away and make smaller tracks than formerly. 2. Getting some first-hand knowledge of the big bears has increased my interest in them. Familiarity may sometimes breed contempt, but it can also dispel ignorance and false beliefs.

If anyone should ask me to name my idea of hunting at its finest, I know just what I'd pick. To my way of thinking you can't beat selecting a certain brown bear—after first deciding that his coat and size are as good or better than those of other bears seen—and then stalking and outguessing this particular animal. Getting close enough for good pictures can be even more of a challenge.

It would be fitting, I think, if among the last man-made tracks on earth could be found the huge footprints of the great brown bear.

Brown Bears *Do* Attack

Ralph W. Young

August, 1959

A few months ago, there appeared in this magazine a well-written and convincing article about brown bears ("Do Brown Bears Attack?", November, 1958, OUTDOOR LIFE). This article interested me considerably because—like its author, Earl J. Fleming—I live and work in Alaska. Unlike Mr. Fleming, however, I have never "interviewed" many bears, but I have had a few bears make solid attempts to interview me. On the basis of such experiences, I have drawn some conclusions that are very different from Mr. Fleming's.

The one conclusion of his I differ with most of all was summed up in these words: "Any bear possibly will charge if sufficiently provoked or disturbed. [But] I believe that most bears accused of charging were not actually charging at all."

It was the lure of the big brown bears that brought me to Alaska, and it's the bears that have kept me here. I started hunting the bears in tbe Kodiak area in 1932, and I suppose it was inevitable that I would take up guiding hunters as a profession. Since 1946, I've been at it on a full-time basis. I figure I've spent more than 2,000 days in the field with the bears—hunting, photographing, and observing their behavior—and I'm still learning about them.

I've guided more sportsmen than I can remember; the number certainly goes into three figures. Most of my hunters have come from Texas, New York, or Wisconsin, but I've had a smattering from nearly every state east of the Mississippi River, as well as from Oregon, Washington, and California. I've had clients from as far away as Austria, Germany, Switzerland, Italy, and Brazil.

Many of my hunters are world-famous sportsmen. They include men like Jack O'Connor and Warren Page, both winners of the Weatherby Big

Suddenly she swapped ends, and with a series of coughing roars came straight at us. We both raised our rifles and fired.

Game Trophy; Carl Goehringer of New Jersey; A. C. Gilbert of New Haven, and Bob Johnson, the Band-Aid man.

I have guided members of the Explorers Club, The Adventurers Club, the Shikar-Safari Club, and the Camp Fire Club of America. My clients have been corporation presidents, businessmen, teen-age kids, women, salesmen, farmers, doctors, lawyers, and airline pilots. One was a service-station attendant, another a barber, and one a genuine baron.

I'm acquainted with half a dozen sportsmen who, though they have hunted big game all over the world, still consider the Alaska brown bear the most dangerous animal on earth to hunt or photograph. On the other hand, I know just as many men with vast hunting experience who don't rate the brownie so highly. Only last fall, for example, I guided a chap from Wisconsin who referred to the brownie he killed as an "overgrown field mouse." He made this profound observation on the basis of having seen exactly 19 bears on a single hunt.

My own attitude toward the brownie is one of tremendous respect and admiration. I base my opinion on the thousands of brown bears I've seen, and on the several hundred brownie kills I've been in on. I firmly believe that no animal is more dangerous to hunt than these mighty monarchs of the northern wilderness.

To begin with, the Alaska brown bear has tremendous size, strength, and tenacity of life. And though attaining about twice the size of an African lion or a tiger, the brownie is just as quick and agile as either of these beasts. A brownie in full possession of its faculties, and making a determined attack, can cover 100 feet in a bit less than two seconds. This statement sounds fantastic, but it's true.

A charging brownie is one of the most dramatic and chilling spectacles nature has to offer. As often as not, bears start their attacks with no preliminary warning, and invariably at close range. Nor do they charge in the classic storybook manner—erect on their hind legs, paws extended to engulf the hapless victim in an apocryphal bear hug. A bear standing on its hind feet is as harmless as a man doing a handstand. A bear charges on all four feet, in great leaping bounds, very reminiscent of a huge, eager dog chasing a cat. When a brown bear charges, it's a life-and-death matter. Nothing short of death will stop the animal. The bear kills you, or you kill the bear. It's that elemental. On the several occasions I've faced charging brownies, I have never had time to get in more than one hastily aimed shot, and the only thing I've seen in my sights is blurred hair.

The single factor—above all others—that makes the Alaska brownie so dangerous to hunt is the complete unpredictability of its behavior. No one, no matter how much he has hunted, nor how much he thinks he knows about bears, can always correctly predict how any brownie will react to any given situation. Every bear is an individualist. Some are cowardly; some are brave. There are foolish bears and smart bears. Most bears panic at the scent of man; a few are indifferent and even contemptuous of man's close presence. Most unpredictable and volatile of all are females with cubs. During the years, I've seen so many bears do so many things that I take nothing for granted when hunting them. It's one of the reasons my wife is not a widow.

Several years ago one of my dudes shot a brown bear late in the evening at the head of a timbered cove. I sent him down the creek to watch our skiff while I skinned out the trophy. Halfway through the operation I looked up and spotted a small male brownie watching me from the edge of the woods, 100 yards away. Sitting on his broad rump, he was evidently greatly interested in what I was doing. While I worked, I kept close watch on my unwanted visitor.

After completing the job, I had to walk to within 35 yards of the bear to wash my hands and clean the skinning knife. The animal made no move to give ground. Then, with the pelt lashed to my packboard, I moved downstream 200 yards and looked back.

The brownie had walked along behind me, picked up the still-warm carcass in his mouth, and was carrying it back to the woods to eat. The whole area must have reeked with man scent and the smell of death, yet the bear was completely indifferent to all this. I can find nothing in the rule book on bears to cover this behavior.

Do brown bears attack? Of course they do. I'll go so far as to say that a wounded brown bear will almost always attack if it gets the chance and is physically able to. Every year, in the normal course of guiding hunters, I trail several wounded brown bears. It's a disagreeable job, and if I didn't get paid for it I wouldn't do it. There are people who enjoy living dangerously; it just happens I'm not one of them.

Although following up a wounded brownie in thick cover is hazardous, it isn't exactly suicidal provided the tracker knows his business and maintains control of the situation. The tracker has one tremendous advantage—the bear doesn't know it's being followed. So long as the hunter keeps this advantage, the odds are overwhelmingly on his side. If, however, the bear locates the man before the man finds the bear, and if the range is short, it's a toss-up who will come out of the fracas alive.

In any situation, Alaska brown bears are most impressive animals. And meeting one that is thoroughly aroused, in the gloom of a southeastern Alaska rain forest, is an unforgettable experience. The bear always looks twice as large as it really is, and has the nightmarish, malevolent look of some prehistoric creature. Each time I finish the job of trailing down a wounded brown bear I feel weak and limp. Sometimes the reaction is so strong that I vomit. I guess I'm no hero.

Will a brown bear attack without apparent provocation? My answer is an unequivocal "Yes." At least three times I have been charged by brownies that had no provocation except that we happened to be in the same area at the same time. In none of the three cases were we hunting the animals that attacked us.

The first unprovoked attack I experienced was in the summer of 1950. I was guiding Dr. Sterling Bunnell of San Francisco, and we were photographing bears on Admiralty Island. One fine, bright day we set up our camera in a likely looking place alongside a salmon stream, and settled down to wait. In due time a medium-size brownie appeared downstream, too far away to photograph. He picked up a dead salmon, ate it, and, moving downstream, finally disappeared around a bend in the creek. I thought we'd seen the last of him. However, in the usual unpredictable manner of the species, the brownie—unknown to us—turned and traveled in our direction through the thick cover bordering the creek. Next time we saw him he was coming out of the woods directly opposite our blind, and hardly 60 feet away. The doctor swung his camera over to get the picture, and I automatically covered the bear with my .375 Magnum. The brownie saw our movements and although he was only a few feet from cover, chose instead to attack. He covered half the distance between us in two mighty bounds before I dropped him with a shoulder shot.

Maybe the bear was just bluffing—but suppose he wasn't! It's about the same situation as if a hoodlum shoved a .45 into your belly and demanded your money. He might be bluffing, but how can you be sure?

In September 1957, I was guiding Lee Doerr of Cedarburg, Wisconsin, on a brown-bear hunt. Lee had made it very plain that he wanted a large, trophy-size brownie or no bear at all. The first day we went afield we walked up a creek on the southern end of Admiralty Island where salmon were plentiful and bears numerous. Right from the start we began seeing bears—small bears and medium-size bears—but nothing that interested us. The farther upstream we went, the more plentiful were the bears. Finally we came to a mean stretch of water where the creek broke up into many rivulets. Hundreds of salmon were stranded in the shallows, and the area was laced with big trees that had blown down in a recent storm. It was just the sort of place bears love to feed, and precisely where an experienced hunter dreads to meet a brownie. We moved through this jungle with extreme caution, and were nearly in the clear.

Suddenly, to our left, we heard a tremendous splashing, and out of a hidden backwash came three bears—a sow and two cubs. They all ran up the far bank, and the two cubs jumped over a log into the woods. The female made as if to follow them, then suddenly swapped ends.

Uttering a series of coughing roars, she came straight at us from a distance of 100 feet. So unexpected was the attack, and so rapid the action, that I think she might have made it to us if she hadn't been forced to cover part of the distance through three feet of water. Lee and I both hit her fair in the chest, and dropped her at a distance of about 35 feet.

If ever there was an unprovoked attack, this was it. The bear had no broken teeth that might have pained her, she was unwounded, her cubs weren't threatened and the avenue of escape was clear. And for our part, with a limit of one brownie to the license, we had no desire to kill her. Yet we had no choice. This sow meant business. She definitely was not bluffing.

A year later almost to the day, I had another experience with a brown bear—this time a near-fatal one. I was hunting with Jerry Kron of Mount Kisco, New York, a well-known scouter, and a salesman for a Rochester photo-supply company. Again this was on Admiralty Island.

We really shouldn't have been hunting that day. It had been raining hard for 36 hours and all the streams were at flood stage. The creek we were on was so high that we could wade it on only a few of the shallower riffles. So we spent most of our time struggling through the almost impenetrable thickets of devil thorn, blueberry, and alders that line the banks of any Admiralty Island salmon stream. Fish were scarce, and on our slow progress up the creek we never saw a track or fresh bear sign. Finally we decided there was no point going farther, and started across a point of land to strike another stream, which we intended to follow back to tidewater.

In a few minutes we found ourselves in the midst of one of the worst jungles I've ever seen. The brush was higher than our heads, and we actually had to force our way through it. Visibility was practically zero in any direction.

Presently I saw a raven fly up out of the brush ahead, perch in a dead hemlock, and begin croaking dismally. Ravens acting this way often indicate the presence of a bear. I climbed up on a spruce log several feet in diameter to look around. I huffed and snorted trying to get any bear that might be in the area to answer me. Nothing happened. The only sound or movement in that dismal, dripping jungle was the raven still perched in the tree. I checked my rifle to be sure the sights were clear, and jumped down off the log. Jerry was directly behind me. I had taken perhaps six steps when I heard something come crashing through the brush in our direction.

As soon as I saw the brute, I pressed the trigger. That was the luckiest shot of my career. The 270-grain bullet passed through the brownie's neck and lodged in the spine for an instantaneous kill. It died just nine measured feet from where I stood. Jerry said the animal went back two feet after I shot. If so, I killed the bear at a range of about seven feet.

We carefully examined this brownie for signs of old or fresh wounds, but found none. It was a perfectly healthy specimen. The only possible reason it could have had for attacking was that we happened to be in the same patch of brush. Furthermore, it must have charged without knowing what manner of creature it was attacking.

It's always startling to meet a brownie at such close range. Years ago I guided a well-nourished gentleman from a small country in central Europe. All the brownies we saw up to one eventful day were mild-mannered, inoffensive, and small. My client wasn't impressed. He enjoyed relating his experiences hunting such exotic game as wild boars, European brown bears, tigers, leopards, and Indian buffaloes. He made it quite plain that he didn't consider the Alaska brown bear in the same class as any of those horrendous beasts from the other side of the Atlantic. Since my hunting experience has been confined to a very small portion of North America, I didn't presume to debate the point.

One afternoon toward the end of the hunt, after another unsuccessful day afield, we were wading down a salmon stream. We came to a large spruce that had fallen across the creek, and were about to crawl over it when a brownie—a really big one—rose up on the other side of the log directly opposite us. I've never been so close to a live brownie before or since. I believe I could have touched the animal.

Both my client and I had our rifles slung on our backs, and were absolutely at the mercy of the bear. In a crisp, firm voice my companion said, "Attention!" I've never figured out whether he was talking to the bear, to me, or to himself. In any case, it was the most superfluous remark I've ever heard.

The brownie glared at us for what seemed a long while. Suddenly it snapped its jaws, making a sound like a steel trap springing shut. It roared once, leaped up on the creek bank, and disappeared into the jungle.

It took my dude a while to recover from this experience. He was visibly shaken, and had trouble lighting a cigarette. Finally he remarked, "I zink zoom day one of zese bears kill you, no?"

I doubt if there's a professional brown-bear guide in Alaska who has handled as many as 20 hunters who hasn't faced at least one bona fide attack by a brownie. I'm acquainted with four guides, ex-guides rather, who were seriously mauled by brown bears.

Allen Hasselborg told me he'd been charged no less than 12 times during his career. His crippled right arm was a reminder of one encounter that had a near-tragic finale.

Hardy Trefzger had his arm nearly bitten off and was practically scalped by a bear that he'd been photographing. This bear attacked the moment it saw Hardy, and without the least provocation.

Ed Younkey and Lee Ellis were both severely mauled by wounded bears, and both consider themselves fortunate to be alive today.

Then there's the classic case of Frank Barnes. Barnes was a guide, and also the mayor of Wrangell, Alaska. Thus he was a well-known and respected man locally. One fall he took a party of sportsmen up the Stikene River to hunt waterfowl. They left their cabin in the morning and were hiking toward a lake where they hoped for a good day's sport, when one of the party discovered he'd forgotten an essential piece of equipment. Barnes volunteered to go back to the cabin for it. A short while later a single shot was heard from the direction Frank had disappeared. His companions waited a reasonable time, and then went back to investigate.

They found the guide wedged so tightly into the crotch of a tree that he had to be chopped out. He'd been fearfully mauled, and his face had been bitten off and was lying in the trail. Incredibly, Barnes was still alive and rational. He kept repeating, "She got me! She got me!" He died four hours later in spite of the efforts of his friends to get him to a hospital where expert medical care might have saved his life.

Of course no one will ever know exactly what happened that day in the gloomy rain forests of the Stikene River. Undoubtedly, however, this was another authentic case of a brown bear making an unprovoked attack. Frank was carrying only a shotgun at the time, and being an experienced hunter would never have shot at a bear with such a weapon except under extreme duress. Probably he met a sow with cubs, and she charged the moment she saw or smelled him, as they sometimes will.

I hope no one gets the impression that I'm trying to build a case against the bears. The only reason I live in Alaska is that there are brown bears here. I consider them the grandest and most interesting animals on earth. I'm dedicated to their preservation. So long as Alaska brown bears live, there'll be at least one creature in North America that cannot be tagged, branded, taxed, or deprived of life, liberty, and the pursuit of happiness without a fight.

I'll go on guiding bear hunters as long as there are bears and hunters and so long as I'm physically able. I have a premonition that somewhere out on Admiralty, Baranof, or Chicagof Island, there's a brownie—perhaps yet unborn—that has my number on him. Someday we'll meet, and it will be one for the bears. It isn't a thing I worry about.

More Brown Bears

Ralph W. Young

June, 1960

It was about 28 years ago that I made my first brown bear hunt, and it was very nearly my last hunt, too. That I wasn't killed that day was not due to any intelligence, skill, or courage shown by myself. At the time I was living on Afognak Island, which is on the west side of the Gulf of Alaska north of Kodiak Island and separated from it by a narrow channel. During this period of my life I was definitely ill housed, ill clothed, and ill fed. But I didn't know it; I thought I was doing all right.

One night it snowed several inches, and the next morning I left the cabin before daylight, taking a handfull of cartridges from one of several boxes I kept on a shelf. I didn't bother to check the ammunition, and this oversight was the first of many mistakes I made that day. No one but a rank amateur would consider hunting any kind of game, dangerous or otherwise, before making certain the ammunition he carried was the proper kind. The rifle I used was a .300 Savage, hardly the weapon for hunting such a large and powerful animal as the brown bear.

There were few bears out so late in the season, but that afternoon, with the light already beginning to fade, I picked up the track of a fair-size brownie on the edge of a creek. I followed the tracks half a mile upstream and noted several places where the bear had dug dead salmon from the snow and eaten them. Then abruptly the animal had left the creek and gone up a flat-topped hill some 300 feet high. I followed directly in the trail instead of to one side of it as an experienced bear hunter would have. At the summit, where the hill leveled off, I nearly fell into a depression where the bear had bedded down. Fortunately for me, the brownie had moved out of this bed and I could see its tracks leading into a nearby grove of spruce trees.

205

It was twilight in the heavy timber, and I hadn't gone far when I heard the bear. It was snoring, almost exactly like a man.Crouching down and peering under the limbs, I saw a huge dark mound in the snow. Very carefully I moved up closer and soon could make out the form of the bear. It was lying on its side in such a position that the top of its head was broadside to me, offering me a clear shot at the brain. This was going to be too easy. I moved a couple of steps closer and was just resting my rifle over the lower limb of a tree when a frozen twig snapped under my foot, making a noise like a cap pistol. Instantly the bear—completely awake and alert—was on its feet, and all I could see was its legs. I stepped out into the open where I could see the entire animal and also where the bear could see me.

Before I could take a frontal shot, the brownie swapped ends and started running away from me. Then I did an extremely stupid thing—I shot the fleeing bear in the rump. Uttering a blood-chilling roar that was part snarl, the mighty brute turned and faced me, the very picture of primitive savagery. This unexpected turn of events, added to the tension that had built up, was too much for me. I panicked and ran! I ran as I have never run before or since, and I didn't stop running until I was out of those woods and into an open meadow.

I blush now as I think of my actions. But if I blush now it's nothing to how I blushed that day more than a quarter of a century ago. I was completely disgusted with myself and was thankful there had been no one to observe my disgraceful performance. I was so scared that my teeth literally chattered, and my legs felt as if they were made of gelatin.

Fear must be the most basic and natural of the emotions, and I think no one is immune. However, it's not pleasant to experience in aggravated form. When I finally calmed down I did some thinking. Unless I was willing to have my bear-hunting career end the same day it started, I'd have to go back and finish that animal. There was no alternative. I decided to follow the bear until I killed it or it killed me.

I jacked the empty shell from my rifle and was about to put in a fresh cartridge when I noticed that the bullet had a steel jacket. I emptied the magazine and found that every bullet was the type purposely designed to inflict *minimum* tissue damage in an animal. Then I did what I should have done that morning before leaving the cabin; I examined every bullet I carried. Only two were the soft-nose, expanding type that I should have been using in the first place. Loading up with these two cartridges I started back for the woods in the fast-fading light. I never got there.

Just as I was about to enter the timber, the bear came out. Instead of going back into the cover when it saw me, it started running across the meadow toward another patch of timber at the opposite end. My first shot rolled the animal over, but it came up running. The second shot put the bear down again, but this time when it regained its feet it was plainly badly hurt. The bear struggled on another 50 feet and crumpled in the snow. Reloading with hard points, I went over to investigate. The animal was dead. My first bullet (the one I had fired in the woods) had entered four inches to the right of the bear's tail and traveled the length of its body.

When I skinned the bear the following day I recovered this bullet, undamaged, at the base of the skull behind the ear. It had probably produced no more pain or shock in the beast than a hornet sting.

Since that day I have seen thousands of bears under every conceivable circumstance. It goes without saying that in the course of guiding big-game hunters through the years I have come into contact with many bears under highly unfavorable conditions. However, since that occurrence on Afognak Island, I have never met a bear I was particularly afraid of. Nor have I ever taken a backward step from one, unless it was to get into a better shooting position. There isn't a season that I don't have to trail wounded brown bears, frequently in cover so thick that I often hear and even smell them before I see them. I know lots of things I'd rather do than trail a wounded brownie that has even partial possession of its faculties and awesome potential to inflict damage. I consider it an unpardonable crime, however, to permit a wounded animal to escape without making every possible effort to locate the beast and put it out of its misery. Also, in my case, it's part of a job I get paid to do.

It is well established that Alaska brown bears are not gregarious. Once past cub stage these animals are solitary creatures. They don't travel in herds, packs, or even family groups. The interesting exhibits we see mounted in museums of mama bear, papa bear, and baby bear are found only in museums. Even where several bears are congregated in a relatively constricted, choice fishing spot, they tend to remain aloof from each other. It's unthinkable that a mature brownie feeding on a moose carcass would share his find with another bear that happened along.

Although brownies are anything but sociable, I witnessed a sight two years ago that I never expect to see again—six brown bears in one compact group. When I first saw them they were sunning themselves on a grassy point about 150 yards away. They were so close together that I couldn't make out how many bears there actually were. Using my 6 × 42 binoculars, I could see there were two sows and four cubs in an area no larger than an ordinary living room. When they finally saw me and departed, they did so as a group. This occurrence only goes to show how futile it is to make hard and fast rules concerning brown bear behavior.

When actually in the field hunting brownies, it's a good idea to keep your rifle in your hands or at least quickly accessible. These bears have a way of appearing in unlikely places at unexpected times. One fall I was guiding a man who had a very bad habit of leaving his rifle in our stand and wandering around unarmed in the brush. Several times I cautioned him about this, but it was plain that he considered me overly cautious and an old fuddy-duddy as well. There are individuals who prefer to learn things the hard way, and he was one of them.

One day we took a stand by a creek where we hoped a fish-hungry brownie would eventually show itself. Presently my friend became restless and decided to investigate a berry patch across the creek, which was about 100 feet wide. He left his rifle at the stand, of course, and I watched for bears while he picked berries. Suddenly there was a commotion directly behind me. I turned just in time to see a grouse fly out of the brush and light in a nearby hemlock. I watched the bird awhile debating whether to shoot it for the pot and then, deciding not to, turned back toward the creek.

There, right in the middle of the stream, was a brown bear. How it got there or where it came from I'll never know, but there it was, directly in line between me and the dude. I could look over the bear's back into the white, scared face of the hunter who was armed with nothing more lethal than a mouthful of blueberries. Even as I watched, the bear raised its head and began testing the air. In a moment it would get the dreaded man scent and bolt for cover—but in which direction? Luckily, the beast scented my companion first and, with an explosive snort, ran for cover in my direction. I stepped behind a tree, and the bear passed so close to me I could have touched it with my rifle.

I shudder to think what might have happened if the brownie had smelled me first and had run toward my client. A nasty situation might have developed which I couldn't have done much about. I wouldn't have dared shoot for fear of killing the man instead of the bear. I might have found myself in the interior of Baranof Island with the mangled corpse of a person who learned one of the basic rules of hunting dangerous game too late.

Stories relating the skill displayed by native trackers of Africa and India have always intrigued me. If I have read correctly, some of these persons can examine the track of a lion or tiger and determine how much time within minutes has elapsed since the animal passed by, its age, sex, physical deformities, and exact size. I have no skill remotely comparable to this, nor do I know anyone who has. A set of tracks made during dry weather in hard sand or mud simply indicates to me that a bear of an approximate size passed by at some indeterminate time. Frankly, under average conditions I can't tell the difference between a track made 10 minutes previously and one 10 hours old. I have seen tracks made by bears clawing up a hard clay bank that remained fresh looking for weeks. Few men can determine the sex of a medium-size bear even when they see the animal. How anyone can determine sex by tracks is beyond my comprehension.

When hunting brownies, I'm far more interested in sign other than tracks. Fresh bear beds are significant. By even the most casual inspection of droppings you can tell the size of a bear and whether it is feeding on fish, grass, or berries. I'm always happy when I see tapeworms drifting downstream. This is a sure sign that bears upstream are feeding almost exclusively on salmon and have been doing so for some time. But the best sign of all are the remains of partly eaten salmon. Such leavings are a sure indication that at least one bear has been around within the hour, as these scraps are speedily cleaned up by eagles, ravens, and other scavengers.

Along this line I must mention the time I guided a hunter who had traveled thousands of miles to Alaska expressly to kill a brown bear. It was a hard-luck trip right from the start. We were handicapped by foul weather, and, although we worked hard, we couldn't locate any bears. On the final day of the hunt, we went up a salmon stream that flows into the ocean on the east side of Admiralty Island. Although there were very few salmon, there was bear sign galore. Every gravel bar was covered with tracks, and countless well-worn trails led down from the hills to the creek. As we slowly made our way up this creek hour after hour without seeing a bear, I decided that all this sign wasn't as fresh as it appeared and that we had come to the place a few days too late. Finally we gave up and started for home. It looked as if my client wasn't going to get his bear.

We were hardly a quarter of a mile from tidewater and the end of the hunt when, coming around a bend in the creek, we spotted a salmon lying on a gravel bar. Blood oozed from wounds where a bear had bitten it, and it was still alive. The bear must have heard us coming and dropped the fish seconds before we appeared. Moving cautiously, we stepped into the timber bordering the stream. Then I challenged the bear in its own language. It answered immediately, and in a moment we saw it coming toward us. The dude dropped it with a nicely placed chest shot, and all was happiness in camp that night.

Complete lack of sign doesn't always indicate there are no bears in the area. On several occasions I have blundered into highly precarious situations because I ignored rule No. 1 of Alaska brown bear hunting: Take nothing for granted. I remember the fall I was guiding a prominent architect from one of our Eastern states. All one day we had hunted a creek and its tributaries without success. We saw no bears nor any sign of bears. Heading for home late in the afternoon we came to a spruce tree some four feet in diameter lying across the stream. It's a prudent thing to look over these obstructions before going over or around them, but I was so certain there were no bears on this creek I was careless. There was a narrow passage formed by the upended roots of the tree and the bank of the stream. I started to go through this pass and then, for some reason, looked back at my companion. He was standing literally petrified with fear, pointing at something on the other side of the log. I turned back to see what he was looking at just as a sow brownie with two cubs appeared at the end of the tree. Had I taken two more steps I would have walked right into her. Probably that would have been my final act on earth.

I studied brown-bear behavior and hunted them for 25 years before I ever saw a pair perform the breeding act. This must be a rare thing to witness, particularly in the heavy cover of southeastern Alaska. Even Allen Hasselborg, who lived alone on Admiralty Island for 50 years and was probably the greatest brown-bear hunter of the century, told me he had never seen brownies breed. June is the mating season, and at this time males and females are often seen together. Invariably the boars are following or pursuing the sows, but in the actual case of breeding that I observed this process was reversed.

I was hunting with Durland Daron, of Luzerne, Pa. We were watching a likely looking cove one evening when a bear came out of the woods and disappeared around a point at the head of the cove. At the time we had no way of knowing its sex, but it was quite badly rubbed and we didn't shoot it. A short while later another bear, smaller than the first, came moving fast along the trail. My friend and I walked to the point for a look and, although only a couple of minutes had elapsed, the bears had already joined. Several times while we watched, the male cuffed the sow on the side of the head with his right paw. They were still together when we left 10 minutes later.

The longer I study brown bears the more amazed I am at their complete unpredictability. They are highly intelligent animals, and every one is an individualist. There isn't a year that I don't see bears do things that I have never seen one do previously. I have always assumed that mature brownies were never playful, but last fall I saw one adult amusing itself by tossing a sun-dried salmon in the air and catching it in its mouth.

A wounded brown bear, in agony from the results of a poorly placed shot, will attack any fisherman, berry picker, or deer hunter it meets. And when one of these suffering bears attacks a man in Alaska, rare as it is and regardless of the circumstances, the occurrence rates headlines in every newspaper in the state. Many Alaskans don't like brown bears and shoot at every one they see without following up and finishing off any they have wounded. Limits and seasons mean nothing to such persons, nor are they concerned with potential danger they've created.

One confirmed bear killer once asked me, "What are bears good for?"

The easiest way to answer that question is to ask another much more difficult. What are human beings good for? That one has puzzled philosophers ever since the first cave man stopped beating the brains out of one of his fellow men long enough to look up at the sky and wonder about that very thing.

I Take Brown Bears Alive

Earl S. Fleming

July , 1960

My head was pressed against the back door of the long iron trap, and my eyes were glued to the peephole. Before I could make anything out of the semidarkness within, however, three things happened simultaneously. There was a terrific explosion, a great flash of light, and I was stunned by a jarring blow on the head.

Three explanations came to mind as I reeled backward into the brush: lightning had struck the trap and I'd been electrocuted, the trap had exploded, or a cub bear was in the trap and its mother, waiting outside, had charged me.

The time of year and type of storm then in progress were not conducive to lightning, I realized as my brain began to settle, and the 10-foot section of culvert couldn't possibly have exploded. Then came the low, angry growl of a nearby bear, and the most horrible of my thoughts seemed confirmed.

As the mental fog lifted, my right hand eased slowly toward the Smith & Wesson .44 Special on my belt. A feeling of sick disgust crept over me when I realized I had come directly to the closed trap without circling it to make sure no mother bear was lying nearby to avenge a caught cub. It was the first time I had forgotten this precaution.

Suddenly there was a coughing grunt and a rattle of metal from inside the trap. Then the truth dawned on me. A captive bear had struck the inside of the steel plate against which my head had been pressed, and the blow had been transmitted to me.

Live trapping Kodiak bears began in 1957 as one step in a study of the

211

famous brownies initiated several years ago by Will Troyer, manager of the Kodiak Island Refuge. Assisting him were Kim Clark, United States Fish and Wildlife Service biologist on the preserve, Ken Durley, a wildlife management student at the University of Alaska who often spends summers working for the U.S.F. & W.S., and myself. I'm a licensed big-game guide and photographer, but I've worked for the Fish and Wildlife Service before as predator-control agent, on law enforcement, and on Alaskan fish and big-game research. For 13 summers I studied brown bears in an effort to evaluate the many contradictory stories I'd heard about the big bruins, and it was largely due to this experience that I was offered the job of trapping them on Kodiak Island (see ''Do Brown Bears Attack?'' OUTDOOR LIFE, November, 1958).

The object of our study was to gain more knowledge of the giant bears and their ways so that more accurate population counts could be taken, more scientific management could be practiced, and the future welfare of the animals assured. How far, for instance, does an individual bear travel in a day? In a season? How much weight does a cub gain in an average year? Does a bear fish in the streams of more than one watershed?

To get the answers to these and many other questions, we intended to anesthetize our trapped bears, weigh them, measure them, and put numbered tags in their ears. The bears would be recognized by these tags if seen through the scopes used in survey work, and in this way their habits of travel could be studied. Also, a tagged bear might be caught a second time, or shot as a trophy. The records for his eartag numbers would be checked to see how much he'd grown and how far he had traveled.

Our traps, generally, were made of sections of steel culvert about 10 feet long and 3½ feet in diameter. Each end was closed by a steel plate sliding up and down in channels. The channel irons for the back door were only about as high as the trap, but the front ones were about twice that height so the entrance door would remain in them when raised above the trap opening. This plate was held up by a tripping device connected to a trigger by a piece of quarter-inch cable. The trigger, to which the bait was tied, was near the back of the trap. Once the animal took the lure, the door would slide right down behind him and he would be captured alive.

The first trap was placed near the mouth of the Thumb River, which empties into Karluk Lake. It was in the latter part of June, and bear tracks were numerous because the brownies were attracted by the sockeye salmon heading upriver to spawn. We weren't sure of the best material for bait, but, knowing that bears like bacon, we chose it for our first try, putting a two-pound slab on the trigger.

The second question was the adjustment of the trigger pull. How much resistance would a bear tolerate before becoming suspicious? Naturally a bear would not mind tugging at a tasty root or some berries in a natural setting, but this was different. Since a very light pull could be set off by any small creature, we tried for a happy medium.

To minimize human scent we wore gloves when handling bait or setting a trap, and we splashed water on the ground to wash away the odor of our footprints.

Several days after our first attempt, we found the door open and many bear tracks around the trap. It was, however, empty. Judging by the tracks and the hair on the lower edge of the door, a bear had been rubbing against it, moving it back and forth until it fell. We changed it so that in a cocked position the door was entirely above the body of the trap and could not be used as a back scratcher.

Some days later we found the door down again, but again the trap was empty. I reset it and made a careful check. The door was loose in its grooves, and it seemed probable that strong winds had moved it back and forth until the rod that held it had moved, allowing the door to slip down past it. Forcing the door against the back sides of the channels, I fitted small sticks into the space between the door and the forward edges of the grooves. These held the door snug but would not keep it from responding to the trigger when a bear entered the trap to take the bait.

When Ken returned from checking a few days later and announced that we had a bear, it was hard to believe. Loading the boat with the necessary equipment, we started for the trap and our first brownie. It was difficult to settle down to work before each of us had taken a long turn at the peephole.

The scales were tied to a tree limb and the weighing ropes made ready, after which we plugged all but two holes in the trap with bits of rag and laid a piece of canvas over the trap to make it more airtight. Then we began pumping ether into the two holes with ordinary insect sprayers.

The first fumes caused an increase in the pitch and volume of the growling inside. This was followed by frantic clawing and sniffing. Our noses and lungs were filled with the fumes too, as much of the ether seeped from under the canvas. The day was hot, and we were covered with perspiration. We had to either lean away from the ether and be chewed by the bugs, or get in close and suffer the fumes. We alternated and suffered both.

Gradually the growling subsided. After 20 minutes it ceased entirely, but another 15 minutes were needed to knock the animal out completely. By then, we too were noticeably affected. The job had taken 35 minutes and 3½ pints of ether.

Grasping the bear by the front feet, we dragged him bodily from the trap for measuring and weighing. Whenever he started to revive, a pail that we kept on hand half full of ether-soaked cotton was put over his nose. A few breaths of the potent gas would return him to sleep. Caution was in order, however, as an overdose could have killed him. In this, as with all aspects of the project, we had no data to guide us. We found that doses recommended for other creatures of the same weight did not apply to the brownie. We were pioneering a new field and were completely on our own.

The animal was 72 inches long, and his hind feet were 5½ × 10. We took a few other measurements and put a numbered tag in each of his ears. That left only the weighing and painting to do. We were experimenting with putting a patch of red paint on the backs of the bears to make identification easier, but this was soon discontinued because the paint rubbed off or became too dirty to distinguish readily.

Turning our attention from the data book to our patient, we found him with raised head eyeing us groggily. We regained control with the aid of the ether pail. Brownies recover from the effects of this anesthetic surprisingly fast, and they caught us off guard a number of times.

A bear's hide is so loose that you can take a firm grasp on the fur and move your hand six or more inches in any direction. This, and the fact that our animal was unconscious, made handling him extremely difficult. Further trouble was added when he twice regained consciousness. On the fourth attempt, we succeeded in keeping him balanced in the tangle of ropes long enough to weigh him. The pointer of the scales stopped at 360 pounds. Six minutes later the bear was on his feet wobbling about.

We had been busy a hectic 3½ hours. Our clothes reeked of ether and were soaked with bear saliva and sweat. We were tired, hungry, bug-bitten, and nauseated. Still, we scrubbed the inside of the trap and let it air out.

Our weak spots in material and technique had been strongly highlighted by this first operation. A sling was definitely needed for weighing the animals as well as a tripod to hang the scales from. Tree limbs and the trunks of bushes were too springy and never conveniently located.

The following day the trap was left undisturbed to air out while Ken built a tripod of three saplings and I made a sling of quarter-inch rope. Then we reset the trap.

Early the next morning Ken returned from checking the trap and yelled, "Bear number two!"

We knew now that catching live bears was going to be easy after all. It didn't take us long to put the equipment into the boat and get started.

Chinking the airholes was well along when Ken happened to think of the flashlight in the pack.

"Just want to take a quick look at him," he said directing the beam through the inspection hole.

"Hey! This bear's got eartags," he shouted.

How a bear could go through the misery of hot, close confinement, smothering ether and its aftereffects, and come back to the same trap two days later was beyond us. To release the animal, Ken climbed on top of the trap and lifted the door while I stood at one side with a camera and my .375 Magnum. The bruin gave us a brief glance and dashed into the brush. He was the only bear we caught twice.

In an effort to find the best bait, we built a contrivance that held four tasty morsels at one time. Disturbing any one would cause the other three to be yanked out of reach by a pulley arrangement in a tree. If the same kind of bait were chosen a number of times in succession, we'd know it was a good lure.

One night a bear broke the lower part of the set-up, climbed the tree (young brownies can climb trees), and tore down the pulley support. The baits fell to the ground and the bear ate them all, leaving no indication of his preference.

Bears are reputed to like well rotted meat, but we found they would often eat meat at a certain stage of decomposition and refuse to eat more of the same piece later when it had become putrid. We found they especially like beef—fresh or nearly so—ham, bacon, fish, and bags of berries. We also tried dog and cat food, lard, fried bacon, honey, clams, and apples. No doubt brownies will eat any of these when their natural foods are scarce, but they were more particular during this time of plenty.

Many foods we tried were unsatisfactory as bait because they spoiled rapidly and had to be changed too often. Fresh fish, fruit, and uncured meats would mold and rot in two days. Bacon became pretty much the main bait.

The larger bears, as we had expected, were more wary than the younger ones. This was good because we could learn more by tagging younger animals and they were easier to handle. A small bear was not apt to be taken by hunters for some years, giving us a greater number of seasons to compute rate of growth and observe travel patterns.

In the summer of 1958 we put a new trap on the west side of Karluk Lake. This trap was built of three-quarter-inch marine plywood reinforced with strips of steel. It was lighter than the culvert type, easier to set up, and had a more natural appearance. We knew there was some danger of a captive bear chewing out or breaking through it, however, so we decided to check this trap first each morning and watch it closely.

The second morning after setting it up, we had outboard-motor trouble and didn't reach the new trap site until 10 o'clock. Only the door frame showed above the brush. "I think we got him," I said as we approached the trap.

"Well, we had him," said Will when we got close enough to see what had happened.

A hole, 22 inches across and looking as if it had been chewed out by a giant rat, gaped through the top of the trap near the back. The ragged edge of the hole had scraped so much fur from the escaping bear that it resembled a big, fuzzy hoop.

It took us a day and a half to repair the trap, but the bear never returned.

Twice we caught cubs, and in both instances the distressed mothers stood by fretfully for several hours and then, either becoming hungry or abandoning hope, left and did not return. This behavior surprised us. It also caused us some concern until both cubs were later seen in the company of their mothers.

We were also able to observe wanderings and habits of some of the bears around us. One large male was seen fishing during the same day in two streams 10 miles apart. A mother and her first-year cub traveled eight miles from one watershed to another in three hours. Contrasted with these travelers were two pairs of two-year-olds, without their mothers, who spent an entire summer in two brush patches, neither patch more than a mile in diameter. The animals had all the food and water they needed and may have feared meeting larger bears if they roamed elsewhere.

For two weeks a bear had been successfully stealing bait from a trap we'd set on the O'Malley River at the upper end of Karluk Lake, about six miles from our headquarters on Camp Island. He gave me so much trouble, and showed such intelligence, that I dubbed him Geronimo.

Now, for two days after the animal's last visit to the trap, a storm prevented travel on the lake. The third morning dawned dark and rainy, but the wind and waves had calmed some. I was very anxious to see if the genius had been back and to find out if his capers were following a predictable pattern.

Some of our bears had been crafty enough to make their capture a real battle of wits, but this particular animal had far surpassed the others in brain power.

On my last visit I had strung progressively larger pieces of meat on the trap floor from the door to the trigger at the rear. I hoped the increasing lure of successive bigger bits of bait would offset the bear's increasing reluctance as he went further into the trap. In addition to this, I connected the next to last morsel to the trigger by a concealed cord. There had been definite indications that this bear knew the bait on the rod was the one to stay away from. There had also been evidence that the animal would abandon meat, even after having it in his mouth, if it seemed to be fastened to anything. Therefore, I had set the pull very light and had arranged the bait on the loose cord so it would be free to move in all directions.

Going all-out in my efforts to catch this wizard, I had also rigged a board under the grass covering the bottom of the trap. It too was connected to the trigger. A pull on either of two pieces of bait, or a step on the covered board, would close the door. Such a set would easily catch a fox or other small animal, so I wasn't especially excited when I saw the door down.

I gave the side of the trap a kick. Except for the noise I made, the silence was unbroken. Going to the rear of the trap I opened the little swinging door that covered the three-inch inspection hole. Pressing my head against the steel plate, I cupped my hands to my face and against the trap to shut out the light so my eyes would more quickly adjust to the darkness inside.

It was then I got the shattering blow that sent me staggering back into the brush.

Drinking some cold water from the river in front of the trap, and rubbing some on my head, brought me back to normal. I was too thankful to pay much attention to the headache I still had.

More cautious now, I pushed aside the inspection door with a stick. Almost instantly a large nose came out, accompanied by a series of hoglike grunts and long, inquisitive sniffs. Without losing any time, I set up the weighing tripod, hoist, scales, and sling. Then I started chinking the air-holes by pushing in the usual rags and cotton with a stick.

The bear seemed to realize I was trying to cut off his supply of fresh air because, as I was plugging the second opening, the rag disappeared inside the trap. Another attempt ended the same way. I tried a different opening, but to no avail. The bear was unplugging the holes as fast as I filled them. He'd first try his rough tongue, and if that failed he'd pull the stuffing out with the tip of a claw. I was a happy trapper indeed, for now there was no doubt about the identity of my prisoner.

Backing quietly away, I tiptoed to the opposite side of the trap and started work again. I was feeling quite clever in outwitting my captive this way when a sledge-hammer wallop struck the inside of the trap directly under my nose. Surprise and fright catapulted me eight feet into the brush. I was glad no one was watching this job.

After that, the bear kept up with every move I made and took out each piece of stuffing before I could pack it firmly in place. If I was to stay ahead, I would have to hatch some new strategy on the spot. Cutting willow sticks into short lengths I forced these into the holes. Before I could remove my hands the sticks would start wriggling about and moving inward, the sharp edges of the holes peeling the bark back in little curls as the bear's teeth pulled the sticks through. Then I cut some more, but this time I got them larger in diameter than the holes and whittled their ends to a taper. When I drove these into the openings they wriggled a little and then were still. The harder they were pulled, the tighter they became. Feeling very successful, I chinked the rest of the leaks without further trouble, though Geronimo tested each stick carefully. I enjoyed watching the plugs move around, knowing that if everything passed the bear's inspection I had done a good job.

Filling a sprayer with ether, and putting the nozzle to a hole left open for the purpose, I started pumping anesthetic. It wouldn't have surprised me much if the bear had put a paw over the inside of the hole to keep out the fumes. If he had, I think I'd have just opened the trap and released him.

After I'd pumped for 40 minutes—and used 3½ pints of ether—the bear went to sleep. I had five or six minutes to work before the animal would start to revive. Since I was working alone, I had to make sure that all my equipment was ready and my procedures were well planned.

My first task was to raise the iron back door 3½ feet and shove a spike into a hole in the channel to hold it up. Since the door was very heavy, I put the spike in my belt so it would be easy to reach and then started to lift. As the door slid up, the handle brushed against my belt and knocked the spike to the ground. At the same time, the bear's head rolled limply over the threshold.

Standing on one foot, I tried to push the big head back in the trap with the other so I could lower the door and pick up the spike. I couldn't budge the massive head, and the door was too heavy to hold with one hand while I bent over to pick up the spike with the other. It was also too heavy to let down on the animal's head without injuring him. My mind worked frantically, but there was only one solution. I had to remove the door completely by sliding it up and out of the grooves.

I strained until I saw black spots dancing in the air, but the big plate was still a foot below the top of the guides. My eyes burned and my vision blurred from the sweat trickling down my forehead and over my face. Glancing down I hazily saw the bear's eyelids flickering, the first sign of revival. Something had to be done fast, I realized as I gasped for air and felt the starch draining from my knees.

The door was loose in its grooves, and the bulk of its weight was now above the top of the channels. Pushing the top of the door back toward the front of the trap with all the strength I could muster, I hoped to lock the bottom in the grooves. If my idea worked, the heavy top would lean back over the trap and the top of the grooves would act as a fulcrum to force the bottom of the door against the front of the channels. Slowly I relaxed my hold on the handle; the door didn't slip.

I reached around the frame, grasped the edge of the door as far up as I could and pulled back on it to keep the pressure in the channels. Then I eased around the side, climbed on top of the trap, lifted the door from its grooves, and dropped it to the ground.

Quickly I jumped down and grabbed the ether pail. I knew without looking that getting the animal back under anesthetic was the next step. The bear had his head up and was calmly surveying the situation.

Lying on his stomach, his left foreleg outstretched and his right foreleg under his body, he offered no objection as I pushed the pail over his head. His attitude changed, however, with the first breath of ether. Reaching up with his free paw, he hooked his powerful claws over the lower edge of the bucket and sent me and the pail tumbling into the nearby brush with a frantic shove. Prepared now for rougher tactics, I rushed in again and planted my right foot on top of his free paw. Then I jammed the pail over his nose, put my right arm under the bottom of the bucket, locked my left arm around his head, and got set to hang on.

The bear threw his head back violently, but the pail stayed on. Then he rolled and pulled his foot from under my boot. With my left knee supporting my weight, I tried desperately to pin down his foot once more with my own. Again his neck went back, throwing me off balance and cracking the back of my head against the side of the trap. My teeth rattled and lights twinkled, but still we remained together. By now, I was on my back with the animal's head on my chest, and I was struggling to keep my body as tight as I could against Geronimo's throat to prevent his grabbing the pail again. In this horizontal position I had lost all chance of using my feet effectively. Not so the bear. His left front paw was squirming and twisting under me and gradually working back. My clothing seemed to tighten suddenly, and there was a ripping sound as the animal straightened his free leg. But the leg was not drawn back. Then I felt his neck weaken and slowly go limp. A few seconds later he was snoring. Wanting no more of his quick recoveries, I left the pail on his nose a little longer.

The animal was 74 inches long. His hind feet were 10 inches long and his front feet 5½ inches wide. With the crude hoist, I was unable to drag the bear from the trap for weighing, but I estimated him at 450 pounds. "He" turned out to be a female.

I wanted some photographic proof of this venture, so I mounted the camera on its tripod, set the timer, and took pictures of myself and the bear together. The final shot was to show me holding the bear's head in my lap. Unfortunately, I had to change film. I hurried because the animal was recovering, but several minutes were needed before the camera was ready. When it was, I hastily put it on the tripod, focused, set the timer, and turned to get into the picture. The bear, however, was watching me with keen interest and clear eyes.

It was evident that any attempt to put my arm around her neck might result in a picture of the bear with my arm in its mouth. Grasping the tripod just under the camera, I got ready to run the instant the shutter clicked. I knew by the changing expression in the animal's eyes that trouble was near.

Just as the camera clicked, the bear gave a snort and raised her head.

Then, with open mouth and a gargling roar, she lunged at me from the trap. I had a fleeting impression that the trap was a huge cannon barrel with a heavy charge of powder blasting the enraged bear in my direction. She snapped at my arm, leaving saliva on my sleeve and a tooth hole in it. She did not, fortunately, try to hang on, but her nose hit me so hard that I was knocked off balance. Still gripping the camera and tripod in one hand, I jumped up with more agility than I knew I possessed and raced around the trap for the river with the bear snorting at my heels.

I plunged through the water to an island in the middle of the stream where I turned to see if I was still being pursued. The bear, however, had given up the chase at the edge of the river. Bellowing and shaking her head, she danced back and forth over $2,000 worth of my finest camera equipment spread out at the front of the trap.

It was a horrible sight.

Having vented her anger, the bear walked slowly to the stream and, after drinking copious amounts of water, lumbered away into the brush.

A few filters and rolls of film had been somewhat mangled and stomped into the ground, but the more valuable pieces had escaped damage.

I left the trap open to air, gathered up my tools, and headed for the boat and camp. I was hungry and tired. I had a sore bump on my forehead, another on the back of my head, and a throbbing welt across the lower part of my right biceps where the bottom rim of the pail had gouged me. The operation had taken four rough hours. It seemed more like a week since I had eaten breakfast and started up the lake.

We experimented continually with bait and scents, because one of our problems was drawing animals to a trap area. Scent travels farther during clear, moderate weather than it does during heavy rains or when temperatures are below freezing. One day when favorable conditions prevailed, we decided to try something different.

We set a gas stove by a trap and began frying and burning bacon until great clouds of smoke, steam, and aroma drifted up the river valley. We threw skilletfuls of hot grease on the grass and quantities of fried bacon into the trap and around it. Then we hung large pieces of the meat in the brush where the odor would carry better on the breeze. These maneuvers created the biggest amount of the most delicious smells I have ever breathed.

It was no surprise to find the trap closed the following morning. Considering the delightful fragrance that still hung in the air, it would not have amazed us much to have found two or three bears in captivity. We were experimenting with an open grid for the back of the trap at this time, and peering through it we saw a well-fed, very contented fox. Such quick response was encouraging, even if the catch wasn't wanted.

Several foxes and one bear were caught after these bacon fries. One fox was caught twice, given a good switching on his second visit, and seen no more. The trick was very effective for drawing bears to the general area, but it didn't lower their intelligence.

The weather, too, played an important role in our work—most often the role of the villain. Heavy rains would destroy bait scents, or a shifting wind would carry them where they could do no good.

On one occasion ominous clouds rolled in from the southeast just as a heavy salmon run was starting in the Thumb River, which flowed past our first trap. Because of the fish, there were lots of bears around, and we were confident we'd catch one as soon as our scent left the area. However, those clouds brought torrential rains that lasted for three days. When the rain stopped the river was in flood stage, and the bears had left.

A week later the river was back to normal, but by then the salmon run was over and the bears had been drawn into the brush by ripening berries. Effective trapping at that spot was over for the year.

It usually took a fortunate combination of circumstances to catch a bear. First, there had to be animals in the vicinity of the trap. Next, a hungry one had to come by the set, and it helped if he was also trusting or reckless. The bait had to be in perfect condition at that exact time, and the trap had to be open, not already sprung accidentally or by unwanted animals. Mechanical parts of the trap had to function perfectly, and there could be little or no human scent nearby.

Then, if the wind didn't cause a dry bush to scrape against the trap or a stick to drop on it from overhead, or something didn't distract the bear's attention at the crucial second, and his suspicions weren't aroused after he entered the trap or bit into the bait, and he hadn't been previously tagged, then—and not until then—would we have another brownie to work on.

The peak period for bear activity was waning during the second season of trapping when we began to realize that, from an economic standpoint, our methods were impractical. While we had caught five bears, and could certainly catch more, our success was not in proportion to the time and effort involved.

We had tagged bears and gained an insight into their natures and habits that would be valuable in further study. Our project had not been a failure, therefore. It had just been too expensive.

We were aware that domestic and some smaller game animals were being subdued with drug darts shot from compressed air guns (see "Knockout Drops," OUTDOOR LIFE, January, 1960). Will Troyer decided to try this on the brownies. We got a gun that used CO_2 cartridges to propel the dartlike hypodermic needles, and we had on hand some nicotine sulphate.

With this drug, an accurate estimate of an animal's weight is necessary; an overdose can be fatal. We had charts showing exact dosages for different weights of farm animals and some data on black bears, but we had no information on the amount needed for brown bears. Judging the weight of a live brownie in the brush isn't easy anyway, but what data we did have was the basis for a start.

We made two attempts to get the big bruins with the nicotine solution, but both failed. We intended to knock the bears out just long enough to use ether, but in each case, though we brought the animals down, we came so close to being mauled by the rapidly recovering brownies that Troyer stopped the experiment as too dangerous.

We continued the study the following year, and success came with the use of two drugs in combination. One of them was used to drop the animals instantly, and the other, with longer-lasting effects, was administered to keep the bears unconscious for as long as two hours. That year—

1959—we tagged 29 bears, and had hopes that even more would be tagged in 1960.

This tagging project is the boldest and most important step ever taken officially in the study of the brown bear. Much credit is due the United States Fish and Wildlife Service, and due especially to Will Troyer for initiating and continuing this study in spite of limited funds and maddening obstacles. Speaking as a trapper, I can say that trapping the brownie has been the most challenging, most confusing, and most dangerous trapping I've ever done, as well as the most interesting and educational.

PART

VI
TO HUNT A
TROPHY
BEAR

Biggest Bear in The East

Robert Avery
as told to Nick Drahos

May, 1963

Th#his story might be called "How To Shoot A Record Bear Without Really Trying". Certainly, on the morning of December 1, 1962, I had no idea that before night I was going to be responsible for a considerable change in Eastern black-bear statistics. In fact, I wasn't even thinking about bears that day. I was hunting deer. And that's an odd part of it, too, because for the past three years I've been after a certain big bear . . .but I'm getting ahead of my story.

As I say, this Saturday morning began just like any other late fall day in my business, which is running Avery's Hotel in Arietta, New York, and guiding deer hunters that come to stay with us. My grandfather started the business when he and my grandmother homesteaded a chunk of this Adirondack wilderness region back around 1840, and it's been in the family ever since. Today, we own about 3,300 acres of land, and our present hotel can accommodate up to 100 if we use the dormitory we call the Ram Pasture on the third floor.

Arietta is located along Route 10, about halfway between Caroga Lake and Piseco near the southern end of the Adirondack Forest Preserve. It's a summer resort area nowadays and there's some logging in the winter, though not as much as there used to be years back. There's good fishing here for trout, bass, whitefish, and pickerel, and good hunting, too. The country is still just about as wild today as it was in granddad's time. The dense forests and mountains hold plenty of deer, bears, cats, and partridge, but it's the deer that bring most of the hunters into the region. Last year, the kill for Hamilton County was 2,448, second highest of the Adirondack counties. There are a lot of road hunters around here in the early season, but by late November you've got to get back into the woods to get your buck. That's the way I like it.

225

This was the last weekend of the season. Conditions were ideal. There was snow on the ground, and we had 40 men for the day's hunt, every one of them figuring it was his day to tag a buck. Some even hoped to get a bear, but I told 'em there wasn't much chance of that.

Sure, there are bears around, and, in fact, besides the local population, the Conservation Department's Black Bear Research team imported seven of the critters into this area and turned them loose as a part of their life-history studies. This trap-and-transfer plan was designed to get facts on bear migration, homing instinct, reproductive ratios, summer and winter ranges, and a batch of other information which would result in better bear management. But knowing bears are around and seeing them are two different things. I've spent a good many years in the woods and I've only shot one—a 180-pounder a few seasons back.

We hunt deer mostly by driving. This is big, rugged country, 30 miles between roads in places, and driving is about the only way to get deer out of it. On this particular morning, I split up our party into three groups. Dutch Smith, who has guided for me for 22 years, had charge of the 14 drivers; Turkey Smith, another of my guides, led one bunch of 14 standers and I was guiding the remaining dozen. Incidentally, Dutch and Turkey Smith both hail from Fort Plain, New York, but they're not related to each other.

We got into the woods about 7:30 a.m., and headed cross-country for Moose Mountain which lies almost dead center between Benson, Caroga Lake, and Arietta near Canary and Silver lakes. With our red coats and rifles, I guess we must have looked like one of those squads of Tory rangers that used to roam these forests 200 years ago. It was a mild sort of day with a south wind blowing, and that, combined with a noisy crust over three inches of snow, made the going tough. It's a good 3½-mile jaunt from camp to the foot of the mountain, and by the time we arrived there around 9 a.m. everyone had worked up quite a sweat.

We weren't through yet, either, because from this separation point each group had another hour and a half of traveling to get to its appointed station. Dutch was to take his 14 drivers around the back side of Moose another mile and a quarter while Turkey and I set our 26 standers around this side of the mountain. When Dutch was set, he was to work through with his gang and meet me at the foot of Big Ledge, the end point of the drive.

The area is a rugged section of mixed hardwoods and softwood pockets all tangled up with blow-down timber from the 1950 hurricane. It's an unholy mess to travel in, and once the hunt started, it would take the drivers at least 2½ hours to cover the 1¼ miles that separated them from the watchers.

That gave the rest of us plenty of time to get set. Turkey and I began methodically placing our standers at strategic points on knolls, beside runs, and at other spots where we knew they'd have a good chance for a shot at a buck. These men were all experienced hunters, and I knew they'd stay where we put 'em and not go wandering off. The crusty snow made conditions ideal for a drive. I prefer to take men into the woods on noisy days—either crunchy snow or dry leaves—because we can move deer better under these conditions. They're more skittish, and the watchers can hear them better and get more shots.

I had the last of my watchers in position by 10:30, and then I found myself a stand overlooking a jack-straw mess of blow-downs near the top of Moose. I scuffed away the snow down to the leaves so I wouldn't make too much noise if I had to turn around. Then I settled down to wait. Everything was as still as only winter woods can be, but in my mind's eye I could see the line of drivers moving slowly forward, climbing over down trees half-hidden by snow and new sprouts of hardwoods and conifers. And I could see the watchers huddled on their stands, eyes and ears straining into the woods. That big stretch of blow-downs had deer in it, and before too long there was going to be some shooting—sooner than I expected, as it turned out.

I couldn't have been on stand more than 10 minutes when I caught a faint sound of breaking crust deep in the woods. At first, I thought it was Dutch working through to meet me, but after a quick glance at my watch I realized it was too early for him to be coming. He still had about 40 minutes of traveling to do. But whatever it was continued to move closer through the crusty snow, and my fingers tightened instinctively around my rifle as I stared toward the sound.

It must have been all of two minutes before I spotted something black flickering among the blow-downs. At that distance I couldn't make out what it was, but it sure wasn't a deer. I squinted my eyes against the sun and I figured it was either a bear or maybe a fisher. Far off, a fisher looks as black as a bear and, you know, some people even call 'em black pekans. In that heavy cover I couldn't be sure whether I was looking at a whole fisher or part of a black bear. I don't use a scope sight, for you seldom need one in this thick, brushy country, but it would have been handy to have had one now.

Whatever it was, it was in a hurry and making a lot of noise, moving about as fast as it could in that mess. A few more jumps and I made it out to be a bear, but it didn't look too big, about like a yearling, and nothing to get steamed up about. I recalled the boys' remarks that morning about hoping to get a crack at a bear, and I wished the darned cuss had come to somebody else because I honestly didn't know whether I wanted to shoot it or not.

I got scattered glimpses of it through the brush and I still couldn't decide what to do. After all, I'm in the guiding business and I had a bunch of deer hunters to consider. I've had past experiences on hunts when some stander would shoot a bear just before the drivers came up. The shooting and the general commotion turn deer away from the watcher line and the whole drive is wasted.

All this flashed through my mind as the bear kept coming closer, but at the same time I could feel my trigger finger getting itchy. By this time the bear was crossing broadside below me about 90 yards away, and I had to make up my mind in a hurry. Glancing ahead of the bear, I saw a small open space through which he would pass. He did, and right then I made my decision. When he hit that opening, I was going to start blasting.

I had a new Remington .30/06 autoloader and I snicked off the safety and snugged the stock to my shoulder. The bear disappeared momentarily behind a blow-down, and I waited with the muzzle aimed at the edge of the clearing. When it roly-polyed into view again I centered the front bead just back of the shoulder and let drive. I got off four quick shots as fast as I could before the bear lunged across the opening and vanished into the brush. It never once flinched, and I cussed as I lowered the rifle. Even if I hadn't been too anxious to shoot, it rankled me to miss. Not only that, the shooting had turned deer from the watchers. I could hear them stampeding through the crusty snow as the blast of my last shot died away.

I was still standing in my tracks when, suddenly, a blood-curdling bellow shook the air—a deep-voiced roar that vibrated through the blow-downs and sent little prickles up my spine. I knew then that at least one of my shots had done some business. Naturally, my first idea was to go after the bear, and I'd already taken a couple of instinctive steps when another thought made me pause. From the ruckus, I felt sure the bear was hard hit and I didn't think it would go far. If it did keep on going, I was sure, with snow on the ground, that we could pick up its trail. I figured, too, that maybe one of the other standers might get a shot at it if it kept on traveling. The drivers would be along soon now, and I was afraid if I went traipsing after the bear I'd scare more deer from the watchers. So in the end I just stayed put, sweating it out. By now that horrible bawling had stopped and in the silence I could hear the harsh scream of a jay.

It seemed like hours that I stood there waiting, but maybe it was only 30 minutes or so until I heard the first shots of the drive. That was when two drivers, Pres Stewart and Ray Meyers, missed shots at bucks, as I learned later. A few minutes after that, Ronnie Kettler on stand took a crack at another buck and ended up with a wad of hair when his bullet grazed the deer's backbone. About then the drivers hove into sight and we thought the excitement was all over. Instead, it had just begun. Ed Smith was coming toward the spot where the bear had disappeared and I hailed him.

"I think I shot a yearling bear somewhere near you," I told him. "You better be on the watch for him."

It was only seconds later that Ed came upon the bear's track and he let out a yell. "Yearling, hell! This is no yearling's track."

Meanwhile, Dutch Smith had come up and overheard our talk. "That wasn't a yearling, Ed," he agreed. "I saw him when I kicked him out. He was fair size."

All of a sudden, Ed Smith began hollering and throwing his hat in the air. "I guess it ain't no yearling!" he whooped. "He's right here and he's the biggest bear I've ever seen!"

That started a stampede. As I scrambled down the knoll, Sam Claflin sung out, "Bob, you've killed the Son of Kong!".

By the time I got there quite a crowd was milling around the bear and Dutch Smith was kneeling beside it, hunting knife in hand. We've got an agreement, Dutch and I, that he is to clean any game I shoot and I'm to clean any he shoots. So far, I think Dutch has dressed more game than I have, and I'd sure given him a job this time. I stood looking down at that great black bulk in the snow and I couldn't believe it. It was the biggest bear I'd ever seen, and I wondered how I'd thought he was small. Looking at him now I felt that prickly sensation all over again.

"Where did I hit him, Dutch?" I asked, fumbling for a cigarette.

"Near's I can figure," Dutch said, "you almost paunched him with one shot. The other hit about 15 inches back and broke his spine. That's the one that really let him down."

Later, though, he found that the paunch shot had smashed the liver, I figured then maybe I should have led the bear a couple of feet for chest shots, but I wasn't complaining. The 180-grain slugs had done a quick killing job and that's what really mattered. Dutch is handy with a knife, and before long he had the steaming entrails lying in the snow. I thought he had the cleaning job about done, but then he reached into the body cavity and began hauling out pounds and pounds of loose fat that lay against the back and sides. It was creamy, translucent, globular stuff that came out in long ropes and coils.

"Look at this fat!" Dutch said. "Gotta take this stuff out. There's no sense in dragging all that extra weight."

When he finished, there must have been 20 pounds or more on the snow. As it turned out, removing the fat was a mistake, but none of us knew it at the time. We still didn't realize what we had on our hands. I knew we weren't going to try to drag that critter seven miles out to the road, though.

I looked at my watch and I said, "Let's leave him lie. We can't get him out today. We need a team or tractor. If we hurry we've got time for one more drive. We'll get the bear tomorrow."

So we left him there in the woods. We put on another drive, and this time George White knocked down a nice eight-point buck. That night I stood the boys a round of drinks, which is a custom we have at Avery's when someone shoots game. I'd stopped referring to the bear as a yearling, but I still thought he was just a good-size bruin.

The next day, Sunday, I had other hunters to guide so I didn't get a chance to go back after the bear. My 21-year-old son, Lyman, and four other hunters went in to drag the bear about a half a mile to a point where John Burgess could hitch onto it with his tractor. There aren't any roads in to the mountain, so John had to zigzag the tractor 6½ miles through the woods.

It sounded like a good idea but it didn't work. It took Lyman and the other fellows 2½ hours of man-killing pulling and hauling to move that bear 150 yards, and the tractor couldn't get within half a mile of it because of the blow-downs. Night was coming on, and there was nothing to do but leave the bear and take the tractor back out. It cost me $100 to hire the tractor for that trip with nothing to show for it.

The bear lay in the woods that night while I arranged to have Jerry Gessinger from Bleecker go in with his tractor the next morning. It cost me only $50 for that trip because a trail had already been broken in. This time 16 men went along with me to drag the bear the last half a mile through the blow-downs where Jerry was waiting. Working in two shifts of eight men, hauling our gizzards out, it took us two more hours to get to the tractor. It was just like trying to wrestle an enormous sack of jelly through the woods, and by the time we got to the tractor, hacking through brush and skidding the carcass over blow-downs, we were soaked to the skin and puffing. Marcus Putnam, the local conservation officer, went in with us to help.

We shoved two stout poles between the radiator and the blade of the tractor and chained them in place. Gessinger raised the blade, wedging the bear tightly between it and the radiator, and, for good measure, we chained the bear on. Then we started off on the long trip home. It was just past 7 p.m. when we finally got back. It was a good thing the tractor had lights or else we'd have had to leave the bear, tractor and all, another night.

We hung him up on the front porch of the hotel and I stood the boys another round of drinks—which we needed. By now we'd come to realize that this was a pretty big bear, especially those of us who'd helped bring him out of the woods, and the gang began trying to guess his weight. Guesses ran all the way from 400 pounds up to my father's estimate of 510. I thought 500 was closer. I'm pretty good at figuring the weight of deer, but bears are a lot harder to estimate because they're built chunkier and their long fur makes them look heavier than they are.

On Wednesday, five days after I had shot the bear, Bill Hesselton and Steve Brown of the New York Conservation Department's Bear Research Program came up with scales to weigh it and to take various measurements. They both agreed that this bear was probably one of the seven which had been released in the Arietta area. The ears had two parallel slits in them, indicating that ear tags had been torn out. Those tags, incidentlly, would have been worth $25 to me if I could have turned them in to the conservation department.

Well, they measured that bear from the end of his snout to the tip of his tail. Then they measured the tail alone. They measured his head and they measured his paws, both length and width. Actually, these measurements weren't too impressive. The bear's total length was 75 inches, his skull, when cleaned, they estimated would score under 20 points, which is far from a Boone and Crockett record, and his paws, 7¾ × 4¼ inches for the hind foot and 5 × 4¾ for the forefoot, were on the small side. In other words, as big bears go, this one was on the short and blocky side, which is probably why he looked small to me when I first saw him in the woods. He was over 4½ years old, how much over they couldn't say because no one has as yet been able to age bears accurately over 4½ years.

It was when they got to the weight, though, that the roof really fell in on us. That bear tipped the beam at 562 pounds! I did a double-take and could feel my eyes bugging as I looked at the scales. They bugged out more when Bill Hesselton glanced up from some calculations he'd been making.

"Mr. Avery," he said, "you have not only shot the heaviest bear ever killed in New York, but also in the Eastern United States."

I digested this in stunned silence. "That's a lot of territory," I said.

"Right," he agreed. "Up to now Pennsylvania had held the Eastern record with a bear that weighed 633 pounds live weight. That bear dressed out 538 pounds. The largest bear we know of in New York is a 599-pounder we live-trapped and weighed near Tupper Lake in 1957. So far as we know, that one is still running around.

"In comparison, your bear, as it hangs, weighs 562 pounds with heart and lungs. Allowing 102 pounds for the innards minus about eight pounds for the heart and lungs, I figure the critter weighed at least 656 pounds alive. We'll never know just how much it weighed because we don't know how much fat was discarded in the woods or how much shrinkage took place during the five days the bear has been dead. It might have gone 700 pounds."

"Seven hundred pounds!" I echoed. "I didn't know they came that big."

"That's a lot of bear," Bill said, "but back in 1885 an 802½-pounder is supposed to have been killed near Stevens Point, Wisconsin. And in 1921, on the Moqui Reservation in Arizona, a man named Musgrave shot a black bear whose weight was estimated at 900 pounds. We don't know how authentic either of these reports is, but we do know that in 1953 Ed Strobel shot a bear in Land O'Lakes, Wisconsin, that dressed out at 585 pounds, and it's the present-day national record. You might have beaten it if you had left the fat in your bear."

I thought that over. And I thought about that big pile of creamy fat lying in the snow. I was going to go back in and get it, but that night it began to rain and it poured for the next two days. So that ended that, so far as the records go, anyway.

But it didn't end the excitement for by now the story of my big bear had gotten around. They say if you build a better mousetrap the world will beat a path to your door. And if you shoot a better bear, people from miles around will flock to have a look at it. The telephone started ringing day and night and the place was full of people, most of them total strangers, poking at the bear and asking questions. I answered so many questions I about decided to make a tape recording and play it.

As soon as we could we skinned the bear and sent the hide to George Lessor in Johnstown to be mounted. Then it seemed as if everyone wanted a chunk of meat. I was glad to let 'em have it, but I spent two days just carving steaks and roasts. Fast as I'd slice, my wife would wrap and call people up to tell 'em their meat was ready. Some folk wanted a hunk of fat for hair tonic, and one man wanted some for rheumatism. As they say in the stockyards, by the time I got through there was nothing left of that bear but his bellow—and that's something I'll never forget.

Sometimes during those days I almost wished I'd never shot the critter, even if it is an Eastern record. But lately I keep thinking about the big bear I've been after for the past three years—the one I mentioned earlier. I swear his prints are twice as big as my bear's tracks, and it wouldn't surprise me if he'd set a new all-time record. Maybe I'll run into him some fall. If I do, I'll tell you one thing—next time I'll know what to do with the fat.

World's Rarest Trophy?

Howard Shelley

July, 1965

We churned out of the harbor at Prince Rupert on a wet, windy September day aboard Alvin Nystedt's 37-foot Aristocrat I. Dark clouds were scudding overhead, rain was pelting down, storm warnings crackled from the two-way radio, and the fishing boat pitched and rolled in a heavy chop.

Nystedt headed south and we came under the lee of the soaring, mountainous islands that guard British Columbia's half of the Inside Passage. The sailing was smoother, but there was no letup in the wind and rain. The weather that afternoon was only a foretaste of what we'd have for the next 12 days while hunting bears in the dripping rain forests and streamside thickets on the lower slopes of those timber-covered mountains.

We had planned this hunt for almost a year. There were four in the party, Art Hutchings and myself, Nystedt, and a young French-Indian deckhand. I'm 55, a wildlife-adventure movie maker and lecturer from Pontiac, Michigan, associated with the Mort Neff hunting and fishing TV show, Michigan Outdoors, at Detroit. Art is in his early 50's and lives in the nearby town of Rochester. He's the owner of an auto-parts plant in Detroit and manages to take enough time off for hunting and fishing. He and I have been companions in the bush for a long time. We paired up on hunting, fishing, and filming jaunts to Alaska, the Canadian Rockies, Northwest Territories, and quite a few places nearer home.

In the fall of 1963, we decided that our big project a year later would be a bear hunt along the Inside Passage. We both have a high regard for bears of any kind as trophy game, although neither of us had ever killed one. The very word bear has meant adventure and excitement to me as

233

Art Hutchings shot twice and the milk-white black bear let out a bawl, changed ends on the log jam, and lunged for the shore.

far back as I can remember. I had photographed blacks in Michigan and Canada and blacks and browns in Alaska. They stand at the very top of my list as interesting and entertaining actors in any wildlife movie. Art shares my enthusiasm, and we concluded it was time we did some bear hunting with rifles. The Prince Rupert section of British Columbia would afford us a chance for blacks and grizzlies. After making films from the Lake Superior country to Nome, I was also convinced that the islands and channels of the Inside Passage had great possibilities for a wildlife-adventure movie.

We contacted Nystedt, a Prince Rupert guide and outfitter, and several letters and two or three long-distance phone calls later, our arrangements were complete for a two-week hunt in September of 1964.

Although he is only 26, and looks even younger, Alvin Nystedt has been aboard fishing boats since he was knee-high to a duck, and we learned that he enjoys a topnotch rating as guide and skipper. His boat was brand-new and had good cooking facilities and bunk room for six or eight. We'd live aboard and go ashore to hunt.

Art and I really prepared for the trip. We had practiced with our rifles until we were shooting well enough to nail any bear that showed an ear.

We left home on Friday, September 11, drove to Detroit, crossed the border at Windsor, and boarded a Trans-Canada airliner for the flight to Vancouver. We stayed overnight there and flew on to Prince Rupert the next morning. Half an hour after we landed, a blockbuster was dropped into our hunting plans.

Nystedt met us at our hotel and we sat down for a brief get-acquainted coffee session with him and some people from the local chamber of commerce. Out of the blue, one of them turned and said, "Well, understand you're going on a white-bear hunt?"

I looked at Nystedt in astonishment. In the year we had corresponded with him, no mention of white bears had been made. Up to that minute, I had thought that the nearest white bears were drifting around on the polar ice fields 1,500 miles or more to the north.

A hazy recollection went through the back of my mind of stories I had heard or read about a white race of black bears somewhere along the British Columbia Coast, but I knew too little about the subject for it to mean much. We had told Nystedt we wanted a crack at blacks, grizzlies, and maybe a mountain goat, plus some salmon fishing and a chance for me to film the hunting and the matchless scenery of the Inside Passage. That seemed like assignment enough for two weeks.

Now he told us something that brought us up on the edges of our chairs. The white bears were indeed the little-known race or subspecies of black bear known as the Kermode, in all likelihood the rarest trophy-game animal on the North American continent. This beast is found only on a few big islands and a limited coastal area south of Prince Rupert. In the old days, a few skins taken by Indians had found their way into the Hudson's Bay Company fur trade, and in recent years a very few of the animals had been shot under special permits for museum groups. Arthur Popham told the story of one such hunt in "Rare White Black-Bear," in OUTDOOR LIFE, April, 1961. That bear is in the Kansas City, Missouri, Museum. Also, one of the white bears, captured alive with the aid of a hypodermic gun, was in the Stanley Park Zoo at Vancouver, Alvin said.

So far as he knew or we have been able to learn since, the Kermode was a trophy that no sportsman had ever taken under an ordinary hunting license because they had been completely protected since they became known to science 59 years before.

But last April, our outfitter went on, the British Columbia Fish and Game Branch had legalized hunting them on the ground that they were a color phase of black bear, and Jack Fox, the game warden at Prince Rupert, had suggested to Alvin that he take us into the Princess Royal and Gribbell Island country where the white bears are found. "If we have luck, and if someone doesn't beat you to the punch, you could be the first hunters ever allowed to take one on an ordinary hunt," Nystedt finished.

It was an exciting thought, but Art and I didn't let our expectations build up too high. From the little we knew about the situation, a bear as rare as the Kermode, limited in range to 1,000 square miles or so of Pacific Coast rain forest and tide flats, seemed too much to hope for on a two-week hunt. For example, Popham said in his story that a fish-icing plant manager who had lived on Princess Royal for 14 years had seen only one of the white bears in all that time, and it had taken Popham three trips to the area by air, steamer, and boat to get the one he killed. We'd need fantastic luck to take one. All the same, we couldn't get the idea out of our heads, and the white bears were the main topic of conversation as the Aristocrat I ran down the narrow, wind-lashed channels of the Passage that rainy afternoon.

We bought our nonresident licenses and left Prince Rupert right after noon on Saturday, only a few hours after we arrived. The licenses cost $25, plus $5 for a grizzly tag. No tag was needed for black bears.

The Aristocrat I carried a device that I had never seen before—two 30-foot poles mounted like masts on the deck about amidship and close to the rail on either side. Known as stabilizer poles, they were carried vertically in good weather, but during bad weather they could be lowered to a horizontal position and fastened there, standing out from the boat at a 90° angle. With an empty gas drum fastened at the end of each pole, they did a lot to check our rolling.

We anchored that night in a sheltered bay on one of the islands, and in spite of miserable weather the next morning, we went ashore to look for bears.

Every stream emptying into the sea along that coast is a potential hangout for either blacks or grizzlies, since all the creeks and rivers are spawning grounds of one kind or another of Pacific salmon. As long as the salmon runs last, from early summer to fall, bears congregate along the streams and on the tide flats where the fishing is fabulously good. We didn't have to go far in search of bear sign. There were well-used bear paths along the stream at the head of the bay, and three or four times in a walk of half a mile we came on freshly caught salmon, tooth-punctured or partly eaten. But for all the abundance of sign, that island did not pay off. Late that afternoon, we nosed out of the bay and headed south.

There was no letup in the bad weather, but we refused to let it interfere with our hunting. Shortly after noon on Sunday, we felt our way into a cove on a small island, put the skiff and outboard over, and started up the stream that emptied into the cove. Less than a mile above the tide flats the stream became too shallow and fast for the boat, so we landed and continued up the valley on foot.

Bear trails followed the stream through brush and tall grass, and there was much evidence that the bears were catching all the salmon they wanted. We had walked about a quarter of a mile when we rounded a bend below a small waterfall and saw our first bear. He was only a cub, and we must have given him the surprise of his young life. When he turned a corner in a bear path and came face to face with us only a few feet away, he set his brakes, took one startled look, and went into the brush as if he'd seen ghosts.

Two hundred yards farther on, we sat down on a log near the water's edge to look things over. "There are bigger bears than that fishing along here," Alvin told us. "If we give them a little time, maybe one will show."

It was a dark, dreary afternoon, with rain pelting down, not pleasant for hunting and no good at all for camera work. But we were snug enough in our rain gear, and I reminded myself that there was just as much chance of seeing bears in the rain as in sunshine.

I was carrying a pair of 7X binoculars in addition to the Weaver K4 scope on my bolt-action Remington Model 700. I started to glass the stream above us, going over both banks foot by foot. The river came down through a stretch of white water and spilled into a big pool. Thick tangles of brush closed in on both sides, and at the head of the rapids, 200 yards upstream, a logjam extended out from the left bank. A big, dark stump or snag at one end of the jam caught my eye. When I leveled the glasses for a better look, I was staring at the broad rump of a big black bear.

He was sitting astride a huge log, four feet above the water, hunched over, watching for salmon. I decided he was big enough to satisfy me, and passed the glasses first to Alvin and then to Art. It took them a few seconds to make him out.

I couldn't have asked for better conditions for a stalk. The wind was blowing in my face and the rumble and roar of the rapids would cover any noise I might make. I started cautiously upstream among rocks, brush, and rubble with Art and Alvin trailing a few yards behind carrying two movie cameras. In spite of the weather and poor light, I wanted a film of my first bear kill if we could get it.

At a point 75 yards from the bear, I came to a protruding tree branch that afforded a perfect rest for the shot. I brought the rifle up, and then Art tapped me unexpectedly on the shoulder. "That isn't a bear, Howard," he whispered. "That's a snag sticking up from the logjam." What a letdown!

I lowered the rifle and went for my glasses again. After all, rain had blurred my vision and I hadn't seen the bear move. Maybe Art was right. But just as I put the glasses on it, the upturned snag came to life. It was a bear shaking himself like an overgrown black dog to rid his head and shoulders of rainwater.

He was still hunched on his log with his rear toward me. I got the bear in the scope of the .30/06, put the Lee dot on his back between the shoulders, and drove a 180-grain softpoint into him. The Remington boomed like a cannon in that timber-enclosed valley, and before the echoes had died away, the bear was in the river, dead.

He was a good male with a fine, thick pelt, heavy enough so that the three of us had a hard time getting him ashore for skinning. Nystedt guessed his weight at around 325, and from what Art and I knew of bears, that seemed a good estimate. I had taken a trophy every bit as good as I had hoped for, and I was a proud and happy hunter.

I'm aware that along the British Columbia coast and in southeastern Alaska, the black bear is regarded with close to downright contempt, hardly worth hunting and certainly no kill to brag about. But where I come from, he's considered about as exciting a trophy as a hunter can ask to take, and that happens to be my own feeling.

There was still the tantalizing possibility of a white bear to reckon with, and we moved south next morning and headed down the west coast of Princess Royal Island. It was there, Alvin told us, that we'd have the best chance of finding a Kermode.

Princess Royal is some 50 miles long, 10 to 25 wide, and, like the neighboring coastal area, is timbered with dense rain forest. There are tide flats only in the bays and coves, and even there the flats are exposed only at low tide, for when the tide comes in it drowns everything up to the bush. The timber was so thick that in many places we could see only a few yards ahead once we entered it. The forest dripped with the incessant rain and fog, and Art and I agreed that it would be hard to find a tougher place for a hunt. The rare white bear has a lot of natural advantages on his side.

We spent two fruitless days along the Princess Royal coast, cruising Laredo Sound and moving from one secluded bay to another. About noon on Wednesday, we anchored in a small bay in the southwestern part of the island, went ashore in the skiff, and found the usual stream running in.

The river was literally full of salmon fighting their way up through the reaches of fast water. We found fresh bear sign everywhere we looked— trails, beds, and a half-eaten fish, some so fresh that we suspected we had spooked a bear away from his meal.

We worked our way slowly upstream, and half a mile from the place where we had left the skiff we came to a fork in the river, surprised a small black bear fishing, and sent him scampering.

The fork of the stream looked like a good place for bear pictures, so I waited there while Art and Alvin pushed on up the right branch. I could see 100 yards up the left branch, and the pool in front of me was full of spawning salmon. But I realized that even if a bear came down to fish, I'd be under great handicaps. The day was foggy and dark and huge trees intertwined to form a canopy over the 40-foot width of the river.

I got my glasses out and settled down to watch the branch to my left. All of a sudden I thought I saw the forepaws of a bear move behind a screen of brush, as if the animal were standing erect to look for salmon. But there was no further movement and I wrote the bear off as imagination. For the next 20 minutes nothing happened. Then, without warning, a big bear dodged out among the boulders in the river 100 yards upstream, lunged for a salmon, and went out of sight again. I had only a hurried glimpse of him, but that was enough to tell me he was worth going after. I had my bear, so I decided to wait where I was until Art and Alvin came back.

Close to an hour went by before they showed up, and when they did I gave them a quick rundown on what I had seen. "But that was almost an hour ago," I warned. "He may have cleared out."

Nystedt shook his head. "Good chance he's still around. Let's go see."

We started up the left fork of the stream, moving cautiously, with Art in the lead and Alvin backing him. I trailed behind with my camera ready. Within a few yards we broke out of the brush onto a bear trail packed down from constant use. At the first bend in the path, we found a salmon so fresh that blood still oozed where the bear had bitten into it.

There's a tension in a situation of that kind that only a hunter can appreciate. We had the river on one side and brush on the other so thick a bear could have watched us three steps away without our knowing he was there. I've stalked a fair amount of big game in my day, but it never loses its excitement for me. I knew Art well enough to be sure that his blood pressure was as high as mine.

We came to the place where I had seen the bear and stopped at the top of the bank where we could look down into a gorgelike stretch. We stood there for a moment or two, waiting and peering into the thickets, but there was no bear in sight. Before we moved on, Art asked me in a whisper, "Would you trade guns? This damn scope has fogged up again."

He was carrying a .30/06 Winchester Model 70. The scope had given him trouble all during the hunt, and when we exchanged guns, I could see nothing through it.

The afternoon was almost gone and the light, already bad, was beginning to fade. The bear trail continued along the river and we followed it to a big, open pool with a submerged beaver dam at the lower end and a jumble of logs, piled up by flood water, 75 yards upstream. We stopped at the edge of the brush to look things over.

Halfway across the logjam a white bear was clambering toward our side of the river, slowly and surefootedly. Neither Art nor I will ever forget that minute. The bear simply materialized as if he had emerged out of the low-hanging fog. Against the background of green timber and rushing water, he looked unreal, a ghost bear from another world.

The white bear had no connection with the black I had seen earlier. It simply had been our incredible good luck to blunder into the trophy we had dreamed about. As Art said afterward, it wouldn't happen again in two lifetimes.

Not quite believing his own eyes, Art took time to turn to Nystedt and whisper one startled question, "Is it a white bear or a light-colored grizzly?"

"It's white," Alvin barked back. "Shoot!"

Art shot twice, so close together that the reports sounded almost like one. Both shots were on target, behind the shoulder, and the range was only 75 yards, but the bear kept his footing on the logs. He let out a bawl, changed ends as nimbly as a red squirrel, and lunged for the far shore like a white streak. He was out of sight in thick brush before Art could fire again.

"He's down," Art shouted, "he's got to be down."

"He should be," Nystedt agreed. "You hit him fair and square. But we won't be sure until we get over there and take a look."

Getting across the river and taking the look would both be ticklish, especially with darkness coming on, but we were too excited to think about that. Art had killed a white bear or we thought he had, and nothing else mattered at the moment.

We tried the logjam first, but the main log, the one the bear had crossed on, was under a foot of rushing water in midstream and the pool beneath it was six or eight feet deep and icy cold. We went down to the beaver dam and Art inched out, but there was a foot of water pouring over it, too. My partner got a boot wedged between two rocks and nearly fell, gave up, and came back to shore. "The jam is better than that," he grunted.

Walking the submerged log was as difficult as trying to balance on a greased slack wire, but we used long poles to brace ourselves against the rush of the current and finally made it. Then, with all three rifles ready— Alvin was carrying a .30 caliber of English make as a back-up gun—we started our search for the bear. We didn't have far to look. He lay dead in the brush 50 feet from the river.

Art will never kill another trophy like that and I'll never see one killed. Save for his strikingly beautiful color, he was a typical black bear in every way, but color converted him into a magnificent animal unlike anything I had ever expected to see.

He was milk-white on the sides and flanks, but the white was washed with bright orange-yellow around the face and on the shoulders and feet. A broad band of the yellow started between his ears, ran back over the shoulders, and faded out over his rump. So far as we could tell, it was natural color, not stain.

His nose, lips, and the pads of his feet were light gray. There was no black on him anywhere, but his small, beady eyes were dark like those of a normal black bear. Plainly this was no albino, but a member of a race apart. Studying him, we knew why the Indians held the white bear in great reverence, as Alvin had told us earlier.

He was a male, heavy and blocky, with the squarish head of a black bear, and we agreed he'd weigh at least 400 pounds. That was no wild guess begotten of our excitement, either. All three of us had seen plenty of bears and knew something about their weight. We measured and considered carefully before we came up with the figure. And when we got home with the pelt and skull, Al Hilde, the Pontiac taxidermist to whom Art took his trophy for mounting, told us he thought our estimate was very conservative.

It was dark before we finished the skinning. We found later that the pelt and head weighed 86 pounds, but Nystedt rolled them into a bundle and shouldered it, and the hike back to the skiff wasn't bad in spite of the darkness and rain. We had only half a mile to go, and the bear trail that ran beside the river was worn and as easy to follow as a cowpath. If bears were using it that night, they cleared out when they heard us coming.

We fleshed out the skull and paws the next morning, salted the hide and put it on ice in the hold of the boat. Two days later, a well-intentioned but uninformed fisheries patrol officer took a lot of the fun out of our bear hunt when he tracked us down along a stream and told us he had gone aboard our boat and had examined the white bear hide. He bluntly demanded to know who shot it.

We explained the entire episode and showed our licenses and credentials, but he was not satisfied. He did not detain us, but warned us that he would report to the proper authorities by radio that night and told us we could expect to be checked as soon as we got back to Prince Rupert.

It was a thoroughly unpleasant spot to be in and we were extremely ill at ease the rest of the trip. Could there have been some misunderstanding between Fox, the game warden, and Nystedt? Had we mistakenly killed a bear that was still under protection? It seemed impossible, and Alvin was absolutely sure he was right. Nevertheless, it wasn't an enjoyable situation.

Art killed a second bear a few days later, a 200-pound black, but the weather licked us when it came to finding a grizzly. We had 12 straight days of rain, plus wind and fog a fair share of the time. It had rained the day we left Prince Rupert and it was still pelting down when we got back on September 25.

We didn't wait for the warden to come to us. We went to him almost the minute we were ashore, and he eliminated our worries immediately. Sure our white bear was legal, he assured us, and every phase of the hunt had been in accordance with British Columbia game laws. The fisheries patrol officer just wasn't up to date on Kermode bear regulations. To two law-abiding nonresidents, that was a relief.

Certain questions will probably bother many sportsmen who read this story. Did the British Columbia Fish and Game Branch make a mistake when it opened the season on the very rare white bears? Are there enough of them to justify lumping them with black bears and stripping them of the protection they have enjoyed since they first became known to science? What were the reasons for that rather surprising action? Will widespread interest in the Kermodes as rare and beautiful trophies result in hunting pressure heavy enough to endanger the race?

Those questions bothered Art and me, and it was our feeling that they also bothered Jack Fox. Obviously we couldn't answer them, but after OUTDOOR LIFE heard our story it went to the Fish and Game Branch to get the answers.

To begin with, almost nothing is known about the size of the Kermode bear population. Indians with whom we talked estimated it from as low as a few dozen to as high as 200, not large in any case. But those are no more than wild guesses. British Columbia game authorities say that because of the inaccessibility of the area where the bears are found, and the wild, rough terrain, no research has been undertaken and nobody has any reliable information on their numbers. Even the exact boundaries of their range are not known. But everybody acknowledges that pure-white bears such as Art killed are far from numerous. One official told us we might hunt 10 years on Princess Royal without seeing another like it.

Then why take a chance of allowing any hunting of such a rare animal? Dr. James Hatter, director of the Fish and Game Branch, replied to that question this way: "Because we thought the Kermode was a species that could stand a limited harvest under rigid controls." No such controls were imposed, however. Any hunter who had a license could kill a white bear if he got the chance.

It seems evident that the game biologists underestimated the amount of hunting that might result and relied to some extent on the inaccessibility of the area to protect the bears. Also involved in the decision was the fact that the Kermode is regarded by scientists as a color phase of the black bear, not a separate race. One biologist compares them with the cinnamon bear, a brown phase of the black common in the West but rarely or never seen in the East, and also with the blue or glacier bear of coastal Alaska. Dr. Hatter says it is believed that two black bears, carrying the white genes as a hereditary characteristic, could mate and produce a white cub, or that a white bear could mate with a black and produce a black cub. Admittedly, however, there is no known case of a white cub being seen with a black mother or the reverse of this.

In any case, the Fish and Game Branch took a second hard look at the whole situation last winter and decided to return the Kermode to the closed list, at least for the next two years. So, after the present bear season expires on June 30 this year, hunters planning a British Columbia hunt in the hope of taking one are out of luck, and there is reason to doubt that the Kermode season will ever be opened again.

That makes our hunt one that no sportsman will be able to repeat, and means that Art's bear was not only the first of its kind ever taken under an ordinary hunting license but that it also may well be the last. That leaves him with a trophy that in all likelihood is the rarest in the world. Al Hilde made up the pelt as a rug with a full-head mount, and it's every bit as beautiful as it is rare.

Polar Bear The Hard Way

John O. Cartier

June, 1982

Bob Matyas and his Inuit (Eskimo) guide, John Kunayuna, saw the strange object at the same time. Moments before, John had halted their dog team near a massive field of broken and wind-jammed ice. The men knew the object might be a polar bear, but it was 400 yards away and white in a landscape of white snow and ice. Even though it was as motionless as its surroundings, something about it seemed out of place.

While the men were staring, the object took a step. "Polar bear," John grunted. Matyas yanked his slung Model 70, .30/06 Winchester from his shoulder. He sprawled on the ice and found the bear in the rifle's 3X-to-9X Redfield scope. One glance told him that the bear was definitely in the trophy class.

"Don't shoot. Too far," John said.

The bear was walking fast and heading for the tangled mass of ice that Canada's arctic winds had jammed against the shore of an island. Boulders of ice, some as big as houses, were piled up along the shore. Great slabs of ice over five feet thick were crushed and jammed into the bigger chunks. There was no way the men could get their dog team onto the broken ice without unloading hundreds of pounds of gear from the sled so they would be able to lift it.

John's assistant guide, Andy Akoakhion, was close behind the two men with their second team and sled. Both Inuits began unloading, but Matyas had other thoughts. High winds, blizzards, whiteouts and other hazards can make staying alive a hard job. The Inuits are used to it, but hunt conditions are too tough for most white men.

The physical hardships include things that the average hunter never thinks about. The normally simple task of pitching a tent becomes a tough

244

job when you have to pitch it on ice. Arctic tents are anchored with steel spikes and cakes of ice. Supplies and gear are limited when everything, including several hundred pounds of dog food, has to be carried on two 15-foot sleds. Canned goods, toothpaste, liquid soap and so forth freeze solid and have to be thawed.

"Setting up and breaking camp is a great deal of work," Matyas said. "I discovered that if I helped with the chores I could get in more hunting time. I did all the cooking and helped in other ways. Maybe a lot of guys wouldn't consider doing KP when the hunting costs $1,000 a day, but I wanted to be out on the ice every minute."

Optical illusions are part of the game, too. Most outside hunters begin seeing things that aren't there after many hours of staring over the polar landscape. Matyas sometimes developed the feeling that he was traveling uphill or down, even though he knew that the sea ice was flat.

Meals during these hunts usually are a combination of traditional foods such as caribou, arctic char and seal, plus polar bear when a hunt is successful, and some "southern" foods, including steaks, vegetables, bread, bacon and eggs.

Matyas left home March 2 and flew on three commercial flights to Edmonton, Alberta. The next day another jet got him to Yellowknife, NWT. His destination was Holman Island in Amundsen Gulf, north of the Arctic Circle. Then he traveled three days by dog team to the hunt area in Prince Charles Sound. He was less than 200 miles from the North Pole. In these days of quick access to almost any place in the world, it took Matyas six days to reach his hunting area.

After the first day of dog-team travel, the three men met two Eskimos on snowmobiles. It's legal for Inuits to hunt bears or anything else with these machines, but they can't use them when they are guiding a white man. The two Inuits had covered more than 250 miles of sea ice without cutting a single polar bear track. Matyas' heart sank. "I figured that if two native hunters on snowmobiles couldn't even find a track, my odds were about zero," he remarked.

No bear tracks were sighted the next day. That evening, after setting up camp, the men established radio contact with Holman Island.

It snowed most of the next day, and again the men sighted no bear tracks. Late that night Matyas had a horrifying experience. He awoke with an urgent call of nature, crawled out of his sleeping bag and stepped out of the tent.

"I couldn't have been outside much more than a minute," he told me. "I got back in the tent and into my bag just as the shakes came on. They were so violent and so rapid, I couldn't get my breath. Then spasms of very deep and unnatural breathing hit me. For about half an hour, I thought I might be dying. Then I slowly got back to normal. The problem was that our two Coleman stoves only held fuel enough for 1½ hours of burning. When they go out during the night, the temperature inside the tent rapidly goes down until it matches the outside temperature. The two Inuits told me that a man should never go outside at night until he heats the tent and puts on his outside clothing."

The next day, hunting prospects improved. The three men found five sets of polar bear tracks, but none of them had been made by a big bear. Matyas was looking for the tracks of a 10-footer. This traditional measurement is made by stretching a tape measure on the flattened bear skin. The hide is measured from the tips of the claws on one front leg to the tips of the claws on the other. Then the hide is measured from the tip of the nose to the tip of the tail. These two dimensions are added and the total is divided by two. A ten-footer is a very big bear indeed.

On March 10, Matyas and his two guides found a big polar bear track near a pressure crack in the sea ice. They agreed that the bruin was at least a nine-footer, maybe better, so they decided to try for it. They unloaded everything from the sleds except the tent, sleeping bags, short-wave radio and a little food. Speed was important. At this point in a hunt, the tracks are followed as rapidly as possible in an attempt to catch sight of the bear. The hunters stayed on the track for six hours, but had to stop when darkness fell. During the chase, they crossed nine other sets of bear tracks, all smaller than the set they were following.

The next morning they had to give up on the bruin because they were almost out of provisions and dog food. They had no choice except to head back to where they'd left their supplies. By the time they got there, the wind had died to almost nothing and the brilliant sun rode in a faultless blue sky. By noon the hunters were looking for the bear's fresh tracks near the pressure crack, which had been caused by expansion when the water froze. It was about four feet high, 40 feet wide, and ran for miles across the sea ice. Seals, the mainstay in a polar bear's diet, come up through holes along the broken ice. That's why these cracks are good places to look for bear sign.

Early in the afternoon they found tracks belonging to a bear that was even larger than the one they'd tried for the previous day. Though Matyas had seen about 40 sets of tracks during his two hunts, he had never seen any as big as these. His excitement grew with each moment of the 3½ hours they followed the tracks, but then disappointment hit him again.

The tracks led off the flat sea ice and into the tangled mass of shoreline ice I mentioned earlier. The men abandoned their sleds, walked into the obstructions and climbed to the top of a huge ice boulder. There Matyas tried unsuccessfully to spot the bear with his 7×35X Bushnell binoculars. He did pick up the animal's tracks, and it looked as though the bear had traveled toward the end of the mile-long field of broken ice along the shore of the island. The men decided to rush back to the sleds, move forward and look for the bear's tracks there.

They had the two dog teams under way when they spotted the odd object that suddenly took a step, and Matyas entered the broken ice alone.

"I had been stalking for half an hour when I came to an inclined slab of ice about 40 feet high," Matyas told me. "It was very slippery, but I knew I'd have a fine view ahead if I could reach its top. I had to walk in a crouch and almost crawl to get up there, but I made it. Then I had to lean over the top edge to keep from sliding back down.

"I stared for several moments, and then a movement caught my eye. The bear stepped out from behind a huge chunk of ice about 250 yards away. I'd never been in such an awkward shooting position. My caribou parka was jammed up around my shoulders. I tried to find the bear in my scope and keep my balance at the same time."

Matyas finally got the scope's crosswires on the bear's heart area from the side and touched off. He heard the unmistakable *whump* when the 200-grain bullet struck, but the huge polar bear gave no indication that he was hit. He just stopped for a few seconds, then headed back toward the flat sea ice in a slow run.

Matyas fired two more shots, but both slugs hit low and threw up tiny geysers of ice. He rushed back to the sleds and told John what had happened. The Inuit decided to head the dog teams toward the far end of the broken ice while looking for tracks, blood or both.

"We hadn't gone a mile when I suddenly spotted the bear coming out of the broken ice about 500 yards ahead," Matyas told me. "I yelled, 'Polar bear running!' and John stopped the sled. He cut the harness off one of his huskies, said something in Inuit, and pointed toward the bear. That dog took off in a dead run.

"We raced ahead on the sleds. When we closed the distance to 100 yards of the bear-dog fight, I got off the sled and raised my rifle. All I could see through the scope was a tangle of polar bear and husky dog. I walked closer, and it now became obvious that my first bullet had seriously wounded the bruin. He was still fighting the dog, but he was slowing down. As soon as I got a clear shot, I aimed for his heart and fired. The bear dropped and never moved again."

The hide of Matyas' bear measured 10 feet 7 inches by 10 feet 5 inches, and squared out at 10 feet 6 inches. Matyas' outfitter estimated that the bear weighed at least 1,000 pounds. It was by far the largest ever taken by a sport hunter since modern sport hunting began in the area in 1976.

As this issue goes to press, it could not be determined if the trophy was good enough to make the Boone and Crockett record book. The U.S. Marine Mammals Act of 1972 prohibits the importation of polar bear hides and all other marine mammal parts. Matyas' bear hide is at a taxidermist's shop in Ottawa where it is being prepared for a full life-size mount. There is considerable pressure to repeal the Marine Mammals Act, but if that doesn't happen, Matyas intends to lend the mounted bear to a Canadian bank where it will be put on display.

If the skull is ever officially scored by Boone and Crockett Club measurers, and if it is good enough to make the club's record book, Matyas will have done something no other hunter has ever accomplished. Every polar bear listed in the record book was downed in Alaska. A bear from NWT has never made the grade.

Matyas doesn't need accolades, but his bear hunting is very unusual in another way. All of the 11 bears he has taken (including a giant black downed last October in Montana) have been males. Though a female bruin sometimes reaches exceptional size, the males are normally much larger. It's plain that Matyas is a real trophy hunter and never settles for less than the best.

High-Climb Kodiaks

Dick Powell

February, 1970

He won't break any records, Dick, but he's a hell of a lot of bear!" So said George, our skipper, as we watched the huge Kodiak bear moseying peacefully along the high, rugged, snow-covered mountains overlooking Uganik Bay north of Kodiak Island.

"That's the same bear we chased across the mountain Wednesday or I'll eat these binoculars, case and all!" I replied. Lou and Jack quickly agreed, but events that followed proved us wrong. But let's go back to the beginning of this hunt.

Our hunt had started on April 27, a day we'd been awaiting for many long, cold months. We'd done a lot of planning and had met our share of disappointments during that record-breaking cold Alaskan winter of 1956. But now everything had worked out beautifully.

Four of us were Navy men stationed at Kodiak Island: Lou Wagner is a native of Grand Rapids, Michigan; Si Simoens hails from upstate New York; Ski Baczkiewicz comes from Pennsylvania; I'm a native of Spokane, Washington, and now live in Garden Grove, California, where I retired. Our fifth hunter was Jack Flanders, who hailed from Florida. He was then a civilian employee of the Navy.

Lou and I had been able to squeeze in a last hunt for the big bruins. I had already received orders from Washington to leave Kodiak for other duty, and I'd had a hectic race against time and the weather before I could make this trip. Now the only thing that might upset our plans was the weather—the unpredictable, changeable Alaskan weather! Particularly during spring.

During the past few months I had talked to practically everyone on Kodiak Island in my efforts to charter a boat for this hunt. I had made a previous hunt by flying in, then hunting out of a base camp on foot, and

248

it left a lot to be desired (see "Too Many Bears," OUTDOOR LIFE, February 1957). Besides, Jack and I wanted to hunt for 10-foot or larger bears this trip, and much more territory can be covered by boat, cruising through the bays and inlets and glassing the mountains, than by any other method.

My search for a suitable boat had been very discouraging until about a week before the hunt when Byrl Clymer, a Kodiak businessman, offered to charter us his Guy Junior, a 65-foot twin-engine diesel. Lou and I looked the boat over. She was ideal: berths for nine, a good galley, excellent facilities, and more important, a good dory and outboard motor. We chartered her on the spot.

Lou's time in Alaska was rapidly coming to an end, and he hadn't collected a bear. Si and Ski, both young fellows who loved to hunt, had dreamed for months of nailing a Kodiak. Jack had come to Alaska from Florida several years before to hunt and fish and had done little else since.

Only he and I had previously hunted the big bears, but Lou, Si, and Ski had a great deal of hunting experience, were better than average shots, and were in fine physical condition. Being in shape is a prerequisite for hunting these huge bears, particularly in the spring when they are just coming out of hibernation and are in the high country.

Our clan had agreed to gather at Jake Foley's Unique Bar and Grill at midnight and to get under way at 2 a.m., weather permitting. This departure would get us through the shallow waters of Whale Passage on high tide during daylight hours.

Everyone arrived at Jake's on time, each carrying his own carefully sighted-in rifle, for a last drink before leaving civilization. Our boat crew, already on the scene, was doing an excellent job of holding down three stools at the bar. George Christoffersen was the skipper; Lawreance Panamaroff, the engineer; and Rudy, the mate, cook, and morale-builder par excellence. The crew were all natives of Kodiak or the immediate vicinity and had sailed these waters all their lives.

After we had met the crew we made our plans. In months of talking to experienced hunters, guides, and game officials, I had concluded that for our type of hunt and for a chance at some really big bears, Uganik Bay would probably be the best bet. George agreed, and we finally got on board and under way about 3 a.m.

We passed an uneventful first day eating, sleeping, and admiring the beautiful and rugged Alaskan scenery. During the day we navigated Whale Passage and Kupreanof Straits, past Raspberry Island into Viekoda Bay and Terror Bay.

During the afternoon we shot our rifles at rocks and driftwood to check our sights. Lou, Si, and Ski were armed with Model 70 Winchesters, 30/06 variety, and were using factory-loaded 180 and 220-grain cartridges. Jack was carrying my old .375 H. & H. that weighed just over seven pounds with its 19-inch barrel, custom stock, and scope, and he was shooting 285-grain Speer bullets pushed along by 82 grains of 4831. I had my pet .300 Weatherby with 78 grains of 4350 behind 180-grain Sierra bullets.

At about 6 p.m. we rounded the headland out of Uganik Passage and headed into Uganik Bay, where we tied up at the San Juan cannery dock in the East Arm.

On the way down the bay we had passed close by Sally Island. I'd seen what I thought was a bear, but it had disappeared before anyone else noticed. All hands said I was seeing things, but by 4 a.m. Sunday, bear fever was running high and everyone was seeing king-size bruins behind every rock. We took the dory and outboard and ran up to the head of the arm. The early-morning air was cold and penetrating, with lots of wind and spray. We went ashore where a small stream empties into the bay. Lou and I took the east bank while Jack, Si, and Ski scouted the west side. We all went back over several ridges and glassed a lot of country but saw no bears or fresh sign. At about 8 we returned to the dory.

On our way back down the bay in the dory, about midway between the stream we had just left and the cannery, I glanced up the mountain and saw a big bear stand and stretch on an overhanging ledge. I yelled at George to stop the motor.

While we lay watching, two other bears ambled out to the edge of the ledge and seemed to stand there staring down on us from their 3,000-foot perch in the snow. After watching them a few minutes, I could see that it was a big sow with two well-grown younger bears.

Ski and Si said that if those were young bears, they would be all they wanted, thanks! Lou was watching the old sow so intently that I didn't bother to ask him if he was interested. Jack and I weren't interested in any bear hide that would square under 10 feet, so we decided to go along as back-up guns for Lou.

For the stalk, we planned to follow a ridge to our left up to about the 3,200-foot level, then cut over to the right, putting the bears below us. George put us ashore at the mouth of a small creek, and the work began.

Below the snowline, an almost solid stand of alders made the steep climb slow and difficult. It took us almost four hours to reach a point where I thought we should cut to our right. By now the snow was very deep and we were sinking up to our crotches.

Though I didn't know it then, I had missed my turning point. We were actually above the bears, and they were hidden from our view by a small knoll.

I was in the lead, with Lou perhaps 10 yards behind me, when he put his glasses on the dory and saw George waving frantically at us. Lou yelled at me, and as I turned to see what he wanted I saw the bears.

They had left their ledge and were climbing the mountain behind and below us on a course crossing the one we had taken coming up. They were about 300 yards away and moving fast.

I shouted to Lou, Ski, and Si to sit down and start shooting. While I watched through my glasses, I saw the sow go down just as she topped the ridge. She was back on her feet in an instant and ran straight down the mountain, where she disappeared into a patch of heavy alders. Then I saw one of the smaller bears flip and the other one disappear over the top of the ridge.

Lou, Jack, and I trailed the sow, while Si and Ski took out after the two others. There was a huge amount of blood where the sow had gone down, so we knew that she had been hit hard and probably in the lungs. We sat down for a smoke to give her a chance to lie down and stiffen up or die.

If you have never hunted in Alaska's alders, they require a brief explanation. They grow profusely in the low country and on the mountainsides up to snowline. They're eight to 12 feet high and grow so closely interlaced and entwined that it's almost impossible to get through them in places. The visibility in an alder patch is almost nil. I have followed trails worn through alders by the bears over a period of many years and I've actually had to crawl on my hands and knees. Alders make an excellent place for a wounded bear to surprise the unwary hunter.

In Alaska, as anywhere else, you just don't leave a wounded bear. So after a short rest we cautiously entered the alders. I was leading, so I changed guns with Jack, wanting the .375.

We had been in the alders for only about 10 minutes when I saw her.

She was lying by a small creek. After watching her intently for a few minutes for signs of life, we cautiously approached. Finally one of us poked her with his gun barrel while the other two covered. She was dead.

Lou's 180-grain slug had entered behind the right shoulder, ranging through the heart and lung area and exiting in front of the left shoulder without hitting any bones, a fine bit of shooting at 300 yards. She was a beauty with long, thick light-colored fur without a single rubbed spot.

But, the work was just beginnng. We were still above the 3,000-foot mark, and she had to be carefully skinned out and her hide packed to the bay.

We discovered there was a thick ice bridge over the creek that would support the weight of the bear. So, we thought, if we could roll her onto the bridge, we could slide her to the foot of the mountain.

We hadn't considered that the lower we got, the thinner the ice would get. So when we arrived at about the 1,500-foot level the ice broke with a crash and we had one big brown bruin in the creek under the ice.

How could we pull her from under the ice and up about four feet through the hole onto the bank?

All of us climbed down into the icy water, and we succeeded in getting her front legs and head up onto the bank. With the bear in a sitting position in the creek, Lou got out on the bank. While he pulled, Jack and I got under the bear's rear, pushing and lifting. After a long, hard struggle we finally wrestled her out onto the bank.

It was almost 3 p.m., a long time since breakfast, so we headed down the mountain, very tired but happy hunters. We'd leave the skinning chore until next morning.

Meanwhile, Si and Ski had anchored the two other bears. Si had returned to the boat, but Ski had encountered a little trouble. He had caught up with the second bear and shot it. But in the process of turning the carcass over to inspect the hide, his quarry had rolled over a cliff into a stream. He'd searched up and down the creek for a couple of hours but couldn't find it. After deciding that it had washed down under the ice, he'd gone to the boat for help.

The next morning, Lawreance accompanied Si and Ski to give them a hand skinning and to help Ski locate his bear. Lou, Jack, and I went up to skin out Lou's bear and take some pictures.

Jonas Brothers in Seattle later told me Lou's bear was one of the best they had ever mounted. We spread the hide on the cannery dock. The steel tape indicated that the pelt squared eight feet two inches—a respectable bear in anyone's book.

Si and Lawreance returned to the boat shortly after noon with Si's bear hide; then they ate and went back up the mountain to find Ski.

George, Jack, Si, and I took the dory out into the bay where we could get a good view of the mountainside. We searched with our glasses and after about 45 minutes saw Ski in a small creek about 2,000 feet up. He had found his bear and was trying to drag it out of the water single-handed.

We put Si ashore to go up and help while we stayed in the bay signaling directions to him. We had planned to take the boat out and hunt the west shore during the afternoon, but the rain began, and the wind increased until we had to give it up.

It was almost 7 p.m. when Si and Ski got back with Ski's hide. They were two tired, dirty, and hungry sailors, but both had grins from ear to ear. Both bear hides were in top condition and squared a little more than six feet.

We considered ourselves lucky. Of five hunters, three had their trophies salted down after only one day of hunting. This left Jack and me free with four days to spend hunting the big ones. Optimism ran high. If only we could have seen a few days into the future!

By Tuesday morning the wind had died down and the rain decreased to a light drizzle. We cruised up to the end of the east arm and circled Sally Island, but saw only two small bears all day.

Wednesday morning dawned bright and clear. We were under way by 6 a.m. After a fast trip through the narrow strip of water separating Sally Island from the mainland, we cruised along the east shore, all hands scanning the rugged mountains with binoculars.

Shortly after 7, I spotted a huge old black Kodiak far above the snowline. He was ambling back and forth on a ledge, looking for a place to lie down for a nap in the sunshine. He was within climbing distance if the snow wasn't too deep, but there was no cover near him. A stalk would be very difficult.

We watched until he lay down. Then Lou, Jack, and I went ashore to try for him. It was a fairly easy climb, with only a few thick patches of alders below the snowline. After that, the snow began to slow us down. By the time we'd reached a spot 400 yards below the bear, the snow was thigh deep. We stopped here for a breather. Then the fickle mountain breeze got in its licks.

We couldn't see the bear, because we were still below his ledge, but we'd left Lou at snowline on a high knoll to watch him and signal us. As we noticed the change in the breeze we watched Lou. Sure enough: he signalled that our quarry was moving out.

Looking up, we saw the bear leave the ledge and cut across the face of the mountain about 600 yards above us to our right. He was in high gear and throwing snow 50 feet behind him, but I decided I'd try a shot. Falling prone in the snow, I touched one off. The bear didn't falter. The last we saw of him, he was two miles away and running.

We had lunch while we were crossing the bay to hunt the west side. I had just finished eating and had stepped out on deck to look around when I spotted another bear—the granddaddy of them all!

Even at a distance, he looked as big as a dray horse. This was the one I'd come for.

He was up over 3,000 feet, and as soon as he heard the diesels he began to run. He wasn't taking any chances. He ran almost straight up over those sheer cliffs and disappeared over the top.

This range of mountains forms a peninsula into Uganik Bay, separating the east arm and the middle arm, or Mush Bay. We put on full speed and rounded the end of the peninsula. There was old Ursus on that side of the mountain, moseying along in the afternoon sun. About the only sensible way to get to the bear was by helicopter, but Jack and I were ready to try for him.

We stopped the engines and watched the bear for half an hour or so until he looked as though he would settle down. Then George put the dory over. Jack and I climbed in and started ashore, but the first cough of the outboard put the bear into high gear again, straight back over the mountain. We cruised back toward the cannery docks but saw no more bears that day.

Shortly before noon on Thursday as we rounded the end of Sally Island, I began glassing the west side of the bay. There in the same spot where we had first seen old granddaddy yesterday, was a big bear! But there was a noticeable difference: this one didn't run from the sound of the engines. He was about 300 yards under the top of the highest peak on the peninsula and in the deepest snow, right under the cliffs where it had drifted heavily.

While we watched, the bear walked unhurriedly behind a knoll. He couldn't possibly go out without our seeing him, and after watching awhile, we decided that he had decided to nap. George took the boat down to the end of the peninsula a mile and a half away and put us ashore.

There a hogback comes down to the beach, so we started our climb right up the ridge, always keeping on the very top, until we reached the highest part of the peninsula. This was a good 2½-mile climb, and we made it in 3½ hours. The top of the ridge was bare rock, and the high winds had kept it free of snow. So, except for numerous breather stops, our progress was excellent. We had the wind in our faces all the way. And when the boat crew signaled that the bear was still there, we began to think that maybe at last our luck was improving.

We were on a sheer rock cliff about 300 yards high. The terrain tapered from the base of the cliff into a not-quite-so-sheer slope to the sea. From the base of the cliff to a point over halfway down the mountain the snow varied from knee deep to 12-foot drifts. Below that were the infernal alders. The boat, lying offshore, looked like a water bug through my 7 × 35 Bausch & Lomb binoculars.

Crawling very quietly to the edge of the cliff, we looked over. There, about 350 yards below us and sound asleep, was our unsuspecting bear. I studied him through my glasses for a few minutes and decided he would be very near the 10-foot class. He had a huge head and hump and very heavy dark fur on his head and neck. The fur faded into a lighter brown down his back and sides.

We got into comfortable prone positions, and I centered the one-minute Lee dot of my 6X Unertl scope on the top of his hump. We had previously flipped for the first shot and Jack had won. I was to hold fire until he had shot, shooting only if the bear appeared to be getting away.

After I was set, I asked Jack if he was ready. He said he was, so I yelled. The bear bounced to his feet and stood looking down the mountain toward the boat. Jack touched off the .375. I saw the bullet strike the snow, short by several feet. I told Jack to aim higher and he shot again, but still too low. This happened three times. By then the bear had concluded that something was decidedly wrong and his instincts told him he'd better move.

He started off fast to my right and almost directly away from me. I held the dot on top of his hump as well as I could and squeezed off the .300 Weatherby.

At the first shot the bear went down. But he was up immediately on his hind legs, snapping at his side and roaring loud enough to be heard back in Kodiak.

I held in the same spot again, and again he went down. He was up again immediately and moving off down the mountain, leaving a very heavy blood trail and snapping at his hindquarters.

By then I knew that the range was longer than I'd estimated and my bullets were dropping too much. So on the third shot I held on the back of his head and broke his back, right behind the shoulders. He died in his tracks. We lay for a long time watching him for a sign of life, but there was none. So we started down to him.

The snow below was over our waists, and we had to lie down and drag ourselves over it. The 200 or 300 yards to the bear took us over an hour.

Upon reaching him we found that all that had kept him from sliding all the way to the bay was a small rocky point jutting up through the snow. So we rolled him over, and he resumed his trip down the mountain. His path made the going much easier for us because his carcass packed the snow considerably.

It was almost dark by the time we got down, and all hands pitched in to do the skinning. The hide squared nine feet, three inches.

After getting back to the beach, we had fired Jack's rifle again and found it was shooting more than two feet low at 100 yards. We concluded that during one of our climbs he must have hit the scope against something, knocking it out of alignment. Probably on Sally Island. Jack decided he was finished hunting; he wanted to get back to Kodiak. We left Friday.

When I left Kodiak a few days later, I took with me many wonderful memories of the hunting and fishing trips I had taken and of the people that I had met.

World's Biggest Grizzly?

Jack Turner

March, 1967

In the summer of 1957, the year we came to our present place on the Atnarko River above Lonesome Lake, my wife Trudy went down to the garden one morning to get vegetables for lunch. She came back worried, and mad as a hornet.

She had surprised a sow grizzly and two young cubs that were tearing the garden apart. Our prized rows of peas, beans, beets, squash, and other vegetables had been half dug up and reduced to a shambles. The bears left voluntarily when Trudy showed up, which was somewhat unusual for a sow-and-cub combination, but a lot of damage had already been done, and it was a sure bet that the old grizzly would be back. We depended on that garden for a big share of our winter's food supply, and we knew we'd have to take strong measures to save what was left.

We kill nothing needlessly—Trudy and I both have strong feelings on that score. But we don't hesitate to hunt for meat or to protect our property, of course. In this case, we especially disliked the idea of doing away with a whole bear family, but there was no choice. Once the mother was killed, we would have to shoot the little grizzlies to save them from certain death by slow starvation. Trudy's parents were our only neighbors for more than 20 miles, and her father, Ralph Edwards, came up with a bit of advice. If we killed one of the cubs, he thought, the sow would be very likely to take the other one and leave the country. That would be much better than killing all three, and we decided to try it.

We started sleeping in the open at the garden, my .30/30 Winchester Model 94 carbine at my side, ready for the bears. For three nights, nothing happened. But the fourth morning, just at daylight, we heard the grizzlies tearing things up again. When I grabbed the rifle and rolled out of my sack, however, the old lady saw me and hightailed for the woods with the cubs at her heels. She was out of sight in the timber before I could get a shot.

I followed and overtook the bears in very thick brush. I could hear them moving off ahead of me, and after a minute or two I caught a glimpse of one of the youngsters and immediately clobbered him, killing him in his tracks.

I had no desire to pick a fight with the sow by walking in on her right then, so I backed cautiously out into the clearing, keeping my eyes peeled, and Trudy and I went back to the house for breakfast. I'd give the old bear ample time to clear out if she was going to.

I went back in a couple of hours to check on things. Walking slowly and carefully, I got to the place where I had killed the cub. It was gone. But I soon found a faint drag trail leading off into the brush. I followed it 30 feet, walking even more slowly and carefully, and it ended in a small pile of leaves and litter. The sow had buried her dead cub.

There was no sign of her or the live one, so I started to do a little looking around. I got the surprise of my life.

I found a second blood-marked drag trail, starting near the first one, and after a minute or so I figured out what had happened.

The two cubs had been running broadside to me, side by side and both in line with my shot, with the old bear following them. I hadn't seen the second cub in the thick cover, but incredibly my one shot had killed the two of them, and the mother had dragged them both off. She wasn't going to be in a very good frame of mind.

I followed the second blood trail about 200 feet until it ended as the first one had, in a raked-up mound of sticks and duff. And in that same instant, I saw the old grizzly standing in a thick windfall 100 feet away.

She wasn't growling or blustering. In fact she didn't make a sound. But her little piglike eyes, riveted on me, were blazing, and she looked mad all over.

We stared at each other for maybe 30 seconds, though it seemed much longer than that, neither of us moving an eyelash. Then she came for me in a rush, businesslike and deadly.

Forty feet away, she stopped and stood erect. She was growling and raging now, sore to the roots of her tail, and I couldn't blame her. I had given her more than enough reason.

In a situation of this kind, you must decide whether the animal can be bluffed or has to be killed. There wasn't much question this time. She dropped down and started for me again, moving at the hair-raising speed with which bears attack at close range (experienced hunters say they can outrun the best horse for a short distance, even in good going).

I decided she was close enough. I smashed a 170-grain soft-point into her heart at 35 feet, and she was dead almost as soon as she hit the ground.

That was my first grizzly encounter at our new home (I'd had a few earlier in other areas of British Columbia), but it was destined to be far from the last.

The Atnarko, rising in the rugged mountains to the south of us and fed by the melt waters of year-around snow and ice fields, is a major salmon stream. The runs start in September, with sockeyes and humpbacks first, followed by the cohoes. When the salmon appear, the grizzlies start coming down off the mountains to fish in the valley where our homestead lies. Salmon make up the main part of their diet the rest of the fall. Bears get pretty numerous around our place.

I once counted 10 adult grizzlies and five cubs along a seven-mile stretch of the Atnarko, all in one day. I figure that on the average there are 10 or 12 adults within a six-mile radius of the house, up the river and down, all through the fall. With that many bears around, you're likely to run into one at any time and any place.

Toward the end of October 1965, for example, when we finished our annual job of packing in grain for the trumpeter-swan flock we feed each winter, Trudy and our eight-year-old daughter Susan and I moved our four horses up to what we call our upper pasture. It's 15 miles up the Atnarko valley, and we sometimes run stock there.

On the way to the pasture, we encountered a female grizzly with three cubs. She got a little too aggressive for comfort, but I put a shot into a tree and scared her off. On the way back, we saw two more grizzlies, one at a time, but they gave us no trouble. Then we got home, only to find a medium-size grizzly walking around the yard, 100 feet from the house, and he refused to let us in. We tried to drive him off but couldn't, and finally I had to kill him.

You never know when a grizzly will decide to pick a fight, so I rarely venture beyond the cleared fields around our house without hanging that battered old .30/30 over my shoulder. That precaution has saved my skin or my family's at least twice.

A few years after I'd killed the garden-raiding bear family, we were finishing the fall job of grain packing, and Trudy and Susan and I began the long hike up the Atnarko from Lonesome Lake to our place after dark. We knew that this wasn't exactly a good idea, and it's something we don't do often. But we were tired from days of packing and rafting wheat in from the road, and we disliked the idea of camping out in the woods another night when we were so close to home. There's a good wagon road along that part of the river, so we decided to risk it.

It was late October, the salmon run was at its peak, and there were likely to be fish-hungry bears all over the valley. I hoped we wouldn't run into any of them.

I was walking ahead, and Trudy was following me, carrying Susan in a small chair lashed to a packboard. Our child was only about three at the time. The night was pitch dark, and I saw nothing of the two cub grizzlies in the trail ahead. The first inkling I had that they were there was the sound of something scampering off into the brush 20 or 30 feet in front of me. Then I heard two small animals crashing through a windfall to our right.

The next things I heard were the unmistakable growl of an angry grizzly and a third animal scrambling up the five-foot bank of the Atnarko on the other side of us. I knew from the noise that this one was not small, and it took me only a split second to figure out that it was the sow, leaving her fishing and barreling up from the river to rescue her cubs.

She hit the trail about 20 feet in front of me, and if she knew where the cubs had gone, she paid it no attention. Instead, she whirled and came for us.

In the darkness, I could see her only as a black shape, almost in my lap. I had the rifle in my hands by then, ready for action, but the light was too poor to see the barrel, let alone the sights. Behind me, Trudy dodged around a tree, hoping that this would give her and Susan some protection.

I pointed the gun in the bear's direction and hammered out three fast shots when she was only about 10 feet away. She didn't bawl or grunt but just spun around and ran, and I didn't know whether I had hit her or not. Half a minute later, we heard her or the cubs clatter up the mountain, breaking brush as they went. The Turner family made it the rest of the way home without incident.

Next morning I went back to see what had happened. One of my shots had connected, but I never learned where it had hit or how much damage it had done. I found a little splash of blood in the trail and a few scattered drops on the leaves in the direction the bear had run, but the sign petered out in a windfall. I hunted along the river and up the mountainside for four hours but found no trace of her or the cubs, and we never saw hide or hair of any of that family again. And that was all right with us.

As events turned out, I guess those two encounters with cantankerous grizzlies were a good thing. They taught me to be alert, and I really needed to be ready for the next bear I met.

In May of 1965, I left the house before breakfast one morning, just at daylight, and started up the Atnarko to repair the log fence that keeps our milch cow from straying 15 miles up the river to join the other cows and our bull in the upper pasture. That same type of fence—eight feet high and built of logs laid up like rails—encloses our garden and the hay land around the house to keep out moose and deer.

Because of the fence job, I was carrying an ax, and I had the .30/30 Winchester slung across my back by a length of nylon cord. I wasn't expecting to see a grizzly, for they rarely come down that low except in the fall when the salmon are running. But where we live there is always the likelihood of running across a black bear or catching a fleeting glimpse of a cougar. And anyway, as I said earlier, I make it a routine practice to carry the rifle on all my hikes—just in case.

I had two miles to walk, on a good horse-and-cattle trail that leads to the upper pasture. Most of the way, the trail is within sight or hearing of the river.

It was a fine spring morning. The Atnarko brawled along on my left, tumbling and frothing down its rock-strewn gravel bed, a little milky from snow melt. It's as beautiful a river as I've ever seen. Bunchberry and a few other early flowers were blooming along the trail, birds were flitting in and out of the brush, and I was enjoying every minute of my walk.

I came to a place where the trail, winding through cedars and cotton-woods, opens out into a little sunny glade no bigger than a house. I rounded a bend, and there in the center of that glade stood the biggest grizzly I had ever laid eyes on (and I have seen more than 200, in just about every part of British Columbia, in the last 20 years). He was staring straight at me, and he was just 40 feet away.

He barely gave me time to be startled. He had seen me first, probably had watched me approach for half a minute or so. I rounded the turn in the trail, our eyes met and locked, and he was on the way. I saw him one instant, and a fraction of a second later he was coming for me in a savage rush, running like a dog closing on its prey. He gave me no warning—not so much as a growl or a single popping of his teeth.

I've been asked since whether he snarled or bawled as he ran at me. I don't know. It all happened too fast for me to remember every detail. But to the best of my recollection, he was drooling as he came, and a low growl was rumbling in his throat.

I dropped the ax and whipped the Winchester off my back, all in one motion. I had to do two things before I could shoot, and I did them very fast. For reasons of safety, I carry the rifle loaded in the magazine but not in the chamber. I had to lever home a shell. And the gun's Lyman peep sight was folded down. It had to be raised.

The bear was almost on me when I slammed my shot at him, and I recall thinking, in that brief flash of time, that I'd have time for only one. I was using 170-grain soft-point factory loads. I hit him dead center between the eyes, just over the bulge of the nose, and that soft-point blew his whole brain out through a hole in the back of his skull. He was still running full tilt when I shot, but then his head went down between his forelegs, and he fell almost straight down. He didn't seem to roll or skid when he hit the ground, and he didn't even twitch. I backed off a few steps, held the rifle on him, and waited until I was sure there wasn't a spark of life left in him.

The sooner a shot bear is skinned the better, so far as the condition of the pelt is concerned. I wanted Trudy to help me skin this one, so I decided to put off fixing the fence, go home and eat breakfast, and come back with her and do the skinning without delay.

Trudy and Susan both went back with me. Even I was a little surprised at what we found. My ax lay in the trail just six feet from the bear's nose. That meant he had been only about three feet from the muzzle of the rifle when I shot. I hadn't realized he'd gotten quite that close.

He was a buster—by far the biggest grizzly we had ever seen. And his pelt, except for being a little thin on the sides, was a handsome trophy, well furred on the shoulders and along the back, and rich, dark brown in color.

What accounted for his furious charge the instant I came into view? I'll never know the answer to that question, of course. The bear was a male, and there was no question of cubs being involved, nor could I find any evidence that he'd been feeding on a dead animal anywhere in the vicinity.

Grizzlies here hardly ever make a kill of their own unless they happen to get the odd chance at a sick or helpless deer, mountain goat, or cow. But they do feed on kills made by cougars or wolves and on deer and moose that die after being wounded by hunters and not found. Once grizzlies take over such a carcass, they usually consider it theirs and run off all trespassers. But there was no sign of anything like that in the case of this bear.

Later that day, however, I did come across his bed, a 10-minute hike up the trail from where we'd met. He had crossed the Atnarko and left the wet imprint of his body where he lay, apparently most of the night.

He must have started down the trail shortly after daylight, met me, and simply made up his mind that he was either going to run me off or teach me a lasting lesson. That I walked so close to him without knowing he was there probably had a lot to do with it. An animal as big and short-tempered as a grizzly is very likely to resent any intruder at short range. He seems to think that if you weren't looking for trouble, you wouldn't crowd him, and if trouble is what you want, he's ready to oblige.

I stretched his hide, and we cleaned the skull and laid it aside. The more I looked at that skull and compared it with other grizzly skulls I'd seen (I have several from kills of my own), the more it puzzled me. It was just too big to belong to an ordinary grizzly.

Finally I started to wonder whether I had killed a rare and unusual hybrid, the result of a chance mating between a grizzly and one of the big brown bears from the coastal country of southeastern Alaska, a brown that had strayed inland from his usual haunts and left a descendant behind. I had never heard of such a cross, but the more I thought about it, the more logical it seemed.

I finally wrote to I. McTaggart Cowan, a dean at the University of British Columbia at Vancouver and a widely respected authority and official measurer for the Boone and Crockett Club, and put the question to him. He replied by suggesting that I ship the skull to him for a detailed examination.

I took his advice. When his verdict came, in May of 1966, I got another surprise. I had not killed a hybrid bear; the skull was that of a true grizzly. But apparently I had taken a new world record for that species.

"According to my most careful measurements," Cowan wrote, "your skull measures 17$\frac{1}{16}$ long and 9$\frac{12}{16}$ wide, totaling 26$\frac{13}{16}$." I had measured it before I sent it to him and scored it 27. I knew that the present world record, listed in the 1964 edition of the Boone and Crockett Club's book, *Records of North American Big Game*, scored 26$\frac{10}{16}$. That skull came from a bear killed at Rivers Inlet, British Columbia, in 1954 and is now in possession of the University of British Columbia.

"Barring the eventuality of another equally large skull having turned up within the last year, this certainly seems to me to be a new record," the dean added.

I have entered my bear in the 1966–67 Boone and Crockett Competition, but whether it will finally be accredited as a new world record remains to be seen. When I smashed that shot into the grizzly's head at two yards, I blew a good-size chunk of bone out of the right side of his skull, toward the back, and the Boone and Crockett scorers follow quite strict rules about damaged skulls.

On that subject, however, Dean Cowan had this to say: "I am sure that the remaining portion of the skull is yielding completely accurate measurements. If anything, the width would have been a little greater had the skull been intact."

That's enough to satisfy me that I killed the biggest grizzly ever taken anywhere. And the fact that he went down three feet from the muzzle of my rifle doesn't rob the affair of any of its thrill, either.

I have the big grizzly's pelt hanging in our log barn. We don't have much use for bearskin rugs where we live. But I figure that one of these days a hunter will come in to Lonesome Lake, fail to get a bear, and want to take home the pelt of the top grizzly on record.

PART

VII
ENTER THE
BEAR DOGS

The Dog Who Forgot to Fear

Jim Rearden

August, 1976

Hook-jawed, humpbacked pink salmon swirled and scuttled in the clear shallow water of the Alaskan stream as hip-booted Alex Brogle, a fisheries technician, waded the riffles and crunched across the bars to tally the fish.

Ahead ran his wolflike black dog Rex. The dog disappeared around a bend, and moments later Alex heard the distinctive alarm bark that said, "Bear!" It was a warning he had heard many times.

Alex scrambled away from the stream toward a clear spot on a knoll. From there he looked down and saw a huge quick-moving brown-bear sow about 75 feet below him. She was standing up on her hind legs and was threatening the barking, dancing dog. Three half-grown cubs clustered nearby.

Danger comes in many forms in the wilderness, but nothing is more fearful than an angry half-ton sow brown bear with cubs. In seconds Alex climbed a tall spruce, and his hip boots didn't hinder him a bit. Knowing he was safe, he called, "Here, Rex! That's enough."

Rex retreated to the base of the tree, watching suspiciously over his shoulder. The ruffled sow, back hairs still up, popped her teeth and whuffed her anger at the retreating dog. Then she gathered her triplets and hustled them out of sight.

For eight summers, from 1968 to 1975, Rex's job was to warn Alex of bears while he waded streams to count salmon in Alaska's Yakutat district on the wild gulf coast. Like Alex, the bears come to the streams because of the spawning salmon. Alex lost count of the number of times Rex had warned him of nearby bears. Rex had a deep fear of the big bears, and he never got close enough for the huge teeth or sharp claws to touch him.

Alex Brogle's partnership with Rex began in July 1967, when Alex was patroling in Yakutat Bay in his Boston Whaler. He was surprised to see two dogs on the beach of lonely Khantaak Island, half a mile from the mainland. He landed and found a friendly black Labrador retriever bitch heavy with pups, and a stand-offish mask-faced Siberian husky male. Alex later learned that their owners, who sometimes lived in an old cabin on the island, had been weeks delayed on a trip.

Brogle is a slim, master woodsman with a lifelong interest in animals, and the plight of the dogs worried him. The husky was fat from beach-combing mussels and other foods from the sea, but his black mate was thin and hungry, and wolfed Alex's lunch. For several weeks thereafter Alex stopped on every patrol to feed and visit the lonely dogs.

One day the Labrador was no longer carrying pups, and she led Alex to the floor of the porch of the ramshackle cabin. There she whined and sniffed at a much gnawed and clawed hole in the floor. Alex reached into the hole and retrieved seven dead black puppies. The Lab had apparently dropped them into the hole for safety, and was then unable to reach them. The blind and helpless pups had died of starvation and exposure.

Alex felt he was partly to blame for their loss, and he comforted the whining bitch for some time. He decided it would be best if he weighted the pups and dropped them into the bay. But just before leaving the island, he removed his jacket, rolled up his sleeve, and reached farther into the hole under the porch. He was astonished to find one more pup, just barely alive.

Alex tucked the puppy inside his shirt for warmth, hurried to his boat, and sped to the village of Yakutat, where he fed the puppy warm milk. The black ball of fur came back to life, wriggled, and snuffled until put into a box by the stove at the fishery station.

The owners of the two dogs on Khantaak Island returned shortly thereafter. Later the Labrador died in an accident on the island. The Siberian, now an old dog, is still alive in Yakutat.

"Rex didn't have a mother to feed and teach him," Alex told me, "and he had no littermates to play with. I became his whole world. He imitated my behavior, and he never did learn to play with other dogs."

The Yakutat region is a wilderness where hump-shouldered moose roam and where the spine-tingling howls of timber wolves are often heard. The focus of Alex's life, however, are the streams that head in the nearby snow-peaked St. Elias Mountains and wind through spruce forests to the violent Gulf of Alaska. Alex has managed the commercial fishery there for the state of Alaska since 1961. When he finds enough spawning salmon in the streams, he announces legal fishing time for the local commercial fishermen, who can then lay their nets for the fat silvery salmon. If Alex decides there aren't enough salmon in the streams, the fishermen have to wait. His counts must be very accurate.

Even when the dog was tiny and almost helpless, Alex often carried Rex in a coat pocket on his aerial and foot surveys of the salmon streams. Humpy Creek, a mile-long stream near Yakutat, is small and brushy. The salmon in it must be counted on foot. Once that summer, Alex carried Rex while surveying the stream. He put Rex in shallow water near spawning salmon, and a splashing fish swam near and knocked the black pup on his side. Rex yipped and yelped, but once he was back in Alex's arms, he growled fiercely at the swirling fish.

Even at that tender age, Rex's hackles lifted whenever his button nose caught bear-tainted air.

These unpredictable fishing bears make stream surveys afoot very dangerous along much of Alaska's coast. Few years pass without someone being killed or terribly mauled by a furious coastal brown. Fishery biologists all have horror stories about the big bears. The Department of Fish and Game has a policy that calls for a rifle-carrying companion to accompany everyone who makes a salmon survey afoot.

Once, when he was counting salmon at Humpy Creek with an inexperienced summer employee as his guard, Alex heard the rifle bolt slam several times. He turned and saw the guard staring in terror at a giant bear that was standing on hind legs on the bank. The bear was peering down at the two men with its piglike eyes.

"Let me have the rifle," Alex said calmly after noticing that the guard, in his panic, had pumped four live rounds of ammunition through the rifle and onto the ground. One cartridge was in the chamber, and the magazine was empty.

The two men backed away slowly. With each step, the bear's hackles lowered. Finally the bear dropped to all fours and disappeared into the thick devil's club and alder brush. The overwrought assistant collapsed and fell into the stream.

Rex was four months old that October when Alex left him in Yakutat with Larry and Caroline Powell and their two children. Alex was heading south for his annual job switch to ski instructor, and there was no place in his winter life for a bird dog. He traveled a lot, mixed with hundreds of skiers, lived in crowded quarters. A dog would have been a nuisance.

Alex returned to Yakutat the following May and drove to the Powells' house. Rex, now nearly full grown, leaped into his pickup truck and, despite commands from Alex and Larry Powell, refused to get out. Alex was his master.

Alex didn't deliberately set out to train Rex to be a bear sentry. The dog trained himself with Alex's encouragement. The dog's awareness of the big bears and his fear of them stemmed from a day during his second summer when he and Alex were driving along a sandy coastal beach in an open Jeep. A huge brown suddenly galloped into sight ahead. Rex leaped out of the Jeep and swiftly caught up with the bear. Alex was amazed when the big dog slashed his sharp teeth into the rear of the galloping bear.

The bear skidded to a stop in as cloud of sand. Out of the cloud came a yipping black dog, headed for the Jeep, closely followed by the enraged bear. Alex drove toward the running animals and honked his horn and revved the engine, hoping to frighten the bear away.

"Rex leaped into the speeding Jeep and damned near broke his neck doing it," Alex remembers. Alex spun the vehicle around and raced away, glancing over his shoulder until the pursuing bear gave up the chase. Miraculously, Rex was unhurt.

Many Alaskans will tell you that it's dangerous to keep a dog in bear country. If the dog tangles with a grizzly or a brown, the dog often becomes terrified and runs to its master for protection. If the bear is angry enough, it often jumps the man. But Rex seemed to learn something from that incident on the beach. He seldom led bears to Alex afterward, but he wasn't infallible. When the dog was really frightened, he wanted Alex to share his trouble, and Alex always did his best—even if he did so while perched on a limb high in a tree. Rex always gave loud and clear warning.

Rex had a special growl whenever he sensed a bear during a stream survey. If the wind was right, the dog could smell a bear as far as 200 yards away, and he invariably warned Alex. When Rex located a bear, he pointed his sensitive nose at it and continued to point the bear while he and Alex walked past. Sometimes Rex even walked backward after passing a bear so he could continue to face the menace, which was usually hidden in brush. Alex could tell how close the bear was by how high Rex lifted his hackles.

By the end of his second summer Rex had reached his mature weight of 85 pounds. He looked like a black husky with small white markings on chest and left hind foot. Strangers often thought he was part wolf. His upthrust ears, deep chest, heavy neck, and thick coat came from his Siberian husky sire. His dense fur kept him warm when he curled up to sleep in the snow with his nose buried in his bushy tail. The Siberian blood made him aloof to strangers, except for children, whom he loved.

Siberian Eskimos developed the husky as a workdog, and the animals were brought to Alaska during the gold rush early in this century. They are valued in the North as sled dogs of great speed and stamina, and Rex often ran behind Alex's pickup truck for as far as 20 miles without stopping. If it was cold, so much the better. Rime often froze on his black face and chest, and his long tongue lolled from his grinning mouth as he leaped along.

From his gentle Labrador dam came his wagging tail, the oil in his black coat, and his soft brown eyes. From her too probably came his hunting-dog sense of smell and his love of the water. It was the Labrador retriever's desire to please that made Rex so tractable. He even retrieved ducks that Alex shot.

That fall Alex again left Rex with the Powells when he followed the geese south. But Rex developed an embarrassing possessiveness. In the Powell's general store he growled at customers, and he constantly fought and whipped visiting dogs. He was overprotective toward seven-year-old Michele and two-year-old Brandon Powell.

When Alex returned in the spring, Larry Powell suggested that it might be best if Rex did not spend the winters at the store. After that, Rex lived and traveled with Alex all year. He guarded the fishery station and Alex's truck. He stood barking into the wind at the bow of the speeding patrol boat. He waited while Alex made stream-survey flights, and he accompanied him when he had to walk streams to make his salmon counts.

Again and again Rex warned Alex of nearby bears. Once, he drove a big sow and her two nearly grown cubs from the garden Alex had planted at the fishery station. Alex watched carefully and observed that Rex always kept a safe distance from the bears. He barked, danced, and threatened, but he was quick to dodge or run.

Alex was apprehensive when he took Rex out of Alaska that winter. The wilderness-bred dog had never encountered crowds, livestock, traffic. But at California's Sugar Bowl ski area, where Alex instructed, Rex quickly adapted. He howled when the ski-school bell rang, and then trotted away and remained off the slopes, where he might have tripped a skier.

Rex disgraced himself once. He resented a huge young St. Bernard dog. At Easter a parade was scheduled, and several hundred skiers gathered on a large porch. Many carried eggs or candy in baskets. The St. Bernard was begging for food and attention when Rex arrived and leaped at the rear of the bigger dog. There he clung—biting, growling, and half riding the frantically fleeing St. Bernard through the crowd.

Skiers were knocked down, Easter baskets and eggs flew through the air, and women screamed. The St. Bernard finally escaped by leaping off a high porch. Rex lost his grip.

Alex was furious. Such behavior in Yakutat was one thing, but at the Sugar Bowl it was unforgiveable. He beat Rex with the handle of a ski pole because he had to make it clear that he was the dog's master and that Rex had to behave. Half the crowd shrieked at Alex for being cruel to the dog; others urged him to destroy the vicious dog.

After the thrashing, Rex lay in a corner, refusing to move or to look at Alex for a whole day and night. But finally he crept to Alex for forgiveness.

Alex never again had to physically punish the sensitive dog. A vocal warning was sufficient.

Rex disliked men with long hair, those with a strong body odor, and people who had been drinking. He probably took his cues from Alex. When he disliked someone who was with Alex, the dog placed himself squarely between the two. He couldn't have made himself any clearer if he had said, "I don't trust you near my master."

The wolfish black dog and the slim fisheries technician-skier were as close as only a bachelor in his 40's and his dog can be. Rex knew about 20 word combinations, including "This way," "We'll go in the jeep," and "We'll go in the pickup." With the last two, he always jumped into the right vehicle.

Rex communicated his mood to Alex by demeanor and facial expression as well as by voice. He had a pleasure growl, an anger growl, his bear growl. He had special whines for attention, and various other tones that Alex learned to interpret.

On August 30, 1975, Alex had to make a foot survey of Humpy Creek. No one was available to accompany him as guard, so he took Rex on a leash, and for last-resort bear protection he carried a .44 Magnum revolver in a hip holster.

Humpy Creek was alive with 15,000 spawning and dying pink salmon. Spawned-out dead salmon lined the banks, and clean-picked fishbones were strewn everywhere. Dozens of gorged seagulls squatted on the sandbars, and their droppings white-washed the shoreline. The smell of dead fish fouled the air, and flies buzzed over rotting salmon. Alex and Rex flushed several overweight bald eagles that had been picking at dead fish.

Here and there a raven or a fish crow quarreled with the gulls for a salmon. Fresh brown bear tracks covered the banks and dimpled the sandbars.

Alex and Rex paid little attention to this life that flowed with the death of the salmon; they had seen it hundreds of times. Alex got busy counting. For every 25 live fish in the stream, he punched his hand counter once.

Halfway along on the mile-long stream, Rex growled *bear*, and his hackles rose. He pointed his nose across the stream.

This too was an old story, and Alex knew what to expect. He watched as a large male brown bear stood briefly on hind legs, peered at the intruders, and then dropped to all fours and silently disappeared into the brush.

Then Alex heard brush crackle and gravel crunch close behind him. He whirled and faced one of the most fearsome sights any man ever sees. A huge brown bear was in full charge toward him. The bear was less than 15 yards away.

Alex dropped Rex's leash and reached for his revolver. The bear came on at full speed to within seven yards and reared up on hind legs to tower over man and dog while still moving forward. Rex launched himself in a tremendous leap at the bear's throat before Alex's gun was out of the holster.

Alex still shakes his head in wonder at Rex's response to the charge. After hundreds of bear encounters, the dog had a healthy fear of the great animals, but he instantly leaped at the great bear.

As Rex leaped, so did Alex. His ski-trained muscles propelled him in a six-foot jump that put him atop a three-foot bank.

He landed with the handgun out and whirled to see Rex on the bear's chest with jaws open and white teeth reaching. Alex aimed to miss and fired a shot over the bear's head, hoping to frighten the animal, but the bear closed its forelegs and pinned Rex to its chest. Then it bit savagely at the dog.

The bear dropped Rex into the shallows, and Alex stood poised, .44 ready, held in both hands. The dog was limp and did not move in the water.

The great bear was through. It dropped to all fours and leaped into the brush. Moments later Alex saw the animal running up a low hill followed by two cubs. Alex believes the sow had scented the male bear they had seen across the creek, but then had heard their steps on the gravel. It seems likely that she thought the scent and the noise came from the same source. The sow probably believed she was going to drive a boar away from her cubs and fishing ground. Because the sow was downwind, Rex had been unable to smell her.

Rex was dead, his neck broken by one savage bite. His life-debt to Alex was paid. When the shaking stopped and the shock lessened, Alex carried the warm body into the forest and placed it deep among the exposed roots of a tree. Rex lay there as though sleeping.

Later Alex nailed a marker on a spire-topped spruce on the bank of Humpy Creek: "In Memory of Rex, Who Here Sacrificed His Life to Save His Master. August 30, 1975." In his official report to Dave Cantillon, his superior in Juneau, Alex wrote that Rex " . . . stopped the bear six yards from me . . . and lunged into certain death in order to save my life."

Shoot, Shoot!

Mike Gallo

December, 1981

I had called five California houndmen and had the same conversation with each of them.

"I'd really like to get a bear," I began.

"I can get you a nice one."

"A big male?"

"How big?"

"Say around 500 pounds."

At this point the guide hesitated. He'd really have to look to find something like that. Then I told him the clincher—I hunt with a bow and arrow.

"A bear that size won't tree," each houndman told me. "It'll stay on the ground and fight." Each refused to let a bowhunter try to take a bear on the ground, but offered to take me if I would use a gun.

Then I called Jesse Turner of Redwood Valley. He knew of a bear with a huge track, and he told me he didn't care what I used as long as I could kill the bear. I booked the hunt.

October 20, opening day of California's general bear season, found me thumping and bumping my way over the potholes of Mendocino County roads. It was long before dawn. The first rain of the season had fallen during the night, turning roads into mushy red clay.

As we neared the hunt area, the road became worse. Finally Jesse said that after one more steep trail we could stop and set out to locate a hot track. If we were lucky it would be the track of the monster bear the 19-year-old houndman knew to be in the area.

Jesse is a bear hunter accomplished beyond his years. He was 8 when he killed his first, and he's hunted bruins ever since. He's 6 foot 2 inches, 220 pounds, and he has a handshake like a vise grip.

Halfway up the steep trail the truck began to bog down. A shower of

271

mud spewed from the furiously spinning front tires. The more they spun, the deeper we sank into the ankle-deep muck. We got out of the cab; frozen breath streamed from my nose as darkness slowly gave way to dawn.

"C'mon, Mike, let's walk," Jesse said in a low monotone.

We climbed to the top of the trail and stopped to catch our breath. Pulling a flashlight from his vest, Jesse becan to scour the road for tracks. I followed at a distance. All I could see was the soft glow of his flashlight. The slosh of boots was the only sound until Jesse whispered, "Come here."

I high-stepped my way over.

"There's your boy," Jesse whispered excitedly.

The track was enormous, a full nine inches long and seven inches wide. I felt a sudden chill.

"I'm gonna get the dogs, and we're gonna catch us a bear," Jesse said. He set off for the truck at a run. I couldn't take my eyes off the print. I tried to cover it with my hand, but two inches of the track showed all around.

I could hear the dogs in the distance, their heavy breathing muffled by tight leashes around their necks. As they pulled Jesse to the top of the hill and then stood at the track, their subdued moans and salivating jaws clearly said, "Lemme at him."

Caesar was first on the track. As soon as his trained nose hit dirt he was off; in minutes his throaty bark was far away. The two other dogs, Poacher and Missy, nearly pulled my arms from their sockets, trying to pull free.

"Turn 'em loose!" yelled Jesse.

They were gone in an instant. We turned off our flashlights and stood there, listening to three separate barks that seemed a world away.

"Those tracks were smokin'," Jesse said. "We must have been right behind him."

The three barks melted into one and became hardly more than an echo over miles of rough country and near-darkness. Jesse listened. Then the barking became quicker and more intense. Had another bear crossed the track they were following and sent them off after fresher scent? I looked at Jesse for the answer.

"They got him," he said. "They're barking in his face."

We hurried back to the truck, winched it free and drove over an old logging road toward the canyon that the barks came from. Jesse powered the four-wheel-drive up the slick trails with reckless abandon. This was no time to bog down. His dogs were on a bear, and we had to get there as soon as possible.

When we got out of the truck we heard a furious battle in the canyon below. The dogs had the bear stopped, bayed in the brushy manzanita. I quickly checked my bow as Jesse holstered his .44 Magnum. As we prepared to set out, a high-pitched cry filled the fog-shrouded basin. Then there was silence. Eerie, unending silence.

"He got a dog." Jesse gritted his teeth and kicked at the ground. "That's a mean bear. He may have been run before."

When the barking resumed, long minutes later, we were relieved to hear all three voices.

"He's still in the creek, and they have him stopped," Jesse said. "Let's go."

We started down the canyon, partly walking, partly sliding. Rain began to fall, first drizzling, then pouring. My heart pounded as we got within a quarter-mile of the dogs. We followed a creekbed, trying to avoid slick rocks and fallen trees. The barking got louder and louder. We rounded a sharp bend, and Jesse pointed to a rocky knoll.

"He's right behind there."

I was ready for the shot. "Can you smell him?" Jesse whispered as I checked my bow once more. I hadn't noticed anything. Then it hit me.

Phew! A rank, sour odor, like a dead animal, the kind of smell that would make a man take an occasional glance over his shoulder if he were in the woods alone.

We crept ahead on hands and knees and peeked over the knoll. The bear looked indestructible. Droplets of water dotted the hairy black pelt that covered a hulking mass of rippling muscle. Saliva streamed from the powerful, clicking jaws, and steam wafted from the hump of his high back.

"Don't shoot yet," warned Jesse, "Poacher is right behind him."

The bear turned toward us. His hard dark eyes fixed on us. He sniffed at the air, then woofed loudly and took off at a trot up the canyon. We followed.

As we climbed we got into thick brush and had to crawl. The rain persisted and turned to hail. Finally we heard the barking coming from one spot again.

The bear was bayed in the worst patch of brush in the canyon. We had to go in on a trail eight inches wide, crawling in the mud until we caught the smell again.

Jesse had his handgun ready. I was close behind, my bow tucked under my arm. I was getting nervous—activity all around, but I couldn't see anything. Jesse pointed to a small, branchless tree 30 yards ahead. A line of smooth white mist streamed from its base.

"He's right there. That's his breath."

I was close enough to shoot, but I still couldn't see the bear. So we crawled closer, sliding on our stomachs through a tunnel of manzanita. One of the dogs, Missy, was an arm's length away. I crawled over Jesse and turned to ask what the next move should be. Silence. The dogs had stopped barking. Something was wrong. I snapped my head back and saw Jesse's wide, searching eyes, open mouth and pointed revolver. I looked ahead again. The tree I had been watching was mowed down in my direction with a resounding crack. Brush exploded, and the dogs went berserk. Missy jumped over me and Caesar retreated to my side. On hands and knees, all I could see was the bear's yellow snout coming right at me. *He's going to run us down*, I thought.

When the bear was an arm's length away I dropped my bow and jumped off the trail, all in one motion. I flew sideways through the air, my head cocked toward the trail. Then things went in slow motion. Out of the corner of my very alert left eye I saw a large black claw swipe at my airborne leg. I hit the ground and crow-hopped again, landing face down in a small bush. I closed my eyes and was afraid to open them. I forced one open, thinking, *If I see black it's all over.* Luckily, the bear had gone on toward Jesse. I heard two blasts from the .44 and then quiet.

I crawled back to the trail and called out to Jesse. No answer. I tried again. Deafening silence. I was afraid to look, afraid of what I might find. The rain started again. I wiped my eyes and called again, this time as loud as I could. I heard some brush break and then Jesse's voice.

"Over here, Mike." Boy, was I relieved. I found him lying in a small bush, on his stomach, his .44 still smoking. When our eyes met it was all we could do to laugh nervously.

"Did you kill him?" I asked.

"I was just trying to shoot him off now. I'm sure I missed him clean, though." He chambered two fresh rounds while I retrieved my compound, which the bear had stepped on as it ran by. I did my best to straighten it out, and we took up the trail once again.

We picked up the barking about a mile farther up the canyon. The bear had followed the creekbed and then started sidehilling up. Jesse stayed close behind the pack, but my bow slowed me. I finally discovered the technique—I threw the bow ahead as far as I could, then crawled toward it. It was all I could do. We reached the bear after 30 minutes of the roughest brush-busting travel I hope I will ever have to do.

Near a break in the brush I had noticed a splash of red—blood, so Jesse must have hit the bear. I met Jesse 30 yards from the bear, where he was waiting for me.

The bear was downhill, in some fallen trees slightly overgrown with ferns, quartering toward me. It was a shot of about 35 yards, quite risky for a bowhunter. The bear shifted slightly, and a huge tangle of dead branches—and Caesar—stood between me and the bear's giant side.

"Shoot! Shoot!" Jesse called. He wanted to get it over with. But I decided against it. There was a good chance of arrow deflection, which would mean a wounded bear or a dead dog.

The bear wouldn't move, and I couldn't shoot. All we could do was watch. The dogs were relentless in their torment of the bear. Missy snapped at his left side, backing him up against a tree. Caesar nipped at his rear, and Poacher barked directly into that huge dark face. The bear's piglike eyes fixed directly ahead. Frozen breath poured from his straining nostrils as he growled and swiped. I was beginning to wonder who would tire first. But the bear slowly turned his triangular head downhill and trotted off.

"There was blood on the hill coming up," I said to Jesse. "You must have hit the bear."

"That was dog blood." He looked uncharacteristically serious. "We have to kill him soon." He took off at a trot. His dogs were taking a beating, and he knew it. I kept up as best I could.

The bear was retracing his steps, going downhill this time. We could hear the dogs at the bottom of the basin; they were headed for the creek again.

We were halfway down when we heard the barking stop, then continue. The dogs had the bear at bay already. He must have been tiring. As we homed in on the barking, a bloodcurdling cry rang out. Jesse immediately identified the source of the scream as Poacher, the dog known for fearlessness.

"I hate to say this, Mike, but if you don't get him this time I'm going to have to kill him myself. My dogs can't take much more."

The bear was bayed on a steep hillside across the creekbed. He was standing in the same kind of eucalyptus-brush cover as before.

We could see the dogs' tails as we crossed the creek. We crawled around and got above the bear. Jesse pointed through an opening, but it was a terribly risky shot. He took my arm and raised the bow for me. I tried to aim for the huge side, but I could barely see it. I let the bow down.

Jesse was beside himself. I wouldn't have put it past him to shoot the bear first, then me. The rain was coming down again, crashing against the treetops. The next dog to cry out was Caesar. I turned my head in time to see the dog fly through the air and land hard against a rock, the victim of a well aimed forepaw. It was now or never.

"Follow me," I whispered, "and shoot to kill if he charges."

I walked directly toward the bear. When I got within 15 yards he turned that monstrous head toward me. Jesse held his trembling .44 directly over my shoulder, pointed and ready.

For a split second I was terrified. Saliva foamed off the bear's lower jaw as he displayed an ivory-white set of canine incisors. His odor was hideous. I brought the compound to full draw and let fly.

Just then the bear turned, heading downhill. The arrow hit slightly behind the front shoulder, angling in toward the chest. It sailed out the other side. The bear took off, the hounds doggedly at his heels, and I was close behind.

When I caught up, the bruin was sitting on his haunches in the middle of the trail. I sank another arrow deep into his chest. He reached down and neatly bit it in half, but it had done its damage. He fell to his side, clawing and biting at the sky, and then he was still. The dogs lay down and rested their heads on their front paws. I dropped my bow and just lay there with them, too tired to savor the moment.

But I savored it later. When we finally weighed the field-dressed bear the scale read 396 pounds, which would mean a live weight of about 550. And the skull's official measurement of $20^{15}/_{16}$ points made this the third largest bear ever taken by a bowhunter in California.

Hardest Way to Hunt Bear

Mike Reynolds

February, 1974

I did a double take when I saw the enormous bear tracks in loose dirt near my bait station. I couldn't clearly make out the prints, because dawn was just minutes old.

I turned a couple dogs loose, and they cold-trailed the bruin to a sandy logging road. By then it was light enough to study the tracks in the damp sand. I've seen a lot of bear tracks, but none ever sent more shivers up my spine. I figured I was hunting the biggest bear of my life.

Harold "Hoppe" Hafenstein, a welder from Lake Mills, Wisconsin, was with me, and he was as worked up as I was.

"Mike," he said, "we've got one brute of a bear going. If we catch up to this one we'll have our hands full."

That northern Wisconsin bear hunt was one of the toughest and most frustrating of the many bear chases I've been on. As a guide I hunt bears with my dogs every day of Wisconsin's September bear season. Years ago I used to fish and hunt everything in season, but now I concentrate exclusively on bears. It almost has to be that way if you're going to succeed. Raising and training bear dogs takes all my free time.

I live near Park Falls, Wisconsin, and I earn most of my living as a gunsmith. I also guide bear hunters. During the last four years my hunters have taken 38 bears.

The largest black bear I've killed scored 19^{15}/$_{16}$ on the Official Scoring Method of the Boone and Crockett Club. It would have scored higher if my bullet hadn't blasted away part of the animal's skull. I told the story of that 1967 hunt in "Bear That Wouldn't Quit" in OUTDOOR LIFE for May 1970. That bear field-dressed at 443 pounds.

A year later three of us rushed in to kill another giant bear that was doing his best to kill some of my dogs. He dressed out at 437 pounds, but his skull scored higher than the slightly heavier bear. His skull was damaged by bullets too, but the measurements still totaled 20%16.

In 1971, while training my pack of hounds in June, I found a bear skull in the woods. It officially scored 21%16. The world-record black bear, taken in San Pete County, Utah, by Rex Peterson and Richard S. Hardy in 1970, scored 22%16. So I feel it's likely that a new world-record black bear is roaming the wilderness of northern Wisconsin. That's why I was so excited when I studied those enormous tracks in the damp sand of the logging road. The date was September 28, 1971.

My dogs cold-trailed down the sandy road for a few hundred yards before they turned onto a deer trail that went up a pine ridge. The scent was still cold an hour later as we followed my Plott hounds through a logged-off area.

Then we worked down into an alder swamp. With a sudden chorus of frantic yelping, the dogs announced that they had jumped the bear. The hound music began a short distance ahead, but it faded fast as the dogs lit out. They raced through the swamp, over a ridge, and into another tag-alder swamp.

When Hoppe and I reached that swamp we heard the hounds far ahead. They had changed from the drawn-out yowls of trailing to high-pitched staccato yelps. When I hear that chorus I really hit the brush running. It means that the bear is treed or is fighting on the ground. Big bears seldom tree. They know how to fight, and they can kill dogs as fast as lightning strikes.

Hoppe and I ran for a mile as hard as we could go. That swamp was so thick and the acoustics so deceiving that we overran the fight. The bear scented us and moved out. The dogs streaked after him.

Half an hour later Hoppe and I closed in on another fight at the far end of the swamp. I couldn't see 20 feet ahead in the thick jungle. Somehow that bear heard us or winded us, and it took off again.

The bruin must have decided to run away from trouble. The animal broke out of the swamp, ran to high ground, crossed a U.S. Forest Service road, and headed into a wilderness that is 10 miles across and 15 miles deep. Only two very bad roads cross that entire chunk of wild country. I groaned when I thought of the problems we'd have.

The Plott hounds went out of hearing in nothing flat. When that happens, you rush back to your vehicle and drive down a road that may get you in front of the chase. I knew of a road leading to an unused fire tower, and I figured that was our best bet.

When Hoppe and I got back to where my four-wheel-drive vehicle was parked, we found Ira Lee waiting for us. Ira runs a window-cleaning business in Wind Lake, Wisconsin, and he was another of the five hunters I was guiding that day.

We bounced our two 4WD vehicles for five miles before we reached our destination. Then I climbed the tower fast. Far off to the north I heard the faint barking of my dogs. I scampered down the tower.

Hoppe went off to pick up our other hunters. Ira and I would try closing in on the chase with my vehicle. Every five minutes we'd stop to listen for the pack. On the seventh stop I heard the dogs far away. We took off through the woods and ran our hearts out, for miles it seemed.

No matter how hard we ran the dogs moved out of hearing again. We rested a couple of minutes—just long enough to stop gasping for breath—and jogged back to the truck.

I drove the vehicle around a big chunk of wilderness and headed up another road. In a few miles we met Hoppe and his crew. Then we heard the dogs barking in the distance. We paused to determine which way the chase was going. Then we took off running again. Soon my lungs were pumping for air, sweat was running down my face, and my heart was banging my ribs.

The bear had decided to fight again. When I ran up to the scene in a cranberry swamp I was dumbfounded.

The bear wasn't as big as I had thought. It wasn't treed, and it wasn't a boar. It was a sow of about 400 pounds, and she was fighting the dogs at the base of a big pine. I knew she was a sow right away because two yearling bears were up in the branches. The hunt was over right then. We don't shoot sows with youngsters.

How come the sow had such big feet? I can only guess that they were abnormal. After all, I've seen huge bears with small heads and small bears with large heads. Anyway that sow wasn't finished dishing out trouble.

I didn't get a chance to call the dogs off, because the old lady lit out as soon as she saw us. The hounds streaked after her. I knew it would be a long run—the sow would surely take the pack as far as possible from her youngsters. We kept up with the chase till dark. Then we had no choice except to walk six miles back to our vehicles.

We returned to camp, ate, and collapsed into bed for a few hours of sleep. We got up at 3 a.m. and got back to the chase scene by dawn. We finally found the hounds walking down an old logging road. They were so tired they could hardly move. They were 20 miles north of where the sow had put her youngsters in that pine.

That's bear hunting. It can be work of the hardest kind, but to me it's also the most thrilling hunting you can find. I particularly enjoy the challenge of hunting with dogs.

Many bears are killed easily by hunters waiting in ambush at bait stations or by deer hunters who see a bear by chance. But a bear chased by dogs knows he's running for his life. Such a bruin can win fair and square in many ways.

A wild bear has great native intelligence. And the bigger they get the smarter they get. Once a black bear outsmarts a pack of dogs he'll never forget how.

Some bears, after being jumped by dogs, will run in a circle about a mile across. They'll run that circle a half-dozen or so times and then jump away from it or cut off down a blacktop road. By then the circular path is so loaded with bear scent that the hounds keep going around and around without realizing that the bruin is long gone.

I can't explain why bear scent won't hold on blacktop roads, but it doesn't. Smart bears know that fact. They also know that something dissipates or overpowers their scent along roadsides that have been sprayed for insects. You chase a bear that runs through such terrain, and you'll have a mighty bewildered pack of hounds.

Big bears know that dogs aren't a really serious problem. They know that the man with the gun is the danger. Often a big bear won't even run from dogs. He'll walk, stop and fight a bit, and walk again just fast enough to stay in front of the hunters. When I get a slow chase going, I can be fairly sure I'm dealing with a trophy-size bear.

And there are some factors that men, dogs, or bears can't control. Weather can be a blessing or a curse. Say a big bear hits some of my baits at night, but a rain comes on before dawn. The rain will wash out tracks and push scent into the ground. When that happens you're usually licked unless you go with a "rig dog," a dog that can catch a scent while riding on the hood of a slow-moving car or truck.

The odds can go the other way too. Take a situation in which the ground is warmer than the air on a dry day. Scent rises on such days, and trailing dogs are in their glory. However, when the air is warmer than the ground, the scent goes into the ground and the dogs are baffled.

One of the great things about hunting with dogs is that a lot of people have a lot of fun. A single hunter who has a bear over bait wraps up all his enjoyment in a short time, but a hunt with dogs often goes all day with total involvement by as many as 20 men. These fellows are usually in scattered groups, and each group tries its best to figure which way the chase will go and what the bear will do. Much of the fun is the competition between groups. A true bear hunter considers it an honor to be the first at the site when a bruin is treed. Why? Because hunting with dogs is about the toughest physical sport going. Once you try it you either love it or you can't stand it. If you have pride in your physical condition and you love to hunt the hard way, running after hounds can become an addiction. We are fanatical in our feelings for the sport.

Many hunters say sheep hunting is the toughest. Well, I say you can lie down and rest once in a while during a stalk for sheep. But once you start a bear hunt, you don't stop till you're worn out or you catch up to the dogs.

Remember that a bear will run in the roughest and thickest swamp he can find, and that's where you have to go if you're going to get him. During the chase you'll be soaking with sweat. You'll be scratched from running through branches. Your hair will be plastered to your scalp, and your exposed body will be covered with mosquito bites.

The astonishing thing is that most dedicated bear hunters don't even want to shoot a bear unless it's a big bear. Such men reason that the more bears they leave alive the more chases they'll have in the future.

So killing a bear is not the most important lure. What attracts a true bear hunter is the thrill of hunting with a good pack of hounds and the tremendous pride a man feels when he knows he has dogs that live for a chance to chase and fight a creature many times their size. I could tell hundreds of stories about the courage of bear dogs, but a couple stand out in my memory.

Jim Olson, who owns a truck firm in Lake Mills, Wisconsin, is a dedicated bear hunter. We're partners in developing our pack of Plott hounds. One day in the summer of 1971, we took some of our dogs on a trail hunt in the Chequamegon National Forest.

We found a bear track alongside the road. We put down Mickey, our strike dog, and Tyee, a young male. They both struck immediately, but neither did much barking. We figured the trail wasn't very hot, so we turned in Spade to help. We held two experienced dogs back to run later with Cade a youngster on his first hunt.

When the first three dogs jumped a bear in a cedar swamp, we turned Buttons, Flint, and Cade loose. We got a line on which way the bear was running by listening to the hound music and then we drove off to get ahead in the chase. We stopped 100 yards from where we figured the bear might cross a road near a tiny creek.

In minutes the bruin flashed across the road and melted into thickets. He was big, 400 pounds or so. A couple of hours later the dogs treed him. When Jim and I arrived the howling dogs were all but tearing the bark off that big poplar. The bear was 20 feet above, growling and popping his teeth with rage.

When the initial excitement wore off, we noticed that the young dog, Cade, was missing. We got the rest of the pack into the truck and spent the rest of the day looking for Cade without success. So we left a jacket at the spot where we had turned him into the chase. If he'd become lost, he'd be likely to backtrack to that jacket, where we could pick him up in the morning. If he'd fought that bear, we figured he was hurt or dead.

The next morning we found no sign of Cade near the jacket. After hours of searching and calling we heard a faint, lonesome bawl. It was late when we finally found the pup, and he was a mess. His right front leg was smashed, and he was unable to walk. It's frightening to realize how a bear can inflict terrible damage with one bite or swipe with a paw.

It cost Jim and me $350 to get Cade patched up. Our local veterinarian decided he couldn't handle the surgery. We sent Cade to a specialist at the University of Minnesota, and after that the dog required therapy twice a day for weeks. But he recovered, and he went back to hunting.

Another incident turned out to be more humorous than serious. This time a treed bear decided to come down and fight the dogs. He hit the ground in the middle of 10 dogs. During the uproar hounds went flying. It was as if they had been tossed down and bounced up on a trampoline. About the time we figured half our dogs would be killed—we were training dogs in July and had no firearms—the bruin decided he'd had enough.

He'd climbed eight feet back up the tree when Bud, one of Ira Lee's hounds, decided he could handle the bear by himself. He hurled himself through the air and grabbed the bear's rump, and he wouldn't let go. Up, up, and up went the bear with Bud hanging on. Everybody except Ira stood paralyzed.

"Let go, Bud—let go, you fool!" yelled Ira.

Dog and bear were about 30 feet up when Bud finally let go. Luckily he hit ground on the swampy side. He got up, shook himself, jumped back against the trunk, and began howling at the bear again. A good bear dog won't give up.

That kind of test is an example of why we begin running our dogs in summer. (We'd start earlier, but we won't allow our hounds to chase cubs that are too small to run and tree.) We want to weed out dogs that won't carry their weight when it's time to hunt for keeps. The only bear dog worth a nickel is the one that will give his all and come back for more punishment. Inexperienced or halfway hounds have no place in bear woods. At best they help make hunts unsuccessful. At worst they can cause good dogs to be hurt or killed by not carrying their share of the load. It takes months of training to determine which dogs will be winners.

Our system of hunting bears with dogs is pretty simple. It's standard in northern Wisconsin to begin with baits set in areas frequented by bears. Baits usually are meat scraps from butcher shops, suet, or bread laced with raspberry jam. Bait sets must be registered with the state's Department of Natural Resources, and they must be cleaned up and removed at the end of each hunting season.

Resort operators often make bait sets and rent them out to hunters who hope to kill bears from stands when the animals approach the baits at dawn or dusk. We use bait differently. We can't put our dogs into a chase until we find a fresh track, and the best way to find a fresh track is to start at a bait that has been hit during the night.

I usually put out at least 20 baits over a very wide area. Before dawn on each hunting day my hunters split into groups, and as soon as it is light enough, they start checking the baits in pickup trucks. If we find more than one set of tracks, we confer and choose the best set to put the dogs down on. We try to get as many hunters as possible in on the chase.

Don't get the notion we spend a lot of time riding around in trucks. As soon as those dogs take off on a hot trail, the only way to follow is on foot. The trail often leads miles into the roughest terrain around. And don't forget that getting back is part of the task. We travel mile after mile on foot.

When my baits fail to show fresh tracks, or big tracks, we often use a rig dog. A rig dog is a hound trained to ride on the hood of a slow-moving truck, and his job is to sound off as soon as he smells bear. A good rig dog has what we call a free mouth: he'll howl when he catches the slightest scent. A tight-mouthed dog won't bark unless scent is strong.

Bears often cross dirt roads during their travels, and when they do they leave scent. If the track is fresh a rig dog can catch the scent in the air when a vehicle crosses the trail. The trick then is to stop, find the track, and turn loose some strike dogs if the size of the tracks justifies a chase.

Once a chase is on, almost anything can happen. Two and three-year-old bruins usually make the longest and trickiest runs. Treed bears often come down when they see hunters. When that happens the race is on again.

Such situations are particularly unnerving for newcomers. When they see a big bear drop out of a tree into a pack of yelping dogs they just about come apart with excitement. The viciousness, the racket, and the tearing apart of the terrain are almost unbelievable.

Unfortunately hunters who don't own trained dogs can't get in on the action unless they hire a guide. But northern Wisconsin has many guides with bear hounds. You can contact guides by writing Jim Rice, Wisconsin Bear Hunters Association, Neillsville, Wisconsin 54456.

The season for hunting bears with dogs in Wisconsin usually runs the last three weeks of September. The non-resident license costs $35.50. Most rifles of .30 caliber or larger will do.

Most bears are shot at a few yards. You won't need a scope. It's a chilling thought, but at those ranges a scope would be dangerous. It's difficult to aim if your entire field of view is filled with magnified bear fur.

Green Mountain Bear Chase

Doug Knight

October, 1969

Three times in two hours we'd been close enough to hear the dogs corner the bear. And three times the bear had sensed us closing in and had broken off with the dogs.

The latest miss had been the toughest to take. For over an hour, Bill Mason and I had climbed up, down, and across the tortuous rocky eastern wall of Styles Peak. We'd heard at least two of the dogs battling the bear near the top and had hoped that this time would be it.

Then we reached the point of fatigue at which we would climb 20 steps and stop to gasp for breath. Bill was doing a little better than I was since he was carrying only a Model 94 Winchester .30/30. I had camera gear in my pack, a camera slung around my neck, and a Smith & Wesson .357 Magnum, a gun belt, shells, and an aid kit hanging from my waist. I may be six-foot-four and 220 pounds, but after 11 hours of this sort of treatment I was completely bushed.

As we closed to within 50 yards of the top the bear broke away, this time into the dense, dark wilderness surrounding Mad Tom Brook. It was 6 p.m., and with darkness closing in we just couldn't press on. Reluctantly we turned back.

It had been a long day. At 7 o'clock that morning we had parked our vehicles at the deep-woods end of an old dirt road northwest of the tiny Vermont town of North Landgrove. To the north of our parking spot lay Pete Parent Peak and to the southwest towered Styles Peak. Up the trail and across the notch to the west lay Mt. Tabor, a long mountainous table topped with lakes, ponds, streams, swamps, and some of the toughest bear country in the Green Mountain National Forest.

Also in this rugged wilderness were some mighty big bears—big because hunters rarely bothered them and food was abundant; mighty because that's what they had to be to get around in this sort of country.

It was Sunday, our second day out. The bear we'd been following was a big one. We knew it because the dogs couldn't hold him. We knew it because he'd refused to tree. Instead, he'd kept turning on the dogs to try to discourage them. And most of all, we knew it because we had picked up his splayfooted tracks where he'd crossed a brook. Bill had guessed he'd weigh 250 to 300 pounds.

My companions on the hunt were Bill Mason of Endicott, New York; Linwood Jones and the late Marvin Brinsfield of Severna Park, Maryland; and my son Chip. Bill Mason—sturdy, round-faced, and full of fun—is a plumbing-and-heating contractor who maintains one of the effective packs of bear-and-cat dogs in the East. Bear hunting is one of his favorite sports, and Vermont is his favorite territory. I work in communications with IBM, and my son was at the time in his senior year at John Jay High School in Cross River, New York. We live in South Salem, New York. Marvin Brinsfield was a husky outdoorsman who doubled as a radio outdoor sportscaster. Lin Jones is a college student.

This Vermont real estate is big, remote, and rough, much of it straight up, with hardwoods, softwoods, and a lot of evergreens—spruce, pine, and hemlock. In the fall the bears like to move up into the highlands, where most of them will den up when winter locks in on the mountains. The high country holds its cold longer, and the bears seem to realize instinctively that their dormant period will last longer and their sleep will be deeper because of it. A bear doesn't like being hungry, and the longer he can sleep, the more food he'll find in the lowlands after he wakes up.

For the early-rising bear the spring pickings are extremely slim. The small ground animals aren't moving, the buds aren't full enough for nibbling, and there are no apples or berries—a bear's favorite food. But on our hunt it was early October, and the oaks in the high country had left plenty of sweet ripe acorns on the ground for bears to stock up on, thereby adding to their already heavy layer of hibernating fat.

On Saturday, our first day of hunting, we took a bear track out of a blowdown on the edge of a fine grove of oaks. This bear wasn't hibernating yet but must have been trying out the snug harbor under the downed trees for size. It was a young bear, lightweight and fast, and he gave us a fine chase before he threw off the young dogs in a series of streambed excursions. Our hounds were wet and tired when we picked them up that first night, but a good rubdown and steaming meals picked them up fast back at camp.

Bill had brought seven hounds on this trip—two Walkers, a Black and Tan, a Bluetick, two Redbones, and a Redtick. You need plenty of dog power in this sort of hunting. If you bring only three or four dogs and they get hung up in a grueling all-day chase, you've got tired noses and sore feet to put on the trail the next morning. Worse yet (and it happens all too often) two or more of your best dogs might just take a straightline bear into the next county. Luck like that will wipe out a bear hunt. The dogs may not show up again for a week.

The weatherman predicted sun for Sunday, our second day, but the day started overcast and cool, perfect for tracking if it held. Bill took along four dogs—two Redbones, the Redtick, and the Black and Tan. The Redtick, a veteran named Old Red who had the scars of eight battle-filled years engraved on his liver-spotted hide, was the strike dog in the team. When Bill Mason turned him loose, Old Red had the job of ranging the woods on both sides of our line of travel in search of fresh bear track. If he found it he'd start to sound—slow at first, maybe one howl every couple of minutes. The more noise he made, the fresher the track was. When Old Red started moving out, we'd follow with the other dogs still on leash.

I find it amazing that veteran strike dogs never take a bear track out in the wrong direction. With a younger strike dog, though, you'll sometimes find yourself trailing the wrong way on a bear. Smart old-timers like Mason allow for this contingency by keeping the rest of the pack under leash until a spot is reached where the bear crossed a trail or mudhole or climbed up a bank. At such spots the clawmarks will indicate whether the hunt is turned around. If it is, the hunters just reverse directions, walk back up the return trail until the strike dog is out of hearing, and unleash the rest of the pack in the right direction. Wrong Way Charlie soon discovers that he's out of the hunt, that no one is following, and that the scent has run out. An hour or so later, sheepish and with his tongue dragging, the missing dog will come tearing back up the trail, heading the right way to get back into the action.

It doesn't take a good hound more than two or three times out to learn his lesson. He either smartens up or gets demoted.

Saturday we'd started on the Wallingford side of Green Mountain National Forest and hunted the swamps and lowlands around Wilder Mountain. Sunday we were starting farther south, from the town of North Landgrove. A small road northwest of town led us past a few small farms along Griffith Brook and soon gave way to an old logging trail that led up toward the base of Peru Peak, a rugged 3,429-foot-high mountain with a reputation, among us at least, for breaking the heart and back of many a stout hunter who went after the abundant bears that cruise its slopes.

Bill led off on the trail with Old Red under leash. Marvin, Lin, and my son Chip held the three other dogs in check, and I brought up the rear. This early in the day, the eager dogs were hard to hold in. At times their pulling power was welcome. But too often their route around a tree was not ours, and a tangled leash was a continual frustration.

We walked about half a mile before Bill turned Old Red loose to cruise along Griffith Brook. A stream is always a good place to cruise a strike dog, especially when it originates far up in a mountain range. Bears traveling that side of the mountain will always stop for a drink and will invariably cross. The crossing point yields good sign for the hunter and good tracks for his dogs. Unfortunately, Griffith Brook produced not a sound from Old Red.

Maybe his nose is gone, I thought to myself. But then, the other dogs didn't bark either, and if the scent were strong enough we'd surely have heard from them.

Slowly, painfully, we climbed the steep tree-studded slope of Peru Peak's eastern wall. In half a mile of climbing we gained almost 1,200 feet in altitude. By the time we topped the ridge, it was 10 a.m. and everyone was looking in vain for his third wind. Ahead and below us lay Swale Meadow, a basin at the 2,500-foot mark with two ponds that fed a stream called Lake Brook. While we sat in a mossy glen overlooking the meadow, Red moved out of sight. The leashed dogs whined nervously, and Bill cussed them quiet. Marvin pulled a silicone rag from his jacket pocket and rubbed the morning moisture from his Remington .30/06. I discovered a sandwich in my pack and tossed half to Bill.

"If you insist," he said, grinning. Bill rarely refuses.

The forest behind and ahead of us stretched out in the green and rainbow hues of fall. Stately evergreens complemented the golds and reds of the maples and the yellow-browns of the oaks. Off in the distance a blue jay objected to some intrusion. Three crows soared across the edge of the sky.

My son lay back, his eyes closed while Marvin and Lin spoke in muted tones off to our right. As I checked my light-meter readings, the lonely howl of a hound echoed up out of the boggy basin ahead.

"Hey, is that Old Red?" Lin eagerly inquired.

Bill grinned, holding up a hand for silence. A minute passed. Another howl. And another. We sat tight, letting Old Red work it out, letting him decide which way the track went and how fresh it was. So far, we couldn't tell which way Red was moving. The three leashed hounds wiggled and whined in anticipation.

"Let 'im sort it out," Bill cautioned, "and give that Squealer a whack to shut him up."

Lin obliged, and Squealer momentarily toned down.

We all listened to Old Red's lonesome tones roll back across the swamp. Bill was gauging the freshness of the track by Red's bark.

"Turn Squealer loose," Bill ordered. "Let's see if we can get something moving. Old Red's out there tellin' us that a bear's been through here today."

The small-boned Black and Tan was away like a soundless arrow. We kept waiting for his crazy voice to open up on the trail, but all we heard was Old Red's mournful howl every minute or so. Even Red's voice was fading now. We looked at Bill.

"Let's move out," Bill directed. "Red's taking that track into the ravine on the far side of the meadow. If we get over to the edge fast enough we can tell which way he's going."

By the time we had slogged around the edge of the swale, Squealer's warbling high-pitched voice was pouring up out of the hollow.

"That's a good track," Bill announced. "Turn in the other dogs."

Seconds later Rebel and Jiggs, the two Redbone speedsters, were off, openmouthed, hot after the now faint-voiced Squealer and Old Red.

From there on out it turned into a very long day. The bear track ran down the ravine paralleling Lake Brook, turned the corner at the base of Mt. Tabor, and then headed up. Halfway up the mountainside the dogs jumped the bear out of an oak grove and pushed him on up over the top. They were in full cry now.

By this time our hunting party was scattered all over the area. Everyone had his own idea about which way the bear was heading, which way the dogs were running, and what the easiest way to intersect their line of run was.

My method for handling this situation comes from many years of hunting with Bill Mason, and it's usually the best. It doesn't require much sense—only endurance. I stick with Mason.

Over the years, he has developed a sixth sense for bear. By listening to the dogs' trailing barks he can tell if they're following a cold trail or a hot trail, or if they've jumped a bear. He knows the country, he knows bear habits, and he has patience.

When the dogs jump a bear, Bill strikes out for a listening post on the high land. He has to hear the dogs to know which way they're going. If their voices fade out as they cross the next hill, Mason moves out to sit on top of that one, too, saving his energy for when it's really needed.

Except for time spent listening, Mason keeps moving from high point to high point. Rarely will he move down into a valley after the dogs unless they are barking treed or unless sounds indicate that a bayed bear may be injuring his hounds. Hounds in danger really move Bill into action. With hounds worth $800 to $2,000 apiece, he likes to protect his investment.

Bill and I kept to the high side of the canyon wall as we made our tedious way up the precipitous side of Buck Ball Peak. Before we had got halfway up, the bear topped the mountain and dropped into Elbow Swamp, a messy tangle of alders and swamp grass sitting at the 2,400-foot level atop massive Mt. Tabor. Four dogs went in, and then mayhem. We could hear the bear plunging and splashing, brush tearing, and dogs barking in ecstatic chops and yelping with surprise when the bear managed to nail one of them. Bill got soaked to the waist trying to reach the dogs, but he slogged back out when he found that the way in was too treacherous. We had to wait for the bear to get fed up with the dogs and move out.

The bear wasn't the first one out. Old Red was, with a deep slash across the top of his nose. Bill checked it over and then sprinkled a little penicillin powder onto it. Then he sent me to one corner of the marsh to stand watch while he moved to the other side. Chip took a stand behind a boulder halfway between Bill and me.

In answer to a hail from Brinsfield and Jones, Bill shouted across the swamp for them to watch the far side. The bear apparently didn't like the way things were shaping up. He broke out of the swamp like a black specter, dripping with swamp water and draped with shards of grass, and charged straight across the grassy edge toward my son, who was armed with only a camera.

Bill and I only heard the bear. But with the dogs on his heels he passed within 30 feet of Chip, who reeled off a series of photos of the tumbling, slashing action.

The bear took off up the mountain. He was big, "at least two-hundred-and-fifty pounds," Bill estimated from Chip's description. The bear crossed the mouth of Long Hole Lake, broke up over Staples Trail, and circled Peru Peak twice before baying once more at dusk near the top of Styles Peak.

We got close, but not close enough for a shot. The dogs took the bear down the other side of Styles Peak and into the dark morass surrounding Mad Tom Brook. At this point, which I described at the beginning, we called it a day.

Fortunately it was all downhill to the cars. We got to them by 7:20. Old Red and Squealer made it out with us but Jiggs and Rebel were apparently still on the bear's trail. We left two dog blankets at the parking spot so that if Jiggs and Rebel returned they'd have a friendly scent and a little warmth to encourage them to stick around until we returned to pick them up.

Back at camp, we fed and watered the dogs and ate dinner. About 11 p.m. Bill and I took my four-wheel-drive vehicle and headed back up the Griffith Brook trail to see if Jiggs and Rebel had returned. As our headlights hit the little vale, two pairs of lights beamed back at us. Both dogs obviously were glad to see us, but they were too stiff even to stand. They only things moving were their tails. We carefully cuddled the two hounds in our arms, put them on blankets in the back of the van, and then turned up the heater full blast. Food, water, and a good night's sleep were what they needed, but the next morning a check of their feet revealed that both dogs were through for this hunting trip.

From his remaining dogs Bill picked out the pack for Monday, our last day to hunt. The Bluetick Rock was well rested, as were the Walkers Rapaho (Rap) and Crybaby. The Black and Tan, Squealer, had endured a hard chase the day before and probably wouldn't last, but Bill wanted his nose in there for the early going.

"Where today?" Marvin asked as he brought back an eager, hard-pulling Rap from a short exercise run.

"Right where we were yesterday," Bill said.

Our faces fell. Bill grinned.

"Only this time," he continued, "we'll pick up that bear's track quick from the south side of Styles Peak. Then we'll hit him hard with some fresh dogs. We'll see just how long he can keep this up."

Bill knows this southern-Vermont country well. An old road west out of North Landgrove would take us right into Mad Tom Notch and just a quarter-mile south of where we had last heard the dogs and bear.

After less than 20 minutes of hiking up the southwest wall of Styles Peak, both strike dogs—Rap and Squealer—opened up on the previous night's bear track.

This was brutally heavy cover, and I was glad we hadn't tried tackling it the night before. The evergreens were so dense that no direct light hit the forest floor. The woods were damp and foreboding, but the dogs' chorus was hot and full of fire. Excitement coursed through our hearts and gave us the energy we needed to drive ourselves up the steep slope after the dogs. Ten minutes later, the dogs jumped the bear. He apparently was well-tired from the preceding day's action and had quickly holed up after Rebel and Jiggs had broken off the chase.

This bear was no slouch, however. He pushed right up through the meanest cover he could find, trying to brush off the hounds. He managed only to brush *us* off.

Lin and Marvin leveled off and cruised north along the western slope of Mt. Tabor, holding at about the 1,800-foot mark in case the bear decided to drop back over. Bill, Chip, and I pushed up over the top, just below the main peak of Mt. Tabor.

The bear half-mooned the peak and dropped into a small swamp 500 yards to the north. He stayed just long enough for us to close in. Then Rap and Rock became so annoying that he couldn't stand it. I got one glimpse of the bear as he backed out of a heavy tangle, grunting and coughing at the ripping and darting hounds. Then, with a coughing, tooth-popping roar, he broke for the edge of the mountain again. I had one glimpse of him as he dropped down over the saddle and headed toward the other half of our party. Almost immediately I heard a shot, then two more. The chase turned back up the mountain, with Lin and Marvin close after the dogs.

The bear was no longer sure where we all were, and he lit into a brook that flowed north from Tabor toward Griffith Lake, hoping to throw the dogs off his scent. But he was too late. The dogs could sight-trail him now. The chase led us back toward Griffith Lake and Long Hole Lake, where we had pushed the bear the day before.

The bear was brought to bay again in the tall grass and goldenrod between the woods and the lake. He charged back and forth from one tormentor to another, twice going mouth-to-mouth with Rock, the ever-charging Bluetick.

Bill, Chip, and I closed in on the action from the east. Marvin crossed the stream just below us. As Marvin broke through from the woods to our left, the bear broke away from the dogs. It was the first open shot we had.

"Take him!" Bill roared at Marvin.

Marv snapped up his Remington Automatic and swung with the high-tailing bear. Just as the bear reached the woods, Marvin let go. The bear was down in a tangle of fur, feet, and dogs. For a moment we couldn't see what was happening just over the little rise, but as we topped it the bear made one last lightninglike move toward the most aggressive of his tormentors, Rock. The Bluetick stood his ground as the 250-pound raging black hulk closed the 10-foot distance. Marvin had his gun up but couldn't shoot for fear of hitting one of the dogs.

Rock tumbled back under the bear's final charge and disappeared, scrambling and yelping, under the heavy black body as the mortally wounded bear swatted and bit at him.

Mason was over the bank in a flash, his Smith & Wesson .357 Magnum suddenly in his hand. Then, holding the handgun practically against the bear's lunging shoulders, he fired one shot into the broad target right where the bear's neck met its bulging back.

It was all over. As Bill heaved at the now unresisting bear, Rock struggled out from under the smothering weight and stood, momentarily mute, on shaking legs. Then, as the rest of the pack charged in to tear at the lifeless bear, Rock came back to life and jumped in to chew on a piece of hide.

It was a sudden but satisfying ending to an exciting three-day hunt. Marvin Brinsfield had his first bear, and my son had his first close-in view of one of our country's finest game animals. It may take Chip and me a year to forget the punishment we took during that hunt. But this fall we'll both be back again. Bear hunting's like that. It gets in your blood.

PART

VIII
BOWHUNTING
FOR BEARS

A Bear Worth Waiting For

**Hawley (Hawl) Rhew
as told to Reg Sharkey**

October, 1969

The northern tip of Michigan's Lower Peninsula is part of God's country. Local residents firmly believe that, and I'll drink to it, for that area south of the Straits of Mackinac is ruggedly beautiful. It's also bear country.

I'd been going there from Flint, Michigan, for a good many years to hunt deer, and I finally made up my mind that driving back and forth was cutting into good hunting time. So in the summer of 1970 I pulled up stakes and moved my wife and five kids to Carp Lake, a village of 200 people. It's only eight miles from the straits, where in 1763 a band of Chippewa Indians wiped out the British troops garrisoned at Fort Michilimackinac.

It didn't take me long to settle into a new job as a meatcutter with the Giant Supermarket in Petoskey, only a few minutes' drive from my home.

Getting acquainted with my neighbors—just about everybody in a small village—was easy because a lot of them were ready to go hunting at the drop of a hat. I even got myself a pack of bluetick hounds and tried coon hunting, but it didn't give me the excitement I expected, so I sold the dogs and concentrated on my greatest love, bowhunting. I'd been doing it for 17 years and had 10 bowkilled whitetails to my credit. I had also taken a 150-pound black bear with a rifle. That bear convinced me that hunting them was my Sunday suit, but I believed that the right way to do it was Indian style—with bow and arrow.

In the fall of 1968 I went to Grand Marais in the Upper Peninsula, drawn there by the ballyhooed abundance of black bears in the area. From a bowhunter's viewpoint it was bedlam. An archer didn't have much of a

293

A split-second before the arrow hit his shoulder, the enormous bear turned his head and looked at me.

chance to pursue his silent sport. There were dogs and hunters all over the country, and things got a little out of hand at times. I don't have anything against hunting bears with dogs, but I believe that a few days before the dog season should be reserved for archers.

After that scoreless trip I decided to concentrate on the bears in my own backyard. And that I did for a few years but without any luck.

In the summer of '72 I heard that huckleberry pickers had seen an outsize black bear feeding in a nearby marsh. I pursued the subject like a hound on a hot track. I found out that this big bear was roaming near Wilderness State Park, almost in the shadow of the Big Mac Bridge, the five-mile engineering wonder that links the two Michigan peninsulas.

Since I lived only a few miles away, I went there often to look for him and read bear sign. There was plenty of sign. Thanks to the protection afforded bears through closed seasons, they were coming back strong all over their range in the Upper Peninsula and the northern part of the Lower Peninsula. Right here I'd like to salute Carl T. Johnson, chairman of the Natural Resources Commission and "father" of modern bear hunting with dogs in Michigan. He is the man most responsible for elevating the black bear from his former unprotected status as a nongame animal to the protected status he enjoys today as a game animal.

I put in every minute I could in the 1972 season without getting a good chance at a bear. I didn't see hide or hair of the big one.

The following summer I forgot about fishing in order to put in more time scouting bear country. I saw bears all right, but not the one I was looking for. About a week before the 1973 season opened, I got a good look at him for the first time. That's when I began calling him Big Mac. He was the largest black bear I'd ever seen.

I put in many hours and hunted hard that season. I even passed up a smaller bear, for under Michigan's one-bear limit I would have been all through for the year had I killed him. Big Mac was the one I wanted, but I didn't see him. I didn't hear of any other hunter getting him, and that gave me hope. If he had been taken, I'm sure I would have heard about it. In this piece of country, news of that sort travels like a crown fire in a stand of jackpines.

I kept looking for him all that summer, and though I didn't see him, I found enough sign to know that he was still around. His big footprints were unmistakable, and the height of his scratch marks on trees convinced me that Big Mac was alive and keeping his territory posted.

Opening day 1974 was September 21, and I was rarin' to go. My hunting gear was in tiptop shape and all checked out. I use a Herter's takedown bow made of laminated fiberglass and wood. It has a 53-pound pull. Some bowhunters tell me that a 50-pound bow is a little light for bear, but let me tell you something. I am 38 years old, of muscular build, and in pretty good shape. I've tried bows with a heavier pull, and I find that my accuracy suffers, so I'll stick with a bow that fits me.

I'm a fanatic about the business end of my aluminum-shafted arrows. I've found out that you just can't get hunting heads too sharp. I believe there are times when a deer or bear takes an arrow and runs off simply because the broadhead isn't sharp enough to give maximum penetration. This can lead to an exhausting chase before the animal is dispatched.

It took bowhunters a good many years to be accepted as legitimate sportsmen by old-time firearms hunters. There were a lot of exaggerated stories told by the hot-stove leaguers about deer looking like porcupines. That's why I make sure my broadheads are razor-sharp. I knew that a lot of arrow penetration would be needed to reach a vital area in a bear the size of Big Mac, so I customized a half-dozen three-bladed Wasp broadheads. I epoxy-cemented single-edge injector razor blades to each edge. If there's a drawback to those heads, it's getting nicked if you're the least bit careless when handling them.

The closer it got to opening day, the more often I checked the big bear's stomping grounds in the Hardwood State Forest. At one spot, three runways came together in a small clearing. It looked so good that I built a blind, using a large stump, a fallen tree, dead branches, and a little scrub brush.

A few days before the opener, things didn't look too good for me and my three hunting buddies. Two of them, Bud and Bob Winters, are close neighbors of mine, while Dick Cushman lives not too far away, in Harbor Springs. Bob works for a small manufacturing plant in Petoskey. He's been bowhunting four years and has taken three deer. His brother Bud is a maintenance man at a gift shop near Fort Michilimackinac, and he was in his first year as an archer. Dick Cushman works as a meatcutter with me, and he too was a newcomer to bowhunting. He probably caught the fever from me.

Two days before the season opened, we gave our blinds a final check and looked around. We were disappointed when we found that bears did not seem to be using the runways. After so many sightings by berry pickers and our own observations, why should they suddenly change their habits? We couldn't feigure it out.

Nevertheless we went ahead with plans for the first day. We agreed our best chance of success would be to hunt from late afternoon until dark, which would come around 8 p.m. Except during the gun season on deer, Michigan game laws limit hunting to the hours between 6 a.m. and 7 p.m., Eastern Standard Time. Because the state was still on Daylight Saving Time in September, the legal quitting time was 8 o'clock. By then the light would be too poor for hunting anyway.

The morning of the first day was anything but encouraging. There was a strong wind and a threat of rain. I puttered around the house and groused about the weather until my wife told me to go away and talk with Bud and Bob. We hashed over archery techniques, equipment, and how we'd make our shots until Dick finally showed up from Harbor Springs. At 4 p.m. we gathered up our gear, and by 5 we were in our blinds.

It had been overcast all day, and the wind started blowing hard again. Then it began to rain. By 6:30 I'd had it. I went to find my friends and head for home.

I picked up Bud, and we went on to meet Bob and Dick. On the way to their blinds we ran across them. Dick had put an arrow into a small bear, and they were following the blood trail.

"I know my shot was good," he said. "It looked like the arrow went clear through him."

While were were looking for the bear, we met John Rirsa, conservation officer for the northern part of the county. He had been bear hunting on one his pass days, and he offered to help us. We gave it a good try, but it got dark, and we had to give up. Disheartened, we drove home in silence, but we were grimly determined to go back bright and early to look for Dick's bear.

The morning dawned cold and rainy, a miserable day to hunt, yet it didn't take long to locate the bear in an alder thicket just a short distance from where we had given up the previous evening. Dick had made an excellent shot on a 130-pounder. The arrow had gone completely through the chest cavity, piercing both lungs. We gutted and dragged the animal out to Dick's vehicle and then headed for Carp Lake.

My wife Lucille made us some lunch. Toward midafternoon the rain let up, and Bob, Bud, and I went on out to hunt. After an hour I realized I hadn't put on enough warm clothes. I was beginning to get the shakes. Finally it got to be more than I could stand, so I eased out to the road and ran a fast quarter-mile, back and forth, to warm up.

Back at the blind, I was just getting settled down when I heard Bud's four-wheel-drive vehicle leaving. I guessed he and Bob had been frozen out. It was getting dark.

The discomfort and abuse hunters endure was in my mind when I caught a movement out of the corner of my eye. Turning my head ever so slowly, I saw Big Mac's dark hulk materializing silently out of the underbrush!

He moved slowly forward in the deepening twilight—a giant of a bear, burly, low-slung, black as midnight. The magnificent trophy I had sought for three years was coming into view as noiselessly as a black ghost, and he was almost within good bow range. He turned and came shuffling down the runway toward me, and I could feel my heart knocking.

Big Mac was edgy. He stopped, sniffed, and then came on again. As he eased into the little clearing in front of my blind, he stopped and turned broadside to me. He was looking suspiciously at the blind, and I didn't move a muscle. Then he turned his attention away. I slowly raised the bow high enough to let the arrow clear the blind and drew.

I had an instant of doubt. Could I plant my arrow where it would kill a bear of that great size? Then I released.

I could see the trajectory of the white shaft, and it looked good. The bear must have heard the muffled vibration of the bowstring. A split-second before the arrow hit him in the shoulder, he turned his head back and looked straight at me again.

Then the razor-armed broadhead stabbed into his vitals, and he wheeled on his back legs and bolted into the underbrush. No bawling, no coughing—only the sound of snapping brush marked his progress as he charged blindly away in the darkness.

Then it was very quiet.

I sat there wondering if my shot had been good and even thought about the possibility that he might make a circle and come up on me from behind, something I guess wounded black bears rarely or never do. I worried about it for five minutes that seemed like half an hour. Then I headed for my car.

I drove back to Carp Lake as fast as I dared and went to Bud's place for help. I was so keyed up I couldn't sit down or stand still. I paced back and forth until Bud said, "Calm down, Hawl! You're making *me* nervous. We'll find your bear."

He phoned Bob, who came as soon as he could. We took flashlights and a gas lantern and went barreling back to my blind. When we got there it was 10:30 and dark as the inside of a cave.

The bear had left a good blood trail, and it was easy to follow with the help of our lights. But we went very slowly. Under Michigan game laws it is illegal to carry firearms or bow and arrows in the woods after legal hunting hours. We were armed only with our hunting knives.

I suppose I was too keyed up at the time to think about the risk we were taking. If the wounded bear attacked in the darkness, I thought, our very lives would be in danger. I had heard and read many times about encounters of that kind. But I had also heard more than enough stories (few if any of them true) of bowhunters wounding animals and letting them die without making any real effort to track them down. I had made up my mind that nobody would ever be able to say that about me.

So Bud and Bob and I felt our way gingerly, a few steps at a time, stopping to listen for any sound from the bear, and I'll admit my scalp prickled. The woods stayed deathly still, and we finally picked him up in the beam of a flashlight. Our feelings as we stood and studied the motionless black shape are easier to imagine than to describe. Big Mac was dead.

With almost superhuman effort we managed to roll him over for field dressing. We removed all the internal organs, along with some fat. My modified broadhead had performed very well, slicing through the top of one lung, and Big Mac had died from a massive hemorrhage, as arrow-shot animals are supposed to. The shaft had broken off eight inches behind the head.

We knew we couldn't possibly drag him out, so we marked a 400-yard trail back to our car and headed to Carp Lake to get help. I couldn't endure the thought of leaving the magnificent bear out in the woods until after daylight the next morning.

Regardless of the late hour, we pounded on the doors of sleeping friends, and when they heard what had happened they came willingly.

Eight of us harnessed ourselves to the bear with ropes, one held a light, and the three others moved logs out of the way. Eventually we got out to the road and muscled the bear into the pickup truck. It was 2:30 Sunday morning, September 22. At 3 a.m. Big Mac was hanging from a maple in my front yard. Then I went to bed.

That afternoon I took him to the market where I work and weighed him on officially sealed beam scales. His dressed weight, witnessed by market employees and by Jim Doherty, editor of the Petoskey News-Review, was a staggering 613 pounds. A lot of that weight was the heavy layer of fat he carried.

Next I took the bear to the district office of the Michigan Department of Natural Resources at Gaylord for inspection and registration. Up to that time I hadn't thought much about the possibility of my bear being a record-breaker. I knew I had shot an exceptional bear, but I didn't know what the record weight was.

I found out in a hurry when Bob Strong, district wildlife biologist at Gaylord, saw the bear.

To begin with, Big Mac had broken by 58 pounds the 555-pound Michigan record for bowkilled bears. That bear had been killed by Dean Lovelace of Hamtramck in 1950. More surprising, he was a pound heavier than the biggest bear ever recorded in Michigan, a 612-pounder, dressed weight, killed with firearms in 1972 by Ed Phelps of Melvindale and Estille Johnson of Romulus.

Finally, Big Mac was 33 pounds heavier than Michigan's No. 2 record holder up to that time, a bear that dressed 580, shot in 1971 by D. S. Pope of the Detroit suburb of Troy. Pope killed his bear near Shingleton in Alger County, in the Upper Peninsula. Phelps and Johnson were hunting in the same county when they downed their record-holder. Of the three biggest black bears ever killed in Michigan, only mine came from south of the Straits of Mackinac.

Strong estimated Big Mac's age at around eight years, and using an official table of weights he calculated that the bear had weighed 694 pounds before dressing. El Harger, a game biologist at the Houghton Lake Wildlife Research Station who is a leading authority on black bears east of the Mississippi, estimated that the live weight had been at least 10 pounds heavier than that. If so, Big Mac had weighed more than 700 pounds.

Extraordinary as Michigan's three top heavyweights were, they fall quite a bit short of equaling what is believed to be the heaviest black bear ever killed in this country. That one was shot in northern Wisconsin in 1963 by Otto Hedbany of Milwaukee and tipped the scales at 652 pounds dressed. Game men calculated the live weight at around 720 pounds.

According to the rules of the Pope and Young Club, which registers bow kills, and the rules of the Boone and Crockett Club, bear trophies are rated by skull measurement rather than weight. On that score my bear was less impressive than I expected.

Measured by Frank Scott, an official Pope and Young measurer, after the required 60-day drying period, the skull scored $20^{12}/_{16}$. That's seventh on the Pope and Young list, but not quite good enough to make the Boone and Crockett records, for which the minimum is now 21.

Regardless of his skull score, however, Big Mac will remain a record-breaker in my book for the rest of my life.

Arrow for a Grizzly

Fred Bear as told to Ben East

October, 1957

The moose was standing shoulder-deep in frost-yellowed willows. Though he was on a slope nearly a mile away across the valley, we could make out with the glasses that he was big as a horse and had a rack as wide as a barn door. We'd seen plenty of moose on the trip, but nothing like this fellow.

"There's what I came to the Yukon for," Judd sighed, "and now we see him too late in the day to do anything about it."

"Moose stay all night. Killum in morning," said George John, Judd's Indian guide, backing his prediction with a confident grin.

We'd intended to move camp right after daylight next day, but if that big bull was still there in the morning camp moving could wait. Somewhat to our surprise, he was. In the first good light, while the autumn-cured grass in front of our valley camp was still white with frost, we spotted him browsing in thick willows on the slope less than a quarter of a mile from where we'd seen him the night before.

The overnight wait had given us plenty of time to map our campaign. Judd would ride across the river with George John and Alex Van Bibber, who was our outfitter and my guide, then up to a bench about half a mile below the moose. There Judd would leave the guides and make the stalk alone. That was the way he wanted it. Don Redinger and I would stay in camp and signal Judd with a white towel pinned to a forked stick. At a distance, the mountain looked free of heavy cover. But we'd been on it and knew it was a jungle of tall thickets. Judd would need help to find the moose.

With the spotting scope set up and our binoculars handy, we were ready when Judd left the guides and started his stalk. Most of the day the moose browse for half an hour at a time, then lay down. Watching our

301

signals, Judd sat tight when the moose was down, then resumed his stalk every time the bull got up to feed.

It was an exciting game of hide-and-seek to watch, and it went on for hours before Judd got where he wanted to be—just 25 yards from the moose. The bull was in the open, and our scope showed us he was staring down at us, possibly puzzled by the white flash of our signal towel. Don and I waited for Judd to shoot. Then suddenly the moose slewed around and vanished in the willows. That was that.

Judd came in alone after dark, disappointed but not dejected. It must have looked easy from where we sat, he agreed, but it wasn't so simple over there on the mountainside. He'd been close enough a dozen times to nail the bull with a rifle of almost any caliber. But this was a bowhunt, and Judd was armed with one of the bows I make, a Kodiak model with a pull of 65 to 70 pounds.

Judd had used every precaution, even kicking his boots off and walking in his socks part of the time. But when we saw him close in to 25 yards, Judd could see only the bull's neck. So he waited for a sure chance to put an arrow into the rib cage. While he waited, he felt a stray puff of wind catch him from behind and chill the sweat on the back of his neck. That was all the warning the moose needed.

"Never mind," Judd said cheerfully. "I'll do better at Devils Lake."

We were after moose, goats, Dall sheep, and grizzlies. We'd left our take-off point on Haines Highway, 93 miles from Haines Junction, on Sunday morning, August 26, 1956. It was now the 31st, and our camp was set up on Blanchard Lake in Yukon Territory, a few miles north of the British Columbia border and about 50 miles east of Alaska. This area is good for goats and moose, fair for sheep and bears.

There were seven in our party, not counting Tiger, the young husky that Alex had brought along to keep grizzlies out of the cook tent. Judd (Dr. Judd Grindell, a bowhunter of vast experience from Siren, Wisconsin) and I were the hunters. Don Redinger, Pittsburgh photographer, had come along in the hope of doing something I'd wanted to do for 17 years—take good action pictures of a big-game bowhunt. Don was using a movie camera with a series of telephoto lenses and had his hands too full to do any hunting. (Don is the cameraman who, a few months later, went to Africa with the Texas sportsman, Bill Negley, to film the shooting of two elephants with bow, the hunt that won a $10,000 bet.)

In addition to guides Alex Van Bibber and George John, we had a wrangler and a cook. Ed Merriam, the cook, came originally from some place in Virginia but liked the Yukon better. Joe House, the wrangler, had quit a $2-an-hour job in town to shag horses, at considerably less pay, for the same reason. He liked it.

About the only time Joe had ever regretted the deal, he said, was on the hunt before ours, when he went out for the horses at dawn one frosty morning and blundered into a sow grizzly with two cubs. She jumped him, and Joe lit out with his hair standing up. Coming to a steep bank, he saw one of the horses at the bottom of it—directly below him—and made a flying leap astride, only to find the horse was one he'd hobbled the night before. Luckily for both Joe and the horse, the bear gave up at the top of the bank. Joe bought himself a rifle the next time he got to town, and now carried it faithfully.

We had 21 horses in our string and they were about as entertaining and companionable as so many humans. Each horse had a buddy, and we had to be careful not to separate pals in choosing animals for a side trip.

Alex has the best horses of any outfitter I ever hunted with. He keeps around 60, building up his stock from time to time from the wild-horse herds that still roam the Yukon. In spite of that, plus the fact that Alex pulls their shoes after the last hunt in the fall and turns the whole bunch out to shift for themselves until early summer, the horses are unusually gentle. The one I rode, Buck, used to stand over me half asleep while I sat on the ground and leaned against his front legs while writing notes on the day's hunt.

Besides the fun that goes with every big-game hunt, this trip had a twofold purpose for me. Most of all I hoped to kill a grizzly bear with an arrow, something I'd dreamed of for years. If I succeeded I'd be the first man, so far as I knew, to take a full-grown silvertip that way since Art Young and Saxton Pope did it in Yellowstone in the early 1920's while hunting down a big trouble-making bear under permit.

On top of wanting to take a grizzly this way, I wanted to test a new type of hunting point I'd recently developed for my arrows—a razorhead, a single-blade broadhead that mounts an extra removable two-edged razor blade, very thin and hard, to do its cutting. We'd experimented with it for three years at my archery plant at Grayling, Michigan, and I'd killed antelope and other thin-skinned game with it in Africa. I was eager to test it on something bigger and tougher. That's why my bow quiver now held three hollow-glass shafts mounted with these new heads, and I also had a reserve supply. Given the chance, I intended to find out just what the razorhead would do.

My bow was a Kodiak model, like Judd's, with a draw weight of 65 pounds. Made with a hard-maple core, faced and backed with Fiberglas, these bows shrug off heat, cold, or moisture, and cast an arrow with great power and speed. So far as equipment was concerned, I was ready for business. The rest would be up to the grizzlies and to me, if the right time came.

The hunt was off to a good start. Before we left the highway, we'd had some first-rate fun with grayling at Aishihik Lake, and I'd put in a lively morning shooting 30 to 40-pound salmon with harpoon arrows. That's fishing to write home about.

Though neither Judd nor I had had a shot at big game in the six days we'd been out, we had seen plenty of sheep, moose, and goats (just couldn't get close enough) and enough grizzly tracks to put any hunter in a hopeful frame of mind. Alex had wound up a successful hunt with another party a few days before, and everything looked rosy for us.

There was just one small fly in the ointment. I knew from the outset that Alex Van Bibber didn't relish the idea of guiding a bowman, and he cared even less for guiding a bowman followed by a photographer. He had made that clear in advance.

Alex had his reasons, and I admitted they were sound. The average

Yukon and Alaska guide figures to put his hunter within 200 yards of a grizzly or brown bear, and the rest is up to the client. If he can't connect with a modern rifle at that range, he doesn't deserve the trophy. If conditions warrant, the guide will move him in to, say, 100 yards. That's about the limit.

Alex understood before we left Champagne that he'd have to get me a lot closer than that. I stopped killing game with rifles 25 years ago; the bow has been my sole hunting weapon since. Whatever I nailed on this trip, grizzly included, would be put down with an arrow. I had no intention of risking a bad shot at a range of more than 50 yards, and 25 or 30 would be more to my liking. The bow, however good it is, is not a long-range weapon. At 25 yards, a hurt grizzly can spell bad trouble if he's not killed in his tracks, and that's something no arrow—however well placed—can be expected to do.

He knew this and didn't like it. It wasn't a question of physical courage with him. He's anything but short on that. His father was a mountain man from Virginia who went to the Yukon many years ago and cut enough of a swath that his name is still legendary up there. Alex is one of 12 children raised in the bush and schooled in the business of living off the land with whatever equipment they could put together. He was brought up to be afraid of nothing.

It wasn't fear of bears that was bothering Alex. It was worry that his reputation as a guide might suffer if things went wrong. For one thing, when you have to stalk as close as you do in bowhunting, there's always a chance of spooking game and losing the best trophy of the hunt, maybe after weeks of waiting and working for it. For another, Alex felt he'd be in a bad spot if he should lose a hunter—even a crazy bowman—to a wounded bear.

I didn't much blame him when he said to me while sipping a screwdriver—an odd drink for a leather-faced Yukon guide, but his favorite—before the hunt started, "I'll see it through and do the best I can for you, but I wish you were using rifles instead." There was no chance of that.

The day after Judd missed getting the big moose, we broke camp for a two-day ride to Devils Lake. Ten days of rain and snow had soaked the mountain tundra like a sponge. The alders and scrub willow dripped as we rode through them, and the weather wasn't getting any better. In five weeks we were to see just five days of sunshine.

Base camp at Devils Lake turned into little more than a place to pick up supplies. With good rain gear and dry bedrolls, we roamed the country in the saddle. My rainsuit is a two-piece outfit of coated nylon, so tough it's almost indestructible and so waterproof I can sit in a pool for hours without getting damp.

Good rain gear came in mighty handy hunting the Devils Lake area. We made side camps and stayed in them for a day or two at a time, hunting in rain, snow, and fog. Many days when we rode high we could see clear weather in the distance, but all of Alaska to the west seemed to be funneling wind and water our way.

We saw no bears.

Now and then we saw moose, but never close enough for a shot, and though goats were fairly plentiful we had no luck stalking them. Except for the lower lakes and valleys, the country was all above timberline.

We hunted canyons, climbed vertical cliffs, waded glacier-fed rivers. We stalked one good billy to within 100 yards on an open plateau, then ran out of cover. He might as well have been on the moon.

But we were finding plenty of small game, getting enough shooting for practice, and having a fine time. Ptarmigan were plentiful and made a welcome addition to our grub list, but were hard on arrows because of their habit of squatting among rocks.

Shooting a bow hunting-style is done instinctively, without sights or mechanical aids, and daily practice is necessary to keep in form. We were using blunt arrows for small game and target work, and after a week I'd broken so many heads that my supply ran out. We found a way to repair them by filing off the necks of empty .30/06 cases so they fitted over the broken shafts. Spruce gum in the cases, heated over a fire, made a fine bonding agent.

The big blue grouse down in the scrub timber were tame enough to be a bowman's delight, and fine eating too. A couple of times we even varied our menu with fresh grayling.

Our only contact with the rest of the world was a bush plane that dropped supplies and mail, including a letter for Alex from his wife, with the latest news from Champagne. A native had lost his entire dog team to a grizzly that wandered into his cabin while he was away for the day. When he came home after dark and went to look after his dogs, the bear came within an inch of clobbering him. Wolves had all but killed a mare and colt belonging to Alex, but Mrs. Van Bibber had sewed them up and thought they'd recover. It seems there are plenty of things to worry about, even up in the Yukon.

At the end of two tough and weary days out of base camp, we finally got a day of blue sky and sunshine. From our side camp on Upper Hendon Lake, right after breakfast that morning, Alex and I spotted three goats—two billies and a nanny—high on the mountain above camp. One billy looked very good, and we voted to make the hike.

It took us three hours to climb to them. By then they were bedded on a bench in the open, so we holed up behind a rock 500 yards away to wait them out. Below us, the Hendon River snaked through a long, narrow willow flat.

We stayed hidden, peering over the rock from time to time, until late afternoon. Finally the goats moved off to feed, and as soon as they were out of sight we started after them. A steep side canyon was in our way. We clambered down into it, waded a brawling snow-melt creek in the bottom, and started up again. Suddenly Alex grabbed my arm and pointed ahead. Above a shelf 30 yards away, I saw the black tips of a goat's horns. I laid an arrow on the string and inched my way up toward the shelf, walking as light-footed as a cat.

Most men who knock over a mountain goat with a rifle feel they've taken one of the toughest-to-get trophies in North America, and nine times out of 10 they've good cause to think so. Mr. Whiskers rarely comes easy. I'd certainly worked hard for this one, but the wind was right at last and the footing good.

Now, only 20 yards from the black-tipped horns, I was climbing slowly and warily, hoping to see the billy's body before he saw me. Suddenly gravel crunched underfoot, and up on the shelf three goats came to their feet like big white jumping jacks. I'd caught the two billies and the nanny flat-footed—at closer range than I'd dared to hope.

They stood broadside, staring in amazement, as if not believing a man could get that close.

I didn't give them time to collect their wits. Even while I was taking in the picture, I was pulling the bowstring back into the angle of jaw and throat. Before any of the three twitched a muscle, my arrow was on its way.

I'd picked the biggest billy, and my razorhead slashed into him diagonally—a little too far back for the lungs. It sliced all the way through, came out his flank, and sailed off down the canyon.

The other two goats went out of sight in a couple of jumps. Mine flinched, pivoted, and started away, running over tumbled boulders. My second shot missed him at about 50 yards, but the third, released as fast as I could nock and draw, knifed up under a shoulder blade. The goat turned downhill, running heavily, and disappeared in a side canyon.

When we found him he was lying at the edge of a ledge. I put another arrow into his back to finish him. But there was no way we could get down to him without ropes, and it was too near dark for us to fool around on the mountain. Unless we got off immediately, we'd have to spend the night there. So we headed for camp.

It was pitch dark when we got there. The river had risen a foot or more during the day, as a result of the glaciers melting in the sun, and we got wet fording it. I was bone tired, but felt pretty good.

Right after breakfast next morning, we started back up the mountain with ropes. "Better take your handgun along," Alex suggested. "If a grizzly found your goat, you might need it." That sounded like good advice, so I followed it.

When we got to the goat, we found he'd kicked himself off the ledge and was lying dead in thick alders in a draw below. Fortunately he hadn't broken his horns. He was a good billy, around 200 pounds, with 9½-inch horns, just what I wanted for a full mount in my trophy room.

When we skinned him, we found that my first arrow had put him out of business. Striking too far back for either heart or lungs, it had gone through the diaphragm and stomach and cut him up enough to bleed him to death quickly.

We rolled the head, ribs, and a front quarter in the skin, stuffed it into a packsack, and started to hike to camp. With the camera gear, we had a sizable load. Alex and I traded packs from time to time. We got to the river past noon and edged across on stepping stones, bracing ourselves with stout poles against the rushing, milky current. By the time we reached camp it was too late to make another trip for meat that day. The following morning we climbed the mountain again and brought down the remaining quarters.

Two days later we rode into base camp in wind and rain and got a warm welcome. Up to now our meat supply had depended mostly on what was left of a moose that had been killed on a hunt Alex handled earlier. That was about gone, and fresh goat looked good to everybody.

Judd and George John came in that night with the pelt of a good blond grizzly, but Judd wasn't satisfied with his kill. They'd stalked the bear to within 150 yards, and then the guide flatly refused to go closer.

George John has a powerful phobia where grizzlies are concerned, and carries some bad scars on his neck, arm, and shoulder to prove it's no idle whim. He had a tight shave on a hunt a few years back, when he tackled a grizzly at close range with a .30/30. The bear grabbed him by a shoulder and came close to killing him before his hunting partner got a shot into its head. George John simply won't go near a grizzly now if he can help it, and he regarded my determination to take one with a bow as downright foolish. Nothing Judd said could make him go closer.

Judd's time was running out (his hunt was shorter than mine by three weeks) and he figured this was the only chance he'd get. The thought of that blond bear pelt on the floor of his study was too much to resist, so he reluctantly asked George John for the loan of his rifle, a 6.5 mm. Mannlicher. When the guide handed it over, Judd asked how it shot at 150 yards.

"Dunno," George John grunted, "Not my gun. Borrowed from cook."

Apparently the sights were O.K., because Judd nailed the bear through the heart and anchored it almost in its tracks.

A couple of days after Judd killed his bear, we stopped for lunch beside a small glacial stream in a pretty little valley. Cold rain was falling but Alex produced a stub of candle, flattened and dark from much carrying in his pocket. He lighted it and held it under a pyramid of wet twigs that dried slowly and finally crackled into a brisk, small fire that licked cheerfully up the blackened sides of our tea-water pail.

We ate cold goat and Yukon doughnuts for lunch, and the stop was pleasant in spite of the weather.

The last drop of tea was gone and Alex was stamping out the fire when he happened to look toward a mountain half a mile up the valley, and spotted a bear working down a steep slope.

He lifted his glasses for a quick look. "Black," he announced. Everybody looked and agreed. Nothing to get excited about, even though it was a big one. However we may feel about black bears in the States, in Alaska and the Yukon they're regarded by guides and hunters with about the same contempt that trout fishermen feel for suckers.

We stood there for 20 minutes, watching this fellow amble down off the mountain. He took his time, stopping every now and then to dig, but finally he worked his way into a patch of willows and disappeared. We climbed into our saddles.

Our course upvalley led along the foot of the mountain, about a quarter of a mile from where we'd last seen the bear. As we rode, I kept turning the situation over in my mind. The more I thought about it, the more unwilling I was to pass him up. He was the first bear I had been close to on the hunt, and big enough to rate as a good trophy. And he'd give me a chance to try my razorheads on tough, thick-skinned game. I knew the guides wouldn't bother with him unless I insisted. Alex hadn't promised to hunt blacks. But I decided to insist.

Just at that point we topped a low rise and saw him again. He was on the side of a ridge across the creek, and while we watched he walked down into a draw, out of sight.

"What do you say?" I asked Judd.

"A bear is a bear," he replied. "Let's go get him."

We climbed out of our saddles, stripped off our rain gear and chaps, and started for the ridge. Don unlimbered his movie camera and trailed us. Alex and George John stayed on their horses, watching with tolerant grins.

Our position as we approached the ridge put Judd on my right. He'd climb that side and I'd circle around to the opposite slope, about where we'd last seen the bear. I rounded the end of a low knoll, and there he was, digging out a marmot less than 100 yards away.

His front legs were down to the shoulders in a hole he'd excavated, and he was trying to watch all sides so the marmot wouldn't pop out and get away. His rump was toward me, so it was easy to back off, crouch down, then creep up behind a small boulder just 25 yards behind him. I made it without attracting his attention, and with my arrow on the string, I rose in a half crouch on one knee. But before I could draw, the bear jerked his head around my way, still looking for the marmot.

Now, for the first time, I noticed a telltale sprinkle of gray hairs in his rain-wet pelt. I'd have seen them sooner in dry weather. This was no black bear. This was what I had come to the Yukon to kill—but the circumstances were anything but what I'd planned. I was all alone and looking into the grizzled, bulldog face of a *silvertip* just 75 feet away.

I'd never intended to tackle a grizzly with the bow alone, unbacked by a rifleman. Alex and I had a clear understanding on that. While I have complete confidence in the killing power of a well-placed arrow, I also know that an arrow-shot bear isn't likely to die then and there.

What I faced now was a lot more than I'd bargained for. I'd even gone to considerable pains to make sure it didn't happen. To begin with, Alex has a good reputation as a rifleman and it was agreed he'd be behind me with his .30/06 any time I got close to a grizzly. But now he was sitting in his saddle on the other side of the creek.

I hadn't wanted to get into any such spot as this without a handgun either. When I started planning a grizzly hunt, I bought a .44 Magnum Smith & Wesson revolver and put in a whole summer of practice with it. The Canadian Government and the Mounties at Whitehorse had been co-operative about giving me a permit to carry it on the hunt, just as Them Kjar, Yukon game commissioner, had readily given Alex an O.K. for carrying a rifle while guiding bowmen. The Yukon authorities didn't want an accident on this bear hunt any more than we did.

But my Smith & Wesson was heavy in its shoulder holster and interferred with the use of the bow, so I had formed the habit of carrying it in another holster on my saddle. It was back there now, with Alex and my horse. I was on my own all the way, no matter what happened.

It was a tough challenge but it was also the chance of a lifetime, and it seemed pretty late to back out. I don't think I weighed it for more than three or four seconds—just long enough to tell myself that if the grizzly charged me, he'd be running downhill and I'd have time to dodge once and get a second arrow into him. Thirty seconds later I was doing some tall wondering on that score.

Still crouched behind the boulder that was barely big enough to break my outline, I brought the string back and let drive.

I didn't know it at the time, but Don Redinger had come up behind me within 150 yards and was covering the whole affair with his camera. The movie film later showed exactly what happened, in even clearer detail than I recalled.

The bear heard the twang of the bowstring and I saw his head jerk around in one of those lightning-quick moves any bear can make. But before he could locate me, the arrow slashed into his rib section.

He growled and whipped sidewise, snapping at his side where the arrow came out. It had knifed all the way through him, slicing off a rib and cutting through lungs, diaphragm, liver and intestines, and still had drive enough to bury itself above the head in the hillside.

The grizzly bit at his side while I could have counted three. Then he swung around, hesitated a moment, and came for me, growling and bawling. I got ready to dodge. But the way he was barreling, I was no longer sure I'd have a chance to use a second arrow.

Then he did a thing I'll never understand. Maybe he changed his mind in mid-charge or simply failed to locate the cause of his trouble. Bears are notoriously nearsighted, and maybe that was what turned him. I can think of no other good reason why he shouldn't have kept coming.

But he didn't. Halfway to me, he swerved up over the ridge. Judd saw him come down the other side. The grizzly spun around two or three times in tight circles, and went down to stay. We paced it off later. After the arrow hit him, the grizzly ran 80 yards before he dropped.

This was my 50th kill of big game with a bow, in the United States, Canada, Alaska, and Africa. I'd dreamed of a grizzly for years, and when I found that Don had photographed the whole thing with the six-inch lens on his movie camera, I was about as happy as a hunter can get. As things turned out, I was fated to share honors with Bill Mastrangel of Phoenix, Arizona. He reported killing a good grizzly with a bow in British Columbia in September, shortly after the hunt I'm telling you about.

My bear was no monster, but he was big enough to satisfy me. Gaunt and thin, but with massive head and shoulders, he had the powerful legs and typical long claws of the silvertip. These mountain grizzlies don't grow as big as their fish-eating cousins at the seaside. But considering location and food supply, this was a good bear, and when we got his pelt off we uncovered a streamline carcass that was all muscle and sinew.

Most of the time it's these medium-size ones, not the big bruisers, that make trouble for a hunter. The big ones know better. Bears like mine are the bad boys—the cocky young toughs. George John remarked that mine was almost exactly the size of the one that had mauled him, and Alex added that it was a bear in about the same class that had killed a hunter in the area only a year or so before.

When we opened this grizzly up to see what the arrow had done, we found a hole in his diaphragm so big that the stomach had jostled through it into the lung cavity as he ran. He had bled white inside from the cuts made when the razorhead slashed through his vitals.

Bad weather continued to pile in, winding up in a sharp temperature drop and an eight-inch snowfall. Judd left for home, flying out from Devils Lake. Alex and I rode a lot, hunted hard, and saw plenty of sheep and moose, but we couldn't make connections. We could have filled my license many times with a rifle. However, I can't say I was disappointed when we rode out to Champagne in the teeth of a bitterly cold wind the last day of September. I figure a goat and a grizzly on one trip are about all a bowman should ask for, and on top of that I'd had a couple of nice demonstrations of what the razorhead will do.

Quite a few times since the hunt, I've been asked whether I'd tackle the grizzly single-handed, with the bow alone, if I had it to do over again. That's a tough question.

Certainly I wouldn't recommend that any hunter try it deliberately. Remember, I didn't do it intentionally. But if I had the same chance again, in the same circumstances—and especially if I was *above* the bear with a rock or cover of some kind to duck down behind after releasing my arrow— I'd have to make the same decision. I guess that's the way it is when you're after trophy game.

My Bear Was Blue

James F. Martin

June, 1973

I was taking one step at a time, and very slowly at that, stopping after each to look and listen. Somewhere below me in the thick brush that lined both sides of the trail was a bear, a rare and beautiful trophy that I wanted more than any other animal I had hunted.

I moved a cautious step, paused—and heard something heavy walking through the thick cover on my left. Then I saw the brush move and knew exactly where he was.

The thickets were chest-high, and all I could see were the tops swaying as he came on. He was only a few yards away, and I was standing in plain sight on the trail. I didn't dare move, not even to bring my bow up to shooting position. I think I held my breath.

The footfalls and rustling came abreast of me and moved toward the trail. Then, no more than 40 feet away, he stopped just inside the cover, and I knew he was listening and looking, just as I was. If I hadn't held my breath before, I certainly held it now.

Nothing happened. I didn't know whether he had seen me, scented me, or was just being cautious. Would he keep coming, or wheel and pound off at a run, or simply vanish in that elusive way that spooked bears can? A light wind was blowing. Save for its low sound, the woods were silent.

Then I heard a muffled sound of movement, and the bear poked a coal-black head—at least it looked coal-black—into sight a scant dozen yards from me. My heart skipped a couple of beats and then started to hammer hard enough that I half suspected he would hear it.

The hunt had begun four days before. This was the third week in September 1972, and silver salmon were running in the Situk River about

311

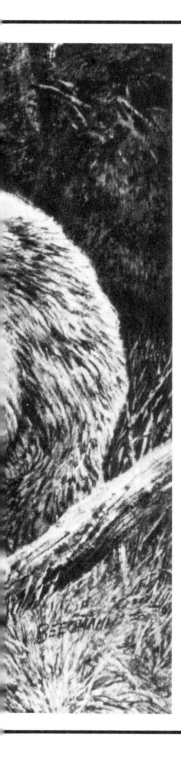

*Holding my 48-pound-pull bow at full
draw until my arms shake, I wait until
at last he steps clear of the brush*

eight miles east of Yakutat, Alaska, where I live. I was helping Bill Fraker, a commercial fisherman, with his salmon fishing. We took a good catch and cruised toward the mouth of the Situk where a cannery truck was waiting to buy the fish.

Bill had a party of friends who were sportfishing for silvers. They were staying at a cabin about a mile upriver from the Situk's mouth, and when our work was finished we hiked up to have lunch with them.

They were taking some beautiful salmon, they said. But they were also having trouble with a bear that was getting into their fish during the day while they were away from the cabin. They were still telling us about the bear when we heard a racket outside, and then the clatter of their trash can being knocked over.

We ran for the door. I was the last one out, and I glimpsed what looked like a dusty black bear lamming into the brush.

"That's a glacier bear!" Fraker yelled.

I didn't know much about glacier bears, but I knew enough to be sure that I wanted a crack at this one.

They are a silver-blue phase of the black and are found only along a stretch of coast in southeastern Alaska. The books say their range extends from Mount St. Elias to the region of Glacier Bay, but the guides I know tell me that these bears are rarely encountered southeast of Mount Fairweather.

Some authorities rate their oddly colored pelt the most beautiful of any of the black-bear family, including the cinnamon and the milk-white Kermode. Glacier bears are decidedly rare, and on the average fewer than two are killed each year. If I took this one, he would be my third bear. I didn't know then that there was no record of any of his kind ever having been killed with a bow.

I'm 25 years old and have bowhunted since my early teens. I was born and grew up at Ogden, Utah. I began hunting with a gun, then joined a Boy Scout troop that was hooked on archery. The troop hunted rabbits together, and shortly after I acquired my first bow I turned to bigger game. When I started after the glacier bear, I had killed six deer, an elk, and two black bears with a bow.

I was discharged from the Air Force in December 1969, and I put in the next year prospecting at Cape Yakataga, about 100 miles west of Yakutat. I'm not married, and I'm free to hunt and fish as much as I like, which is a great deal. I have a small gold-mining operation about 80 miles north of Yakutat. When I'm not at the mine or hunting, I work at construction. It's a way of life I like.

I killed my first black bear while I was at Yakataga, taking four arrows to do it. He was a nice one, and ever since then I have considered bears among the most exciting North American trophy animals.

That first hunt was lively even if it didn't last long. Pop Eggebroten, a good friend who lived near me, saw a hefty black walk across the road near his place one early-spring day in 1970. He knew of my interest in bowhunting, and he came after me in a hurry.

"I've just seen a bear I think you can get," he said.

That was all the invitation I needed. We trailed the bear through thick stuff, got near him, and I worked in close enough for a shot.

My first arrow sliced into his right shoulder, but the heavy bone of the shoulder blade stopped it. The cedar shaft broke on impact, so quickly that it appeared to bounce off.

The bear lit out, and I sent another arrow on the way fast. It hit low in the right front leg, hard enough to break the bone, but it didn't seem to slow him a bit.

The next arrow glanced off a small tree and missed clean. Then I put one where I wanted it, square in the lungs. The bear ran a short distance, collapsed, and was dead in two or three minutes.

"I'm sort of glad he didn't turn on us when he felt that first arrow," Pop said with a grin.

We had no gun, and it hadn't occurred to us that neither was carrying even a knife.

"Next time I go after a bear with one of you bowhunters, I'll have something along for backup," Pop added. "You can kill 'em, all right, but you don't do very well at knocking 'em down."

The next bear I took, later that year, I did a better job on. I was hiking back to my cabin and surprised him raiding it. I put my first arrow into his heart, and he died almost in his tracks. I was sorry Pop wasn't there to see it.

When we boiled out of the fishing cabin that day and Bill Fraker shouted that the bear vanishing in the brush was a glacier, I was inclined to doubt him. I had never seen a bear of that color phase, but this one had looked like an ordinary black bear to me. I said as much.

"He was a little dusty," I told Bill, "but are you sure he's a glacier bear?"

"You bet I'm sure. He was in shadow. Catch him out in the sun, and you'll find he's a silver-blue all the way from his head back."

We had no more than started back to our boat when Fraker was proven right. We rounded a bend in the trail, and our bear was standing on the river bank about 100 yards downstream. I couldn't mistake his odd gray-blue color in the full light. I made up my mind that I was going to gather him in.

Bill had the same idea.

"That's a trophy worth going after," he told me.

I didn't mention it, but I was thankful that no one had had a gun. I'd have a chance to take the bear with a bow.

Fraker's friends were leaving the cabin later that day, but he and I talked it over and agreed that the bear would likely hang around for a few days, since he had found food there. He'd be hoping to find the garbage can refilled or a fresh cache of salmon.

I could see that Fraker wanted the bear as much as I did. But he made me a very fair offer.

His son Bob was also a bowhunter.

"Tell you what I'll do," he said. "I'll give you first chance at him if Bob can hunt with you. Whichever one of you kills him, you can share the honor of taking a glacier bear on a bowhunt. So far as I know, it's never been done."

I accepted on the spot. Having thought things over, I was sure Bill was right. From all I had heard, if Bob or I connected, the bear would be the first of his kind ever taken by a modern bowhunter. It was an exciting prospect.

It was agreed that Bill would back us up with his rifle. If Bob or I had a chance and muffed it, or if it seemed likely the bear was going to get away, Bill would take a hand.

The three of us were back on the Situk the first thing the following morning, and we hunted hard all day. But we could find no sign of the bear. Bob had a moose hunt planned, and that night he decided to give up on the bear and go after moose.

His dad and I went back to the Situk and put in another hard day looking for some hint that our bear was still hanging around the cabin. We didn't find so much as a fresh track, and the next morning Bill announced that he too was quitting the hunt. I felt he had decided that there was no longer a chance of taking the bear.

But I wanted to make one more try. I went back alone that morning but had no luck. I left the cabin about noon and headed for the beach. On the way I stopped for a last look at the bear's four-day-old tracks along the river bank. It was a farewell gesture—I had resigned myself to the fact that we had drawn a blank.

As I studied the old tracks, I wondered where their maker had gone. For some reason, I raised my head and glanced downstream, and my heart skipped. About 350 yards away a bear was walking slowly upstream toward me. When the sun touched him, I could see that his pelt was an unmistakable silver-blue.

I was in plain sight, and I stayed rooted in my tracks. The bear was feeding on salmonberries. I watched him for more than half an hour. It took him that long to move 150 yards in my direction. All that time I didn't dare make a move.

Finally, 200 yards from me, he turned and disappeared in the brush and timber. I dodged into the brush too, hoping to head him off.

I moved carefully, a step or two at a time, stopping to listen. I came out on a bear trail that I had found earlier and turned onto it, working my way downstream toward the place I had seen him last. It was easier to move quietly on the well-used trail, but still I knew better than to hurry.

I figured I must be getting pretty close to him when I came to a place where I could hide within good bow range of the trail. If he had made up his mind to follow it back to the cabin, as I suspected, I wouldn't have long to wait.

I waited more than an hour and I saw or heard nothing except a beautiful bald eagle that perched in a dead cottonwood, watching for salmon in the rapids, and a pint-size red squirrel that made me jump almost out of my boots when he exploded into furious activity 10 paces behind me. For an animal of his size, that squirrel was incredibly noisy. He stirred up more commotion than I had expected from the bear.

That was as long an hour as any I can remember. I gave up finally.

Wherever my quarry had gone, it was evident that he did not intend to walk past me on the bear trail. I figured he had probably turned back downstream, so I moved off in that direction, still walking cautiously. I had very little hope of making contact with him now, but I couldn't afford to overlook the basic rules of bowhunting.

I hadn't taken a dozen slow steps when I heard him coming. I stopped and waited, my pulse racing, while he walked abreast of me, turned toward the trail, and poked his head cautiously out of the brush.

I thought he was a different bear, for all I could see of him looked jet black. But then he moved a bit, and I made out the telltale bluish color at the base of his skull.

For an eternal two or three minutes, we didn't move a muscle. I was sure he hadn't made me out, but I was equally sure that if I tried to bring my bow up, the movement would catch his eye. And anyway, so long as I could see only his head, I had no intention of risking a shot.

My two earlier bears had taught me that with such a big, tough animal, there is only one place to put an arrow for a quick and certain kill. Aim for the rib cage, trying for the lungs and heart. Until this blue bear showed me the right part of his anatomy, I'd wait.

Finally he swung his head and looked straight at me, and it seemed impossible that he could fail to discern the man shape in the trail some 35 feet away. But he showed no hint of alarm, and looked the other way. I raised my bow a few inches, moving in slow motion.

We repeated that performance half a dozen times, as he looked toward me and then away. At last I was ready for the draw.

I drew the bowstring back to my jaw while he was looking away, but still he wouldn't step clear of the brush. My bow was a 52-inch Kodiak Magnum, made by the Bear Archery Company, pulling 48 pounds. It's hard to hold a bow of that power at full draw for more than 10 or 12 seconds, and my arms started to shake. But I was waiting for what I knew would be the chance of a lifetime, and I wouldn't risk a shot until I could send my arrow where I wanted it to go.

The wait lasted hardly more than a minute, but it seemed a quarter-hour. At last the bear looked down the trail at me once more and then stepped clear of the brush, standing almost broadside, angling a little away from me—exactly the target I wanted. The bowstring slipped smoothly off my fingers, and the razorhead flew as if it knew where it was going.

It knifed in about two inches behind the right shoulder, sinking almost to the feathers. I learned later that it split one rib, cut a two-inch gash across the top of the heart, and went all the way through both lungs. I had made a perfect bowshot.

The bear made no sound. He whipped his head around, bit angrily at the arrow, and then for the first time he appeared to see me. He leaped sideways into the brush. When I saw blood gushing from his mouth I knew he was as good as dead. I did not shoot again.

He made two or three jumps, as if trying to get away from what had hurt him, and then I heard him collapse in thick brush. After a brief thrashing everything was quiet. I realized then that my knees were shaking so hard they could barely hold me up.

I heard voices moving along the trail from downstream, and Johnny Nelson and his wife, local Indians, came into sight. They were picking highbush cranberries. If they'd arrived a minute or two earlier they would have cost me my chance at the bear. I still shudder when I think of that close turn of fate.

Johnny and his wife walked up to me, and I blurted out my big news.

"I just killed a bear," I said.

Johnny all but dropped his berry pail.

"With that?" he said, pointing to my bow.

"With this," I assured him.

His next question was logical enough. It was also urgent.

"You sure it's dead?" he asked.

"He has to be dead. He isn't making a sound. You can't even hear him breathe."

The two Indians waited while I walked carefully into the brush. The bear was lying stone-dead just 40 feet off the trail, the most-beautiful animal I had ever seen.

A male, he squared six feet three inches. At first, I believed he would rate top place in the glacier-bear category in the Pope and Young Club's record list, since he would be the first one of that kind recorded as killed with a bow.

But I learned that Pope and Young, like the Boone and Crockett Club, does not have a separate category for glacier bears. Instead, the blue bear and even the white Kermode are lumped in with other color phases of the black bear for purposes of record-keeping. So there seems no chance that my bear will be No. 1 on any official list.

The skull has not yet been measured. But he was a big bear, and those who have seen it say he will undoubtedly end up somewhere among Pope and Young record blacks. Whatever happens, he was all the bear a bow-hunter could ask for.

He is to be mounted whole, and I have arranged to loan the mount to the Fred Bear Archery Museum at Grayling, Michigan. It is to be on display there for 10 years and then will be returned to me.

I expect to bowhunt the rest of my life, but I doubt I'll ever take another trophy to match that magnificent blue pelt.

No Guns Allowed

U. J. Mackarain

October, 1956

My brother Bill rounded a bend in the trail 100 yards ahead and came hurrying toward us with eyes bugging.

"Did you see that?" he bawled as soon as he was within hailing distance.

"See what?" I yelled back.

"That bear. He went right through here."

I looked at him closely. June and I had seen nothing all forenoon except a lot of magnificent autumn color, and for a minute I thought he was pulling my leg.

"He was the biggest black I've ever laid eyes on," he blurted.

I shook my head. "We've seen nothing. Not even a porcupine. You sure it was a bear?"

"Sure I'm sure," Bill said with some heat. "He looked as big, as big as a black submarine. And that's not all. The place is crawling with bears. I've seen five since I left you this morning."

Bill is a truthful character, but nevertheless I found his story hard to believe. Five bears in a morning would set some kind of record in the upper peninsula of Michigan.

The time was October and my wife and I were on a deer hunt with bow and arrow. Bill was along as an unpaid guide. His turn at hunting would come a few weeks later, when the gun season opened on deer. But because he's a top-notch woodsman and knows the country south of his home at Chassell—the area we'd picked—he'd offered to try to put us in touch with a deer or two. Nothing was farther from our thoughts than a bear.

I became a convert to the bow four years ago, mainly because I like October weather and like elbow room in the woods. Room is a little hard

319

to find in Michigan during rifle season nowadays, what with some 450,000 licensed hunters on the prowl. But still I haven't given up hunting with a gun.

June took to the bow when we were married, in 1954. She carries a 37-pound-pull laminated model. Mine is a recurved model pulling 20 pounds heavier. I had one deer to my credit, killed in 1953 in the Sand Lake district west of Tawas City. June had yet to fire an arrow at trophy game.

The three of us walked up the old woods road to the car, opened a package of sandwiches, and sat down to eat lunch. I was taking my first bite when I suddenly realized that Bill hadn't kidded us. Out of the corner of an eye I saw something bulky and black move at the edge of the brush, and out lumbered a bear that looked as big as an Angus bull. He vanished back in the brush, though, before Bill and June could get a glimpse of him.

I flipped my sandwich onto the car seat, choked on the bite I'd taken, grabbed my bow, and raced up the trail, fitting an arrow on the string as I went. I hoped to head him off.

Fifty yards up the road I caught sight of him again, but only his rear end—round, black, and big as a barn door. Lacing an arrow into that area, assuming I could hit him through the trees and undergrowth, didn't seem exactly a bright thing to do. So I pulled up and held on him, hoping for a better shot. But I'd crowded in too close. He'd been lumbering along, swinging his head and rolling his fat fanny, when suddenly he heard or smelled me. He took one startled peek over his shoulder, pivoted, and was gone in a flash.

I followed him into the thicket, but not far, for it occurred to me that I had only one arrow along. I didn't belong in there with a bear of that size. Maybe there was little chance he'd turn on me, but I wasn't anxious to prove it.

I hotfooted back to the car, all thought of lunch forgotten. The last I'd seen of the bear was when he headed up a long ridge to the west.

"Do you suppose there's a trail on the far side of that ridge?" I asked Bill.

He got the idea instantly. "Let's go see," he suggested. "If we can get ahead of him and find a couple of good stands, you might get a crack at him yet."

Backing the car around, we roared down the woods road, but before we'd gone far a windfall blocked our way. So we took off on foot, heading for a swamp at the bottom of the ridge where the bear had disappeared.

Bill found a spot for June, where she had an unobstructed view in three directions, and we left her there. I wasn't sure she'd take to the idea, for we'd started out to hunt deer, not bears, and her bow pulls only 37 pounds. But she was as excited as we were.

"You go on another 150 yards north," Bill directed me. "I'll drift back the other way and we'll see what happens."

It occurred to me that there wasn't much Bill could do no matter what happened, since he was toting nothing more deadly than a pocketknife. But I said nothing, figuring he'd spent enough time in the woods to know what he was doing.

At the end of a five-minute walk from June's stand I found an open spot and settled down. For an hour nothing stirred. Then I saw movement down in the bottom of a big ravine and I instantly became as taut as my bowstring. But when it moved again I realized it was Bill, making his way slowly in my direction.

"Our bear either got through ahead of us or doubled back," he said, when he reached me.

"Seen anything of June?"

"I signaled her a little while ago," he answered. "She'll be along in a few minutes."

She joined us and we stood debating our next move. The bear had eluded us and there seemed little chance we'd see any more of him. I started to think about deer again. "I suppose we might as well—" I began, but that was as far as I got. Bill lifted a hand in quick, silent warning, and pointed behind me. When I spun around there was a bear shambling down the side of the ridge. He wasn't the big one I'd seen earlier, but he was big enough.

The bear went behind a clump of brush, and I took a few hurried steps his way. I glimpsed a patch of black through the trees, not enough to shoot at, but a few more steps would bring him into an opening only 35 yards away. It would be then or not at all, and I'd have to shoot fast, for there was no cover between me and the place where he'd appear.

I brought the bow back to full draw and held the arrow on that open lane. The bear stepped into sight and stopped, looking straight at me, and in that same instant I let the taut string slip off my finger tips.

I was shooting a four-bladed broadhead, a hunting arrow with two full blades and two smaller ones. It hit solidly, and the bear went down as if I'd slammed him with a soft-nose bullet from a .30/06. He hit the ground with a sharp, loud grunt, and on the heels of that he ripped out a series of growls, snorts, and roars so horrible that every hair on my head stood up.

He was rolling and tumbling around, all four feet flailing the air, and the first thought that raced through my head was that I was woefully short of arrows. I'd left my home in Flint three days earlier with only five broadheads, but that seemed enough for a deer hunt. Since then, however, I had lost two when we jumped a couple of deer, and then accidentally broke a third.

June had reminded me only this morning that I was down to two, but I brushed her off with the airy comment that if I failed to kill a deer with one, I wouldn't likely get a second shot. I knew now I was wrong. I had a few field points in my quiver, useful on a rabbit or porcupine, but certainly not right for a bear.

I'll likely be criticized for taking on a bear at all with only two hunting arrows. But before you judge me, please remember that I was on a deer hunt. I hadn't even thought of bear until Bill reported blundering into five that morning. But when one came along and I had the big chance that every archer dreams of, I wasn't going to pass it up.

June was a dozen feet or so behind me, and I yelled at her to shoot before the bear regained his feet. Realizing I was in her way, I dropped to one knee with my second arrow strung and ready, waiting for a sure bet.

June's first arrow struck the ground inches from the bear's head. Her second seemed to shave black fur, it was so close. Then the bear reared half up and I had my chance. I drove my arrow at his rib section, but it thudded harmlessly into a tree beside him. The next thing I knew June was shoving one of her arrows into my hand. I released it and missed again. The bear finally rolled upright on his front legs and went out of sight in the brush, dragging his hind quarters.

I'm not sure yet just what happened to all our arrows. June broke the head off of one trying to pull it out of the tree. She and Bill found two or three that had missed the bear and brought them to me, which I reshot without hitting. When the bear finally disappeared, June's quiver was empty and I was down to three field points. The rest were either broken or lost.

We followed the bear, but didn't crowd him, armed as poorly as we were. At first he left a plain trail, with plenty of blood, as he dragged himself through the dry leaves. But after 100 yards or so it faded. Bill, a far more experienced tracker than I, took over, with June and me walking warily beside him. Suddenly my wife grabbed my arm and pointed.

"There he is," she whispered, "coming down from that tree."

Sure enough, there was a bear standing on his hind legs at the base of a big oak 50 yards ahead. But I knew instantly he wasn't the black we were following; ours wasn't in shape to haul himself up like that. Then I saw ours—stretched full length and motionless beside a log to our left.

If I hadn't seen what happened next I wouldn't have believed it. The bear at the tree dropped to all fours, shuffled down the slope to the wounded bear, and sniffed him carefully. Then he lit out, full gallop, and by sheer chance came our way.

He wasn't charging; he didn't even know we were there. He was just leaving the neighborhood and we happened to be in his path. I wasn't sure of that at the time, and it was blood-chilling to stand there with only a field point on my drawn bowstring and watch him come at us. When he was within 10 feet of me, he swerved sharply to the left and shot past like a black streak.

Then we found to our amazement that our cripple was gone too. Bill picked up his trail again and we soon spotted him, but he was traveling faster now and we had to run to keep up. We edged in as near as we dared, all three yelling at each other not to get too close. I kept hoping for a finishing shot with a field point, but before long he went out of sight in swamp and windfalls so thick it was unsafe for us to follow.

We circled around and picked up his track on the far side. There was just a spot of blood here and there where he'd crawled over logs, and it was slow trailing. The track finally ended at a small, swampy stream, which we had to bridge with a couple of dead trees. Finding where the bear had crossed lost us almost an hour.

His trail led to higher ground, and the next time we saw him he was sprawled on his haunches, front feet planted wide apart, growling and popping his teeth as we approached. He sat there, rolling his head from side to side, making a queer blowing noise between snarls.

I worked to within 20 or 30 yards of him, still looking for my big chance with a field point, when he hauled himself around and went sliding down into a pit—the kind called an exploration ditch up in Michigan's copper country. Such pits, dug long ago by early prospectors, are open at one end, with steeply sloping banks on three sides. They average eight to 10 feet deep and about twice as long. It was a good place for the bear to make a stand.

What I did next sounds crazy and foolhardy, and likely some of you won't even believe it. But I'll go into any court and take oath that it happened.

I wanted that bear and I also wanted to finish the hunt. Knowing that there was almost no chance of killing him with my field points, I did some figuring. I'm six feet three and weigh just over 200. He didn't weigh much more than that, and he was obviously disabled from a spine shot. Under those conditions I decided I was a match for him. So I picked up a dry club about four feet long and went into the pit.

He was cornered, but he was also a pretty sick bear. He growled and popped his teeth but didn't come for me. I inched in until I was close enough, then clouted him over the head for all I was worth. The club broke in three or four pieces, but it also knocked the bear down and stunned him.

I whipped out my hunting knife and stepped in, but as I bent over he came up like a boxer climbing off the floor, mouth open, swiping at me with one foreleg. I got out of the pit fast.

Bill found me a greener and stouter club. June urged me to quit. "You can't kill him, Mack, and it's foolish to keep trying," she argued.

But I still thought the bear was too far gone to be dangerous, so I went after him again. This time, however, he came to me, fighting mad, snarling. I swung at his head, but the club was too long and clumsy and he batted it out of my hands.

I'd had enough, so I turned and started to run but tripped on a root and landed flat on my belly. I wasted no time in getting out of the pit on all fours. Bill and June said afterward that the last snap the bear made missed my rear by less than a foot.

It was almost dark now, and we'd all had enough. We hated to leave him wounded in the woods, but we had no choice. As we turned back in the direction of the car, a mile away, the bear proved he was still able to travel. He climbed slowly up out of the pit and moved off.

On the way out of the woods I asked June, "If you hadn't been with me and I told you the story of what happened, would you believe it?"

"I don't know," she said thoughtfully. "It wouldn't be easy."

"You'll have plenty of trouble on that score," Bill predicted with a grin.

Every rule of decent sportsmanship demanded that we kill the bear, and we planned doing just that. Left in the woods, he'd be a menace to anyone who blundered into him. But I had no suitable arrows, and Michigan game laws forbid carrying or using firearms when you're hunting big game on a bow license.

Back at Bill's house we hurried through supper and sat down to go over the situation again. Bill called the sheriff's office in Houghton to ask for permission to go back with rifles and flashlights and kill the bear that night. But the law was adamant.

"The only way that bear can be shot legally is for us to send an officer along to do the job," the deputy on the phone told Bill, "and there's nobody around here so tired of living that he wants to go after a wounded bear in the woods at night."

That left us exactly where we'd started—on our own. "We'll kill him ourselves in the morning," Bill grunted, but he didn't say how. I felt it better not to ask him.

Next he tried to reach a couple of sporting-goods dealers and hardware stores in Houghton and Hancock by phone, in the hope of locating some hunting arrows. But by that time it was after closing hours on Saturday night, and his calls went unanswered. There isn't a great deal of archery gear sold up in that country, and unless we could find a store with broadheads in stock and persuade the owner to open up and sell us a dozen, we simply didn't know where to turn for more arrows of the kind we needed.

June stayed in bed the next morning. She'd had it. Bill and I agreed we could use a third man, so we drove into Hancock after daybreak and picked up another of the Mackarain brothers, Eino. We made another last-minute attempt to find a store owner and buy some hunting arrows, but again without success.

We returned to the ridge where we'd last seen the bear, and took his track. Blood was scanty and far apart now, and even Bill found it hard to follow. In fact we were ready to give up two or three times, but each time we circled out, found fresh sign, and kept going. When the track finally petered out, after more than a mile of slow trailing, we separated—Eino following one ridge, Bill another running parallel to it, and I combing the swampy ravine between. We kept in touch by whistling back and forth, and finally I heard a series of signals from Bill that sounded urgent. My hunch was good; he'd found the bear.

If the critter had lost any steam during the night he didn't show it. He backed in under a windfall, and as soon as he saw us he came up on his front feet, growling and rolling his head. "He sure looks ready and willing," Eino commented.

Under any other circumstances we'd have been a comical-looking trio as we closed in. I was in the middle with my bow, a field point on the string, two more in my quiver. Eino was on my right, carrying a light ax. Bill had cut a green pole eight or 10 feet long and lashed his hunting knife on one end of it to make a crude lance.

What we'd like to have known but didn't was how completely was he disabled, and how fast and far he could move after a night's rest.

He didn't show as much fight as we expected and we took heart from that. He sat, weaving from side to side, occasionally popping his teeth loudly.

We stopped 20 yards off and I drew a bead on his chest. The arrow whistled toward him but he ducked, likely at the sound of the bowstring, and the field point smacked him in the center of the forehead and bounced off like a toy arrow. It did no damage, but it moved him out from beneath the windfall and I knew then what I needed to know. He was still dragging his hind quarters.

The rest happened fast. I raced in and drove an arrow between his shoulders at 10 paces. He whipped around, bit savagely at it, and tried to come for me. But by then Bill was close enough to prod him with his homemade bayonet, and the bear turned on him, clearing the way for the kind of shot I'd hoped for. I stepped up within a couple of paces and hammered my last arrow in between his ribs just behind the shoulder. At that range even the field point went all the way through a lung and did its work quickly. The bear reached around, snapped at the shaft, lurched a few steps, and went down for keeps. He was dead in a minute or two.

We learned a couple of interesting things when we got him out of the woods. My broadhead had gone deep in his back just below the spine and caused enough bleeding to have killed him during the night. Even more important from our standpoint, that first arrow had put his hindquarters out of use permanently. That was the first time I'd realized just how much damage a hunting head can do.

The other thing we learned was that the bear and I were exactly the same weight class. He went a few pounds over 200.

The real pay-off I didn't hear about until I was home. Bill, a lifelong rifleman, bought a bow and set of hunting arrows right after June and I left Chassell, got in a little practice, and went back the next week looking for the big black that got away. He didn't find it, but he's been shooting target ever since and is making plans for another bow-hunt. All I can say is, the Mackarain boys learn hard.

IX

EXPECT THE UNEXPECTED

Grizzly in No-Man's-Land

Alann B. Steen

February, 1979

For a moment the grizzly wore an expression of almost pure contentment, sitting there in front of the tent eating that granola bar. Moments later, when it was all over, I was left scared to the soles of my boots and almost incoherent. But in those 30 or so seconds that constitute an eternity in such situations, I learned the true meaning of the wilderness. . .

I had seen bear tracks all summer. Kayaking the Teslin River in central Yukon Territory, then on down the Yukon River to Dawson City with a group of college students in tow, I had set up camp on sandbars and islands crisscrossed with bear, lynx, wolf, and the ubiquitous moose. Those tracks were sometimes very fresh, but there was safety in numbers. Besides, it seemed as if those kids never slept in the 24-hour light of the Klondike summer.

Now it was different, I was on the Porcupine River heading west for the Yukon River, about 60 miles above the Arctic Circle. I was tired. I had paddled my 17½-foot canvas-covered kayak more than 40 miles that day, 400 miles in the last 10 days, against a stiff head wind on water that was almost devoid of current. I was hungry; a can of beans and half a granola bar go just so far. And I was alone. Around me were the cliffs of the Ramparts, and 150 miles behind was the Indian village of Old Crow, Yukon Territory; 150 miles ahead was Fort Yukon, Alaska. I had seen no one since Old Crow. Not even a plane had flown over. As far as I was concerned, I was the sole occupant of the river, surrounded by 50,000 square miles of uninhabited subpolar terrain—the tundra.

Off the river, however, one is never alone. Mosquitoes are continual companions ashore, and a welcoming swarm had descended even before I put down my paddle. Insect repellent kept the mosquitoes at bay as I

jumped out and stretched for the first time in hours. The combination of mud and sand sucked at my boots. Then the sand firmed as I walked up the inch-high terraces created by the receding river. The topmost terrace was a dune of eroded white sand, not too level, but dry . . . and still warm in the midnight sunset.

As I retrieved my gear from the kayak and set up camp, I noticed tracks. Most common were the sandpiper tracks that paralleled the river. Worried parents piped out from their willow-bush nests when I ventured too close. One bird came out with the old broken-wing routine, dragging itself along the water's edge, following the tracks left by a wolf the night before. Three sets of moose tracks emerged from the river just downstream from the boat and trotted over the dune and up the bank. Then there were the bear's.

They weren't as sharp as those left by the moose; they were made when the river was higher and the shore less firm. The rounded front paws and elongated hind paws were unmistakably bear, and their size—larger than my stretched-out hand—and the protruding claws left no doubt that they were grizzly tracks. Now partly dried between the falling river and the dune, with some filled with windblown sand, I reckoned the prints to be at least a week old. However, to satisfy myself that the bear was just passing through, I followed his tracks upstream until they angled into the river and disappeared. Then, with nothing on my mind except beef stew and sleep, I returned to the kayak, pulled my camera from beneath the splashboard, picked up the paddle, which needed some retaping, and climbed the terrace.

Man always has been a soft touch for bears, whether it be in Yosemite or Yukon. Salmon left unattended on a riverbank or moose meat drying behind an easy smokehouse door are open invitations for any passing bear to help himself. Rarely will he decline. In return he leaves splintered wood and bone, lots of tracks, and sometimes a stinking pile of black droppings.

To that extent, then, I shouldn't have been surprised to find the grizzly in camp. No doubt he was just passing through when invited to stop by the half-eaten, unattended granola bar—honey and oats. What bear could refuse? In that instant before recognition, he did wear an expression of utter satisfaction. He sat dogstyle, his left paw on the sand, his right shoving the granola into his mouth. Between his hind legs rested my single-burner stove and can of beef stew.

When he saw me, however, everything changed. His expression dissolved into fear. Panic would be a better word. His ears went back and his bottom jaw seemed to just hang there. But his eyes told the story—an amber mixture of surprise, panic, and uncertainty. He stood up. A very quick move it was, yet almost graceful, considering his 600-pound frame. He raised his head, as if to look over his nose, and began to snort in short gasps, the green granola wrapper still in his mouth. He wasn't growling, though. Rather, it seemed he was desperately trying to gather more information through his sense of smell than through his seemingly not-so-sharp sight. He pivoted left and right; the characteristic hump of his shoulders was unmistakable. Then he turned back, looked down, and met my slack-jawed stare—a hazel mixture of surprise, panic, and uncertainty. . .

I'm not a Klondike native. Certainly I'm no professional guide, trapper, or hunter. I'm a cheechako—a green-horn—a teacher from California who will remain a cheechako until, according to Northern lore, I watch a river like the Yukon or Porcupine freeze over in the winter and remain to watch it thaw in spring.

I had kayaked the Yukon River 460 miles from Whitehorse to Dawson during the summer of 1977 and met a canoeist at an abandoned Northwest Mounted Police outpost who mentioned the Porcupine region. He talked about its fast rivers and wildlife. And he talked about the Ramparts of the Porcupine—cliffs of varying colors and shapes that rise hundreds of feet from the flat tundra to tower over the river for miles, then melt back and dissolve.

Naturally, I thought about the Porcupine drainage throughout that winter. My imagination ran rampant to the extent that by the time I landed my kayakers at Dawson, it was an obsession ready to turn compulsion. A few hours later I was standing on a bridge, 260 miles north of Dawson. Close by ran the invisible Arctic Circle. Below me ran the Eagle River; it wasn't what I expected.

This "fast river" of the Porcupine region was low and slow, a brown ribbon squeezed between high mud banks. The high water mark stood 15 feet above its surface. I learned later I was a month late, due to the absence of a substantial snowpack the past two years.

I would be stretching my memory to say the Eagle was 100 feet wide on its straight portions, narrowing to 30 feet around the bends guarded by sand and gravel bars. The V-shaped chutes that marked the channels between the river-bend shoals were rarely more than five feet wide and sometimes so shallow that my kayak scraped the gravel bottom. These chutes were the river's only offerings of current, 50 to 100 yards of seven-knot water that tried to yank the kayak into the outside bank. Usually these banks were completely undermined by the current, so that trees, their roots firmly held by the heavy soil, fell into the river, becoming immediate snags and spears, some barely seen beneath the surface.

In one especially fast, snag-infested curve, with the setting sun and its reflection obliterating everything before me, my kayak was pushed over a half-submerged alder, its aft line getting tangled in the branches. Not only did the boat come to a quick halt, but the current pulled the stern so far down that the river flowed over the deck. I tried to stretch out over the deck to reach the fouled line, but my weight pushed the stern down and the river rushed into the cockpit.

Frustrated and frightened, I knew the only way to freedom was to cut the line. I wasn't concerned with flipping the kayak; it was nearly three feet wide. But I was concerned with the amount of water that would come in during the operation with a not-too-sharp knife and the momentary lack of control I would have once free.

About a cubic foot of water rushed in during the couple of seconds it took to cut the line, but in the seconds it took to pull back from the stern, turn over, sit down, and grab the paddle, the kayak shot forward, then careened broadside to the current dragging the stern across the shoals. I felt rocks beneath my feet as I tried to paddle in the four-inch water, but had no control. The kayak missed one snag whose glistening claws sat unmoving in the current but didn't miss the uprooted willow that hung over the channel from the right bank. It entered the branches obliquely, right into a tenement of waiting mosquitoes. The nightmarish introduction to the Arctic was prolonged.

They descended on me like a shroud, a thousand mindless creatures unaffected by the insect repellent that coated my skin and clothes. Through frenzy and sheer pressure of numbers, they flew into my ears, eyes, nose, and mouth. They got to my body through an open collar and untucked-in shirt. They walked across my belly and bit me at random. I slapped at them and slapped at them, and I yelled at them at the top of my lungs, as if it would do any good. Alternately flailing my arms and furiously paddling on an again sluggish river, a man possessed of devils, I was a black cloud silhouetted by a setting sun.

Then, suddenly, a breeze kicked up before me, and the mosquitoes were gone. I rejoiced.

But, it seems, there's no such thing as moderation in the Arctic. The breeze became a wind, then something stronger. Within moments white water was coming over the bow. If I stopped paddling for only a moment, my forward motion stopped quickly as if I were still tethered to that alder. I found a sand bank, jumped out, stretched, and scratched. A moment later the wind died and the mosquitoes returned.

I wonder, did Jack London ever talk about mosquitoes? Elihu Stewart did, briefly, in his "Down the Mackenzie and Up the Yukon in 1906," one of the few books on northwestern Canada that describes the Porcupine region. The problem was that Stewart, then Canada's commissioner of forestry, didn't publish his accounts until 1913, allowing such "discomforts" to become more tolerable with the passing of time. As I put these words down, I can still hear the panicked whine of trapped mosquitoes in my ears and taste their crushed bitterness in my mouth.

Perhaps I belabor the subject of mosquitoes; they are indeed a scourge of the North yet are a fact of life of an Arctic summer. They have no favoritism, they give no mercy. They live where warm-blooded animals live, drawing the blood they need in order to reproduce their kind. I saw sandpiper chicks attacked and completely covered by mosquitoes the moment they hatched. I was also told mosquitoes had killed caribou calves and driven men mad. . .

A cloud of mosquitoes enveloped the grizzly. Some perched on his nose, others walked in and out from under his jowls. From my distance of maybe 10 feet, I could see he was easy pickings. But he seemed oblivious to them. His eyes were locked on mine.

Seven feet high, three feet wide, he was Death in a brown-gray overcoat. With two-inch claws extending from catcher's mitt paws, he was Doom up close. Never had I experienced fear as I experienced it that day. Nor had I felt so helpless, cold, and alone, all of which added to an unforgettable sensation of overall weakness. My legs became rubbery; to stand erect became such an endeavor that I found myself "shaking in my boots." No other words would fit the situation: I was a living cliche. And when my heart began beating so fast that I thought it would burst, being scared to death no longer seemed absurd.

With effort I pushed the thought from my mind and tried to think of escape and survival. I thought of turning around and making a dash for the river just 15 feet away. No, back up slowly and sink gradually into the water. No. How about falling into a fetal position and playing dead? But something said don't lose his gaze, and I kept my eyes on his. To support my wobbly legs, I slowly raised the paddle to a vertical position and anchored its blade by my left foot. At the same time, the grizzly took a quick step toward me. . .

Along about the height of the Klondike gold rush, Robert Service wrote: "This is the law of the Yukon and she makes it plain: Send not your foolish and feeble; send me your strong and your sane. . ."

Encounters with large, indigenous wildlife indeed tax one's sanity. Going into the Porcupine drainage alone, I learned later, was not-so-tactfully deemed foolish by the Royal Canadian Mounted Police. And relying on the adage that God protects small children and fools is no insurance— particularly when you look down a river that is 1,000 feet wide and surrounded by a billion acres of virtually uninhabited wilderness. The few words that I read on the region and that little map still hanging on the wall back home quickly became near-meaningless abstractions.

You see, the Porcupine region is true wilderness. Its rivers won't carry you to peaceful solitude at a rate of six knots. There are no well-used campsites, no trails, no mileposts to give the distance traveled and the distance to go. It's a region where the way in and the way out is by water, due mostly to the marshes above the rivers, the mosquitoes, and the *tete de femme*—the woman's head hummocks.

At times you're against an antagonistic wind, upon an uncooperative current, sandwiched between the sun and its reflection. You scratch mosquito bites and gingerly dap at an occasional blackfly bite.

Perhaps it's a journey without fun. But it is exciting. It's a combination of trepidation, because once committed there's no turning back, and exhilaration, because you're alone, traveling the course of early-day traders, trappers, and goldseekers. Perhaps some of them saw the Porcupine high and fast, when the rivers were thawing and filled with ice floe, when the wind was low and the mosquitoes few. Perhaps they saw things differently; their accounts vary. But nothing has really changed. Dwellings built and abandoned along the river bear witness to the fact that we are all just visitors. And above the river, the tundra goes on forever.

Initially, I had planned to follow Stewart's 1906 route, starting on the Little Bell River and Summit Lake in northeastern Yukon Territory. This was the route of John Bell, a Hudson Bay Company trader, who in 1842 discovered the river named after him, then followed it to the river he called the Porcupine. In 1844, Bell paddled down the Porcupine until it flowed into the huge river the Indians called Youcon—"The Greatest." However, because of the expense of a floatplane to Summit Lake, I took the Eagle route. From the Dempster Highway, the Eagle River zigzags 150 miles to the Bell, which empties 30 miles later into the Porcupine. From that point the Porcupine flows about 430 miles to join the Yukon. . .

The compass always hung around my neck, beneath binoculars, and a 35-mm. camera. All three would have accompanied me into the water, if I had the need—or the luck—to reach the river. But the bear stopped as suddenly as he started.

Looking back, I believe raising the paddle had something to do with his stopping. That little figure before him suddenly became eight feet tall. Also, the figure before him was a silhouette against the sunset. With no color perception, and having his depth perception reduced at dusk, the grizzly saw a dark object against a very bright sky.

Finally the wind came from behind him. I could smell him better than he could smell me. And what a smell, the odor of a pack of dogs in dire need of a bath.

He was perplexed and frustrated. His snorting grew louder. For a moment I thought he might charge, as he seemed to peer at me more closely by extending his head. Then I wondered if he could really see me. There was a haze of mosquitoes between him and me, closer to him than me. Whatever, my mind raced to escape. The river was fewer than 10 steps away. . .

The banks of the Eagle and Bell are mud, but the Porcupine's are rock, sometimes giving way to sandstone bluffs that have eroded away to look like giant loaves of white bread. Swallows inhabit some of these bluffs, darting after insects that flutter above the water. Among the swallows the peregrine falcon flies, the predator whose cries tell of a seemingly continual hunger, with relief "just a swallow away." Below, Canada geese and pintail ducks lead the kayak away from their nestlings, paddling almost effortlessly 30 yards ahead, then beating the water furiously to become airborne. American eagles in flight take your breath away.

Along the Eagle and Bell, and along the upper portions of the Porcupine, moose watch the kayak approach. Bear cubs are dispatched up trees by unseen mothers, but wolverines come to the water's edge to sit and watch, afraid of nothing. After sundown, wolves trot along the banks, checking territorial boundaries and seeking food. At a trapper's cabin about 20 miles upriver from Old Crow, I found wolves lying down with sled dogs, which were tied to posts along the river, waiting for the season's first snow.

At the village of Old Crow, the Indians were awaiting the caribou, as they had for centuries. Men lined the high banks to ask if I had seen the migrating herd that would keep them in meat for the winter. I had to say no. The hunters of Old Crow take 10 or more caribou per family, freezing the meat in lockers for year-round consumption.

They live in log cabins built on mounds above the permafrost. Though there is no radio, a satellite beams in color television, exposing them to Canadian news and drama, British humor, and American soap. All supplies are flown in. The barges that used to come up the river are long gone, a consequence of progress, even on this far frontier. . . . .

The grizzly was even more agitated, rocking back and forth, making mini-lunges. He wouldn't take his eyes from me. He intimidated through the mosquito screen. Just a few running steps to the river—the thought tempted me, but I resisted for all sorts of disjointed reasons, all of which added up to suicide.

He became even more excited, and I felt what coherence I had left slip away to panic. I trembled all over and my thoughts began to stutter. I took a slow step backward. The grizzly didn't follow.

For a moment I thought I had a chance for escape. Then, for a moment,

I wondered if I should try. If I bolted for the river, would he give chase? Maybe not. . .but if he did, he'd be running on four feet; I'd be running on two.

I took a second step back. This time the grizzly growled. Almost instinctively, I lowered the paddle and grabbed it with both hands, realizing at the same time that I had a defense weapon, something I could use to keep the grizzly four or five feet away, until I could retreat to the river.

But if I reached the water, would I escape? I'd leave behind everything. The grizzly would peel the yellow kayak like a banana to get at the food inside. A similar fate could await my tent and gear. Once in the water, I would be at the mercy of the river, its current, and 48-degree temperature. Survival would depend on quickly finding a beach and a way back to camp.

The paddle shook with all the symptoms of buck fever, yet I could look up its shaft into the bear's mosquito-ringed eyes. Sweat began to run into my eyes and I fought to keep them open, not daring to blink. Yet I know that I did, for the next thing I knew, he had broken off contact.

He merely turned his head slightly and blinked his eyes. Then he closed his eyes and popped himself in the face with both paws; a plume of mosquitoes erupted from his head. He shook his head violently, and the granola wrapper fell to the ground. He lunged forward onto all four feet, and I leveled the paddle to meet his charge. But he didn't come close. He veered sharply to the left and ran down the terrace to the river, shaking his head wildly. In a small splash he was in the water. A moment later he was almost in midstream, his head and humped shoulders very visible. He never looked back.

A mosquito penetrated the repellent on my right wrist and I slapped at it, dropping my paddle. There was no strength in my hand, nor in my legs. I was sick to my stomach and couldn't think clearly. Moments ago I was confronted by a creature noted for its viciousness, now I had the privilege of wondering why I was still alive.

Maybe he couldn't see me, maybe he couldn't smell me, maybe he didn't know what I was. But for some reason he didn't stay around long enough to find out.

My wrist began to itch and I scratched it, flicking away the remnants of a mosquito, one of those creatures that have no favorites, give no mercy. At the same time I felt two more bites on my forehead. I ran to the tent and jumped in, leaving behind a can of beef stew and a half-eaten granola bar.

Weak and sick from fear, I remembered Robert Service's words, "I have clinched and closed with the naked North . . . yet the wild must win in the end."

But not this time, I thought.

This Grizzly Climbed

Napier Shelton

April, 1968

There's something about a bear track. This one was almost as long as my foot and a lot wider, and the mark of four-inch claws was clearly imprinted in the wet sand. All of a sudden I felt small and weak and alone. My interest in meeting a grizzly face to face was evaporating like a patch of snow on a hot tin roof.

I was alone, walking over the wide gravel bars of the Toklat River in Mount McKinley National Park on a June evening in 1961. Low-hanging clouds and a light rain gave a somber, brooding aspect to the dark mountains enclosing the valley. Mist veiled the form of things. I was sure the maker of this track could not be far away, and in the twilight of that wet evening every shadow seemed to have the humped shoulders and dished face of a grizzly.

I turned back, walking faster than usual. This was not the time or place to meet such a bear, I told myself.

I was 29 at the time, unmarried, a graduate student at Duke University at Durham, North Carolina, and working on my master's degree in botany. I was in McKinley Park to do research on plant life. My wife Elizabeth and I live now at Ann Arbor, Michigan, where I'm studying for a doctorate in geography, and teaching, at the University of Michigan.

I had hoped to join a scientific expedition that summer, but had not been able to find an opening, and so Jack van Wyk, a fellow student at Duke whose home was in South Africa, and I loaded my small camping van and headed for the Alaska Highway on a 4,900-mile drive.

We removed the rear seat, rigged a table that could double as a bed, stocked the van with canned stuff, and camped on the way. We pulled off the road wherever night overtook us, heated up a can of something, and slept until morning. It was a good trip.

For me the summer in Alaska was the fulfillment of a dream. That part of the world had fascinated me as far back as I could remember. I'd be studying vegetation, but it was the wild animals I was most interested in, and above all the bears.

As a boy growing up in Washington, D. C., I had read Ernest Thompson Seton's Biography of a Grizzly, and ever since I had longed to encounter this awesome brute and get to know him at first hand. It had never occurred to me that the meeting might prove more than I bargained for.

Jack and I reached McKinley early in June. The night we arrived I went for a walk along the Toklat and saw my first grizzly track, as I related at the beginning of this story. That track didn't really put a damper on my enthusiasm, but it did give me a few second thoughts.

We went on to the park campgrounds at Igloo Creek and put up our tent. Jack was not a partner in my research project. He had made the trip only because he wanted to see the country, and he thought it would take him about as far from his home in South Africa as he'd ever get. He planned to stay with me for two weeks, then fly back to Duke, where he had studies of his own to work on.

Because we were in a national park, we could not legally carry firearms. Anyway, the idea of taking a gun along had not even occurred to me. I saw no reason for taking a gun, for I did not believe that wild animals, even bears, would bother people unless they were given some good reason. And I did not intend to give them a reason.

I'd meet the bears on a friendly footing, and I was sure they'd reciprocate. Maybe I was overly influenced by Seton's books, for he had said flatly, "The grizzly never attacks man, except when provoked."

Jack did not altogether share my trusting attitude. He'd had a few experiences at home that had convinced him that wild creatures of many kinds can be dangerous, sometimes without cause. A cobra had spit venom into his eyes and blinded him temporarily, and another time he had shot the head off a deadly mamba that was upreared almost face high and ready to strike.

His father had killed a leopard with an ax as it leaped at him; and on a hunt Jack and his companions had come on a group of bushmen in a tree, with the half-devoured body of a woman lying on the ground below. A lion had killed and fed on her just before the whites came along.

These encounters had made Jack cautious where all animals were concerned, and he carried a hatchet wherever we went. It wasn't much of a weapon, and I now know that it would have been worthless against a grizzly, but he felt safer with it along.

After he left for North Carolina I was entirely by myself, but that didn't bother me. In the next few weeks I saw so many grizzlies that they became a familiar part of the landscape. They seldom showed up near the campground, but up at the head of Igloo Creek and farther to the west it was not unusual to see half a dozen or more in a day, often from the gravel road that ran part way through the park. Many were sows with cubs; others were males traveling alone. In color they ranged from dark chocolate brown to a startling palomino blonde.

Every bear I had encountered so far was at a comfortable distance, and I was enjoying them hugely. They had fascinating traits of personality. I watched with deep interest the placidity of a mother nursing her young, the playfulness and devilment of the cubs, her savage ferocity if she suspected anything threatened them.

Gradually, however, the idea was being instilled in me that the grizzly is indeed king of the tundra, and everything about him shows it. He walks over his windswept domain with a haughty and powerful arrogance, his gait a slow, bowlegged swagger. I was coming to realize that he would retreat only from man, and then grudgingly.

As the summer wore on I heard stories of grizzly encounters that made me wonder whether my theories about peaceable bears were sound. For instance, there was the bear that took a swipe at Hank Pallage on his own back porch for no reason at all. And another gave my neighbor Joe Hankins a good scare.

Joe worked for a big logging outfit on the West Coast, but every summer for nine years he had been quitting his job and coming to Alaska for a long vacation. His hobbies were hiking and taking pictures, and he had seen a lot of grizzlies.

He was camped near me, and we talked often about bears. Finally he got too close to one and it came for him without warning. Luckily, it chased him only a short distance, then quit. But it left Joe pretty shaken up. I found myself wondering what would have happened if there had been no tree handy.

I also heard the usual stories of hunters, guides, and prospectors who had blundered into sows with cubs at close quarters, or who had shot a bear and failed to kill it and were no longer around. But I still doubted that the bears attacked unless they were provoked.

I still wasn't afraid of them, and I still wanted to meet one face to face. I did, however, take the precaution of filling a beer can half full of pebbles for a noisemaker and carrying it with me wherever I went.

As the blueberries ripened in July, the bears moved down from the higher country and were seen more and more often on the berry-covered slopes where I was doing my plant studies. There were places so thick that the bear trails were tunnels. The only way a man could get through those tangles was to follow the paths the grizzlies had made.

I walked out of such a tunnel one morning and confronted a big blonde bear that was raking in blueberries only a few yards down the mountain from me. Luckily the wind was blowing uphill and he was so busy with his berrying that he didn't see me. Otherwise, as I know now, I'd most likely have had trouble right then.

I stared at him just long enough to discover that a grizzly at close range imparts an overwhelming sense of power and danger. For the first time that summer, I really understood that there was risk involved in meeting these bears. I was above timberline, with no trees nearby, so I backed carefully out of sight, retreated quietly for 50 yards, and then made all the sudden racket my beer can was capable of.

It worked. The bear disappeared at a gallop, without even looking back my way. But it took a few minutes for my hair to lie flat again.

About that time I was warned that people had seen a sow grizzly with two cubs, new arrivals, on Igloo Mountain, where I was working. After that, I very carefully watched for her. I had seen enough to know that if we should meet, I wanted to give her plenty of room to run without losing face.

We had a couple of days of rain at the start of August, and I stayed near my tent. But the morning of the fourth dawned sunny and warm, and after lunch I parked the camping van on the road above the campground, walked across Igloo Creek on a fallen log, and pushed up into the spruce. I was after sample borings from trees all the way from the creek up to timberline, a distance of 300 yards, to determine their age.

It was a bright still day with only a light wind in the treetops, and I was enjoying the peacefulness of the forest. By midafternoon I had worked up to the edge of the timber and was poking through a very thick understory of brush.

I found a four-inch tree, and another that measured eight inches, making a wind-blown stand on the mountainside. I took borings from them, and then noticed a larger spruce, at least a foot in diameter, with dense willows around it. It was the largest tree in sight, but only about 20 feet high, and the branches were twisted and scraggly.

I left my pack on the ground about 10 yards from the big spruce, pushed through the brush, sat down, and went to work with my boring tool. I had no warning, no breaking of brush, no sound of movement at all. But suddenly, a few steps down the slope below me, where my pack lay, the stillness was shattered by a loud, vicious *Warf*!

It was a sound of surprise and rage, half bark and half snarl. I knew what it came from without looking, and I acted without thinking. My hands and feet reached instinctively for the nearest branches, which grew almost to the ground. I went up that shaggy spruce with the speed and agility of a red squirrel.

But even as I climbed desperately, the thought flashed through my mind that I was safe. Grizzlies, I had read and been told more times than I could remember, can't climb trees once they are past the age of cubhood. If I could get high enough before this one grabbed me, I had nothing to worry about.

I was eight or 10 feet up the tree when I looked down for the first time. A big snarling grizzly was scrambling awkwardly up after me. I suppose the branches, growing horizontally almost like the rungs of a ladder, were helping him. Whatever the reason, he was coming fast.

I reached for a branch above my head, but even while I pulled myself higher I felt the bear bite the calf of my left leg. I learned later that its teeth tore out instantly, ripping loose a big flap of skin and muscle. But at the moment, I felt no pain from the bite.

Again I tried to pull myself out of reach, but then the bear's teeth caught a firm grip in the heel of my boot. I felt a heavy weight loosening my hold and pulling me down. Branches started to break in my hands and under my free foot, and I had the horrible sensation that I was about to fall into an abyss.

The words "This is it!" flashed through my mind as if I had shouted them aloud. Then the pull on my foot suddenly ended, and below me I heard a crash and a thud as the grizzly tumbled through the branches to the ground.

I frantically started climbing higher, but almost at once I felt the whole tree shake and knew the bear was coming up again. I reached a height of about 15 feet this time and had only a couple more branches left above my head.

I paused to look down.

The bear was just below my feet, the most horrifying thing I had ever seen. The coarse blonde hair on its head and shoulders was all standing the wrong way, its yellow teeth were bared in a savage snarl, and its small eyes were blazing. As the grizzly climbed, it kept up a continuous low growling, like the sound two dogs make while fighting. I could see that it was straining every muscle to reach me.

I smashed my boot down on its head, but that had no more effect than kicking a brick wall. For a moment I had a strange feeling of outrage. This bear had no fear of me as a human. It was trying to kill me as it would kill any animal it had treed or cornered. It had no business behaving that way. Then my feeling changed to one of disbelief, as if my mind could not accept the fact of the attack.

Teeth slashed into me again, high in my right thigh, but again I felt no pain. The animal bit down hard, then lost its footing in the branches, let go of my leg, and tumbled to the ground for the second time.

The grizzly did not try to climb again. For long agonizing minutes it prowled around the tree, snorting and growling like a dog worrying a squirrel, seemingly insane with fury and frustration. At last it moved slowly into the willows, still snarling, watching me over its shoulder with a look that said as plain as words, "I'm not through with you yet!"

Until now I had felt none of my wounds and done very little coherent thinking. The attack had been so sudden and furious that it seemed to have overwhelmed me. Although I'd been sure when the bear grabbed me the first time that it would pull me down and kill me, I can't truthfully say that I was much aware of being afraid.

But now I realized that my legs were hurting, and I was shaking very hard. I was in the top of a scrawny spruce, with none too secure a hold, and I was sure the grizzly was still in the brush nearby, wating for me. When I looked down at my legs, my trousers were hanging in bloody rags and I could see a row of round tooth holes in my right thigh. A torn chunk of flesh hung from my left calf.

I didn't dare to climb down, but I realized I was close to the limit of my endurance and couldn't stay in the tree much longer, no matter what happened.

Down at the foot of the slope I could see my little van parked on the road. Those 300 yards of forest separated me from safety. One of the few thoughts that penetrated my stunned brain was the full realization that I had no immunity to wild-animal attack simply because I was a human being, as I had always believed. I knew better now.

While I watched, a car drove past on the road, I yelled at the top of my voice, but the distance was too great.

I waited 20 minutes and could endure no more. I climbed down, step by step, filled with dread and terror every inch of the way. I put one foot on the ground, looked around at the brush that hemmed me in on every side, and lost my nerve. I labored up again, as high as I could go.

I waited a few more minutes, trying to peer into the thickets for some hint of the bear. At intervals, I yelled and rattled my can of pebbles.

Down on the road a second car passed. I shouted but it went on. I soon realized I could not stay any longer in the tree, whether the bear attacked me again or not. I was growing very weak, and I'd better go down while I could still climb, rather than risk a fall.

I descended slowly . . . watching . . . listening . . . hardly breathing. Nothing happened. At the base of the spruce I grabbed my hat and hobbled for the road as fast as my wounds would allow, yelling, breaking brush, making all the commotion I could. Every second I expected to see a shaggy palomino-colored brute come roaring at me.

It seemed to take a lifetime to get to Igloo Creek. I slid down the bank, splashed across, and climbed to the road. I still had 200 yards to go to reach my car. I tried to run, but couldn't, and the specter of the grizzly haunted me every painful step. When I finally climbed into the car and slammed the door behind me, a hoarse "Thank God!" welled up out of my throat time after time.

From there on I had plenty of help. The first person I saw was Dr. Adolph Murie, a park service biologist and eminent scientist who had been studying grizzly bears for years. He was coming up the road in his green jeep, and as we met I hollered out the window of my car. "One of your friends bit me!"

"Well, I'll be . . ." I heard him yell back, and then he spun the jeep around and followed me to his cabin, just across the road from the campground where my tent was pitched.

Dr. Murie and his wife Louise gave me first aid and then drove me the 30 miles to the park hotel. A nurse in the infirmary there bandaged my wounds and gave me a tetanus shot. Then she checked through the hotel's guest list, found an M.D., and summoned him. He walked in, very professional looking, took a hurried look at my legs, and walked right out again. I learned later that he was a psychiatrist. I guess he figured that what had happened to me wasn't exactly in his line.

The park people phoned for a bush plane from Fairbanks to pick me up. Sam King, the park superintendent, loaned me a pair of his pants for the flight. There wasn't much left of mine.

The plane flew me to St. Joseph's Hospital in Fairbanks, and there Dr. Paul Haggland, a surgeon and hunter who had repaired many injured outdoorsmen, stitched me up, telling me stories of his own encounters with bears while he worked.

My injuries were not so bad as they seemed. The calf of my left leg was severely torn, and the bear's teeth had left deep puncture wounds in my right thigh. But my heel was not hurt. There was just a hole punched through the pac, and no bones were damaged.

I had a small cut on my rear end that I didn't even know about until

Dr. Haggland found it. A tooth had clipped me there. Luckily, the bear had not used its claws. I suppose it had needed them to hang on to the tree.

When Dr. Haggland finished, he summed things up in three simple words.

"You were lucky," he said with quiet emphasis.

I left the hospital after five days and went back to the park hotel. By August 24, or 20 days after the encounter, I was able to drive and left for my home in Washington, D.C. One of the park rangers who wanted to go to Philadelphia went along, and we had a pleasant, leisurely trip.

Nobody will ever know what accounted for the vicious attack. Dr. Murie told me that I was the second person to be attacked, and the first to be injured, by a grizzly in McKinley Park. The bear was a pale blonde, exactly the color of the female that had been seen on Igloo Mountain several times in the preceding week or two.

But many bears of that color were in the area, and there was no way to tell whether this was the same sow. I saw no cubs, and to this day do not know the sex of the grizzly that mauled me. But the sow-with-cubs theory seems the most logical.

Some of the park rangers were inclined to believe, however, that the bear simply walked out of the brush where I had dropped my pack, was startled by the smell of man, located me instantly, and flew into insane rage. Others suggested the bear might have been attracted when it mistook the squeaking of my boring tool for some small animal in distress.

What happened to the grizzly is also a mystery. It wasn't hunted down and destroyed. In fact, so far as I know, nobody ever saw that bear again.

The day after the attack, rangers went up after my pack. They saw no bear. After I got back to the hotel, the Muries and two other companions went back to the scene with me to retrieve two or three items of equipment I had dropped. I went with my heart in my mouth, imagining a grizzly behind every bush, but my fears proved groundless.

One thing we could not find—my boring tool. I have no idea what became of it, and I still don't know the age of the scraggly spruce that saved my life. But there was bear hair clinging to the branches 14 feet above the ground, and big limbs were broken off where the grizzly had fought its way up to me and fallen out twice. I had proof now of what I had known all along. This grizzly had climbed, not just stood on its hind feet and then reached up toward me.

Just the other day, rereading Seton's Lives of North American Game Animals, I came across the following bit of information:

"This bear never climbs. The hunter who succeeds in getting up a tree is as safe from a grizzly bear as he is from a bull."

All I can say is, I wish Seton—and anybody else who believes that— could have been along that day in McKinley Park.

The grizzly is not the only big North American bear supposedly unable to climb that can go up a tree if it decides to. Its overgrown kinsman, the giant Alaska brown, has that same ability. Like the grizzly, however, the brown seems to use it very rarely.

Ralph Young, renowned Alaska guide and one of the greatest living authorities on brown-bear behavior, tells of a medium-size brownie that he and one of his hunters surprised eating a dead salmon on the bank of a small stream. With an explosive snort, the bear climbed a tall spruce tree, not stopping until it reached a stout limb 40 feet above the ground.

My encounter with the grizzly has a little sequel. In 1965, Elizabeth and I went to Canada on a canoe trip in Ontario's Algonquin Park. We did not know it, but other campers had buried their garbage near a campsite we chose. A black bear had found the garbage. Unwittingly, we set up our tent only a few feet away.

The bear returned shortly after dark. I had hung our packs on a tree limb as a precaution, and he tried first to pull them down. He was so close to the tent that I could plainly hear his heavy breathing.

When I yelled and drove him away from the packs, he started digging up garbage and padding around the tent, grunting and grumbling. He kept it up the rest of the night in spite of all I could do. I didn't sleep a wink until he left at daybreak. I don't think I've ever put in a worse night.

I have news for anybody who's interested. I'll never trust any bear again as long as I live.

Bears in My Hair

Olive A. Fredrickson

January, 1970

When I had my first argument with a black bear, the bear won hands down. But I'm happy to say I have evened the score quite a few times since.

That first run-in happened while I was living alone with my three children, Olive and Vala and Louis, on our homestead on the Stuart River in central British Columbia, a few years after my husband Walter Reamer, a trapper, drowned in the wilderness of northern Alberta, leaving me to support myself and three little ones as best I could.

I left the kids at home one day toward the end of summer and walked two miles to the house of a neighbor, Jack Hamilton, to pick up mail and groceries he had brought out from town for me. Because I'd have enough to carry on the return trip, I didn't take the old .30/30 Winchester Model 94 that went with me on most of my trips.

The country along the Stuart was wild and sparsely settled. You never knew when you were going to meet a quarrelsome moose, wolves, or something else in an unfriendly frame of mind, so I usually carried the rifle as a precaution. But that day I went without it.

When I was ready to go home I took a shortcut across the fields and through timber along the river. I hadn't walked far when I saw a bear and three cubs grubbing ants out of a rotten log at the edge of a small burn.

Both my father and husband had been trappers, and I had lived most of my life in the woods and wasn't really afraid of bears. I had met lots of them, but I had yet to come across one that didn't run at sight of me. Nevertheless, I knew enough about them that I didn't think it would be wise to walk on past that family. I was fully aware that a sow with cubs is likely to be short-tempered.

346

"Get!" I yelled at the top of my voice. "Get out of there!"

The old bear responded with a loud *woof*, but she and two of the cubs took me at my word. They lit out in the opposite direction. The third cub got confused. I guess he was so busy with his ant-hunting that he didn't know where I was. He came straight for me.

The old female ran only about three or four times her own length before she looked back. Then she swapped ends, started after the cub, and let out a roar that fairly lifted me out of my tracks. I turned and ran for Jack Hamilton's open fields as fast as my legs could carry me, but it seemed to me right then that I had lead weights on my feet.

I looked back once and she was gaining fast, but the cub stopped, and then she stopped. When I got out into the field, she was nowhere in sight. I went back to Hamilton's house, borrowed a horse, and rode home. So far as I can remember that was the last time in the years we lived there on the Stuart that I ever went into the woods on foot without a gun.

That was my first encounter with a quarrelsome bear but it was far from the last. In "I Had to Have Moose," OUTDOOR LIFE, May 1967, and "The Wolves Were the Worst," OUTDOOR LIFE, June 1967, I told of leaving the homestead, of moving to a gold-mining camp at Germansen Landing, of Louis's death, of Olive and Vala growing up and marrying, and of my own second marriage to Big John Fredrickson. John and I have a home in Okanagan Falls, B.C., now. I have lived most of my life in Alberta and British Columbia, on the homestead, a ranch, or at mining camps and sawmills. Even when I was living in town I made frequent trips off into the bush, fishing, hunting, camping, or prospecting. Looking back over the last 40 years, it seems to me I have had bears in my hair a fair share of the time. Some of the encounters were funny; some sent a few chills up my back. None were dull.

One of the most unusual encounters happened shortly before John and I were married. We were both working in Prince George. One Sunday in May we went for a walk along the Fraser River. We came to an abandoned field grown up with a few pines. Just as we reached the edge of it, a big black bear walked into the open, trailed by two cubs.

We were hidden in brush, and for the better part of an hour that family put on as entertaining a show as I have ever watched. They tore an anthill apart and lapped up ants until the two youngsters got into an argument that wound up in a battle royal. The mother tolerated that for a minute or so, then broke it up by swatting one of them on the behind hard enough to send him flying through the air. He brought up head-first against a stump, shook his head a few times, and patted one ear with a paw, making a noise as if trying to whine with his mouth full of bubbles. When peace was restored the sow sat down with her back against a small tree and suckled both cubs.

The whole bear family was showing signs of getting sleepy, when all of a sudden the old girl swung her head to one side and sniffed. Then she was streaking across the clearing and John and I caught a glimpse of a doe and small fawn running into the brush. There was a wire fence ahead of them. The doe turned and followed it, but the poor fawn smacked into it and bounced back literally into the bear's arms. There was one long bleat before that old sow sank her teeth into its head. We were just close enough to here her crush bones.

I had seen more than I wanted, and it seemed likely that if she got wind of us right then she wouldn't be in a very friendly mood, so we played it safe. As she started back to her cubs with the dead fawn, we sneaked away. In all the years I have spent in the woods, that was the only time I ever saw a bear make a kill. I'll say one thing for her—she did it quickly and cleanly, without any of the tearing and tormenting I had watched wolves inflict.

A few years after that John and I were running a logging-and-sawmill operation west of Prince George, and bears became so numerous around camp that they were a major nuisance. I had just acquired a dog, a fox terrier named Jeep. That dog wasn't big enough to deal with bears, but he was determined to run them out of camp as fast as they showed up. He had more grit than sense. Every time I heard him barking, I'd scurry out to give him a hand or call him off.

We had bears at the garbage dump, bears around the buildings, bears at the door at night. Finally one big one started ripping the screens off the meathouse, then climbing in and helping himself. He didn't seem to like fresh beef, but he cleaned up our bacon, summer sausage, and pork. John and I agreed he'd have to go.

We cut a four-inch opening in the cookhouse door overlooking the scene of his raids. The peephole was just big enough to poke as gun barrel through. We'd keep watch for him out of the cookhouse window.

He didn't keep us waiting long. He came in shortly after dark the first night and walked straight to the window where we were posted as though aware we were there. Then he stood up with his big muddy paws on the glass and stared into the cookhouse. We had ducked back into a corner.

I'm not really afraid of bears, as I said, but I'll admit that it made my scalp prickle to look that one in the face only six or eight feet away with nothing but a pane of glass between us. John could have killed him easily, but he didn't want to break the window, so he waited until the bear dropped down and started for the meathouse.

John poked his .30/06, a Winchester Model 54, out of the peephole. The bear was only a step or two away from the muzzle. The shot hit him in the ribs, and he bawled and rushed between the cookhouse and the meathouse. The alley wasn't more than two feet wide, and there was more bear than that. He slammed into the side of the cookhouse so hard that every dish on the shelves rattled, but he squeezed through and ran for the brush.

John ran out after him, but I wanted no part of chasing a wounded bear at night, so I stood at the window and tried to help by pointing a flashlight. When John heard him break brush beyond the clearing, he gave up and came back.

As soon as daylight came, we went out and let Jeep take the blood trail. We jumped the bear half a mile from camp, and John stopped him with a hip shot. He was still full of fight, snarling and thrashing around, and the fox terrier came within a hair of getting himself converted into dogburger before John wound things up with a 180-grain softpoint in the side of the bear's head.

The next one that gave us enough trouble to get himself killed came along after we had moved to a ranch on the Stuart River. In April, shortly after our lambs and calves arrived, we began losing them to a bear. We did everything we could think of, keeping watch of the stock during daytime and penning the animals near the barn at night in the belief the killer would not come close to the buildings. But he was bold and persistent, and we continued to find dead sheep almost every morning.

Finally we decided to go looking for him. Because it was still early in the spring, it seemed likely he'd be hanging around near his winter den. Maybe we could find that. We still had Jeep, and he was as dedicated to bear fights as ever, so we took him along.

Jeep made the find. We heard him barking in a thick stand of young aspens, and when we got there he was fussing and fuming around a big hole under a stump. There were claw marks on all the nearby trees. We had discovered a bear den, all right, but whether it belonged to the right bear, or whether the owner was in it remained to be seen. Jeep, however, seemed very sure that the owner was home.

If the bear was home he paid no attention to the racket our pint-size dog was making, and John didn't get any response when he poked into the den with a long pole. But his next move started things happening.

John peeled off the old shirt he was wearing, wrapped it around the end of the pole, set it afire, and rammed it down into the hole. There was a brief silence, then a loud sneeze, followed by a throaty grunt, more

My scalp prickled when the bear leaned against the window to look in.

sneezing, and a gruff cough. At that point, the pole started to shake, and I shoved John's .30/06 into his hands. A split second later the head of a very upset bear emerged from beneath the stump. John didn't let him come any farther. He slapped his shot between the eyes at six feet. It turned out that we had killed the right bear too. We lost no more sheep.

Although bears deserve the blame for a lot of deviltry, in fairness I want to emphasize that they are by no means the only troublesome characters in the woods. It took a buck deer to give one of my brothers the closest call any member of our family ever had with a wild animal, and over the years I have had almost as many arguments with moose as with bears.

I remember a story by the late Eric Collier in which he complained that the big soreheads drove him off his trapline trail, chased him over his own garden fence, kept him from the outhouse, and even barged in on him when he sat down on a block of wood at the back door to hatch a story.

At that time Collier was living at Meldrum Lake, about 150 miles south of us, and when I read his story my heart went out to him. We had depended on moose meat, fresh and canned, for our winter food supply those first few years after I was widowed, and it had meant the difference between eating well and going hungry. John and I still hunt moose every fall and enjoy it. And yet there have been times when I was as sick of moose as Eric Collier ever was.

The deer encounter took place while I was still a girl at home. We were living in northern Alberta at a small settlement called Moose Portage on the Athabasca River 165 miles north of Athabasca Landing. Freighters with horse teams took mail and supplies north to the Peace River in winter at that time, traveling the ice of the Athabasca. They would stop overnight at Moose Portage. In summer most of the freighting was done by steamboat.

My brother Lea Goodwin went hunting one morning, leaving instructions that if we heard him shoot we were to hitch our team to the sleigh and follow his tracks down to the river. We had been brought up not to waste ammunition. If he shot, it would mean venison.

About a mile from the house he heard a racket in a thicket, worked in close for a look, and found two muledeer bucks fighting a ding-dong battle. They were both big deer and fairly well matched for size, but one looked old and past his prime, and his rack was not so good as that of the other.

The younger animal seemed to be getting the better of the fight because he was quicker on his feet. As often as they met head-to-head, the older buck backed the younger one into a windfall or toppled him sideways, but the younger deer could maneuver faster, and he kept ramming his horns into the rump and flank and neck of the oldtimer.

Lea watched them for a few minutes and then decided to lay in a supply of venison while he had the chance. He was carrying a Winchester .32 Special, and he floored the younger buck with a shot behind the shoulder. The old fellow was a bit slow taking off, and Lea levered in another shell and dropped him too.

He walked up to that one first. There was no sign of life in the deer, so he leaned his rifle against a tree, took out his knife, and bent over to cut its throat. The buck came to life at the first prick of the knife. The deer brought his hind feet up into my brother's belly. The hoofs caught in Lea's clothing and he was thrown onto his knees. At the same time, a blow from one antler sent his knife flying into the snow. Then the deer was back on his feet and charging.

Lea managed to stand up again, but the deer slammed into him and drove him back against a tree. My brother broke off a short piece of dry limb and jabbed it at the buck's eyes, but that didn't do much good. The deer was too enraged, too intent on killing, to be stopped that way.

The deer's next rush knocked Lea down and banged his head against a pine stump so hard that he saw stars, but as he fell, his right hand closed around a piece of the stump hefty enough to serve as a club.

The deer lowered his head, and Lea brought the club down behind the buck's ears. Then he grabbed an antler, swung himself back of it, held on with his left hand and clubbed the buck as hard as he could with his right. The deer was weakening but still had enough strength to reach forward with his hind feet and pound my brother on the legs and back. One of those blows caught Lea on the neck and cut a deep gash. That almost finished him.

In the end, neither buck nor man was able to do any real damage. They broke apart and staggered drunkenly around each other, sparring for an opening. The deer was first to go down. The buck fell dead, and Lea fell across the animal and passed out. That was how my younger brother and I found him half an hour later when we arrived on the scene with the team and sleigh. He was lying across the buck like a sack of meal with his head hanging down in the snow.

By the time we revived him and got him into the sleigh, his teeth were chattering. We wrapped two horse blankets around him, loaded a deer on each side to help keep him warm, and ran the horses home at a lope. Lea was so bruised and sore he couldn't walk for days, but by a miracle he escaped serious injury.

That affair taught me a lesson. Since then, I have never gone close to an animal I have shot without keeping my rifle on it until I was positive it was dead. John and I like to walk in from the back with a rifle ready, reach around, and touch the animal in the eye with the muzzle. If there is a flicker of life left, it will blink. A deer or moose or bear that doesn't blink is really dead.

In recent years I have gone even farther. In my early days, when ammunition was hard to get, I never felt I could afford to waste a shell, but now I always play safe with a final head shot.

Of my many moose encounters, two in particular stick in my mind. The first was my own fault and happened because I was guilty of about the same kind of carelessness that got Lea into his scrape. It happened while I was working at the gold-mining camp at Germansen Landing. A trapper came by one day and reported that he had found a cow moose that had a broken hip, the result of getting a foot caught in a crack in the ice. She was in such bad shape that she should be shot, he said, and he'd have taken care of it but he hadn't had a gun with him. I hated to think of the poor thing dying a lingering death, so I loaded the .30/30, and my daughter Vala and I set out.

We found the moose without difficulty. She was in a deep hollow with vertical rock walls on three sides and a 50-foot drop over a creek bank behind her. She was down and couldn't get up, so I worked in close to make sure of my shot. I was on snowshoes and should have known better.

I wasn't much more than her own length away with the creek bank behind me when she lurched to her feet and made a sudden, staggering lunge. I couldn't dodge, so I stood my ground and drove a shot into her head. She fell so close to me that I could have reached out and touched her with a snowshoe.

Vala screamed, "Mama!" and for a minute I had all I could do to keep my knees from buckling. In all the years since, I have never made that kind of mistake again. Any injured or wounded animal I have to put away, I'll do it from a safe distance.

Moose encounter No. 2 on the list of those I remember best was connected with a fishing-and-hunting trip on the Stuart that John and I made while we were living in Prince George. We were camping in the open under a lean-to tarp. There was an old hunting cabin nearby, but we didn't want to use it because of the pack rats.

Along toward midnight, we were awakened by a sudden loud crashing in the willows. We jumped up and heard a heavy animal coming straight for the lean-to. It stopped at the edge of the brush no more than 30 feet away, but we couldn't make it out because of deep shadow. Then it let out a hollow bellow that sounded half cough, half roar.

"That's a bear," John said, but I knew better. I had heard too many moose on the warpath not to recognize that bawl.

"It's a bull moose," I told my husband, "and he means business."

I know of no other animal in the woods that has a vocabulary as expressive as a moose's. A cow coaxing her calf along uses a soft grunt. Calling to a bull in mating time, she sounds a lot like a domestic cow mooing through her nose. The bull talks back with low guttural snorts, much like those of a stallion in like circumstances. But when he gets his dander up, he warns the world with a roaring, chopping-on-a-hollow-log bellow that makes your hair stand on end.

Moose or bear, that loudmouth was too close to our camp to be tolerated. John went after him with the .30/06, and the moose retreated slowly toward the river, keeping in the thick brush and blasting out a grunting bawl every few seconds. In the end he bluffed John out, and we skedaddled for the old hunting cabin.

John still thought we were dealing with a bear, but when the moose season opened two days later, I won the argument. We had counted 36 moose along the river by that time, and the first afternoon of hunting we found a place where two bulls had been fighting on an open hillside. The sign was very fresh, and we could even smell moose. We moved up the hill as stealthily as we could, but we must have made a little noise, for the next thing we knew, a big bull came crashing over the ridge straight for us. His ears were laid back, his eyes were blazing, and the hair on his neck and shoulders was standing up the wrong way. Every couple of steps, he let out the same kind of bellowing grunts we had heard in front of our lean-to.

I suppose the bull had driven off a smaller rival only minutes before, and he was in no mood to put up with us. The whole thing was over in less time than it takes to tell it. He kept coming, and my legs were beginning to feel rubbery. When he was 15 or 20 yards away, crashing through the brush like a runaway freight train, John belted him down with a shot in the heart. The next thing I saw was the cow that was the cause of it all. She was running over the ridge after taking the whole thing in from a vantage point a little way off on the hillside.

"Do you know now what we heard in the brush the other night?" I asked when the excitement had quieted down.

"The same thing we heard just now," John admitted with a grin, and you can bet that he never forgot that sound. Very few people do.

Doctor's Orders

**Frank Glaser
as told to Jim Rearden**

September, 1954

Billy Fraim had just started hauling passengers—or trying to—from Valdez to Fairbanks over the Richardson Highway. The road was a veritable quagmire—really suitable only for horses. The Black Rapids Roadhouse, which I owned and operated, was on this road. One spring day in 1921 Billy arrived at the roadhouse. He came from the direction of Valdez in a Model-T Ford, having taken all day to drive from Yost's, an abandoned roadhouse 25 miles to the south.

As he pulled to a stop the mud-spattered car was spouting steam two feet into the air. And Billy was excited.

"Frank, you've got to do something about those bears down by Yost's," he said.

Billy was in his 20's then, rather small, with sandy hair. He looked like a very serious schoolboy.

"Who, me?" I said. "That's way out of my territory, Billy."

"But somebody's got to do something. It isn't safe to travel that road." Billy was almost shouting.

The three passengers, two women and a man, stood next to Billy and loudly agreed with him. They kept shaking their heads and looking at the hood of the steaming Ford.

I wasn't too surprised to hear Billy's complaint. I'd heard that the grizzlies near Yost's were thicker than fleas, and every now and then someone traveling the old road was scared pink by one of them.

Billy went on to tell me what had happened. "Frank," he said, "this morning I came around a bend near Yost's, and one of those white-colored bears—a reg'lar monster—was right in the middle of the road. I guess I got excited, and instead of slowing down I yanked the throttle and went faster. You know, the road's pretty good there for a ways.

"I scared the bear all right—at first. He ran down the road ahead of us, but I gained on him. That was a mistake."

The three passengers stood behind Billy, nodding and looking solemn.

"All of a sudden," Billy continued, "he stopped running and stood up. Lord, man, he must have been eight or nine feet tall—I looked *up* at him—and he wanted to fight the car!"

Billy reached over and patted it like it was a horse or something.

"I slammed on the brakes and the reverse pedal both at once. Practically threw my passengers through the windshield."

By then Billy was waving his arms in my face and the passengers were all talking at once, trying to help Billy tell the story.

"I'll bet I wasn't five feet from that monster when I stopped. The women screamed and I yelled and honked the horn and raced the motor— and that bear, on his hind legs, walked right up to the car. Snarling! It happened so quick I didn't have time to back up. He swatted the hood once, then I guess the noise scared him and he took off into the willows. I got out of there fast, believe me!"

I looked at the hood of the Ford, and sure enough it had been bashed in and there were deep claw scratches in the metal.

That fall Dr. E. W. Nelson, chief of what was then the U.S. Bureau of Biological Survey, spent about a week at Black Rapids collecting small bird and mammal specimens. He was a tall, gray-haired, distinguished-looking man in his 70's.

I was interested in his work and took time off from my market hunting to show him around. One day, as he was searching the country with his glasses, a cream-colored grizzly wandered out along a gravel bar of the Delta River.

"Frank, isn't that an unusual color for a grizzly?" he asked.

"Gosh no, Doc. Most of them around here are that color," I told him.

"How common are they?"

"Too common, as far's I'm concerned. They give me a scare every now and then. Why, there's a place up the road that's just alive with 'em," I said, and mentioned the flat river bar near Yost's abandoned roadhouse, where Billy Fraim had been.

Dr. Nelson was excited and made me tell him more. Remember—this was 1921, and museums and other scientific outfits were still finding new species of birds and mammals. Many expeditions were made to Alaska simply to collect specimens.

As a rule the cream-colored grizzlies were not especially large, I told Dr. Nelson, but they showed a nasty temper at times. While market hunting, I often killed two sheep and cached one on a glacier while packing the other out. Too often, when I returned, a cream-colored grizzly would be feeding on the second sheep. I killed a few that refused to leave (those whose meat was worth reclaiming), and occasionally one charged me. Most of them would high-tail it when I yelled, but there were too many that wouldn't. As far as I was concerned, they were a nuisance.

The Alaska Road Commission teamsters hated them and complained

bitterly about the runaways and near runaways of their four-horse teams—
especially around the river bar near Yost's. Somehow they didn't appreciate
it when all four horses tried to turn and climb on the wagon with them.
And they didn't enjoy trying to rein down four terrified runaways that
bolted when they saw or smelled a grizzly.

After I told Dr. Nelson all this he asked if I'd be willing to collect a
large group for the Biological Survey. The Survey had bears from other
parts of the Alaska Range, but none from that particular area. I had long
wanted to hunt there anyway, so I agreed to do the collecting job for him
the following spring.

There was little traffic over the Richardson Highway during that winter
of 1921–22, and the shells I ordered from Fairbanks never showed up.
Come spring, I rummaged around the roadhouse for a full day hunting
for ammunition, finally coming up with an assortment of about every kind
of .30/06 cartridge ever made. I think some of the stuff was at least 10 years
old. I had a few 220-grain loads, some 180's, and others of 150, 145, and
172 grains. Some way to start a grizzly hunt!

I started out May 15 by dog team and drove up the Delta River on the
ice toward Yost's old place, where I planned to set up quarters. It was
about noon when I pulled into an Army signal station a couple of hundred
yards from Yost's.

The two soldiers stationed there were just leaving to visit another
station 20 miles down the trail where they planned to stay awhile. I told
them why I had come and got permission to tack any hides I collected to
the Signal Corps station buildings. These included a log telegraph station,
a log barn, and an oversize cache.

Isabella Pass, where Yost's is located, is one of the windiest places in
the Alaska Range. The wind howls through it from the south, then whistles
back from the north. Snowdrifts build up to remarkable heights, and when
I continued on to Yost's I drove my dog team right up to a second-story
window, removed it, and went in. I could easily have driven the team over
the roof where the winter's snow had drifted up to the eaves.

The downstairs, I discovered, was filled with snow—someone evidently had left the door open the previous fall. I found where the kitchen
stovepipe ran through an upstairs room, disconnected it, and hooked up
my little Yukon stove. I was perfectly comfortable there for the two weeks
I hunted. When I left I stood on the drifted snow and replaced the window
I had removed without even having to stretch.

Yost's is gone today, likewise the fence and the bell. The bell, mounted
on a 20-foot post directly in front of the roadhouse, was huge. It was
balanced so that when the wind blew it tipped back and forth and rang
so loudly that it could be heard for miles. The Signal Corps had thrown a
six or seven-foot woven wire fence across the Delta River bar to a 50-foot
bluff opposite the roadhouse. During blizzards—which are still quite common in the pass—people coming from either direction hit the fence and
followed it, on their hands and knees at times, right to the bell and, of
course, to Yost's. A year or two before the fence was put in, 12 people lost
their lives by passing the roadhouse in a blizzard.

The fence is gone now, but was still standing that May of 1922 when

I hunted bears there, and I well remember hearing the insistent clanging of the bell every time the wind picked up over 10 miles an hour—which was most of the time.

The mile-wide river bar where I planned to hunt was blown almost clear of snow. That made it easy for the bears to dig the plentiful pea-vine roots that attracted them to the place. Spruce timber and thickets of sapling birch grew right to the bar on each side of the river, and snow had formed big drifts here and there in the dense growth.

A long ridge poked up between the bar and the road, which used to be the Valdez trail and is now the Richardson Highway. After fixing up a comfortable "camp" in an empty upperstory room at Yost's, first thing I did was to climb this ridge and look at the flat.

I had no sooner reached the top and glanced at the bar than I saw three grizzlies—cream-colored, with brown legs. They were what Dr. Nelson wanted. I glassed them for a few minutes and decided it was a female and twin yearlings.

I wasn't keen to shoot yearlings or cubs, but Dr. Nelson had specifically requested a representative series—young bears as well as old ones. I made up my mind it was for the good of science, so started out to collect the three if I could.

The wind was in my favor, and I waited until the bears went into a dry wash, then walked to within 40 or 50 yards of them. I gathered them in with three shots as they came into sight. It was as simple as that.

I measured them carefully, recording the figures in my notebook, then skinned them out and packed the hides back to the roadhouse. I left the skulls, which are fully as important as the skins for scientific specimens, thinking I would pick them up the next day.

Next morning I fleshed the three hides clean and nailed them to the buildings at the signal station. Then I went after the skulls. First, I walked up on the ridge for a look-see at the flat. I hadn't gone 100 yards along the crest when I saw three more grizzlies in about the same place the first ones had been. Two of these were also cream-colored and apparently they were another sow with yearlings. One of the yearlings was almost white, with blackish legs—kind of a freak.

I worked in close and collected the three with three shots again. I was pretty cocky that night—six grizzlies with six shots was fair shooting, even if four of them were yearlings.

It was near midnight and barely dark when I finished skinning those three and packing the six skulls and three skins back to the roadhouse. I cleaned skulls and fleshed and nailed up hides all the next day. A snowstorm set in then and I didn't get out for two days.

On the third day it was clear and I sat on top of the ridge glassing the flats for a couple of hours before I spotted a single big cream-colored bear digging roots. I had a lot of confidence after my luck with the first six bears, so decided to see how close I could get to him. He was the largest I'd seen until then, and I was sure he was a male.

I moved down into a dry wash and worked upwind toward him, bending over to keep out of sight. Now and then I went to the edge to look at him. He was more cautious than the others had been and occasionally he stood up to look around, then calmly went on feeding.

After half an hour of alternately sneaking and watching, I was surprised to find that I was within 40 or 50 feet of him. He apparently had moved toward me as I sneaked the last few yards. He was much closer than I liked. He looked as big as a horse.

When I stuck my head up to look at him he saw me and stood still, staring. A spindly willow bush about four feet high was near by—the only cover of any kind for a long way. And that huge bear walked over and tried to hide behind it!

He was too close for comfort, but I had one of the 145-grain, bronze-capped shells in the barrel and I had had good luck with them. I thought they were pretty skookum grizzly medicine. One good chest shot should finish him off nicely.

I talked to that bear, trying to get him to stand on his hind legs. Instead he crouched behind that skeleton of a willow, peeking around it at me. This is ridiculous, I thought. I talked, whistled, moved my head back and forth, waved a hand—did everything to get him to stand up. I wanted his chest exposed. After what seemed like a long time of playing peekaboo, he did stand to get a better look at what he must have taken for an idiot.

I usually line up a rifle with my right eye, then open my left and fire with both eyes open. I did this, and squeezed the trigger. A wall of flame hit my face. At the same time, my gun burst out of my hand and spun backward over my head. I thought both my eyes had been knocked out. They were full of tears and I couldn't nerve myself to open them.

At that moment I didn't know or care where the bear was—he might have been breathing down my neck, for all I knew. My eyes burned something fierce, and a continuous stream of tears poured out of them. All I could do was lie there and cover my face.

After a while I forced my eyes open, but all I could see was blackness and stars rolling around. I was sure I was blind, and I wondered if I could get back to the highway for help. I listened for the bear. I felt he was still standing behind the lone willow looking at me. I bagan to panic then, thinking I was blind, with an angry and wounded grizzly ready to pounce on me any second. But I made myself lie still and fight off the temptation to rub my eyes. Finally, after I don't know how long, I could see light and the pain began to go away.

It must have been at least an hour from the time I fired until I could see again. Everything was blurred. I picked up my rifle, expecting to find a hole blown in the side of it or something equally serious, but it didn't seem to be damaged.

Trying to open the bolt, I managed to lift it all right, but I couldn't draw it back. I finally had to put the rifle butt on the ground and use my foot to force the bolt. The shell, split in three places, fell out—and the primer fell out of the shell. No doubt the aged brass of the shell had caused the trouble. Fortunately, the gas port had functioned properly. I had never before been quite certain why that port was there. I worked several shells through the action, looked it over, and decided it was undamaged. Then I started looking for the bear.

He had been hit—I found blood where he had stood behind the lone willow. I went toward the nearest patch of brush about 250 yards away, looking for his trail. My eyes still watered badly and everything was blurred, but I could see.

He had crossed a snow-packed dry wash, leaving a good blood trail as he made a beeline toward the nearest cover. I have often wondered why he didn't charge when I crippled him. I've had many grizzlies come at me for less.

The trail went into thick brush and I followed it slowly and carefully, keeping my rifle ready. Ahead I saw a big snowdrift, and it looked to me as if the bear had walked right alongside the edge of it. I walked toward one end, planning to climb the half-rotten snow and look around. Just as I reached the end of the drift I heard a rumbling noise behind me. I whirled, expecting to see the bear charging. But he was standing on top of the drift, about 25 feet away, with his big head swinging back and forth, growling at me. I shot, and he disappeared.

When I got to him he was dead. He had originally turned just short of the snowdrift, gone around to the other side, climbed it, and dug a hole almost on top. I'd walked not more than five feet directly under where he was curled up on the drift. I quit using 145-grain loads after that.

That flat by Yost's seemed to be a bear hunter's paradise. I killed one or more bears almost every time I went out. In all I picked up three sows, each with two yearlings, and eight males. All were of the same color. None was extremely large.

But I ran into a couple that *looked* awfully big for a while.

I had climbed the ridge as usual and watched the flat for a couple of hours before I saw them. They turned out to be big males, and when I first saw them they were fairly close together, working south, busily digging pea-vine roots. I decided to try to collect both of them.

The wind was in my favor, so I walked directly toward them. Every time one of them looked up I froze in my tracks until he went on feeding. I only had about 400 yards to go to put me in fair range. A deep dry wash ran between the bears, and I ducked into that, crouched over, and ran. I checked frequently to see where they were—I had learned my lesson about getting too close. Each of them was about 50 yards from the dry wash. While they were busy feeding I worked along the dry wash until I stood directly between them. There was no cover on the gravel bar and I could see them clearly. I was certain that I could drop one, whirl around toward the other one, and drop him too.

I bellied up the bank of the wash till I could see over, and drew a fine bead on the bear to my left. He was standing still, broadside, clawing up pea-vines. I held for his shoulder, hoping for a heart shot. He dropped as I fired and I was positive that he was dead.

Without a second glance at him I whirled and saw the second bear standing on his hind legs, looking at me. His chest was exposed and I quickly fired into it before he could drop to all fours again. I must have fired too quickly because he was knocked sideways by the slug—I was using the last of my 180-grain ammunition—and then he bounced to his feet, biting savagely at his shoulder and running toward me. I was certain he hadn't seen me and I think he came in my direction only because he was headed toward his partner; or possibly he just happened to be facing my way when he bounced up after being hit.

A grizzly can travel mighty fast even on three legs. I rammed another shell home and carefully put another slug into his chest. He was within 50 feet when he dropped, kicking and biting convulsively. It was then that I heard the noise behind me.

Something had gone wrong.

I whirled with another shell in the rifle, ready to shoot, and saw the first bear about 20 feet away, staggering toward me. He was looking at me, his head swinging from side to side, lips curled back in a snarl. Those big yellow teeth looked like walrus tusks to me. I took a quick bead on his chest—I was low enough in the gully to shoot up at him—and pulled the trigger.

Snick went the hammer. One of the shells had misfired.

The next shell *had* to be good—it was the last one in the gun. I yanked the bolt open, slammed that last shell home, and fired. He dropped, his nose plowing gravel and sand. Then he kicked a few times and lay still. After I got a wad of snoose in my mouth and calmed down, I measured the distance from his nose to the dry wash. It was just eight feet.

I think each of those bears, after being wounded, had headed for the other, and I was right between them. The first shot, instead of killing the one on the left, had glanced off his shoulder blade, gone forward through muscle, and come out of the lower part of the neck without hitting a vital spot. It was just a freak shot that probably wouldn't happen again in a lifetime.

When I had about 12 hides nailed to the buildings at the signal station, one of the soldiers returned. I was there when he arrived. He looked at the hides and his jaw dropped and he swiveled his head back and forth, staring. Then he walked around each of the buildings, counting hides.

"Where did you get all those hides?" he asked.

I had a hard time convincing him that I'd killed all of them right there in the seven or eight days since he left. Next day he headed for Fairbanks on Army business.

Before I left Yost's I spent a day weighing those bears. The carcass of the heaviest one, without skull or skin, weighed just 350 pounds. It was a full-grown bear. I figured the hide weighted about 75 pounds and the skull around 20. The carcass of one fat, nearly toothless old female weighed 250 pounds. The yearlings' carcasses came to around 125 pounds each. Hides of the adults were as long as about 7½ feet.

I look back on that hunt with mixed feelings. It would be a terrible thing for a man to go out today and kill 17 grizzlies just for a scientific collection. It was different then. Market hunters occasionally shot bears and sold the hides, but not as a regular thing. There were practically no sportsmen hunting them. Consequently, grizzlies were extremely abundant and they were generally regarded as pests. At the time, I received thanks from the Alaska Road Commission, the teamsters and car drivers using the road, and of course Dr. Nelson.

The soldier who'd been so amazed to see all my hides, told the story to a reporter in Fairbanks. Not long after, someone sent me a clipping from the Fairbanks Daily News Miner recounting the hunt, and I'll never forget one line: "Glaser says there is nothing to killing grizzlies and has not had a bit of trouble during his hunt."

Did I say that?

Truce of
the Bear

Eric Collier

July, 1959

I was perched on the old spruce stump a couple of
feet from water's edge, my chin in my hands, my
sight and thinking on the beaver house. When a timid puff of wind rippled
the sheen of the lake, the balm of Gilead tree behind me shivered, and a
shower of frosted leaves pattered down into the slough grass. The sun had
bedded 30 minutes ago, and the mallards that had been scattered in their
individual flocks on the beaver ponds upcreek since dawn were now flying
low and noisy over my head, causing me momentarily to quit staring at
the beaver house and glance up, thinking, "Maybe I should get the 10
gauge and shoot a couple for the pot."

But that was only an idling thought. My real interest was in the beavers
breaking water out from the lodge. My eyes were following their wakes
as they lined for the cottonwoods over on the east side of the lake, a swim
of about half a mile from the lodge. With September half gone and overnight
frost rusting the slough grass, the yearling and two-year-old beavers that
scattered over the watershed when the ice went out last May had now
returned to the colony to give a helping hand with the cutting and storing
of a winter's cache of food.

Anyone with a good arm could stand at the front door of our cabin
in southern British Columbia and heave a pebble that would hit the beaver
lodge plumb center. It's only half a dozen ax handles from the door. Despite
the fingers of shadow reaching across the water, I had no trouble spotting
the beavers as one at a time they surfaced. I was curious to find out just
how many were in the colony, and by counting them away from the lodge
I'd get a fairly accurate census.

I'd just tallied eight and was staring real hard for the ninth when I

362

heard the bawl of a range cow quite a piece off. It came from away back in the fir timber, across the lake and beyond the cottonwoods where the beavers were skidding out their cuttings. It wasn't the bawl of a Hereford cow that has lost track of her calf, nor of one bawling just to hear itself bawl. It was the kind of a racket they make when a hot branding iron is pressed against their flank. It was the bawl of a range beef in trouble.

I forgot about beavers and stared hard across the water. The noise stopped all of a sudden. I was about to shrug my shoulders and bring my thoughts back to the beaver lodge when it began again, louder now and closer to the lake.

I heard the screen door slam, and my wife Lillian called, "Something is chasing it!" By "it" she meant the cow that we could hear but not see.

Lillian crossed the bit of green between house and water and moved alongside the stump. "It's running toward the lake," she said. "Just like a deer chased by coyotes."

I slid down off the stump. Now we could hear hoofs knocking on windfalls and the bawl of the cow was louder and vibrant with desperate fear.

My boat was tethered to a cottonwood stump a step or two away, a single paddle across the seat. But the outboard motor was up in my log warehouse. I hesitated, wondering whether to use the paddle or take time out to get the motor.

But, by paddle or outboard, I guessed I'd be too late to do any good. For bawl after frantic bawl was coming from one fixed position maybe 50 yards back from the far shore of the lake, about where cottonwoods and fir timber met. I figured the luckless animal was down by now.

So I ran to the house, picked up the .303 Ross rifle, dropped some shells into the magazine and went back to the stump. I fired three quick shots at the sky above. But there was no letup to the bawling, though it was a mite feebler now.

"Do something," Lillian urged. "Shout, fire some more shells!"

"Fired three already," I said. "Could maybe fire another 33, but that wouldn't do any good from here."

Next we heard a huffing sound a bit like the grunting of a pig. But there are no pigs in these parts. And the weaker the bawl of the cow, the louder the huffing noise.

I knew now that a killer bear was in action over across the lake, and that the thing he'd been hunting was prostrate beneath the big predator's forepaw.

I raised the Ross to my shoulder and squinted along the barrel. By aiming it at the western skyline I could line up the sights, but against any background of timber I'd not see the front sight at all.

It was quieter now, except for the hungry huffing of the bear. I reckoned the cow beast was dead, from fright if not from wounds. For all the good I could do over on the other side, I might just as well stay where I was. However, I got the outboard, clamped it on the boat, and after three or four useless pulls on the lanyard got the motor running. Five minutes later I beached the boat on the east shore of the lake. I slipped a cartridge into the rifle chamber—more from habit than for any other reason. Then

I eased through the gloomy woods to the spot where I figured we'd last heard the bawling.

I found a whiteface steer dead but still limp and warm. Its tongue was lolling away from its frothing jaws, and horror of the thing that had killed it was still fixed in its eyes. A yearling steer it was, weighing 700 pounds maybe. The brand mark of its owner was just traceable against the fall-thickening hair on its flank.

Then a puff of wind hit me in the face, coming from the northeast, and on it was the fetid stink of the bear. "He's squatted down on his haunches back there in the fir timber," I silently surmised. And there he'd continue to sit until I pulled away from the scene. Soon the pitch dark of night would allow him to fill his gut at the carcass unhampered by any two-legged hunter.

"Maybe I'll have a chance at daybreak," I thought, looking about for some bit of a knoll or boulder to which I could slide on my belly and get within fair shooting range of the carcass. There was a wind-felled tree with needles still green some 70 yards off, and I allowed that by sneaking in on it from the north I'd stand a 50-50 chance of getting a shot at the killer if he happened to be on the carcass at daybreak.

I live at the headwaters of Meldrum Creek, in the Chilcotin district of British Columbia. I'm a trapper. When I first came to this watershed 30 or more years ago there were plenty of bears here. And wild horses, too. But no cattle. The cattle stayed on open range away off to the south.

But competition for the available grass gradually brought cattle drifting north to graze in the timber and along the beaver ponds I'd restored by restocking and years of controlled trapping. Where rightly there was only sufficient summer browse for one white-face, two were crowded in to crop it. And cattle ate or stomped out blueberries, huckleberries, peavines, and timber mushrooms—much of the growth bears rely on for food.

Bears, like all creatures, must eat to live, so it was only a matter of time before some of the oldsters took to killing and eating cattle.

A killer bear can be just as destructive as any full-grown timber wolf— more so in a way. No timber wolf will break into a trapline cabin and either eat or foul up most all there is inside, as will a bear with an appetite for meat. Old Al Parker, who traps 40 miles to the north of me, had one such cabin broken into one spring when there were 40 beaver hides stacked up inside. What was left of the fur after the bear got through chawing at it wasn't worth shipping charges.

An old killer bear is also a menace to the beaver colonies. Bellied down alongside the skid trail, he waits until some foolish yearling or two-year-old comes waddling up the trail, then kills the luckless furbearer with a single swipe of his paw. There's neither profit nor satisfaction in raising beavers for bears. Since it's difficult to tell a killer bear from a harmless one, most Chilcotin trappers and ranchers alike shoot every mature bear they can line sights on.

I'd wrapped the blade of the paddle with gunny sacking so there wasn't much of a splash as the boat glided across the lake the next morning. A crisp dawn was breaking and a heavy mist shrouded the lake. I was within

15 yards of the east shoreline before the willows along the edge took on definite pattern. The mist was partly an asset. If the bear was at or around the carcass, it certainly wouldn't see what was happening out on the lake. Neither would it hear me beach the boat if I eased in quietly.

On the other hand, I doubted that I'd be able to see remains of the steer from the sniping point behind the blow-down—not unless the mist thinned out some. The grass was silver with frost. I'd get plenty chilly stretched out behind the blow-down, waiting for the fog to lift.

As I bellied up to the tree, I could hear the bear's heavy breathing as the brute's huge strength tugged the steer carcass this way and that. But I could see nothing save the ghostly outline of the trees a few yards ahead. The wind was right, and the stalk was right. With the gun barrel resting easily but steadily on the tree, my aim was right too. Only the mist was wrong.

On most any clear fall or winter morning, sunup is the coldest hour of the day. I was wearing a pair of light cloth gloves, and the frost soon got past them and began investigating my fingers. To lessen the chance of the bear hearing me as I moved in from the lake, I'd put on buckskin moccasins with low rubbers drawn over them. But there had been a couple of inches of water in the bottom of the boat and my right foot was wet. I was quickly and painfully reminded of that when the frost began stiffening the sock. But I lay there without movement, figuring that if the mist would lift a little I could see through to the kill. One good shot at the bear would be ample compensation for the discomfort I was now enduring.

I'd been there all of 15 minutes, getting colder by the second, when the sudden quiet at the kill told me the bear was about through eating. In a few moments he'd cover the remnants of the steer with trash and then go off a piece into some thicket and bed down for the forenoon. Maybe he'd be back at the feast come sundown. It was the time of the year when bears take on the layers of fat that must carry them through the long winter months in their dens, so their fall appetite is voracious.

There would be little but bones left of the steer after the bear had a couple more meals off it. If I didn't get him at the carcass this morning, I'd likely not get a shot at all.

I heard him scraping moss and other trash over the remains. Then, after a moment or two of quiet, there was the swish of frosted grass as he moved off from the kill. And the rifle was tight into my shoulder, my finger touching the trigger. The black brute was coming fair and square toward me. The rustle of the grass told me that. My eyes watered from the strain of staring. Now I heard the thud of his pads against the slightly frozen ground and knew that only 40-odd steps separated us. The fog hid him. Then I saw—or thought I saw—his head and shoulders take on weird shape alongside a clump of dwarf saskatoon bush.

But there was no movement to the silhouette. I was just convincing myself that I was seeing things when the head shifted slightly. That sudden movement was what tripped off my shot, for I sensed that the bear had winded me.

Maybe it was on account of the mist, or maybe the chill in my veins.

Anyway, I missed. It was as clean a miss as has come my way in all my years in the woods.

Before the bolt of the .303 had tossed out the empty and rammed a live shell back in, the bear and the mist were as one. I saw no more. The swish of the grass or the snap of a stick told me the course the running bear was taking.

I stared foolishly at the gun, thinking, "My fault, not yours." Then I came upright and walked quietly to and fro, bringing circulation back into my feet and hands.

It was another 20 minutes before the sun hoisted above the trees to burn away the mist. As the air cleared, I began a wide circle of the kill, not in any hope of catching a glimpse of the bear but merely to locate one clear imprint of its pad marks. That I found 200 yards away, where the killer had crossed a bare patch of wet alkali mud. The tracks were as clear as if they'd been fresh made in melting snow, and for half a minute I stood perfectly still, eyes fixed on them. I'd recognize the tracks of that particular bear again no matter where or when I might see it.

By daylight the following morning only a scatter of well-picked bones remained at the scene of the kill, coyotes having come along to help themselves at the left-overs. But a week later, while hunting mallards along a beaver slough three miles east of the house, I stumbled onto the remains of another whiteface that had died no natural death. There wasn't enough of the carcass left to determine whether it had been steer, heifer, or cow, but the tracks of the thing that had killed it were plain in the mud. One swift glance at them informed me the identity of the killer—the same big bruin I'd missed at the lake.

It was September, 1955, when the bear killed the yearling within shouting distance of my house. Almost two years were to pass before I'd get another chance at him. But I often saw his sign. He killed a two-year-old heifer on a hogback a short piece north of the house. He pulled down a runty yearling to the east and another two-year-old in the woods to the west. I saw many an old cow with swollen udder traveling the trails bawling for a calf it would never see again. I was losing beavers, too. The more I saw of this bear's work, the greater my hankering to get rid of him by fair means or foul.

There were quite a few bears killed in my locality during the fall of 1955 and spring and summer of 1956. I knocked over half a dozen myself. Each time I took one good look at the pads and shook my head. Some of them might have been killers, but not the killer I was hoping to catch up with.

In October, 1955, Wilferd Hoffman came from Pennsylvania to hunt moose with me. He killed a fair-size bear on the slopes of Fisher Mountain, but it was an old sow. In the fall of 1956 Wilferd was back again. He fetched his brother Willard with him this time, and Willard dropped two blacks, both of them boars. Neither had pads to match the killer's.

During spring and summer of '56, Don Ward, who traps in the woods north of me, tacked the scalps of 10 bears to the log walls of his barn. He'd shot them as they were snooping around his beaver colonies. But from what Ward told me I was fairly sure that he hadn't connected with the black that was raising merry cain on my trapline.

In late spring of 1957 my brother Jack and his wife spent a month back here in the woods with us, Jack having come from England to eastern Canada on business.

His wife Mary owned the sharp eyes that next spotted the killer bear. He was among the aspens on the east side of the lake. We'd been cruising around the lake, eyes peeled for beavers, for Mary had never seen a beaver. So the three of us piled into the boat as the sun was going down, since sundown is the time when beavers start coming out from the lodges and bank runs to eat and work. Beavers we saw, too—blankets, mediums, and small. When I heard one thump the water with its tail I'd open up the motor and crowd it this way and that, on the water and under, until finally the beaver wearied of the game and sulked off to his run.

It was dusking when we beached the boat and returned to the house. We were seated in the living room drinking coffee and talking when Mary, who was seated close to the window, said, "Is that a moose lying down over on the other side?"

I followed the point of her finger and saw the object. Jack saw it too, as did Lillian, my wife. We all went outside, down to water's edge, me packing the binoculars. But there wasn't enough light left to say for sure whether it was a boulder or moose, clump of brush or a bear. Objects look strangely different when most all the light has drained out of the sky.

Although we watched for several minutes, the object never moved. So I cased the glasses and said, "Must be a rock." Yet somehow I doubted that it was.

Next morning Jack and I launched the boat and went across to make sure. We found the bed, and tracks leading to and away from it. There were a couple of ant hills leveled here, a punky blow-down turned over there, and bear sign galore, fresh as the morning dew.

Sizing up the tracks, I told Jack, "It's him." Then I went on to explain how the bear Mary had spotted the night before bedded in full view of the house was the one I'd fired at and missed in September, '55.

It was no hard chore following the tracks in the knee-high timber grass, and follow them a piece we did. They took us deep into the heart of a spruce swamp with such a litter of windfalls that I knew it was useless to follow them further.

Three days later I said to Jack and Mary, "I've a trapping cabin four miles east of here, but I haven't been down that way since we were beavering there in early May. Heck of a place for pack rats, so I left half a dozen traps set on the shelves to catch any that came along. How about us jumping into the Land Rover (English jeep) this afternoon and going down that way for a look-see. Might spot a bull moose wallowing in one of the swamps or an old buck deer fighting flies in the water. Might even see a bear."

So after lunch we stowed binoculars, camera, and my Ross .303 in the Land Rover and lit out for the cabin. Our road isn't much, even as roads go in these parts. When I first came to these woods it was only a game trail. I widened it some then so I could get over it with a packhorse without ripping up the pack. Then I widened it a bit more to accommodate a team and wagon. In 1948 I brought a jeep back onto the trapline, and now I do 70 percent of my beaver trapping with the help of a jeep. This meant more work on the old game trail, blasting rocks and stumps until I was able to get the vehicle over it. It's a road you drive at four miles an hour.

We saw our moose, not churning mud in a wallow but snoozing the afternoon away beneath the cool overhang of a spruce. It was a three-year-old bull, horns still in the velvet, and Mary had a good look at it as it lunged away from the spruce and plowed up muskeg crossing the swamp.

There were four pack rats in the traps. I heaved them out and re-set. When down there trapping in May, I'd dumped some 40 beaver carcasses down over the hill a short piece from the cabin. We walked to this burial ground, thinking maybe a bear might be hanging around. But there was nothing left of the beavers, not even a skull. We saw a scattering of old bear tracks and here and there the round track of a lynx.

We were on our way back, only a mile from the house, when it happened. I was nursing the Land Rover along, gently easing a wheel over a rock that would have ripped the belly out of the vehicle had I straddled it. Yet I saw the quick blur of movement 200 yards ahead. It was off the road in a scattering of jackpine.

"Whoa," I breathed tensely, pumping hard on the brake and rearing back on the steering wheel. Prior to the fall of 1948, I'd never handled a vehicle such as this. An up-and-coming son had sold me the jeep idea, but I'd driven horses too long to forget my "whoa" in tense moments.

I wasn't quite sure just then what the blur might be, though I doubted that it was the back of a moose. I cut off the motor, set the emergency brake, and fumbled for the door latch. Then I glimpsed movement of a type and color that set me in prompt but silent action.

"Bear!" I breathed, easing the door open. "Hand me that gun, Jack."

He slipped the gun into my outstretched hand. I eased out of the vehicle and gently fed a 180-grain softpoint into the chamber.

"Stay put," I cautioned Jack and Mary, for you can never tell about bears.

The bear was in broad view momentarily, angling down toward the road, obviously unaware of the Land Rover. Then it was out of sight, down in a gulch running off at right angles to the road. I raced forward a few yards, coming to a stop behind a pine tree. I paused there, gun at my shoulder, trying to decide whether to stay put or hurry to the rim of the gulch.

It all lay in the breaks of the game. One has to be in the right spot at the right moment—that's half the battle of hunting, and partly decided by chance. Had the bear ambled off down the gulch then, maybe he'd still be killing. But he didn't amble down the gulch; he went down one side and up the other. He came out in plain view 125 yards away, head-on and coming straight toward me.

"Strut your stuff," I told the Ross, which was an old, second-hand rifle when I got it back in the early 1920's. That bullet hit the bear somewhere in the chest and knocked the brute down.

I heard the door of the Land Rover squeak, and glanced back across my shoulder. Jack was half out of the vehicle. I held up a hand and yelled, "Stay put!"

The bear was up again now, staggering. I'd reloaded but was in no great hurry to shoot. The range was good, and I knew exactly what the .303 could do at such range. Then the bear growled and broke into a run, beelining for the tree I stood under.

Maybe I've licence for saying he was actually charging, if not at me then at the point from where the shot had come. But I won't say that, because I've a hunch he was running blind, too stunned to know whether he was going east, west, north, or south.

Forty steps away from me the bear slowed down and went upright on his hind legs. He stood there, swaying, blood dribbling down his chest. It was then that the lines of a poem flashed through my mind. The poem, which I once knew by heart as a lanky school boy in England, says something about a bear that stands up as pleading . . . veils the hate and cunning in his swinish little eyes.

I shot again, and the bear spun around, went down. He came up again, still heading toward me.

Again the door of the Land Rover squeaked. Jack was clear of the vehicle now, Mary just getting out. "Stay put!" I shouted, for I didn't know what the outcome of this deal would be.

The bear stopped again a mere 20 yards from me. Again he got up on hind legs, huge forearms lifted and held tight against his chest. The poem said, "That is the time of peril, the time of the truce of the bear."

I fired again, putting a bullet in the bear's forehead. He fell dead.

"O.K.," I sang out, beckoning Jack and Mary.

Then I walked over to the bear, staring long and thoughtfully at its pads. Like human fingerprints, no two bear pads leave identically the same tracks, and a lifetime spent in the wilderness can tutor the human eye to tell one from the other. The pad marks of this bear had been photographed indelibly in my mind since the time he killed the steer within hollering distance of my house, and I could never forget them.

I lifted my head and said quietly to Jack: "We feuded for two and a half years, this bear and I, but it's all over at last."

X

DIFFERENT EXPERTS, DIFFERENT ANSWERS

A Warden's View of Bears

Fred G. Smith

June, 1965

I spent 40 years of my life hunting and guiding in Maine and, for nearly half that time, was a member of the Maine game-warden service. As one result of this long experience, I have come to the conclusion that the black bear in the wild is almost entirely harmless to man unless cornered or in a trap. From being a highly aggressive animal, as apparently it was in early frontier times, it has become one of the most elusive and furtive denizens of our forests, shunning man and keeping to the thickest and most inaccessible woods and swamps. Seldom does one hear of an unprovoked attack by a wild bear on a person or domestic animal.

Nonetheless, like the wildcat, the black bear can never be completely tamed and is wholly unpredictable and extremely treacherous. Seemingly tractable and friendly, he may instantly turn into a raging killer. A full-grown black bear is a very powerful animal, and his great paws, armed with long, wicked claws, can deliver a shattering blow.

I have lived most of my life in Maine. I was born in Ellsworth and, when I was a boy in the 1880's, a farmer named Ransom Bonsey, who lived only a few miles from my home, owned a big bull which was killed by a bear with one blow from its huge paw. Not only was the bull's neck broken, but so powerful was the force of this terrific stroke that its head was twisted to a right angle with its neck.

To prove further the fury of an enraged black bear and that he is a respectable adversary even for the so-called king of beasts, the lion, I recently received a letter from my younger brother, Frank, a retired naval officer who now lives in Bradenton, Florida, relating an incident that happened in 1956 at the winter quarters of the Ringling Brothers Circus in Sarasota. A Maine bear and a lion were being trained together in an animal act and, when the trainer turned away for a moment, the big cat lunged at the bear and ripped his shoulder open.

The circus people thought they were out a bear, as they believed the bruin would prove no match for a lion. To their astonishment, the bear reared up on his hind legs and gave his attacker such a tremendous blow with his paw that he knocked the lion backward several feet and nearly tore his shoulder off. The lion was injured so badly that he had to be destroyed, but the bear was back on the job in a few days.

Formerly found throughout the country, black bears have now disappeared from a number of states and were at one time nearing extinction in the rest as a result of indiscriminate bounties placed on their heads. Their recent classification as a game animal in several states, however, has reversed this trend and today they are holding their own and even increasing.

Blackie is a very adaptable creature and has grown up with civilization. His diet is probably more varied than that of any other animal. He is both herbivorous and carnivorous and may be found lunching on apples, having himself a juicy deer steak, fishing for suckers or trout in some brook, eating watercress, tearing up an anthill for succulent ants, feasting on raspberries, ripping up a dead stump for white grubs, or raiding the town dump for garbage. His favorite food, however, is honey, and he will travel miles to locate a bee tree, rip it apart, and feast.

He is truly the hog of the woods, and if his existence depended upon food alone he would survive all other creatures of the wild. This is not only because of his varied diet, but because when winter comes and snow is high in the woods, making it difficult for most animals to obtain enough food to save them from starvation, the black bear has already found himself a den, filled his belly with food, and crawled in to sleep through the long, cold months.

Though I know of many instances of bears eating and sometimes dragging away deer left in the woods by hunters, I have never come across a deer killed by a bear. I have no doubt that they sometimes kill young deer, but a fawn would be only a light lunch for a bruin.

While a bear's eyesight is not overly keen, he can, like a deer, detect the slightest movement at a great distance. But for obtaining his food and foiling his enemies, he depends almost entirely on his unbelievably acute sense of smell. He not only can locate the direction but also the exact spot from which the scent is coming.

Bears breed once every two years, and the end of the seven-month gestation period coincides with the time of hibernation. The young, averaging one to four in number, are born about mid-winter and are the smallest, comparatively, of the young of any of our woods animals, weighing only half a pound at birth.

Common among novice hunters are stories of being charged by bears they have wounded, and these tales usually end with the infuriated beast being finally brought down by a desperate shot at five feet. If one of our Maine bears comes toward the hunter after being wounded, I believe it is because he is death-struck and doesn't know where he is going. I have seen where a 500-pound male bear, after being shot, took hold of small trees with his teeth and claws and dragged himself along in an effort to get away.

My grandfather, Moses Smith, who lived in Eastbrook, Maine, was a noted hunter in the 1830's and 1840's and killed a great many bears. He died a few years before I was born, but I've heard my father tell about gramp's oldtime hunts. He raised and trained a small breed of dogs—I don't know the breed—that were ideal bear dogs.

John Haslam, a relative of my grandmother's, who was the grand-daughter of Capt. George Haslam, one of the first settlers of Ellsworth, usually accompanied my grandfather on his hunts and carried a muzzle-loading gun while grandfather carried an ax. When a bear stood at bay and the hunters arrived, the dog really went to work. He would bite the quarry so viciously that the bear, unable to catch or strike the dog and unable to run without having its sore and bleeding heels nipped, would do the only thing left. It would climb a tree. As it started to climb, my grandfather would dash up and drive his ax into the top of its head, killing it instantly. If the bear got up the tree too fast for my grandfather to reach its head with the ax, John Haslam would shoot it.

I've never tried killing a bear with an ax, but I have hunted them with dogs over many years, and in so doing I have learned much about their habits. A bear is very agile and can whirl and strike unbelievably fast. When coming to bay and facing dogs, he will suddenly dash at one of them so swiftly that sometimes it cannot get away and loses its life with one lightning sweep of the bear's paw. The ideal dog is one that is very fast and has grit and brains enough not to attack head-on. Instead, it will continually nip the bear's heels or the pads of its feet and immediately jump away. Some terriers make excellent bear dogs.

After having had his heels bitten for a few minutes, a bear will get sore and ugly and will come to bay. Then the dog, darting in and out, nipping, will force it either to climb a tree or to stand until the hunter comes up and shoots it. A good dog quickly learns not to fight in a dense thicket, since in trying to avoid the bear's rushes it is likely to collide with a tree or bush that will delay it the split second it needs to get away.

One day in January, 1923, I was cruising the woods near the old Boggy Brook settlement north of Ellsworth looking for bobcats. There was over a foot of snow on the ground and neither tracking nor running conditions were good. One of my cat hounds was getting old, so I had bought a young redbone hound in Kentucky and I was breaking him in by running him with my other two dogs. I had the three on leashes that day and I had snowshoes on my feet, so I couldn't get into the really dense thickets.

When we were nearly out of the woods in late afternoon, my hounds suddenly began to pull at the leashes, almost dragging me off my feet. A short distance ahead, I found where a big bear had come out of the thicket the previous day and had walked along a narrow brook. He'd turned over rocks as he went, evidently looking for frogs. Some of the rocks were half as large as a barrel. After following the brook for 100 yards, the bear had turned upstream again. The dogs yanked me back that way. Retracing my steps, I saw where the bear had come from the woods to the brook. It was late in the afternoon and I had no intention of letting the dogs loose on the trail until the following day.

I started home again and had gone only a few yards when my old gray hound suddenly "yelled" and lunged ahead, breaking the ring on her collar. As she went baying away, the other dogs began plunging against their leads. I let them go and followed as they disappeared among the firs. About 100 yards ahead, I came to the place where the bear had denned. It was a poor shelter, being nothing but a hole dug in the snow under a lodged poplar tree and lined with boughs and cedar bark.

By now the air was full of music from the three baying dogs, and I knew they had jumped the old bruin. He didn't run any great distance, but just cut back and forth through the dense fir and spruce. On several occasions, the dogs drove him directly toward me, but he turned before coming into sight. Just as it was getting dark, I was able to cut off the dogs and catch them. That evening I called a neighbor, Willis Dunn, of Ellsworth, who had been on a number of bobcat hunts with me. Willis had some purebred Airedale dogs that he was anxious to try on bear.

"I jumped a big bear near Boggy Brook," I told him, "and I'm going back after him tomorrow. This is your chance to run those Airedales. What do you say?"

"I'll be there," Willis agreed.

The following morning we drove to within a couple of miles of where I had caught the dogs the previous day. Willis had his Airedales and I had my two veteran cat dogs but not the redbone. Arriving where I had left the bear tracks, we found the scent was too cold for the Airedales to follow. We decided to lead all four dogs until we jumped the bear.

He had traveled so far that night that it was noon before we finally caught up with him. Since the Airedales had never chased a bear before, they were not greatly interested. However, one did swing in with my hounds after a while. The bear, after circling for a time, took one long run down Hurley Ridge almost to the Billings field. I ran on my snowshoes along an old wood road parallel with the course the bear was taking, hoping to get a shot at him when he crossed the field.

When I reached it, I heard the baying dogs going back in the direction from which they had just come. I was soaked with perspiration, but I raced back up the old road. After going half a mile, I caught a glimpse of the bear as he crossed the road 200 yards away. I took a quick shot with my .33 Winchester Model '86, but failed to connect. From then until dark, he cut back and forth through the thick growth. It didn't make a bit of difference which way the wind blew, he would turn every time before coming into sight.

During the last half an hour of daylight, he lay down and faced the dogs six times. He was so hot that the beds where he lay were yellow and glossy. The last two times he came to bay in dense thickets where the dogs didn't dare crowd him. Both times I crawled in beyond them and each time I was within 20 feet of the bear when I heard him go, but it was so dark in the thicket that I couldn't see him. We finally had to give it up for the night.

"Let's come back early tomorrow," I said. "He's too tired to travel far tonight and we ought to be able to jump him in the morning."

Willis agreed, but that night it snowed a foot and kept on snowing, so we never did get to chase that bear again. I have never known a bear to select such a poor place to den up for the winter. The leaning tree under which he had built his bed was not over 10 inches in diameter. Bears usually have a spot located some time before they actually hole up and often have their beds prepared. Since there were several good denning places in that immediate locality, I believe this bear had been driven from his original shelter by dogs and was either too scared or too tired to go back, hence the makeshift den.

Another hunt with an even less happy ending took place in 1938. Harvey Moore, a man who had hunted bobcats with me on several occasions, phoned me one fall evening.

"Fred," he said, "how about loaning me your dog Bob White tomorrow?"

"Sure," I agreed. "Going cat hunting?"

"No," Harvey replied. "I want to teach my hound to chase bears, and I figure the best way is to run him with a good dog like Bob White."

Early the following morning, Harvey went to the orchard with the two hounds and, finding fresh bear sign in the light snow, let the dogs go on the track. They jumped the bear within half a mile, and not long afterward Moore heard loud barking and snarling. He knew the bear was at bay. As he ran toward the commotion, he suddenly heard a shrill screech followed by the furious barking of my dog fading in the distance. Farther on, Harvey saw blood on the snow and along the trail the bear had left as it carried off his hound with my dog still barking at its heels. Fearing my dog would also be killed, he ran after the chase and, by shooting his gun several times and shouting, induced my dog to come back to him. Leashing Bob White, Harvey Moore came home, a sorrowful but wiser man.

A black bear in the wild is an entirely different animal from one in captivity. A captive one, even though taken as a cub, usually can never be trusted and is likely to go bad overnight. A striking and horrible example of this happened in Ellsworth on October 15, 1936. I received a call that morning to go to a roadside stand called the Whistle Inn near the Ellsworth-Dedham town line. Arriving there, I learned that one of two bears kept in separate enclosures had killed the owner of the inn, George Langley, and also an employee, James Virtue, who had come to Langley's aid.

If I remember correctly, the bears, a male and a female, were four years old and had been reared by Langley. The enclosures in which they were kept consisted of 12 × 12-foot yards having wooden floors. The sides and tops were of heavy woven wire. At the rear were small sleeping houses with openings large enough for the bears to enter.

It was Langley's custom to take a shovel and a pail of ground oats into the yards, shoo the animals into their houses, and, reaching through the small doorways, dump the oats on the floor. While the bears were eating the oats, he would scrape up the litter in the yards, then shovel it through the doorways to be wheeled away.

Though there were no witnesses to George Langley's death, conditions at the bear yard told the tragic story. He had evidently gone into the male bear's enclosure as usual, shooed him into his house, and turned the ground oats on the floor inside it. However, the bear had not eaten the oats, as the peaked mound remained untouched.

Langley had apparently just finished scraping the refuse into a small heap when the bear came from the house and attacked him. The victim evidently got through the door and closed it, for new, deep claw marks on the inside frame of the door showed where the bear had struck it, knocking it open. Langley managed to pull out his pocketknife and open it before the bear killed him. His body lay about 30 feet from the cage.

James Virtue, who was employed by Langley, was doing chores at the stable about 75 yards away. Hearing the commotion, he ran to the scene without a thing to protect himself. Upon seeing Virtue, the bear left Langley's body and attacked him. As it was raking and chewing him on the ground, two men drove by and, seeing the tragedy, raced to the home of Joe Willet a mile away. Grabbing his rifle, Willet rode back with them and shot the bear, which was still mauling Virtue's body. The commotion and smell of blood had driven the female berserk and it was necessary to shoot her also.

I talked with Langley's wife and grandson that day. "I told gramp how ugly the bear acted," the boy declared, "but he said he was all right."

At the request of Mrs. Langley, I took the grandson to the Jordan Undertaking Parlors in Ellsworth to get the victim's personal effects. While there I viewed the remains of the unfortunate men whose bodies were cut, slashed, and broken from head to foot. I was told by an attendant that there were over 200 wounds on one of the bodies. The next Maine legislature passed a law prohibiting anyone from keeping wild animals at roadside stands, but this law has since been changed so that today it is legal to exhibit wild animals upon payment of a $50 annual license fee.

Much has been written concerning the courage and ferocity of mother bears in protecting their cubs, but I know of three cases where a female, upon being disturbed in her den, ran away and left her young and never came back. The first case of this kind I personally checked was in the winter of 1938. In answer to a call, I went to Otis and talked with Arthur Moore, who told me he was chopping wood that day a short distance from his home. Nearby, two small boys, four and five years old, were looking for porcupines under stumps.

All at once he heard one boy say to the other, "Come here quick! There's about 100 under this stump!"

The other boy joined his companion and they both stood peering into an opening beneath a felled tree. At that moment, a large bear came out of the hole, brushed by the two boys, and ran away. Moore went to the stump and discovered two small cubs. Taking them, he went to his home to show them to his family, after which he returned the cubs to the den.

He and I went to the spot and found that the mother was not there. Following her tracks, I saw that she had taken a four-mile circle before coming back to within 75 yards of her young. Then she had turned and run away. Though I left the cubs there for three days, she did not rejoin them. I finally took the cubs to Chief Warden Raymond Morse, of Ellsworth, who reared them with three other cubs whose mother had abandoned them.

On January 2, 1941, Earl Webber, of Ellsworth Falls, while hunting raccoons with his dog in the Nicolin area, came upon a large bear in a rock den a short distance from the Maine Central Railroad tracks. The following day I went there with him. There was over a foot of snow and we wore snowshoes.

Arriving at the den, I found it an ideal spot to take pictures since it consisted of two boulders about five feet apart with a ledge roof and a back wall. It was open on the south side. About three feet in front of the bear were two large rocks about four feet high within four inches of each other. By standing here, one could see the entire bear about six feet away. It was a large animal, weighing between 350 and 400 pounds.

The bear knew we were there and, at any sudden movement we made, she would raise her head, ears forward and black eyes shining, and stare at us for about 10 seconds. Then, with a drowsy look in her eyes, she would lower her head, work her nose under her foreleg, and lie quietly until we moved again.

Three days later, I told a national park naturalist about the bear. He said he would like to take some pictures of her, so we made arrangements to go the following day. Next morning, the naturalist, with a minister friend, Rev. James F. McElroy of Seal Harbor, went with Warden Wilbur Ricker and me to visit the den.

The bear was in the shadow of the rocks and it was necessary to use a flashbulb to get a decent picture. It was also necessary to stand the camera tripod against the outside rocks and focus on a downward slant. The bear had changed position in her bed since my last visit and was now lying with her back toward us.

The young minister acted as though he had always been used to bears and gave no outward sign of nervousness, but the naturalist, evidently fearing his camera would get broken should the bear leap from its den, was pale and his hands shook. Unfortunately, his camera and flash were not synchronized and he spoiled every film he had without getting a picture. After parking his camera in a safe place, the naturalist took up a position on top of a high boulder some 25 yards away. From this vantage point, he suddenly remembered that bears cannot see during hibernation. I disagreed with him, as previous experience had shown me that they can see very well.

Since the bear had not attempted to rise on either of my previous visits, I decided it would be a good idea to climb over the barrier and pat her to let her know we meant her no harm. Hauling myself over the rocks, I stood beside the bear. I waited until she buried her snout under her foreleg, then stooped over and started to put my hand on her shoulder. When my hand was within six inches of her body she drowsily raised her head. I slowly drew my hand away as she stared me in the face. After a few seconds, her head went down but she raised it again as soon as I moved my hand. This occurred three consecutive times. Reverend McElroy was standing outside the rocks looking over my shoulder.

Meanwhile, the naturalist was urging me on. "Go ahead, Fred," he called confidently from his rocky perch. "She won't hurt you."

I leaned forward once more. This time, when the bear raised her head, I put my hand down on her shoulder. With a roar like a lion, she leaped at me. All I could see was a fiery red cavity that looked as large as a barrel lined with ivory white teeth. Luckily, she struck her head on the rocky roof when she leaped and that drove her downward; otherwise I would have been in her embrace. I never knew how I got out of there, but I guess it was by a backward somersault over the rocks.

When I picked myself up I saw Reverend McElroy lying in a heap in the snow a good 10 yards away. His broad jump would have won a gold medal at the Olympics, but he gave me the credit for it.

When someone asked him about his record-breaking leap, he explained, "The impetus came from a butt I received in the stomach from Warden Smith when he left the den."

The bear went round in circles a few times, but did not attempt to scale the rocks.

On January 16, I called Warden Supervisor Joseph Stickney and told him about the bear. He asked me to check the den and, if the old lady was still there, to call him and he would be at my home with his camera on the 18th. The following day I worked with Warden Ricker and it was almost dark when I got to the den. However, I could see the bear and I also heard tiny cries from two cubs.

Supervisor Stickney came on the 18th and, accompanied by Chief Warden Morse, we went to the den. He had a fine camera and got some excellent pictures of the mother and one of the cubs.

Wishing to settle the controversial subject of whether a bear will eat during hibernation, Warden George Bradbury and I went to the den on January 30. I took some sweet russet apples and a section of ribs from a deer that had been chewed by dogs. We found everything as it was on my last visit. Going to the rocky roof, I tossed the apples down one by one. Since this did not disturb the bear in the least, I dropped the meat, but a sharp piece of bone stuck in the hard snow, preventing it from sliding down.

Cutting a slender sapling, I reached down and loosened the ribs which slid down and lightly brushed the bear on the leg. With a tremendous leap, she cleared the rock barrier and disappeared into the woods faster than it seemed possible for so large an animal to move through the deep snow.

Three days later, I took a wide circle around the den and found that the mother had not returned to her babies. I went there with the intention of taking the cubs, but found that an owl had beaten me to it and had killed both cubs and carried one away.

Most Dangerous Bear? I Say Polar

Fred Bear as told to Ben East

December, 1962

I have killed five bears above the black-bear class with a bow in the last six years and tackled two others that proved too much to handle that way and had to be stopped with a rifle. From those seven encounters, I've formed a rather firm opinion on a perennial question: What is the most dangerous game animal on the North American continent? I believe I know.

I took my first grizzly in the Devils Lake country of the Yukon in September, 1956, dropping him with one arrow from a 65-pound bow.

What happened, briefly, was that we spotted the bear half a mile away, mistook him for a big black, and my hunting partner, Dr. Judd Grindell, and I climbed off our horses and went after him. Because we thought he was a black we didn't have the backing of a guide or rifle, and I even left my .44 Magnum Smith & Wesson, intended for use in emergencies, hanging on my saddle. When I caught up with the bear it was on the far side of a ridge digging for a marmot. I crept up until I was crouched behind a rock only 25 yards away. Then he looked my way and I discovered my mistake.

The situation was one I had never intended to get into, and I realized the chance I was taking if I drove an arrow into him at that range. There was almost no chance, no matter where I placed it, that it would kill him before he could travel the 75 feet that separated us, and there was no gun behind me. Even Judd, also armed with a bow, was 150 yards away.

But I had come too far, hunted too hard, and wanted a grizzly too much to back down. I let fly and the arrow sank out of sight between the

381

bear's ribs. It sliced all the way through, cutting lungs, liver, and intestines, emerged and stuck in the hillside beyond.

He growled, bit at his side, swiveled around, and made two leaps my way, snarling and bawling. But before I could get off a second arrow he lost track of me or changed his mind, swerved, ran 80 yards, and fell dead.

Three years later, in the fall of 1959, I killed my first brown bear, along the coast of Prince William Sound north of Cordova, Alaska. Medium size, he gave me no more trouble and even less of a scare than the grizzly. I laced an arrow into his lungs at 60 paces, he ran 50 to 60 yards away from me, went down, and stayed.

Then, in April of 1960, I tangled with my first polar bear on the ice off Point Barrow. That turned out to be a different kind of affair.

Bob Munger, a sporting-goods dealer from Charlotte, Michigan, a bow-hunter and cameraman as well as a rifleman, and I flew up to Barrow that spring, hoping to collect two trophy-size white bears.

Flying over the ice fields of the Arctic Ocean 50 miles offshore, we spotted a good one following a pressure ridge across a big floe. George Thiele, my pilot-guide, landed on smooth ice nearby, and once we were safely down Bob and his pilot also landed. We decided I'd shoot the bear while Bob took pictures.

Thiele and I moved in, hidden by the ridge, with Munger behind us with two cameras. George was carrying a .300 Magnum as bear medicine if anything went wrong. We inched up within 17 yards of the bear. He was facing away from us and all we could see was his rump over the top of a block of ice. There was no way to work around for a shot at his rib section without great risk of spooking him.

I looked at George for instructions. "Shoot him in the hind end," he urged. "He'll turn to fight the arrow, and you get in a good one."

Shooting a polar bear in the rump at 17 yards to make him turn around didn't seem to me like the best procedure, but George knew a lot more about this business than I, so I did as I was told.

The bear turned all right, but the rest of it didn't go according to plan. When I drove a four-bladed broadhead into his rear, he whipped around and came at us in one motion, bawling his rage. We hadn't even realized that he knew we were there.

Thiele blasted a shot into his chest and it stopped but didn't floor him. I got off a second arrow that cut through a foreleg, glanced off the bone, and stuck in his neck, not deep enough to do damage. He chewed and tore that arrow out in one second flat, and then started for us again. Before he had made two jumps George slammed another 180-grain bullet into his chest, and again he stopped but didn't go down. He was in shock now, however, and stood with blood gushing out of him until he fell over, just nine steps from us.

The whole thing left me in possession of a filled polar-bear license, a trophy I couldn't claim as a bowhunter, and some brand-new ideas about ice-bear behavior.

Those three encounters, with the grizzly, the brown, and the white bear, so different in outcome, set me to wondering about the matter of dangerous big game and which North American animal is most likely to make trouble for a hunter. Now, four bears later, I still don't claim to be sure of the answer, but I find myself leaning more and more to the opinion I formed that day on the ice.

Hunters who have shot most or all the big game of Canada, the United States, and Mexico may argue about which is the greatest trophy, but there is little disagreement among them on one point. The most touchy and danger-fraught characters an American hunter can go up against are the three big bears.

They're all short-tempered and unpredictable, slow moving one minute, lightning and fury the next, with the brute strength to kill a man with one swipe of a paw and the vindictiveness to maul him as long as they can see him breathe. They have all done those things, and they rate at the top of every hunter's list when he thinks of animals capable of retaliating.

That's as far as agreement extends, however. Ask which one of the three is most likely to try to get even with whatever hurts him and you get varying opinions.

I strongly suspect that any general poll among sportsmen would give top place to the brown. He reaches tremendous size, has a hair-trigger temper, and has maimed or killed more men than any other animal Americans encounter—partly because he is hunted more frequently than either the grizzly or the polar. The tales of brown bear ferocity and attacks, provoked and unprovoked, are legion. Legends have grown up around this animal and he is feared more than any other carnivore in this part of the world.

But I'm not sure the choice of the brown for maximum vindictiveness would be right. More than one hunter who has taken all three bears would question it, I among them. I have more than a sneaking suspicion that the one that fears man least and is most ready to fight, once his anger is aroused, is the polar bear.

I'll make one claim in defense of my ideas. I get well acquainted with the game I hunt. An animal is likely to do things at close quarters that it wouldn't do at 200 to 300 yards, and if anybody has a chance to study the temper and behavior of game threatened or wounded at very short range it's the hunter who uses a bow, as I do.

Despite the fact that I make several hunting trips each year, I have not hunted with a rifle in more than 25 years. I put my rifles away around 1935, when I went into the business of making archery tackle at Grayling, Michigan. Every trophy I have taken since—and the list includes deer, elk, antelope, moose, Dall and stone sheep, goats, caribou, black, brown, and grizzly bears, plus three kinds of African antelope—has been killed with a bow.

That means I have done almost all my shooting at 50 yards or less, the bulk of it at 15 to 30 yards, and I have had plenty of opportunity to observe animals in tight spots. It's when you have your target in your lap and he knows you are there that you find out exactly what sort of critter he is. My opinion regarding the relative fierceness of the three big bears is based on situations of that kind, and all seven of my encounters tend to bear out the theory that the polar is the one surest to come for you if you give him cause.

On the way home from the polar-bear hunt in 1960, Bob Munger and I stopped off at Kodiak and put in 10 days with Ed Bilderback, a Cordova outfitter and guide, on Kodiak Island and along the Alaska Peninsula looking for a good brown. The one I had killed the previous fall had turned out to be too small a trophy to satisfy me.

You may remember my story of that spring hunt, "You Go, I Stay" (see OUTDOOR LIFE, March, 1961). We saw a big brown on the beach and I went after him, with Ed backing me with his .375 Magnum. We made the stalk through a patch of alders, came out on the beach 50 yards from the bear, and I went on alone, creeping to a spot behind a pile of driftwood 20 paces from him.

He turned broadside to me and I sent an arrow into his liver section the full length of the shaft. He let out a roar and spun around, biting at the arrow, giving me time for a second shot. That one hit him in a front leg and did no real damage, however, and then he came straight for me. Up to that time he hadn't seen me, but when he was exactly five yards away and I was ready to blast him with my .44 Magnum sidearm, Ed yelled at me to hold my fire. The bear heard him and spotted me in the same instant.

He could have been on top of me in another jump or two, but for some reason he swerved and ran into the alders. He traveled 200 yards in all and was dead when we got to him. Why didn't he finish what he started, when he had only 15 feet to come to do it? I still don't know.

That made two browns and a grizzly I had taken without any real trouble, unless you call being scared half to death trouble, in marked contrast to what had happened with the one polar.

A year from that fall I went to British Columbia for another grizzly, hunting on the Kispiox River out of Hazelton. I came across a good silvertip (he weighed around 500 pounds) fishing in a creek, got up to him until I was on the bank only 15 yards away, and whacked an arrow into him point-blank. But it hit a little too far back for a quick, clean kill.

He reared upright to fight the arrow and gave me time to get another on the string. I'm not sure whether he located me (that's one advantage of bowhunting; you make very little commotion), but if so he did nothing about it. Instead, he dropped back on all fours and lit out for the opposite bank.

Trying for a lung shot, I led him too much and the arrow punched a hole in his skull, slashed all the way through the brain, and lodged against heavy bone on the far side. He was dead on his feet but ran another 40 yards by reflex. My opinions about the bahavior of grizzlies, browns, and polars in a showdown were growing stronger.

In the spring of 1962, I gathered some additional evidence of a very convincing nature. I went back to Point Barrow for another try at a polar bear with the bow, and again Bob Munger accompanied me. He had killed a good polar with rifle on the 1960 hunt and didn't want another. He'd do only camera work this time.

Flying over the ice 20 to 30 miles offshore, we found one of the size I was looking for. George Thiele was my guide and pilot again, and he buzzed the bear to see what would happen. The animal wasn't a bit afraid of the plane. As we slanted down on him he came raging toward us, mouth open, defiance written all over him.

He lined out across the ice and Thiele set the plane down a long way ahead of him. We picked a spot behind a jumble of ice blocks where we thought we could intercept him and hunkered down. It was a good place for everything except moving in a hurry. Snow had drifted in and was piled to our hips.

The bear came on at the rolling, shuffling walk that takes one of the big white brutes across as many as 25 or 30 miles of ice in a day and started past us only 25 paces off. Just before he reached our position he saw us.

I had an arrow on the string. Thiele was beside me with his .300 Magnum, Bob a few yards behind with two cameras. The bear didn't even hesitate. He kept on at the same unhurried walk, turning his head to watch the three men crouched in the snow.

Hunters and arctic explorers have sometimes theorized that a polar bear attacks because, roaming remote off-shore ice fields all his life, he has never encountered a man before, mistakes the human for a seal or some other food animal, and attacks out of hunger. In support of that belief, ice bears have been known to stalk and kill Eskimos watching at seal holes, and have also come boldly around frozen-in ships and camps searching for food.

In the case of the bear we were after, the part about him having had no previous contact with men may well have been true. I can only conjecture about that. But hunger played no part in what he did, and he certainly didn't think we were seals or anything else edible for he showed us only indifference until we made the first move. On the other hand, he was not afraid of us.

He changed course at a slight angle to veer off but didn't quicken his pace or show any sign of alarm, just watched us over his shoulder as he walked. When he was directly opposite us I let my arrow go.

The range was short and I held where I wanted to hit, but he was moving faster than I realized. I knew instantly I had shot too far back. We had a wounded bear on our hands.

That can be a nasty situation, but he gave us no time to worry about it. The arrow was sticking out of his rump, but he didn't pay any attention to it. He didn't even bawl. He just changed ends and came for us like a thunderbolt.

George didn't let him get far, but for a second or two his charge was as determined as anything I've ever seen, head low, coming to kill. Then Thiele's 180-grain bullet smashed into his skull at less than 15 yards and he folded like a wet rag. His head went down under his forelegs, he rolled in a half somersault with his own momentum and slid to a stop. When we were sure he was dead, we walked around the hummock of ice and measured 10 steps from where we had crouched to where he lay.

He was a good bear, well up toward the record class, but for the second time in two years I was left with a filled license and a trophy I couldn't claim because it had had to be stopped with a gun. And for the second time, I'd seen a demonstration of the lightning-quick rage of a wounded ice bear, their contempt of man, and their readiness to turn on him and kill or be killed in a no-quarter fight. "They're white dynamite," Thiele told me, "and timed with a damn short fuse."

With that experience fresh in our minds, Munger and I left Barrow and flew to Cordova to join Ed Bilderback for another brown-bear hunt.

We left Cordova at the end of April, aboard Ed's boat, with Harley King along as second guide and Dan Corea of Hawaii doing the cooking. We ran down the Kenai Peninsula and crossed over to Afognak Island, but spring was late, with the deepest snow in 20 years, and hunting was slow. Bob and I finally collected a black bear apiece with our bows, and then he put down a recordbook brownie with his .375 Magnum. At the end of two weeks I had been within 30 yards of four bears, none real monsters but all good trophies. I'd even gotten within 15 feet of one. But something had gone wrong each time. Either the wind shifted or the bear spotted me and spooked before I could get a shot. Bob had to go home, and I was ready to call quits and leave with him. But the snow was going now and the hunting getting better, so I decided to stay on and give it another whirl.

It took 10 days to make a contact, but it was worth it. We drew a blank on Afognak and finally crossed Shelakof Strait to the Alaska Peninsula, in the same area where I had taken my big brown in 1960.

There, running into a shallow, rocky bay rimmed by steep mountains, Bilderback, King, and I saw a good bear walk out of the alders onto the beach.

We were in a skiff with an outboard. Ed shut the motor off and started to row quietly for shore. If we could gain the cover of the alders without spooking the bear, we'd have an excellent chance for a stalk.

The brush came down to high-tide line all the way around the bay, but the tide was out now, leaving a narrow strip of rocky beach uncovered between the alders and the water's edge. The bear was working among the rocks, pawing in the sand and kelp, stopping every few minutes to rest.

Harley kept binoculars on him, lifting a warning hand each time he looked our way, and Ed stopped rowing until the bear resumed feeding. He finally did something I'd never seen a brown do. He waded out into the sea, lay down and rolled over on his back with just his head and feet sticking out, and splashed like a kid in a pool.

We beached the skiff and slipped along the alders while he was dunking himself. A point jutted out into the sea about halfway to the bear, affording perfect cover for the stalk. The wind was right and we wasted no time.

Ed and I went ahead, with Harley following about 25 yards behind. Now that Bob had gone home, Harley was our cameraman. He was carrying my 16 mm. movie camera on a gunstock mount and, attached under it on the same stock, a 35 mm. sequence camera that exposes 24 pictures with one winding. It's triggered by a button on the gunstock, so the photographer can take movies and stills simultaneously.

I had only my bow. In addition to the two cameras and their mount, Harley had his .300 Magnum slung on one shoulder. Bilderback was carrying his favorite bear rifle, a sawed-off .375 Magnum. That's a good gun for brownies, and it suits Ed perfectly. He figures that any shooting he has to do on a bear hunt will be at extremely close range, where a short barrel is as good as a long one.

We hadn't gone more than 50 yards from the skiff when the bear's blond ears came into sight over the point. He had left his bath and was walking into our laps. My first thought was that he was very wide between the ears and must be quite a bear. He was.

Just ahead of us was a rock about four feet square, hardly big enough to hide two men but better than nothing. We went for it on our hands and knees, motioning Harley to squat where he was and stay put. He was far enough back that we counted on the bear not noticing him until it was too late.

The beach was open save for the big rock. We knelt behind it, I with an arrow ready and Ed clutching his rifle. The bear came into sight, approaching at a walk, and we pulled our heads down between our shoulders like turtles. Unless he changed course, he'd pass between us and the sea, and the wind would be blowing from him to us.

The minute or so it takes for an animal of that size to walk up within bow range is packed with suspense and thrills, and questions race through the mind like fleet shadows. Would this big fellow keep coming or would he spot us and gallop off? Two weeks before, hidden at the edge of a spruce thicket on Afognak Island, I had started a slow careful draw on a bear at 17 yards. Out of the corner of one eye he saw the first movement I made and was off in a flash, bounding over big rocks like a huge rubber ball. He put 40 yards between us before I could release my arrow, and I missed. Would this one behave that same way? Or when he saw me would he stand and stare in puzzlement?

He did neither. He lumbered on, arrogant and unconcerned. He was 25 feet away and still coming—and then he saw us.

He stopped and swung to look us over. His head lifted, swinging from side to side in typical brown-bear fashion, and his muzzle wrinkled as he tested the wind. But it told him nothing, and Ed and I stayed as motionless as two driftwood stumps. We held our breaths and waited. Finally, satisfied, he turned broadside and started to walk past us.

The 65-pound bow came back to full draw, and the bear did not even glance our way at the movement. I decided to put the broadhead through his ribs, close to the shoulder. There is no better shot for a quick, clean kill. I held just back of a foreleg and the arrow sank to the feathers. The range was only 20 feet.

I'm convinced the bear knew what had hurt him and where we were, but he made no attempt to fight back. He let go a hair-raising roar and streaked down the beach, the way he was headed. I ducked back to give Ed room to swing his rifle to cover King.

The bear still had Harley to reckon with, or rather Harley had to reckon with him. The beach was no more than 20 feet wide at that point, and Harley was squatted in the middle of it with the cameras going. The bear galloped straight for him, and if he hadn't moved he'd have been run down. He stood his ground until the brownie more than filled the finder, then dived for the alders. It wasn't funny at the time, but we had a good laugh about it later. The bear went past him 10 feet away without even glancing aside.

He turned up the beach and tried to climb into alders but couldn't make it. He fell and rolled out of the brush, and in less than a minute after the arrow knifed in he lay dead almost beside our skiff. The four-bladed arrowhead had nicked a rib, sliced through a lung, cut off a big artery near the liver, passed through the diaphragm, and through the skin near the back ribs on the opposite side.

We managed, with considerable difficulty, to roll him into the skiff. From there, we winched him aboard Ed's boat for skinning and weighing. He tipped the scales at 810 pounds, the pelt squared nine feet, and the green skull scored 27 inches, an inch under that of the brown I had taken in 1960. That one went into the records as the biggest ever killed with an arrow.

This brownie had run off without a fight, at far closer range and under as great provocation as the polar I had wounded a month earlier, the one Thiele had to put down with his .300. That one had come for us without a split second's hesitation. This bruiser, close enough to have been on us before Ed's .375 could have stopped him, had not even turned our way. Why? I have no answer.

But I'll go back to what I said before. I'm convinced that the polar bear is just naturally the one to watch out for. It's true, of course, that one swallow does not make a summer, and by the same token maybe seven close encounters with brown, grizzly, and white bears do not qualify me as an expert on their behavior. But at least those seven brushes entitle me to an opinion.

I realize there are exceptions to every rule, and even if I'm right in rating the ice bear at the top as a dangerous trophy I know there'll be many future occasions when a grizzly or brown will go out of his way to disprove my theory.

We had a spine-chilling example of that on our British Columbia hunt in 1961, the fall I killed my second grizzly.

On two occasions we had seen a sow silvertip with three cubs in tow and had stalked her for pictures, getting up within 25 yards. Each time she had winded us and run off.

A couple of days after we saw the bears, Bob Munger and Dick Mauch, another member of our party, made a fishing trip to a small lake with their guide Bill Love. When they left the lake they started up over a steep, rocky point on the way to camp. Bob and Dick were carrying their rods and bows. Bill had a light pack and .270 Winchester Model 70 slung on his back.

Bill was in the lead, Bob behind him, and Dick was bringing up the rear. They were no more than away from the shore when they heard a low snarl behind them. Then brush broke and they saw the sow grizzly, clawing her way up the moss-covered rocks as fast as she could, growling and raging.

The poor footing slowed her down and that was all that saved them. Bill barely had time to shuck the pack and whip his rifle up. The 150-grain softpoint dropped her just 15 feet away.

There were only two of the cubs left. She had lost one in some fashion, and maybe because she had smelled us in the area a couple of times she blamed us for its disappearance.

Whatever her reasons, she picked the fight without being molested or provoked in any way. That's grizzly behavior for you, under the right circumstances. Other silvertips will do the same thing again, and other browns will stand and fight instead of running away as my three have done.

But I still lean to the belief that the one most likely to come for you if he gets the chance is the big, fearless bear of the ice fields, maybe for no better reason than that you will be the first man he has ever encountered and he has no reason to respect you.

One of these days I'll collect a polar-bear pelt with no bullet holes in it, one I can count on my list of bowhunting trophies. When I do that I'll consider that I have killed the most dangerous animal a hunter can tangle with on this continent.

My 40 Years With Bears

**Carl Williams
as told to Jim Rearden**

February, 1980

Food was low in the Indian village of Old Iliamna. The men were at Bristol Bay for the summer salmon season, and the women and children were hungry for meat. I promised to get them a brown bear.

The bear I found for them was slopping across the muddy tide flats of Iliamna Bay, on the Pacific side of the Alaska Peninsula. He was hump-shouldered, hulking, bow-legged, golden-brown, ivory-clawed—typical of the bears found in the region. Wind ruffled his shaggy hair as he plodded, head down, about 80 yards away.

I knelt, readying a new .270 Winchester. The bear was broadside when I fired.

At the shot, the plodding bear was transformed into half a ton of furious action. He roared and bit at himself where the bullet had struck. At the same time he whirled into an angry charge. I knew he had seen me, but I didn't know how quickly he would blame me for hurting him. He was in a full run before the echo of the shot stopped rolling in the nearby mountains.

At about 50 yards I fired again. He kept coming. As he neared I had to get into the rhythm of his run to keep the sights on the vital chest area, and I bobbed the rifle up and down as he plunged toward me.

At about 30 yards I fired again. He kept coming.

I stood, and when he was about 15 yards away, fired again. He kept coming. He looked as big as an elephant.

When he was within about five yards, I slammed a desperation shot into the back of his neck as his head bobbed down. He dropped, skidding and rolling. I stood shaking as I fumbled more shells into the rifle, half expecting him to get up.

I found the bear's heart and lungs in tatters when I butchered him. Any one of my shots would have been fatal. But bears have incredible vitality, and I have since learned that it is not unusual for a lung or heart-shot bear to travel hundreds of yards before dying.

That was in 1935, and the few seconds of that charge taught me things about brown bears that probably saved my life many times during the next 39 years.

I hardly knew what an Alaskan brown bear was when, as a 6-foot-2, 190-pound 21-year-old, I arrived at lonely mountain-backed Cottonwood Bay on the west side of lower Cook Inlet, Alaska, in 1934. No one could have been greener. A doctor had urged me to leave my home at South Dansville, New York, and head north. Uncle Bill Duryea, a distant relative, made room for me in his tiny cabin at Cottonwood Bay.

My new home was in the heart of some of Alaska's finest brown bear country. Alaska's coastal brown bear, the world's largest land carnivore, is a member of the highly variable grizzly clan. Exceptional boars may weigh as much as 1,300 pounds, although most are much smaller. Sows weigh about half that much.

Although grizzlies in the Lower 48 are endangered, Alaska's brown bears are still abundant. They're even increasing in some areas. The state's annual, strictly controlled sportsman's kill averages about 300. Alaska's big bear numbers are still high because the alder thickets, the conifer-clad mountains, the salmon streams, the vast tundra—their home—is still essentially untouched by man.

Uncle Bill, a trader and trapper who lived at Cottonwood Bay from 1902 until 1950, started teaching me how to live safely among the big bears. The most important thing I learned was to always have a rifle within reach. If I hadn't learned that, I probably wouldn't be alive today.

Another lesson I quickly learned was that a brown bear isn't dead until it quits kicking.

Two days after I arrived at Uncle Bill's, I saw three objects far out on the bay, rising and falling with the swells. Light flashed regularly from them, and with binoculars I determined they were *bidarkas*, native-made kayak-like skin-boats. Wet paddles reflected the sun with each stroke.

Half an hour later, three Aleuts—Wanka, Peter Mike, and Black Pete—dragged their boats onto our beach. Wanka had a bloody rag around his head, and he was staggering from pain and loss of blood. I don't know how he managed to paddle.

Uncle Bill led the injured man into the cabin and untied the rag. The scalp was all but torn off. Leaves, twigs, clotted blood and dirt lay across Wanka's wet, smooth, white skull. His hair was matted with blood and debris.

"I shoot big bear. Start to skin 'im. Front foot jerk hard. Claws tear hair off," Wanka weakly explained. Black Pete and Peter Mike nodded. They'd tossed the 10-foot-square hide and 500 pounds of meat into their *bidarkas* before heading to Uncle Bill's for help.

Indians and Aleuts of the region then hunted brown bears mostly for food, although there was some trading in hides, which were used for bedding, clothing, leather and rawhide. Wanka carried a single-shot .45/70 black powder rifle. Peter Mike carried a .30/30 Winchester Model 94 lever action rifle, and Black Pete had a lever action .25/36 Marlin. Though I had little knowledge of firearms and bears, it struck me that these were brave hunters to tackle the world's largest land carnivore with such guns. When I learned more about how the Indians and Aleuts of the area hunted big bears, I developed even greater respect for their guts, if not their hunting prowess.

Uncle Bill's hands were full of tremors, so it fell to me to work on Wanka. After cleaning his head I used a needle and catgut Uncle Bill kept in a sealed vial of alcohol and crudely stitched the scalp back into place. There was no anesthetic.

Wanka lived for years with a scar like a halo surrounding his full head of hair, and he often joked with me about how nervous I had been as I stitched. I'll never forget his stoic face, pain-glazed eyes and sweating brow as I fumbled at the slippery task.

I had lived with Uncle Bill for only a few weeks when Second Chief Gregoriof Nicholi, from the village of Iliamna on the shore of 80-mile-long Iliamna Lake, invited me to go with him native-style night hunting for brown bears. He wanted to salt some bear meat for winter.

I had no rifle, but Old Nicholi, a kin of Gregoriof, loaned me an old black powder rifle, for which he had four cartridges. I think it was a .40/68. The old relic tossed a punkinball that seemed to me to be about the size of a baseball—and about as fast. It was rusty, but Old Nicholi bragged, "That's a fine rifle. Kill many bears."

I was young, eager, green and willing to try almost anything, so I shrugged and followed Gregoriof up the Iliamna River with the old smoke-pole over my shoulder.

We found a party of Aleuts hunting there. Gregoriof conversed in sign language, Aleut, Kenai Indian and English with the Aleut leader. They came to an agreement—Gregoriof and I, under the wing of an Aleut, Little Pete, would use an Aleut scaffold for our night hunt. But first we were invited to dinner at the Aleut camp, where we found a five-gallon gas can full of boiling brown bear meat, with about three inches of fat floating on the top. This, with tea and hardtack, was our meal.

I managed to gulp enough of the tough meat to keep from being hungry during the night, but I have never been crazy about brown bear as food.

Little Pete took us to the river. Each of us cut a long, straight willow withe, which we peeled and lashed to our sides. The peeled willow, visible in the dark, was to help us to aim. Poke shooting, they called it—you poked your rifle in the direction of bear sounds and yanked the trigger.

The system was evolved in the Iliamna Lake area by the Indians and Aleuts. Since the bears were most nocturnal, they had to be hunted at night. Day hunting was difficult because the bears were not active, and the country is heavily timbered, with thick brush.

There was virtually no sport hunting for brown bears in that part of Alaska then, and I'd guess that the Indians and Aleuts killed for food about as many bears 40 and 50 years ago as are killed in the same area today by sportsmen.

The scaffold we were to use was built between two trees and stood seven or eight feet off the ground, with room for three men. It was about 20 feet from a centuries-old, foot-deep bear trail, near a hole in the river where the bear fished for salmon.

We settled on the platform at dusk. While it was still light Gregoriof and Little Pete had me point my rifle repeatedly at a place on the trail where they expected a bear to pass, memorizing the spot so I could shoot blindly in the dark. Since it was only 25 or 30 feet to the spot, I decided I could aim close enough to the sound of a walking bear to hit it.

After a couple of hours it was pitch dark, and sounds seemed magnified in the calm, cool air. An owl called from a nearby ridge. Spawning salmon splashed in the nearby river; we could hear the murmur of flowing water. Soon all three of us were chilled.

Finally a hand tapped my knee. Little Pete had heard a bear. I couldn't see or hear a thing, but I lifted the old coal burner and sighted down the white willow stick, holding where I thought the bear would pass. I knew that Gregoriof was doing the same.

Then I heard the bear. His feet squished in the mud of the trail, and he brushed against some willows. He growled. Brown bears talk to themselves a lot by growling.

Suddenly I was very nervous, sitting in the pitch dark, holding a rifle that belonged in a museum or a junk pile, wondering if the verdigris-mottled brass cartridge I had fed into the dirty, rusty old barrel would fire. And I knew that a large bear standing on its hind feet next to our scaffold could look *down* on us.

Then Little Pete squeezed my leg, and I yanked the trigger. With a roar, a Vesuvius of flame spouted from my octagon barrel, matching the flame from Gregoriof's rifle. We heard the bear run off, his feet *thump-thump-thumping* into the distance. I was convinced that both of us had missed.

We remained on the scaffold. Gregoriof and I fell asleep, but Little Pete remained alert. Sometime after midnight he poked us, saying, "'Nother bear, he come."

I heard the bear, but again couldn't see him. The bear leaped off a bank into a boggy area, and I could tell from his splashing where he was. Finally he padded down the main trail, just as the first animal had. Again the two old rifles exploded into flame and smoke, and again I heard a bear run off. This one crossed the gravel along the stream. I was sure that both of us had missed again.

At daylight we were happy to leave the scaffold and walk the mile or so to the Aleut camp. The leader greeted us with a big grin. "You got two bears," he told us.

I doubted it very much but didn't argue. After more boiled bear meat and tea, which tasted a lot better this time, all four of us walked back to our hunting site, searched, and found both bear dead.

To my knowledge, none of the Indians or Aleuts of the Iliamna Lake area poke-shoot bears now, but it was a method used for probably close to a century. Instead of scaffolds, hunters sometimes built a log crib, three or four feet high, near a trail. They would lie behind the crib and shoot at the sounds of brown bears in the dark. I once accompanied an Indian on a successful all-night hunt from such a crib and decided it was even more dangerous than shooting bears from a scaffold. A hunter on the ground is more vulnerable.

The dying vestiges of a spear-hunting-for-brown-bear tradition also still existed when I arrived in the Iliamna area. Old Nicholi, the part-Russian Kenai Indian from whom I borrowed the .40/68, had hunted brown bears with a spear during his youth. The one bear spear he still owned had a razor-edge 12-inch-long double steel blade, lashed with rawhide to a sturdy 6-foot shaft.

"I tease bear, get him to charge. Then set spear into ground and let bear spear himself," he explained to me. The old man died in a cabin fire in 1936. His spear went with him.

A few years later Gregoriof took me on another hunt up Iliamna River. It was fall and we traveled light, living off the country. We used a 12-foot skiff with a four-horsepower outboard to go upstream as far as the boat would go, and then we walked. We snooped along bear trails, tippy-toed here and there, expecting to see a bear any moment. Salmon were spawning in the river, and bear sign was everywhere.

We stopped at a big horseshoe bend where high water had piled logs and driftwood. It was clear and warm. As we rested Gregoriof held up a hand. "Listen."

I could hear nothing but salmon splashing in the river. "Bear come. Follow our trail," he warned.

I listened intently, watching, for I had learned that Gregoriof knew bears. Finally, in the distance, we saw a small adult brown bear following our tracks. "Maybe he mad bear," Gregoriof said, uneasily.

"Naw," I said. "I don't think so."

Nevertheless we waded a nearby small creek and sat on a gravel bar, in the open, so we could see in all directions. As we watched, the little bear continued to follow our tracks, like a hound on a trail. Soon I heard him grunting and growling to himself as he shuffled along.

He came to the drift pile, and he put his front feet on a high log, head in the air, sniffing. We both fired and dropped him right there. "Meat for 'te pot," grinned Gregoriof. Many familes would eat from this bear.

That little bear looked well used. His teeth were worn smooth, and his face was deformed, with his left eye drooping. He was obviously old, and his hide was scarred with many hairless spots. In recent years Alaska's game biologists have learned how to age bears by counting rings in a thin cross-section of tooth; some wild brown bears and grizzlies apparently approach 30 years of age, and this one looked all of that to me.

We found 13 bullets encysted under his sad-looking hide, including one that I guessed came from a .22 Hornet, and several .30/30 slugs. On the left side of the head I found a huge lead bullet that I later weighed at more than 600 grains. Perhaps it came from an old trade rifle. I still have it.

During at least two summer seasons in the early 1970s, my son Raymond and I saw probably close to 100 different bears—which is not much different from the numbers I commonly saw there in the 1930s and 1940s.

I think that bears are, on the average, smaller and younger today because of sport hunting pressure. Numbers seem to remain steady.

I've never been threatened by or have had any trouble from big old bears unless I started the fight. The problems with troublesome bears have almost invariably come from half-grown boars, which behave like some teenagers. They're out to prove they're tough, and they seem to be looking for trouble.

One half-grown boar's intentions seemed pretty clear. I was cleaning a culvert and had noticed the bear on the side of a hill perhaps 300 yards away. I bent to my work and later glanced up to see the bear slowly heading my way. I watched as I continued to shovel. When he got about 75 yards from me, he bristled up and walked more rapidly.

I rapped my shovel on the truck bed. But I was ready to leap into the truck cab, because in my experience a sharp noise occasionally causes a bear to charge.

The bear ignored the clatter and continued to swagger toward me.

I didn't argue. I gave him the culvert, got into the truck and left. I returned later to find his tracks all around where I had been working. That bear was clearly looking for trouble.

The most impressive example I know of a bear's courage was that of a big sow that attacked a 1½-ton dump truck I was driving. The truck was empty, and I was scooting along at about 40 miles an hour, which was fast for the narrow gravel road. Suddenly a huge sow leaped into the road ahead. I don't know whether she was attacking the truck or just happened to get in the way. I couldn't stop, and both the front and rear wheels bounced over her, almost putting me in the ditch. I was certain the bear was injured, so I grabbed the rifle I always carried and stepped out and walked to the rear of the truck, where I had last seen her. She growled from deep in the brush near the road.

I leaped on the bed of the truck to see better. Suddenly she burst from the brush and charged the truck. She was hurt, but she was bellowing angry, too. I started shooting. She was after the truck, not me. At my fourth shot, when she was just in front of the bumper, she crumpled and skidded under the old International, where she died.

I don't know how many brown bears I killed during the 40 seasons I spent on the Alaska Peninsula. During one period of about three years, I had to kill 16 nuisance bears that threatened or attacked my horses and goats, or that were too aggressive around my family. I also killed a few bears that threatened workers along the Portage road, and in the early years I shot a number of bears to give to local Aleut and Indian villages for food.

I have seldom hunted the big bears for sport or trophies, although I killed two bears with hides that squared more than 11 feet (greatest length and width averaged), a size rarely equaled by brown bears anywhere in Alaska in these days of widespread sport hunting.

The best way to hunt brown bears is to let the bears do most of the walking. Their sense of hearing and smell is uncanny. I think that when the wind is wrong, a bear can scent a man literally miles away. A bear that knows a man is near can become as elusive as a ghost. Hunters who tramp the hills and valleys seeking bears leave their scent with every move, spooking every bear that crosses their trail.

I prefer to get up high where I can see miles of open or semiopen country, then use binoculars until I spot a good bear. I plan my stalk around the terrain, the bear's movements and the wind direction.

I do my best to stay high, out of the brush. I don't like to surprise a bear, for a surprised bear is unpredictable. He may flee, or he may charge.

I have used many different caliber rifles to kill the big bears. Years ago I field-tested ammunition for a large American company—not seeking bears, but simply using the ammo on nuisance bears that we had to kill around camps or along the highway.

In my view, a rifle that is satisfactory for use on Alaska's brown bears must be at least .30 caliber and throw a bullet of at least 220 grains. The .270 I used to kill the charging bear in 1935, while fine for most other Alaskan big game, isn't enough rifle for the big bears. Good rifles that I have used include the .35 Newton (with which I used a 250-grain delayed expanding hollow-point bullet), the .450 Alaskan (a modified .348 Winchester) and the .375 H and H Magnum, especially with the 350-grain bullet. At close range I've had good results using the .405 Winchester with a 300-grain bullet.

Perhaps the best big bear rifle I have used was the .450 with a 300-grain bullet. This bullet just keeps pushing when it hits a bear, and it doesn't blow up.

A wounded brown bear is dangerous in many ways. He may charge the instant he is hit, or he may flee and get into dense cover. Most wounded bears guard their back trail, and many circle back to lie in wait. When a hunter gets close, the waiting bear charges.

One fall when we lived at Iliamna Bay, on the Pacific end of the Portage, my wife, Wilma, had salmon in a smokehouse not far from the main house. Salmon were spawning in the nearby stream, within 100 yards of the house, and they were scattered up and down the half mile or more of stream, where brown bears commonly came to feed on them. Except for one bear. He decided he liked smoked salmon.

Generally bears respected our buildings and home unless food attracted them, which was the problem with this bear. He raided the smokehouse several times, batting the door open with a slam of his big paw, and then, even with smoke flowing around him, he would gobble the hanging morsels.

I ran him off with warning shots several times, but it became clear that if we wanted any smoked salmon, we would have to eliminate him. Further, we weren't sure he would stop at eating smoked salmon. Our goats and horses might prove a temptation. Also our children often played in the yard.

One day Wilma called to me that the bear was heading toward the smokehouse. I grabbed the nearest loaded rifle, a .300 Winchester Magnum, sprinted into the yard and slammed a shot into the bear, expecting him to drop.

He didn't. Instead, with a savage growl, he swiftly disappeared into the thickets of the nearby stream bottom.

We had three men visitors at the time, all of whom had hunted. I knew we had to finish that wounded bear, for it would be unsafe in the area until he was killed.

We waited a couple of hours, and then the four of us went after him. I chose to carry a .405 Winchester, and since I had wounded the bear, I told the others to stand in various spots around the thicket the bear had entered. "I'll go in and drive him out. Shoot until he stops moving," I warned.

I found the blood trail, made sure my rifle was fully loaded and stepped slowly into the gloom of brush and trees.

I walked noiselessly, paralleling the trail 20 to 30 feet to one side or the other, knowing it isn't wise to walk directly on the trail of a wounded bear. I kept to the small openings between the trees and the head-high brush. I moved like a ghost, every sense alert.

I stepped across the bear's trail and saw where the bear had swung to his right.

I stopped, backtracked, and kept well left of his trail.

I eased through a patch of thick brush and stopped just before entering a small opening. I could see the bear's tracks where he had crossed the opening. The bear had continued to swing right, and I knew then he had doubled back to guard his trail.

I was about to take another step forward when I saw a tiny flicker of movement across the clearing, perhaps 40 feet away. I stopped, my heart racing, alert, but expecting to see a small bird or a squirrel. Instead I was facing the bear, which lay close to the ground, facing me. I think it was one of his ears that flicked, drawing my eye.

The instant I saw the bear and our eyes met, he exploded into a charge. The .405 swung smoothly to my shoulder and seemed to fire by itself. The bear, halfway across the tiny clearing, collapsed, still struggling, and I emptied the magazine into him to be sure. I sold the .300 Magnum soon after, having lost my confidence in it as a big bear rifle.

The Alaskan brown bear is everything a sportsman could want in a trophy—huge and powerful, intelligent, dangerous, vindictive when angered, stubborn, courageous and unpredictable. I'll always treasure the memory of my 40 years with him.

Disneybeast or Mankiller?

Ben East

October 1978

On a Sunday and Monday in mid-May of this year, a search party of between 200 and 300 men combed the bush at the northeast corner of Ontario's Algonquin Provincial Park. The group was reinforced by four military helicopters and a tracking dog.

The object of the search was three boys, sons of officers at the Canadian Forces Base at Petawawa: George Halfkenny, 16, his brother Mark, 12, and William Rhindress, a friend, 15, who had gone trout fishing in the park on Saturday.

Just how they spent their last hours and exactly what happened will never be known. When the three boys didn't come out of the woods at dark, it was assumed they were lost. Searchers took to the woods at dawn Sunday, but it was not until Monday that the search ended in a grisly find.

Shortly before dark on Monday, searchers led by Constable Ray Carson of the Ontario Provincial Police and his tracking dog came upon three mutilated and partly devoured bodies near the bank of the creek. The bodies were covered with leaves and debris that had been raked over them. Lying beside them was a medium-size black bear. It retreated slowly into the undergrowth.

Conservation Officer Lorne O'Brien of Pembroke was flown in by copter to kill the bear. He and Constable Carson posted themselves near the bodies. The bear came in just before dark, circling through thick bush as if stalking the two men, and O'Brien killed it. It was a male, weighing about 300 pounds.

On a night back in August, 1967, two grizzlies in Glacier National Park in Montana dragged two college girls out of their sleeping bags and killed them in separate and unrelated attacks at campgrounds 10 miles apart. That tragedy had been regarded as the most terrible example of animal attack known in this country or Canada.

Now a single black bear, a species far less feared than the grizzly and even regarded as harmless by many persons, had done something fully as horrible.

The question that baffled Ontario authorities was: Why had a black bear made this attack?

Opinions varied, and still do. But one thing is clear. The bear was a man-eater. All three bodies had been fed on. The bear's behavior when the boys were found, its return to the scene and apparent stalking of the two men waiting for it, all lend strong support to the belief that it had struck down its victims because it was hungry, just as it would have killed a sheep or other domestic animal.

But the common belief that among black bears only sows protecting cubs are ever to be feared dies hard. Several reporters covering the Algonquin Park killings wrote that male black bears are not dangerous. That is a widely held and hazardous misconception. Yet it is deeply rooted in the public mind (nurtured by pictures of tame bears seen on television and the fearless panhandlers at park campgrounds and garbage dumps). Many residents in the area believe that the boys encountered a sow with cubs, that she did the killing, and a larger male came along later, drove her off, and took over the bodies. This theory persists despite the fact that searchers reported they could find no cub tracks in the area.

The possiblity has to be admitted. All bears are notorious for taking over kills they themselves have not made. Finding a bear on a kill does not prove, by itself, that the bear did the killing.

But all the evidence in the Algonquin Park case pointed to the male bear that was shot as the killer. And as if to reinforce that belief, and prove that it killed because it was hungry (bear food is in short supply in the Ontario woods in mid-May), two weeks later another black-bear attack occurred in western Canada that was clearly prompted by hunger.

A bicyclist riding along the Alaska Highway near the British Columbia-Yukon border rounded a bend and saw a black bear on the shoulder of the road ahead. A 37-year-old Italian, Giorgio Mazza, who was on a bicycle tour from Whitehorse to Dawson Creek, knew little about North American bears. He had encountered one earlier on his trip, but it had run into the roadside brush as soon as it saw him. This one didn't run, and Mazza was frightened. When it started to walk toward him he threw some luggage onto the road to distract it, dropped his bike, and took to his heels.

The bear caught him almost instantly, knocked him to the ground, and mauled him savagely about the head, back, and arms. Then it picked him up by the back of the neck, dragged him under a barbwire fence at the roadside, and started into the woods with him. When a bear does that, it has one thing in mind—a meal.

Nothing but good luck saved the man's life. A car, driven by Wolf Seidler, of Edmonton, came by. Seidler saw the bear dragging the man, jumped out of his car and ran toward the animal, shouting at the top of his lungs. The bear dropped Mazza and started for Seidler, but just at that instant he saw a pickup truck approaching. He ran back to the road and flagged it down. The driver had a .30/06 rifle.

By that time the bear had picked Mazza up again, and the pickup driver did not dare shoot for fear of hitting the man. But the odds against the bear were mounting. After a moment, it dropped its victim and raised its head. Killed with one shot, it proved to be a male weighing about 200 pounds.

Taken to a hospital at Fort Nelson, the victim required 150 stitches about the head and another 150 in the back and arms to patch him up. But he had no broken bones and was able to leave the hospital in a week. Yet there are people who insist that male black bears are never dangerous.

The trait above all others that makes any bear potential dynamite is complete unpredictability. No one can say what bears will do under any set of circumstances. Most woodsmen I have known who have dealt extensively with them believe the bears themselves do not know from one minute to the next what their behavior will be. They can go from peaceable tolerance of man to red rage in a second, and for no reason that humans can understand. The black is no exception. He is not the good-natured clown of the woods or the friendly wild thing of television. There is urgent need for the general public, and especially for those who hike, camp, or fish in bear country, to revise their image of this animal and to realize what to expect of him.

A few years ago I had a letter from K. B. Mitchell, superintendent of Jasper National Park in western Canada, in which he described the killing of an eight-year-old girl by a black bear at a campground near Calgary. The bear had hung around the campground all summer, begging handouts, and was considered to be harmless.

It walked out of the brush and approached the girl, who had cookies spread on a small cloth. She grabbed them up and ran for a cabin. The bear caught her at the steps. Two older girls working at the place whipped it with switches until it dropped her, but the girl died of her injuries.

"What a dreadful thing that this child had to lose her life to prove there is no such thing as a gentle bear," Mitchell commented. "They should always be treated as dangerous animals."

Something like 999 times out of 1,000, probably more often, a black bear will flee from the sound or scent of a human. The next time he will make a murderous attack. The big problem is that the incidents never come in logical order. The dangerous one may be the first. And the fact that it's only one case in 1,000 is no comfort to the man who becomes a bear-attack statistic.

There is wide disagreement among woodsmen and wildlife researchers on what constitutes a provoked attack. Many wild-animal apologists, who can find an excuse for any four-footed behavior no matter how dreadful the consequences, argue that *all* attacks are provoked. Just the fact that a human is in an area near a bear is provocation enough, they say.

I do not agree. If the bear is not wounded, cornered, or threatened, and if the safety of cubs is not at stake, I rate the attack as unprovoked.

The sow-and-cub combination is notoriously dangerous, but the sow's behavior is unpredictable. In live-trapping, drugging, and handling more than 300 black bears, El Harger, one of Michigan's pioneer bear researchers, encountered only four that were determined to run the men out of the neighborhood of their cubs or kill in the attempt. Many made abortive charges, growling or blowing, but stopped short of actual attack. But after he told me that, Harger added the clincher.

"Don't think a bear with cubs is ever to be taken lightly," he warned. "I advise any unarmed human who encounters one to clear out if she will give him time. Not all will attack, by any means, but some will and there is no way to tell in advance which one it is going to be."

The same holds true for any bear, male or female, and whether or not cubs are involved.

Michigan had a freak case last June that illustrates the point. A 19-year-old backpacker, camping by himself in the roadless Porcupine Mountains State Park in the state's Upper Peninsula, was attacked and clawed and bitten. The circumstances of the attack will never be known, for the bear was not identified and the man was dead when found, but the bear had not killed him. He climbed a tree and fell or was pulled down. I suspect the latter. Medical examination showed it was the fall, not the mauling, that caused his death. Nevertheless, the fatality has to be considered the result of a bear attack.

A state park official came forward with an astonishing statement. He was widely quoted in Michigan newspapers as saying that it was the first case on record that a bear had caused a human death in Michigan. Actually, there had been several earlier cases, one involving a three-year-old girl.

"I don't suppose this park man ever heard about that," a veteran bear hunter said to me. "But if he doesn't know what he is talking about, he should keep his mouth shut and not go on leading people to believe that there is no reason to be afraid of bears."

To suggest that the black bear ever becomes a true man-eater is to invite disbelief and ridicule from many persons. After all, bears are supposed to fear human scent, they argue, and that alone would stand in the way of man-eating.

Not always, by any means. There can be no question that the bear shot in the Algonquin Park tragedy was a man-eater, and it is only one of a number of which I have verified records.

The earliest I know about happened at a lumber camp in Alberta in 1906, but I am sure there had been others before that. The 1906 case was vouched for by Ernest Thompson Seton, one of the foremost wildlife writers of the early years of this century and not a man to attach blame to a wild animal for its actions if he could avoid it.

The lumber camp was on the Red Deer River. The bear, a black, walked out of the brush on the far bank, swam across, and came in a headlong rush for three men watching him from beside the cook shanty. Two of them made it to shelter inside, but the bear overtook the cook and killed him with a blow on the back of the neck. It dragged the body into a thicket and started to feed. Revolver shots that missed failed to drive it off, but by the time somebody found a rifle, the bear had run into the brush.

Seton cited a second case. In that one a black bear killed and fed on a trapper in western Ontario in 1924. The bear had porcupine quills in its face and neck, and Seton believed it was starving as a consequence.

In almost every case in recent times, wildlife researchers have suggested that the bear may have attacked because it was rabid. But in every instance, laboratory tests proved that was not the case. I do not believe a man-eating bear suffering from rabies has ever been recorded.

In July, 1948, a year when the blueberry crop failed in northern Michigan, a black bear that weighed only 150 pounds walked into the yard of an isolated firelookout cabin in the Upper Peninsula, chased a three-year-old girl up the back steps of the cabin, grabbed her by the neck as she was reaching for the screen door, and ran off with her.

The bear carried her into the woods despite the frantic efforts of the child's mother, who gave chase with a broom in an attempt to make the bear drop the child. A quarter of a mile from the cabin, the bear put the victim down and started to feed.

Alex Van Luven, and experienced predator hunter, was called in. He put his best hound on the track, and the leashed dog led him directly to the kill. Van Luven posted a companion to guard the body, sent word back to the other searchers to keep out, and followed his dog on the bear track. Before he was beyond hearing of a rifle shot, the bear came back to finish feeding and was killed.

In the fall of 1961 an Ohio man was killed and partly devoured by black bears at an isolated cabin in the Sudbury district of Ontario. The circumstances of the attack were never learned, but certainly it was made by one or more man-eaters.

In 1965 a fisherman in the Duluth area of Minnesota was killed by two or more bears that fed on their kill. Two years later, in southern British Columbia, a 10-year-old girl fell victim to a lone man-eating black. In 1968, there was a similar case involving a 53-year-old Indian guide in western Ontario.

In 1971 a clear-cut case of intended but thwarted man-eating occurred at a campground on the western slope of the Colorado Rockies. A 31-year-old Denver man was attacked by a black bear in his sleeping bag and killed almost instantly. The bear then dragged the body under a barbwire fence and started to carry it off. But another member of the party intervened by pummeling the bear on the head and muzzle with a heavy iron skillet until it dropped the victim and left. Otherwise, it would have gone into the records as a true case of man-eating.

Similar cases of attacks by hungry black bears have increased dramatically in the past two years.

In June, 1977, Sean Clement, a five-year-old whose parents operated a fishing camp 65 miles north of Wawa, Ontario, went into the camp kitchen to get a piece of cake. The door had been left open, and he encountered a bear cub that had found its way in ahead of him.

Scared, the boy turned to run, and found himself face to face with the mother of the cub. She grabbed the child and bolted for the bush. Sean's mother was working outside. She and the family dog, a German shepheard-wolf cross, heard his yells at the same time. The dog attacked the bear with such fury that it dropped the boy. The boy's mother, an experienced hunter, ran into a camp building, grabbed a rifle, and killed the bear in its tracks. It turned out that two cubs were involved, and because they were too young to survive on their own, she shot them as well. Sean was not seriously injured, but it took 100 stitches to close the bites and cuts on his neck and one arm.

Incidentally, this is the only case I know about in which a black bear attacked in defense of cubs and then tried to feed on the human being it attacked.

A few weeks later, an attack on another child in Waterton National Park in southern Alberta just north of the Montana border, ended far less fortunately.

A five-year-old girl from Regina was playing along a small stream with her eight-year-old sister. Their father was fishing from shore in a lake close by. A black bear that the father estimated weighed 300 pounds walked out of the brush, seized the younger child, and started off with her. The father rushed the bear, shouting, and the bear dropped the girl and fled. But she died of her injuries on the way to a Calgary hospital. The bear got away unharmed.

Not long after, a young boy, also with his father on a fishing trip, was attacked and killed on the spot under almost identical circumstances. Again the father forced the bear to drop its victim.

In late summer of that year, a 31-year-old woman from California who was working in the Fairbanks area of Alaska for the U.S. Geological Survey, suddenly saw a small black bear looking at her from a thicket 10 feet away.

The bear knocked her down and bit her in the neck. When she played dead, as she had been told to do, it began ripping flesh from her right arm. Then it dragged her off, through brush and over rocks. When she screamed in pain, he let go and sat down a few feet away to watch her. She managed to reach the radio in her knapsack and called for help.

"I'm being killed by a bear," she cried.

In the few minutes it took a chopper pilot to locate her, the bear resumed its attack. In the end, the woman had to have both of her arms amputated. Alaska game officers killed the bear, a female that weighed 170 pounds. No cubs could be found. Whatever the initial reason for the mauling, the bear certainly proved itself to be a man-eater.

So runs the record of man-eating black bears. One point needs to be made, however. They differ from man-eating lions and tigers in one important respect. Once the big cats feed on their first human victim, they often keep it up. According to official records, several Indian tigers killed hundreds of human beings. A bear of any kind may kill and devour a human under the press of hunger or because of an unusual opportunity and never harm another.

One major question emerges from the record. Is the black bear losing its normal fear of man? The increasing frequency of attacks, especially those resulting from a hungry bear's realization that an unarmed human is easily killed and good to eat, makes it seem certain that the answer is yes. If so, the reason is not hard to find.

To begin with, in the national parks of this country and Canada, and in some state and provincial parks (such as Algonquin) carrying firearms is prohibited, though in most American parks, cased, unloaded guns may be possessed. A bear can live out his life in those places and never hear a gun fired. Man is no longer his enemy, and he has forgotten the lesson of fear. The National Park Service sometimes shoots "nuisance bears" in American parks. The kill for 1977 was 25 black bears and one grizzly. But in the vast expanses of the federal parklands, these control measures are not enough to restore a healthy fear of man among the bears.

Outside the parks, in 37 of the 38 states of this country that still have black bears, and in all the provinces of Canada, the bears have been elevated in recent years from the category of predators to that of game animals or furbearers, and given the protection of closed seasons. Maine is the only state that still allows bear trapping. Many states and provinces ban hunting with dogs, and there's nothing like bear hounds to teach bears to stay away from humans, and everywhere blacks are hunted far more lightly than they were 15 or 20 years ago.

Many old woodsmen believe they are growing brazen as a result. It should be noted that the two child killings in 1977 occurred in a park where firearms are banned, as did the triple killing in May, 1978.

Ted Updike, an old friend of mine who has lived all his life on the edge of clearings in northern Saskatchewan and trapped the bush there for many winters, believes that no bear is more to be feared than one that prowls remote wilderness and has never encountered a human.

"He thinks he is king of the woods, and he doesn't know what a man is," Ted says. "Give him a wide berth if you can."

What can humans do to protect themselves in bear country? There is no sure way. Among the actions recommended by many wildlife biologists is to make noise, talk, sing, whistle, or rattle stones in a can. All these have been tried and have sometimes failed.

The surest way to avoid bear trouble, of course, is to avoid bears. But as an old hunter recently said to me, "In 99 percent of the bear country I have been in, a bear can lie down behind a log or in a depression and be out of sight until you are close enough to step on him. In the best moose and deer cover I know, he can have his paw in your back pocket before you know he is there."

Tree climbing in case of attack by a black bear offers little hope of safety. That same hunter commented that campers are sometimes told to pitch their tents with the opening near a tree they can climb.

"If a black bear comes into your tent at night, a forest of trees you can climb will do you no good," he said. "He'll likely come in at the open end of the tent and go out the other end, and if you climb and he wants you he'll come up and get you."

Many sportsmen (and some game researchers) think the surest safety measure is to carry a firearm adequate for the job it may have to do. I agree. As a California fisherman said to me after he and two companions had been terribly mauled in Canada's Jasper National Park by a sow grizzly that came out of nowhere and struck without warning, "Never again! If the place where I want to fish or hike is in a park where I can't carry a gun, I won't go."

Recently I got an interesting letter about bears and their erratic behavior from an Oregon man, Warren Vanderberg, in his 70's, who has lived all his life in bear areas, either in that state or Alaska. He killed his first black 55 years ago, and has shot some 25 for meat or fat.

He says flatly he will not venture into a bear area without a gun, and the gun must be up to what he expects of it in a pinch.

"I have never killed a grizzly," he told me, "but if I were hunting ptarmigan in grizzly country, which I have done quite a few times, I'd carry a 12-gauge pump shotgun, unplugged, with three rifled slug loads in the front end of the magazine." Anywhere there are grizzlies, he wants either that combination or a rifle big enough for the job. For protection against blacks he rates a .357 or .44 Magnum sidearm adequate.

"I'll admit that if everyone packed a gun in the woods there'd be problems," he said, "but those who live or work in bear country should be required to learn how to use firearms or kept out of the woods.

"An old Alaskan hand warned me when I moved there in 1955 never to go even 100 yards from my car without a rifle. 'You may wander around in bear country for 40 years and not need it,' he said 'but if you do there won't be time to go home and get it.' That's a rule that still holds with me. If I see a bear coming I'll never let him get closer than 20 feet before I shoot. That's about two jumps and two shots and that's close enough."

Vanderberg tells of a black he was forced to kill in Oregon years ago when it threatened him with an unprovoked attack.

"He came out of the brush shuffling cornerwise," he said. "His hair was standing on end, his back was humped up, and he was popping his teeth. It was July and I didn't want him for meat, but when he kept coming, I decided that he intended to make a meal of me. I let him get close enough so that I had time for just two shots, but I didn't need the second one. I put a .30/30 bullet between his eye and ear. He was 18 feet from the muzzle of the rifle when I shot, and I don't ever want a bear with a chip on his shoulder any closer than that."

What it all adds up to is that all bears, the black included, are short-tempered, unpredictable, and deadly dangerous. Quite a few have been mankillers, and every now and then one becomes a man-eater. People who live in or visit bear country need to know that.

There is need, too, if ways can be found, to rekindle in all bears the natural fear of man that many of them seem to have lost. I know sportsmen who think that even national park policy is going to have to be changed to allow some regulated hunting to instill in bears the healthy respect for men they once had. The loss of human life and the terrible consequences of maulings are becoming too frequent to be brushed off as unavoidable mishaps while wildlife theorists continue to assure the public that black bears are never really dangerous.

Index